Rock Brands

Rock Brands

Selling Sound in a Media Saturated Culture

Edited by Elizabeth Barfoot Christian

LEXINGTON BOOKS

A division of
ROWMAN & LITTLEFIELD PUBLISHERS, INC.
Lanham • Boulder • New York • Toronto • Plymouth, UK

Published by Lexington Books
A division of Rowman & Littlefield Publishers, Inc.
A wholly owned subsidiary of The Rowman & Littlefield Publishing Group, Inc.
4501 Forbes Boulevard, Suite 200, Lanham, Maryland 20706
www.lexingtonbooks.com

Estover Road, Plymouth PL6 7PY, United Kingdom

British Library Cataloguing in Publication Information Available

Library of Congress Cataloging-in-Publication Data

Rock brands : selling sound in a media saturated culture / edited by Elizabeth Barfoot
   Christian.
     p. cm.
   Includes bibliographical references and index.
   ISBN 978-0-7391-4634-7 (cloth : alk. paper) — ISBN 978-0-7391-4635-4 (pbk. : alk.
paper) — ISBN 978-0-7391-4636-1 (electronic)
   1. Rock music—Marketing. 2. Branding (Marketing)—Social aspects. I. Christian,
Elizabeth Barfoot, 1971-
   ML3534.R62 2010
   781.66068'8—dc22   2010039845

Printed in the United States of America

A Note on the Epigraphs

.

The quotations appearing on the pages separating the three parts of the book did not originate in published articles or interviews, and there is not a readily available context that would affect the interpretation of the quotations. All the same, below is some reference information that was most recently accessed July 21, 2010:

Part I: Ozzy Osbourne quotation appears on ultimate-guitar.com; Paul Stanley quotation can be found on musicbizacademy.com and rockstarmindset .com.

Part II: Marilyn Manson quotation can be accessed at allgreatquotes.com, quotationspage.com or bebo.com; Adam Jones quote was retrieved from brainyquote.com and appears on quotehash.com and iqpedia.com.

Part III: Elvis Presley quotation can be found at brainyquote.com, quotationspage.com, and thinkexist.com; Christopher Knab quotation appears at barryrudolph.com and audioaddictiononline.com.

Contents

Introduction

Rock Brands: Selling Sound in a Media Saturated Culture will explore how different genres of popular music are branded and marketed today. The book's core objective is to understand how established mainstream artists/bands are continuing to market themselves in an ever-changing technological world.

The chapters in this book will look at several key artists/bands and how they have addressed challenges brought on by changes in the industry and technology-driven media overload. What makes them stand out and succeed when so many fail? How do you find a niche that isn't just kitsch and can stand the test of time, allowing the musician to grow as an artist as well as grow a substantial fan base?

When one thinks of KISS, Bon Jovi, Elvis, or Ozzy Osbourne, a specific sound or image is produced, but few ever consider why or how that happens. Most of us, too, think either positively or negatively about these bands and often associate a specific happening in our lives with one or more of their songs. Subsequently, fans come to feel a personal connection to bands that personify ideals similar to their own or that allow them to fully express who they are. Therefore, it is imperative to the success of a band to know who they are and who their audiences are.

"The record industry is dead," KISS's Gene Simmons declared at a press conference in 2008. "It's six feet underground."[1] No, KISS would not be recording new material until the problem of illegal downloading of music for free was fixed, he declared. So in one year's time, what changed the mind of one of the most formidable rock groups of all time? Well, nothing . . . and everything.

Illegal downloading hasn't stopped, though prosecution of offenders is occurring and sites are being shut down. That doesn't stop others from popping up, as the law struggles to keep up with technology. However, the digital technology that has created this problem has also created new and exciting means of communicating to fans and that means money. Something Simmons gets very excited about.

The first decade of the twenty-first century did see a significant shift in not only how people purchase music but also how bands and wannabe rock stars communicate with fans and potential consumers for their products. Digital downloading of music, of course, is the most significant change the music industry may have ever experienced, but it hasn't killed the recording industry as Simmons suggested. But it has shaken it to its foundations, and successful bands can no longer rely on simply recording catchy tunes to stay relevant in today's pop culture.

Classic rock's audience is aging but still a significant source of traditional album sales. And older groups, while not dependent on new music to stay profitable, must remain relevant to younger, more technologically savvy listeners. Young people have grown up in a world that has always been downloadable. True, classic tunes will be new to them but delivery must be easy for kids. They won't expend a lot of time and energy looking for it—it's got to be easily accessible. Today's listeners aren't just buying songs, they are buying experiences, memories, and emotions. How else can one explain shelling out $2.49 for a 4-bar measure of a song for a ringtone? Or paying fifty dollars for a band T-shirt at a concert? Logically, these don't make rational sense. We don't need these things. But we buy them without question for those rock band brands with whom we feel a kinship.

Brand loyalty does not happen overnight. It takes several repeated interactions with the band and its message, and that holds true even in today's fast-paced Internet culture. Far more musical groups fall by the wayside every day due to a lack of a clear, focused identity than due to lack of talent. You not only have to reach your target audience, you have to know what you are reaching them for—who are you and why should they listen? To form lasting bonds with consumers, there must be something for fans to get passionate about.

The growing marketplace, not just the Internet, but all facets of media have grown exponentially during the last quarter century. And all these avenues create places to showcase sound. Cable and satellite television channels now number in thousands. Movie soundtracks often produce number one hit tunes today, and bands are sometimes specifically sought after by directors to write songs directly for a movie tie-in. The video game industry, perhaps, is one of the newest outlets for popular music. Commercial opportunities for both classic and current songs abound as more games are created solely for music fans, including the Rock Band and Guitar Hero series of games. *Rock Brands* includes chapters that delve into these changing outlets for popular music: gaming, reality television, and social networking sites.

Rock Brands is divided into three sections. In the first section of the book, specific rock bands will be showcased for their creative contributions to the successful marketing of music. Chapters will focus on the commodification of popular music through technologies, licensing and exclusive deals with mega-retailers, like Walmart.

In the second section, chapters will focus on bands and popular music genres that have utilized the power of singing to the choir, so to speak. Through lyrics, images, and their own words and deeds, successful brands know the importance of appealing to their fan base.

Finally, in the last section, chapters will address specific avenues available to artists that simply weren't there a generation ago. As the retail industry dries up, wannabe rock stars and rappers have taken it to the streets—literally—lining up by the tens of thousands for the long shot chance to prove their pipes on reality TV. Others have posted pages on MySpace and offered up YouTube videos hoping they would go viral. But as more people utilize these social networking sites, it becomes increasingly difficult to stand out for more than a minute. And as more of us achieve our "fifteen minutes of fame" as Andy Warhol said we all would, it becomes harder for bands to remain relevant for the long haul.

So what sounds draw us to what we are willing to purchase? The concerts we crave come to our city? The band shirts we must wear?

In this media saturated world where anyone can create a band and upload music anytime, how do newcomers stand out? Not every good singer can be the next *American Idol.* How does one stand out from the crowd? And with so much happening so fast, the audience is even more fickle than ever. How do older bands survive and keep thriving? *Rock Brands* gives you an inside look at how older and new popular music acts are not only able to function but to thrive in this new fast-paced culture in which we live.

—Elizabeth Barfoot Christian, Ph.D.

NOTE

1. Geoff Barton, "Sonically Speaking," *Classic Rock*, Issue 137, October 2009, 59.

1

LEAVING A LASTING IMPRESSION—
WHY BRANDING WORKS

I don't want you to play me a riff that's going to impress Joe Satriani; give me a riff that makes a kid want to go out and buy a guitar and learn to play.

—Ozzy Osbourne

"We're the McDonalds of rock. We're always there to satisfy, and a billion served."

—Paul Stanley, KISS

1

KISS Your Money Goodbye: Why Fans Can't Get Enough of the Biggest Rock Brand in History

Elizabeth Barfoot Christian

AUTHOR'S NOTE

In May 2006, I was shopping in an Atlanta Walmart when I came across a KISS T-shirt, with the original fiery red logo that the members designed in 1973. This struck me as odd because I wasn't looking at a worn T-shirt at a yard sale or a collector's item on ebay, but a rack of dozens of shirts for sale at the largest retailer in America advertising a heavy metal band whose heyday was some thirty-five years ago.

Shortly thereafter, I bought my children the latest DVD release of Scooby Doo cartoons. The first episode— a Halloween special—came on, and the story was about the gang going to a KISS concert. The members of KISS make an appearance and perform in the program. Again, I was surprised to see this band make an appearance on a cartoon targeted exclusively to children. I wanted to know more.

I started doing research and began to realize the magnitude and reach of KISS' marketing strategy. This was no ordinary rock band; it is a rock "brand," as Gene Simmons said, in every sense of the word.[1]

In 2008, the band held a tour in Japan, and Simmons and his family filmed Season Three of the hit reality show chronicling the lives of his rock star family, Gene Simmons Family Jewels. Simmons also now does marketing work for Indy 500 and appeared on the 2009 season of Donald Trump's hit TV show Celebrity Apprentice. He has authored two recent books on the history of prostitution and the art of war, in addition to his previously penned KISS-related books, and has announced the release of KISS' latest collectables: PEZ candy dispensers and refrigerators.

All of this has been occurring, mind you, from a band that hadn't released new music in a decade. Fortunately, for music fans the days of waiting on new KISS tunes ended in 2009 with a Sonic Boom. KISS released its nineteenth studio album in October 2009 as an exclusive with Walmart, one of the newest and most effective venues for marketing music for big-name bands.

NEVER-ENDING KISS

From its humble beginnings placing small advertisements in New York's *Village Voice* magazine to attract fans to its early concerts in Manhattan pubs,[2] to an international marketing phenomenon, the heavy metal band KISS has managed to stay in the spotlight for more than three and a half decades. Today, KISS is as recognized for its marketing genius as for it musical prowess.

In the early 1970s, heavy metal was still a new musical form. Heavy metal has been controversial since its beginnings in the late 1960s, just as rock and roll was. Only this musical form was even louder, harder and faster.[3] Robert Gross authored a study of heavy metal in 1990 and found that it was financially lucrative.[4] KISS showed the world just how true this statement was. In his study, he found the most popular way to advertise heavy metal was through stories and photographs, not actual advertisements. It was actually "clever marketing strategies" that sold heavy metal to its audience, and these strategies sold products, which produced as much income as record sales.[5] A study of KISS showed that decades before other bands caught on and many years before the term integrated marketing communication became a buzzword, KISS was using this in effective marketing and public relations campaigns.

With the members' flashy costumes, black-and-white freakish makeup and 7-inch heels, it is not hard to understand why the band was not easily assimilated into mainstream music culture in the 1970s—even among other rockers.[6]

In 2006, KISS performed a world tour, selling out many venues in Japan. A new KISS coffeehouse opened in the summer of 2006 in Myrtle Beach, South Carolina; Gene Simmons is the spokesperson for Indy 500; and "Gene Simmons Family Jewels," a reality television program chronicling Simmons' family life began August 7, 2006, on A&E network.[7] It marked its 100th episode in early 2010 during its fifth season.

Few unfamiliar with the music scene or non-KISS fans realized the band was still playing music, much less that the band and its members was still capitalizing in a big way until *Gene Simmons Family Jewels* premiered in 2006. Since that time, Simmons has also appeared on the 2009 season of

NBC's hit TV show *The Celebrity Apprentice*, and KISS performed live on the Season 8 finale of *American Idol* with runner-up Adam Lambert. During the 2010 Super Bowl, watched by 106.5 million people—the most watched American television program ever and featuring the most anticipated commercials of the year—KISS appeared in a commercial for Cherry Dr. Pepper with tribute band Mini Kiss to the song "Dr. Love." And if there remained anyone out there unaware of KISS, in May 2010 the raging FOX hit *Glee* combined the music of reigning pop queen Lady Gaga with rock gods KISS[8] in one of the most highly anticipated and watched shows of the series to date.

This study is important because little serious literature exists about heavy metal music overall.[9] Virtually none pays credence to the fact that KISS—arguably the most popular heavy metal band of all time—transformed the rock music industry from one that primarily sold music products, to one that sold a "brand" and anything that could go with it. However, this band has proved it has staying power, despite its never having had a No. 1 hit record. This chapter will explore and explain why the band is secondary to the brand that is KISS, the most iconic '70s metal rockers still not only playing but thriving and more successful than ever due to creative genius and employing the practice of integrated marketing communication long before anyone in the music industry realized its value.

KISS has influenced dozens of the leading music acts of today, and many credit the band with the inspiration behind their own showmanship on stage. Britney Spears, Kid Rock, and 'N Sync all put on an experience for which they pay homage to KISS' creative genius.[10] The use of pyrotechnics in concerts was not done before KISS, and many bands have tried to emulate this.

Moreover, KISS is the epitome of what Ragas and Bueno call a "cult brand"[11] and serves as a "surrogate family filled with like-minded individuals" to the die-hard members of the KISS Army.[12] A cult brand is "a support group that just happens to sell products and services" and in KISS' case, music. Successful brands come from creative minds with a great understanding of the human mind and behavior. People are drawn to other people, places, and things that they can relate to and that can help them achieve their self-actualized state. In other words, people don't need Coca-Cola soft drinks. They don't need to stay at the Holiday Inn or watch *Oprah*. They don't need an Apple computer. But they want the intangible things that go along with these and other well-known iconic brands. True cult brands are daring and new in their approach. They sell a lifestyle not just a product. And they pay attention to their loyal customers first before trying to reach out to potential new fans. Cult expert Rick Ross said these brands often give outcasts a way to feel part of a group and a sense of identity that they lacked.[13] These brands give fans a chance to commiserate and revel in nostalgia. At KISS conventions, concerts, and now online at kissonline. com, genesimmons.com, and numerous other fan and social networking websites, members of the KISS Army can rock and roll all night and buy KISS music and merchandise every day.

HISTORY OF KISS

In the early 1970s the most popular musical acts included the Captain and Tenille, the Carpenters and John Denver—very light rock and folksy sounds.[14] Cofounders of KISS Gene Simmons and Paul Stanley met in 1970 and formed the band Wicked Lester. The partnership between the two would become one of the most prolific songwriting and recording teams in music history. Wicked Lester was not as edgy as the two dreamed of, and they left the band in hopes of finding a drummer and lead guitarist who shared their passion for becoming a band to be reckoned with.

Interestingly, KISS credits classified advertising with bringing the band together.[15] The first advertisement Simmons and Stanley came across was one in *Rolling Stone* for a drummer willing to do anything. Simmons called him. Peter Criss became the drummer for the group that would become KISS.[16] Shortly thereafter, the group placed an advertisement of their own in the *Village Voice* for a "lead guitarist with flash and ability."[17] After auditioning more than fifty guitarists, Ace Frehley[18] became the final member of the fiery foursome.

The group was bandying about names while driving around Manhattan one afternoon, and it was Stanley who threw out "KISS." They all decided it had just the ring that they were searching. They also wanted something to set them apart from the other rock bands, and they decided to wear makeup and flamboyant costumes with platform heels as to appear larger-than-life. Another group, the New York Dolls, already wore makeup, and KISS did not want to be a copy of them. The Dolls had a very "fem" appearance, so to stand apart the group decided to let each band member choose his own "character."[19]

Gene Simmons became "the demon." Paul Stanley became "the star child." Ace Frehley was "the spaceman" or Space Ace, and Peter Criss became "the cat man." These personalities took on lives of their own, and the members very quickly did not appear anywhere in public site without their makeup on. This, in itself, became an important marketing strategy.

Creating a successful and unique brand was important to Simmons and Stanley from the beginning. This required more than a catchy name, good music or a gimmick. It required time and a monetary investment. During the day to make ends meet, Simmons worked as a secretary and learned to fix office equipment. Simmons, who can speak four languages and spent time as an English teacher, could also type ninety words per minute. He proved himself invaluable in an office setting, even working as an editorial assistant for *Glamour* and *Vogue*. At night, he worked the register at a delicatessen. Stanley drove a taxi cab. Stanley would literally pick up patrons and drive them to their destinations on breaks between music sets. Both believed in working to achieve their dreams and were smart enough not to quit their day jobs.[20]

KISS quickly became known for its hard-rocking great show, even as the critics were pummeling its sound and look.[21] KISS biographers David Leaf and Ken Sharp describe the experience this way: "The bombs explode, the lights flash, the fireworks shoot into the sky. To the uninitiated, a KISS concert is an assault on the senses, a decibel blitz and a visual invasion. To their fans, a KISS show is a high mass and most anybody attending their first KISS concert is converted. The lure of the carnival is irresistible."[22] KISS became a religion for millions of fans. Only the devoted and those in the music industry realize KISS broke box office records set by The Beatles and Elvis and remains the American band with the most gold records of all time.[23]

According to Blackwell and Stephan, "KISS never set out to be the best musicians the world has ever known. Nor did it set out to change the world with deep social messages and complex lyrics."[24] What they did set out to do was raise the standard for rock concerts and give the audience an experience they would never forget and would talk about the rest of their lives, and in effect, form a lasting bond with the fans. And it shows—KISS has produced 37 albums in as many years and sold more than 100 million albums worldwide—not counting concert and product sales.

ROCK MUSIC ADVERTISING

Rock 'n roll music was traditionally advertised through magazines published for music consumers, such as *Billboard* and *Rolling Stone*. Initially, KISS advertised on both flyers posted around the neighborhood bars and clubs it played in and in local music magazines. As its popularity grew, the group realized rather quickly it was not the darling of the mainstream press of the 1970s. However, it did not seem to matter. Even the negative press—especially in a teen-driven counterculture business—like heavy metal was positive.

According to an interview Simmons did with the *Indianapolis Star*, "There's no such thing as good news and bad news. There's only news. You're either important enough and you become the water cooler conversation, or you're nobody and you don't count."[25] Simmons was never disheartened by negative coverage. People were talking and wondering what all the fuss was about, and in turn KISS gained fans.

KISS reached out to a much larger audience and in very creative ways. For instance, KISS paid a visit to *The Mike Douglas Show*, a popular talk show among American housewives in the 1970s. The band not only sang "Firehouse," but Gene Simmons also did an interview in full makeup with the host.[26] This created a huge national buzz even if it did not win over any mothers.

When heavy metal came on the scene about 1970, it was viewed by many as even more subversive than traditional rock music. With its loud decibel levels, bright lights, and association with all things evil, one would probably have thought this heavy metal king, KISS, was the last thing America would still be talking about more than a decade into the next century. But KISS wanted to stand out from the crowd. It would not just be KISS' music that kept them alive and a popular culture phenomenon. In fact, KISS and its founding member Simmons are recognized by multimillion-dollar financial companies and *Fortune* 500 as a keen marketing genius.

KISS, however, became an international success without the help of the music industry as a whole who just did not "get it." KISS has still not been inducted into the Rock and Roll Hall of Fame and has never appeared on the cover of an American issue of *Rolling Stone* magazine. The purists in the music business believed it was art—not image—that made a band. KISS broke that mold with its edgy business practices, realizing far ahead of its time, that music just as any other part of the entertainment industry should provide fans with more than just records for them to enjoy. "Image and marketing are integral parts of promoting music."[27]

In 1975, KISS literally changed the way records were made in the rock music genre by recording and forcing a live music album phenomenon. KISS had been experiencing mediocre record sales. Its record company, Casablanca Records, was on the verge of bankruptcy after its first three records— *KISS*, *Hotter Than Hell*, and *Dressed to Kill*—all produced in one year's time did not sell as expected despite huge concert ticket sales and sold out shows.

Because KISS believed its live show was its strongest selling point, KISS decided to record a double live album at a time when live albums were viewed as cheap records and killers of a band's reputation. The band believed it could capture that energy of the live experience and prove live albums could be successful. Even Jimmy Buffett, creator of one of the most successful music cult brands himself with "Margaritaville," has paid homage to the rock legends in his 1978 song "Manana" by urging listeners not to try to describe the experience of a KISS concert if they have never seen it.[28]

At the same time, KISS also began a groundbreaking and genius market-ing plan for a band, licensing its name to carefully chosen products. Today, KISS' logo can be found on just about anything one can think of—lunch-boxes, caskets, KISS my ass toilet paper, and condoms[29] are among the more than 3,000 products available with KISS on them.[30]

INTEGRATED MARKETING COMMUNICATION (IMC)

At a time when the term integrated marketing communication had not been coined, KISS—the clownish-looking, fire-breathing, hard rockers—were taking the band's rock and roll brand as seriously as the music they played. Integrated marketing communication is defined by the following character-istics: it is customer-based; advertising and promotion are driven by cross-functional marketing; the advertising and promotional messages are all con-sistent in what they are trying to "sell," brand positioning is integrated into all brand messages; and all customer touch points impact the brand—not just advertising and promotion.[31] It is a holistic approach to advertising that ad-heres to a consistency in brand messaging through every aspect of a product's packaging and at every touch point.

In integrated marketing communication, a term that has come into vogue in the early twenty-first century, each transaction is a relationship-builder or breaker. It strengthens or weakens the relationship the consumer, or in this case, the fan has with the product. A brand is defined as a "name, term, sign, symbol or design, or a combination of those intended to identify the goods and services of one seller or group of sellers and to differentiate them from those of other sellers," according to the American Marketing Association. To have a successful brand, one must understand the needs and wants of custom-ers and potential customers. This is possible through perceptive integration of the brand image throughout every area of contact with the public. An effec-tive brand cannot be separated from a product because it is so interconnected in the hearts and minds of consumers. "It is the sum total of their experiences and perceptions, some of which you can influence, and some that you can-not."[32]

IMC is not a new concept. While the traditional marketing formula has focused on product, price, place and promotion, IMC focuses on promotion and all that goes into building that ever-important relationship with the con-sumer and in the mind of the consumer. It is what had led to the success of corporate giants like McDonald's, Apple, and Walmart.[33] In the last ten years IMC has become standard marketing practice in all kinds of companies and organizations. However, KISS did it first—and incorporated it first—in the music industry.

KISS showed rock bands that its image and "branding" was as important or more than its music in terms of staying power and economics. All its messages were consistent: KISS was not about an ideology, it was about having fun—period. The youth of the 1970s bought into this. Many remain lifelong fans and followers of the now-aging rockers. They related to this philosophy that wasn't about making a statement.

From traditional advertisements, to television appearances, made-for-television movies and cartoons, to KISS dolls, lunchboxes, and clothing—KISS sent the message that everyone could be a part of this KISS "Army" (as the band's large fan base is known). Everyone is the same and wants to have a good time, or as the KISS theme song states, "I want to rock and roll all night and party every day."

In fact, Simmons wrote a song for the fans for the 1998 *Psycho Circus* album called "We Are One," telling them that they are just like the band members and are "one" with them. Again, this was a clever marketing strategy to sell the image, and in turn, records. This was further evidence for fans that they were integral ingredients in the band's success.

Simmons touts hard work and frugality as the secret to not only his success but also the success of some of America's most familiar rich and famous. The best business education comes from the street, he said in an interview with *BusinessWeek* magazine in 2008.[34] He flies economy, stays in regular hotels and doesn't guard himself from the public with security. He wants to be relatable to the public that has made him so successful, and the public can buy into that. Again, more evidence that he is just like the rest of us.

KISS' MARKETING STRATEGY

KISS has grossed more than $1 billion since 1974 from record sales, concert tickets, and the sell of more than 3,000 licensed products.[35] Simmons believes KISS' continued success has more to do with its promotion and consistent message and always giving the fans what they want (more KISS)—than it has to do with the band's songs and the lyrics. Considering the band has never produced a No. 1 hit in the United States and did not record any new music from 1998 to 2009, Simmons has proof that the KISS brand is much more than just the KISS band.

"Most people think [KISS] is a rock and roll band, but it is actually the only rock and roll brand," Simmons told *BusinessWeek* in 2007. "Because no matter how much you love U2 or the Stones or McCartney, you're not buying Rolling Stones condoms, and you are not going to buy U2 comic books. But all those things and more, you can get from KISS."[36] Simmons and KISS went on a ten-city tour to promote KISS fragrances for men and women for sale in middle- to high-end retail establishments in 2007. When people suggest he has gone too far with pushing the KISS brand, he points to his continued success because he continues to test what people will buy by adding more products. "The people will tell you what they want. You have to be blind not to see that America's biggest export is pop culture." And KISS is "not about guitars. It's something much bigger."[37]

Warner Brothers produced a "KISS Babies" cartoon, and Hanna-Barbera produced "KISS Meets the Phantom of the Park," a made-for-television movie. The movie was a bomb, but it put the band before an even larger audience. A KISS camera was sold in Japan, and the band appeared in the commercial promoting it, on billboards and posters. KISS has had its own comic book series, has done commercials for Pepsi-Cola and Holiday Inn, and had its picture on Coca-Cola bottles in France. Consumers can even get KISS on their VISA cards at some banks.[38]

Paul Stanley summed up KISS' business philosophy this way:

A band is limited in its potential to diversify, by its lack of multidimensional appeal. If music is the sole connect a band makes with a fan, music is all the fan will buy. In the case of KISS, in addition to music and video, we can market the iconic images of the band through products that allow fans to show their affiliation and allegiance to the band's music, image and philosophy. That said, for a band/brand to sustain, the band must remain viable and credible as a music entity to maintain the brand's validity.[39]

Toy figurines of the KISS characters have been released twice—first in the band's heyday of the 1970s and again in 1997 following a smash reunion tour.[40] KISS mini-figurines and Potato Head dolls, along with a new line of the more traditional fan items of T-shirts and posters, were released for Christmas 2009 in conjunction with Walmart's exclusive release of *Sonic Boom*.

The band appeared live at the closing ceremonies of the 2002 Winter Olympic Games in Salt Lake City, and in 2005 put on a show in Iraq and Afghanistan to support American troops as part of the Rockin' the Corps concerts.

The KISS brand was performing even more steadily. In 2002, Simmons began publishing *Gene Simmons' Tongue*, a magazine similar to *Maxim*, which he defines as a rock and roll lifestyle magazine.[41] Stephen Dessau, the CEO of New York's Track Entertainment, a music and event marketing company, described KISS as a classic example of a successful brand development strategy. KISS was ranked No. 41 in earnings on Forbes' Celebrity 100

Index in 2001.[42] *Billboard* magazine did a special report in 2003 on KISS' thirtieth anniversary, citing the group as "internationally known icons," nodding to the KISS brand even more so than its music.[43] In the article, the author mentioned the controversy surrounding the band for the suggestion by some that KISS' business and marketing creativity long ago eclipsed its musical creativity. The blurring of the line between art and commerce, however, has always been part of the band's marketing strategy and something for which the members do not apologize.

In fact, KISS has been instrumental in changing the way heavy metal is marketed today. Hundreds of KISS websites, online fanzines, and www. genesimmons.com are devoted to marketing the band and connecting fans. Most heavy metal music can now be found online, even though it is well past its height of popularity.[44] One can even find articles online about "crossover marketing" of hard rock—another way to describe what KISS did thirty years ago. Ozzy Osbourne has licensed his name to a line of action figures, and both Osbourne and Nine Inch Nails have sold their images to video game producers. KISS had a computer video game long ago. Alice Cooper and Rob Zombie have licensed their band images to comic book publishers.[45] Two other hard rock bands popular in the late '70s and '80s, AC/DC and Aerosmith, have also recently re-branded their images. Aerosmith has licensed its name to the Guitar Hero game, and AC/DC released its new album, *Black Ice*, exclusively to Walmart in 2008—along with T-shirts and children's pajamas. The irony, with the AC/DC branding, is that a band once considered extremely hard-core and the scourge of religious groups in the 1980s is now available only at the family-friendly retail magnate that has refused to carry other bands with lewd records and imagery on its covers.[46] Another '80s hard rocker, former Poison frontman Bret Michaels, is happily reinventing himself to stay relevant. From bad boy reality quasi-porn star in VH1's *Rock of Love* to 2010's illness-plagued sympathetic *Celebrity Apprentice*, the new and improved Michaels' next starring role will be as "Dad." *Life As I Know It* debuts in the fall of 2010 on VH1 in conjunction with Michaels' new country-rock DC, *Custom Built*, and portrays the more sensitive family man that Michaels says he is striving to become.

KISS has never changed its brand-image to accommodate anyone. And Simmons would say this is imperative in successful branding. Effective integrated marketing communication strategies may include a change in look or sound as styles and preferences change, but the core message of who you are and what you are about should never change. That is what the public is buying.

"Credibility, schmedibility—anyone who thinks popular music is about artistry is kidding themselves," Simmons said in an interview in the *Los*

Angeles Times.[47] Simmons believes in the following marketing strategy and has used it to much success with KISS and is now also using it to promote Indy racing.[48]

- Keep the message in the forefront.
- Image matters.
- Stir discussion.
- Simplicity works.

KISS's business prowess often precedes its musical prowess. Companies now approach Simmons and the KISS brand about new products and ideas.[49] And when Simmons calls CEOs, they listen. Simmons values the rights to the KISS logo and faces at $500 million, and he continually puts his own money where his mouth—or his iconic tongue—is. While Simmons cannot create or license any KISS product without the approval of Stanley, who is an equal partner in KISS, it is Simmons who is constantly at the forefront of the business ventures. Dell Furano, the CEO of Signatures Network, the band's licensing company, told *Billboard* that Simmons networks and pushes KISS 24/7, 365 days a year, at times putting up his own money for a project he was especially passionate about.[50]

WALMART OFFERED KISS AN EXCLUSIVE DEAL
FOR ITS 2009 ALBUM RELEASE

Greg Hall, Walmart's vice president of media and services, told reporters right before *Sonic Boom*'s release that he thought "the Walmart mom loves KISS and looks fondly back on that as one of the first concerts she went to."[51] And these moms and dads are introducing their children to KISS culture now, creating a new generation of fans.

"Look at KISS culture," Simmons told the *USA Today*. "People tattoo their bodies with KISS faces, name their children after our songs . . ."[52] Simmons said one of the reasons the band did not record new material for so long was because of the problem with illegal downloading, and he blames the destruction of the music industry on the crime. Simmons doesn't do drugs or drink and has no tolerance for self-destructive behavior or handouts. "I don't believe in socialism and the last time I checked what we do isn't charity," he said.[53]

He does believe in good value, though, as does Walmart, which offered the three-disc set, including a fifteen-track greatest hits collection, a concert DVD along with the new material, for $12.

All of KISS' successes come back to incorporating a communication exchange with their consumers at every step. From its early days of wearing the KISS makeup on stage and off—anytime they were in public—to create the aura that it was not just a "show" and that fans could participate with the band. Fans loved it and showed up in costume at concerts and appearances to see the band. They were experiencing the band not merely listening to music. KISS and fans fed off one another. This kind of interaction has come full circle. KISS took off the makeup eventually, and then to fans' delight put it back on. Early on KISS also played in any city that would listen. Unlike many bands trying to break into the big time that perform in large metropolitan areas, KISS toured small-town America, places where people often feel forgotten and left out of mainstream entertainment. They may sing about the "New York Groove," but this was grassroots groove, and it worked. Young people loved that this flashy rock group visited their hometowns. And again, KISS brought it full circle when in 2009 they allowed fans to go online and vote for the cities it would play on its tour.

THE FANS SPEAK

John Whiddon is a forty-year-old KISS fan from Milton, Florida, and has been a fan since he first heard the band in 1977 when he was eight-years-old. He said he remains loyal to the band because of KISS's loyalty to the people who continue to support them. "They have the 'we are you, you are us' mentality, and I believe that's the way it should be for a band," Whiddon said. "Without fans, no band would survive thirty-five days, much less thirty-five years."[54] Whiddon, who teaches high school percussion, had students in 2003 do an indoor percussion production of a KISS show. He has seen them in concert five times and owns dozens of KISS products in addition to albums and T-shirts and keeps up with the band online.

Whiddon met the band members—Simmons, Stanley, Tommy Thayer and Eric Singer—in 2009 before a concert and was impressed at the amount of time they took with fans and how friendly and approachable they were. According to Whiddon,

> Being a drummer myself, Eric and I talked drums for about five minutes. I was really amazed that they actually took time to talk with all of us in the room, especially knowing they had to head to the stage shortly. There is nothing about KISS music that is technical, especially from a musician's standpoint. It's always been just good time, feel good music for me. I think that was the original point of rock music, and somehow that's gotten lost over the years. I think a lot of artists are taking the genre too seriously now, and it just doesn't seem fun

anymore. With KISS it's not only the music, but it's the visual assault that goes with the music, that makes it fun. I know that when I go to a KISS show, I'm going to get my money's worth. I've heard many people talk about how KISS has sold out with all of the merchandising they've done over the years, but I think it's a case of people being envious because they didn't think of it first. I'll say this, if I could've made my living playing the music I loved, and sold millions of dollars in merchandise, no one could have stopped me. I'm loyal to the band because it goes back to the band's loyalty to the fans.[55]

Ryan Moore, a thirty-four-year-old KISS fan from Portland, Oregon, said some of his earliest memories are of listening to KISS LPs and 8-tracks with his father. Moore saw the band in concert once in 1997 and says the experience was unbelievable. He is a believer in the band's "Keep It Simple, Stupid" philosophy but doesn't agree with some of the over-the-top antics they have tried. His most expensive KISS memorabilia is a belt buckle he bought on eBay because it reminded him of one he owned as a teenager that he had purchased at a garage sale for a quarter. "KISS is rock and roll, and nobody can take that away from them," Moore said.[56]

Keith Lambert, a forty-five-year-old fan from Columbia, Mississippi, has been a fan nearly as long as KISS has been a band and has seen the band in concert five times. "I saw them on *Dick Clark's Rock Concert* and *Midnight Special* when they were just starting out," Lambert said.[57] Lambert credits the music—vocals, drums, and guitars with keeping him a fan—but considers the theatricality a huge bonus. Lambert has dressed in KISS garb several times as a teenager and as an adult for parties and owns KISS comic books, every record album, mugs and drinking glasses, pajamas, a cigarette lighter, and more.

Lance Christian, a 39-year-old fan from Ruston, Louisiana, said he has seen the band more than a dozen times and jokes that he even dated women named Christine, Shandi, and Beth—the women named in KISS's songs. Christian said,[58]

I have been a fan since I was four in 1976. I've kind of lost count of how many times I've seen them, probably around 12 1/2 or 13 1/2 times. The 1/2 comes from when I saw The Ace Frehley band, with Peter Criss opening in Baton Rouge, Louisiana, in 1995. I get on Kissonline.com every day. I had backstage passes on Dec 12, 1979, in Biloxi, Mississippi, but they left immediately following the concert so I did not get to meet them. It was four days before Peter Criss's last show, so I don't believe they were getting along too well and probably didn't want to hang out back stage. Either that or they had a bunch of groupies and didn't want to worry with an eight-year-old boy wanting to meet them. I like their music, even though it is nothing groundbreaking or anything, but it does rock.

I am loyal to them because they are loyal to their fans. They give their fans their money's worth. Any band can throw on some jeans and a hat and go stand on stage for two hours and sing. KISS puts in two hours a night just getting ready for the show.

TODAY'S KISS

Fans take KISS very seriously, and once they are "brand loyal" it makes no difference if the music sucks, the albums and products sell.[59] Simmons told *Forbes* magazine, "If someone likes you, they'll buy what you're selling, whether or not they need it. No one needs *Forbes* or KISS, but they buy it anyway."[60]

Through the use of integrated marketing communication strategies, KISS is one of the most iconic cult brands ever. And Simmons said he isn't finished yet, even though KISS holds more licenses than any band in history. He is working on a Broadway play based on the band, a KISS casino and KISS toothbrushes.[61] KISS has released three in a series that will number 10 KISS-OLOGY DVD collector sets. "No one—and that includes the Beatles and Elvis—can touch our merchandising and licensing," Simmons said. "Outside the music world, it's only Disney and Lucas. But in the music world, they can't shine our shoes."[62]

The first KISS Coffeehouse opened in June 2006 in Myrtle Beach, S.C., where both Stanley and Simmons appeared for the grand opening, introducing fans to flavors like French KISS Vanilla, Demon Dark Roast, and Rockuccino. A fan told a reporter with Fox News at the grand opening, "It's just like seeing Jesus for me."[63] National media covered the event, and press releases abound on the Internet, which translates into more dollars for KISS.[64] In 2009 KISS held a first-ever fan-routed tour and let fans dictate what cities the band played for the entire tour.[65]

Today, only Simmons and Stanley remain of the original band members. The others have come and gone, and this chapter will not name them all here. The band has gone through several hard times and tried to reinvent itself in the 1970s during disco and even removed its makeup in 1983, put it back on when it reunited in 1996 with its original members for a reunion tour, and continues to write books and release DVDs to keep its name out there. The message has remained constant, however.

In February 2006, KISS announced the launch of a KISS fragrance by Gemini Cosmetics, New York. Television and print advertisements promote the cologne, and in turn the band. The fragrances for men and women were initially marketed at department stores like Belk, Dillard's and Nordstrom.[66] KISS wine, skateboards and shoes are some of the newer products available.[67]

As recently as March 4, 2009, KISS was featured prominently in *TIME* magazine for its frontman Stanley's gallery opening. In the past six years, Stanley, now fifty-seven, has developed into a renowned artist with quite a following—and owed in large part to his legions of KISS fans. "The Kiss Army has grown up, has children and is now ready to buy art."[68] While Stanley's paintings lean to the abstract, he also paints KISS-related works including a self-portrait and painting of his fellow band members in full Kabuki attire.

Stanley earned $3 million in 2008 on his artwork, according to an interview on FOX Business Network.[69] He also made an appearance on CNN American Morning in March 2009. Just like Simmons, Stanley is all about cross-promotion, and the KISS brand is always front and center.

In 2008, Gene Simmons released two books: *Ladies of the Night: A Historical and Personal Perspective on the World's Oldest Profession*, and *The Art of War*, an updated version of the centuries-old military treatise. *Gene Simmons Family Jewels* is in its fourth season on A&E. Fans of the show or the band can get interactive on the show's website and watch unreleased episodes and see Simmons' plastic surgery video. This is truly for the fan who can't get enough.

Like or loathe, KISS symbolizes the epitome of the American Dream. Simmons came to America at the age of eight and had to learn English. He took his first job as a paper boy in Queens at thirteen years old making sixty dollars a week for two paper routes.[70] He met Stanley in the inner city of New York as a teenager and worked hard, played hard and made it to the pinnacle of financial success. KISS has faced changes in what's popular in music, clothing, politics—but has remained true to its fundamental mission: work hard, play harder.

NOTES

1. Friedman Joan, "The Outrageous Entrepreneur: Gene Simmons of KISS has built a mini-empire with his in-your-face media marketing," *Los Angeles Times*. March 4, 2006.

2. Dale Sherman, *Black Diamond*. London: CG Publishing Ltd., 37.

3. Robert Gross, "Heavy Metal Music: A New Subculture in American Society," *Journal of Popular Culture*. 24:1, 1990, 119–20. (119–30).

4. Gross, 127.

5. Gross, 128.

6. "VH1 Ultimate Albums: KISS Alive." Casaboontha Records & Filmworks production, 2003.

7. David Lindquist, "The 500's Frontman: Gene Simmons, the blood-spitting rock 'n' roll icon, is on a mission to promote the Indy 500," *The Indianapolis Star*, May

13, 2006; Alan Snell, "Kiss Rocker Lends Voice to Indy Races," *The Tampa Tribune*, April 1, 2006; Sarah Talalay, "Kiss star Simmons drawn to IndyCar," *Sun-Sentinel*, March 26, 2006; "Indy Racing League Forms Innovative Marketing Agreement with Gene Simmons & Richard Abramson," Simmons Abramson Marketing press release, Jan. 10, 2006 (genesimmons.com).

    8. *Glee*, "Theatricality," Season One, Episode 20, May 25, 2010.

    9. Chuck Klosterman, *Fargo Rock City*. New York: Scribner, 2001, 3.

    10. Roger Blackwell and Tina Stephan, *Brands That Rock: What Business Leaders Can Learn from the World of Rock and Roll*. Hoboken, New Jersey: John Wiley & Sons, Inc., 2004, 89–92.

    11. Matthew W. Ragas and Bolivar J. Bueno, *The Power of Cult Branding*. New York: Prima Venture, 2002.

    12. *Ibid.*, xxvi.

    13. *Ibid.*, 3.

    14. "VH1 Ultimate Albums: KISS Alive."

    15. David Leaf and Ken Sharp, *KISS: Behind the Mask, the Official Authorized Biography*. New York: Warner Books, Inc., 2003, 18.

    16. C. K. Lendt, *Kiss and Sell: The Making of a Supergroup*. New York: Billboard Books, 1997, 47.

    17. Sherman, 31.

    18. Peter Criss changed his name from George Peter Criscuola, and Paul Frehley took the name Ace to keep down the confusion from having two named Paul in the band.

    19. "VH1: KISS Beyond the Makeup," Casaboontha Records & Filmworks production, 2003.

    20. Blackwell, 95–96.

    21. "VH1 Ultimate Albums: KISS Alive."

    22. Leaf and Sharp, 2.

    23. "Gene Simmons Bio," genesimmons.com; "VH1: KISS Beyond the Makeup;" Carla Hay, "I Don't Like Handlers, Because They Can't Do Things As Well As I Can," *Billboard*. 116:24, June 12, 2004, 74.

    24. Blackwell, 96.

    25. Lindquist.

    26. "VH1: Kiss Beyond the Makeup."

    27. Kenny Kerner, "KISS and Kontroversy: Giving Yourself a Marketing Edge," *TAXI Transmitter*, January 2005, (www.taxi.com).

    28. "KISS: The Loyal Legion," *Billboard*. 121: 39, 30–32.

    29. "Gene Simmons Tongue Magazine Launches," *The Write News*, June 14, 2002, (www.writenews.com).

    30. Gene Simmons, *KISS and Make-Up*. New York: Three Rivers Press, 2001, 130.

    31. Steven Strauss, "Naming Your Business," *Home Business Magazine,* June 24, 2006, (www.homebusinessmag.com).

    32. American Marketing Association website (marketing power.com).

33. Michael V. Laric, "The Role of Integrated Marketing Communications in Sustainability Marketing," paper presented at the ASBBS Annual Conference, February 2010.

34. "KISS and tell: Gene Simmons talks business," *BusinessWeek*, Sept. 11, 2008, (www.msnbc.com).

35. *Ibid.*

36. "The KISS Machine: Gene Simmons on Branding," video interview with *BusinessWeek*'s Diane Brady. (feedroom.businessweek.com). From March 23, 2007. Retrieved June 22, 2010.

37. *Ibid.*

38. "Gene Simmons Bio."

39. Kevin Carroll, "Rock Star Rockin' the Business Speak," *Brand Autopsy Marketing Practice* online magazine. Sept. 8, 2005, (http://brandautopsy.typepad.com).

40. Steve Traiman, "Kiss' Huge Comeback Goes Miniature," *Billboard*. 109: 47, March 1, 1997, 47.

41. "Kiss and Tell," *Newsweek*. 139: 6, Feb. 11, 2002, 12; Larry Getlen, "Gene Simmons' financial kiss-and-tell," *Bankrate.com*, Sept. 22, 2003.

42. Jon Fine, Ira Teinowitz, and Wayne Friedman, "Tongue Tied to Brand," *Advertising Age*. June 17, 2002.

43. Wes Orshoski, "Band Gives New Meaning to 'Branding'," *Billboard*. 115:32, Aug. 8, 2003, 20.

44. Tim Henderson, "Marketing Metal: Getting the Music to the Minions," *Billboard*. 111:23, June 5, 1999, 20–21; Clay Marshall, "Metal Fans Unite . . . Online," *Billboard*. 113: 25, June 23, 2001, 38.

45. Sandy Masuo, "Tapping Into the Metal Mainstream," *Billboard*. 112: 49, Dec. 2, 2000, 68.

46. Namewire.com, Oct. 31, 2008.

47. John Friedman, "The Outrageous Entrepreneur: Gene Simmons of KISS has built a mini-empire with his in-your-face media marketing," *Los Angeles Times*, March 4, 2006, (genesimmons.com).

48. A. J. Foyt, "The IRL's KISS Method," *Weekly Wisdom, Tips and Tidbits from Hetrick Communications*, May 31, 2006, (genesimmons.com).

49. Wes Orshoski, "Band Gives New Meaning to 'Branding'," *Billboard*. 115:32, 20.

50. *Ibid.*

51. Chris Burritt and Adam Satariano, "Walmart to Sell Kiss's First New Music in 11 Years," *Bloomberg.com*, Aug. 17, 2009.

52. Edna Gundersen, "With 'Sonic Boom,' Kiss will roar anew," *USA Today*. Oct. 6, 2009.

53. *Ibid.*

54. John Whiddon e-mail interview, July 1, 2010.

55. *Ibid.*

56. Ryan Moore e-mail interview, June 29, 2010.

57. Keith Lambert e-mail interview, June 30, 2010.

58. Lance Christian interview, July 6, 2010. Christian is married to the author of this chapter.

59. Chuck Klosterman, *Killing Yourself to Live.* New York: Scribner, 2005, 216–18.

60. Tom Van Riper, "First Job: Gene Simmons," *Forbes.* May 23, 2006, (genesimmons.com).

61. Dorothy Pomerantz, "Heavy Metal Marketing," *Forbes.* Feb. 13, 2006, (www .forbes.com).

62. "Gene Simmons: college kids killed music biz," *Reuters.* Nov. 14, 2007, (www.reuters.com).

63. "KISS Hopes Frozen Rockuccinos Will Be Hotter Than Hell," from the Associated Press reported on FoxNews.com, June 28, 2006 (www.foxnews.com).

64. Dawn Bryant, "A Caffeinated KISS Rewards Zealous Fans," *Myrtle Beach Online.* June 28, 2006, (www.topix.net).

65. "KISS Announces the First-Ever Fan-Routed Tour," ticketmaster.com, April 6, 2009.

66. Sandra O'Loughlin, "Rock 'n Roll Band KISS to Launch Fragrance Brand," *Brandweek* online magazine, Feb. 13, 2006.

67. www.kissonline.com.

68. Carolina Miranda, "From KISS frontman to gallery artiste," *TIME*, March 4, 2009 (www.kissonline.com).

69. www.paulstanley.com, Feb. 27, 2009.

70. Tom Van Riper, "First Job: Gene Simmons," *Forbes.* May 23, 2006, (www .forbes.com).

BIBLIOGRAPHY

Blackwell, Roger, and Tina Stephan. *Brands That Rock: What Business Leaders Can Learn from the World of Rock and Roll.* Hoboken, Jew Jersey: John Wiley & Sons, Inc., 2004.

Bryant, Dawn. "A Caffeinated KISS Rewards Zealous Fans," Myrtle Beach Online. June 28, 2006. (www.topix.net)

Burritt, Chris, and Adam Satariano, "Walmart to Sell Kiss's First New Music in 11 Years," *Bloomberg.com*, Aug. 17, 2009.

Carroll, Kevin. "Rock Star Rockin' the Business Speak," Brand Autopsy Marketing Practice online magazine. Sept. 8, 2005. (http://brandautopsy.typepad.com)

Fine, Jon, Ira Teinowitz, and Wayne Friedman. "Tongue Tied to Brand," *Advertising Age.* Vol. 73, Iss. 24, June 17, 2002, pp. 4–14.

Foyt, A. J. "The IRL's KISS Method," *Tips and Tidbits from Hetrick Communications.* May 31, 2006. (www.genesimmons.com)

Friedman, Joan. "The Outrageous Entrepreneur: Gene Simmons of KISS has built a mini-empire with his in-your-face media marketing," *Los Angeles Times.* March 4, 2006. (www.genesimmons.com)

"Gene Simmons Bio," on www.genesimmons.com.

"Gene Simmons: college kids killed music biz," *Reuters.* Nov. 14, 2007. (www
.reuters.com)

"Gene Simmons Tongue Magazine Lanches," *The Write News*, June 14, 2002. (www
.writenews.com)

Getlen, Larry. "Gene Simmons' financial kiss-and-tell," *Bankrate.com.* Sept. 22,
2003. (www.bankrate.com)

Gross, Robert L. "Heavy Metal Music: A New Subculture in American Society,"
Journal of Popular Culture. Vol. 24, Iss. 1, 1990, pp. 119–30.

Gundersen, Edna. "With 'Sonic Boom,' Kiss will roar anew," *USA Today.* Oct. 6,
2009.

Hay, Carla. "I Don't Like Handlers, Because They Can't Do Things As Well As I
Can," *Billboard.* Vol. 116, Iss. 24, June 12, 2004, p. 74.

Henderson, Tim. "Marketing Metal: Getting the Music to the Minions," *Billboard.*
Vol. 111, Iss. 23, June 5, 1999, pp. 20–21.

"Indy Racing League Forms Innovative Marketing Agreement With Gene Simmons
& Richard Abramson," Simmons Abramson Marketing press release, Jan. 10,
2006. (www.genesimmons.com)

Kerner, Kenny. "KISS & Kontroversy: Giving Yourself a Marketing Edge," TAXI
Transmitter. January 2005. (www.taxi.com)

"KISS Announces the First-Ever Fan-Routed Tour," *ticketmaster.com.* April 6, 2009.

"Kiss and Tell," *Newsweek.* Vol. 139, Iss. 6, Feb. 11, 2002, p. 12.

"KISS and tell: Gene Simmons talks business," *BusinessWeek.* Sept. 11, 2008 (ms-
nbc.com)

"KISS: The Loyal Legion," *Billboard.* Vol. 121, Iss. 39, pp. 30–32.

"KISS Hopes Frozen Rockuccinos Will Be Hotter Than Hell," from the Associated
Press reported on FOXNEWS.com, June 28, 2006. (www.foxnews.com)

"The KISS Machine: Gene Simmons on Branding," video interview with *Business-
Week*'s Diane Brady, March 23, 2007 (feedroom.businessweek.com). Retrieved
June 22, 2010.

Klosterman, Chuck. *Fargo Rock City.* New York: Scribner, 2001.

Klosterman, Chuck. *Killing Yourself to Live.* New York: Scribner, 2005.

Laric, Michael V. "The Role of Integrated Marketing Communications in Sustainability Marketing," paper presented at ASBBS Annual Conference, February
2010.

Leaf, David, and Ken Sharp. KISS*: Behind the Mask, the Official Authorized Biography.* New York: Warner Books, Inc., 2003.

Lendt, C. K. *Kiss and Sell: The Making of a Supergroup.* New York: Billboard
Books, 1997.

Lindquist, David. "The 500's Frontman: Gene Simmons, the blood-spitting rock 'n'
roll icon, is on a mission to promote the Indy 500," *The Indianapolis Star.* May 13,
2006. (www.genesimmons.com)

Marshall, Clay. "Metal Fans Unite . . . Online," *Billboard.* Vol. 113, Iss. 25, June 23,
2001, p. 38.

Masuo, Sandy. "Tapping Into the Metal Mainstream," *Billboard.* Vol. 112, Iss. 49,
Dec. 2, 2000, p. 68.

Miranda, Carolina, "From KISS frontman to gallery artiste," *TIME*. March 4, 2009. (kissonline.com)

Newcomb, Michael, Clairel St. Antoine Mercurio, and Candace Wollard. "Rock Stars in Anti-Drug Abuse Commercials: An Experiment of Adolescents' Reactions," *Journal of Applied Psychology*. Vol. 3, June 2000, pp. 1160–1185.

O'Loughlin, Sandra. "Rock 'n Roll Band KISS to Launch Fragrance Brand," *Brandweek* online magazine, June 24, 2006.

Orshoski, Wes. "Band Gives New Meaning to 'Branding,'" *Billboard*. Vol. 115, Iss. 32, Aug. 9, 2003, p. 20.

Pomerantz, Dorothy. "Heavy Metal Marketing," *Forbes*, Feb. 13, 2006 (www.forbes .com).

Ragas, Matthew W., and Bolivar J. Bueno, *The Power of Cult Branding*. New York: Prima Venture, 2002.

"Revered Rock Legend, Gene Simmons Named Grand Marshal of Honda Grand Prix of St. Petersburg," *The Miami Herald*. (www.genesimmons.com)

Sherman, Dale. *Black Diamond*. London: CG Publishing Ltd., 1997.

Simmons, Gene. *KISS and Make-Up*. New York: Three Rivers Press, 2001.

Snell, Alan. "Kiss Rocker Lends Voice to Indy Races," *The Tampa Tribune*. April 1, 2006. (www.genesimmons.com)

Strauss, Steven. "Naming Your Business," *Home Business Magazine* (online), June 24, 2006. (www.homebusinessmag.com)

Talalay, Sarah. "Kiss star Simmons drawn to IndyCar," *Sun-Sentinel*. March 26, 2006. (www.genesimmons.com)

Tomasson, Chris. "Partnership between Anthony, rocker Simmons is curious," *Rocky Mountain News*. March 14, 2006. (www.genesimmons.com)

Traiman, Steve. "Kiss' Huge Comeback Goes Miniature," *Billboard*. Vol. 109, Iss. 47, March 1, 1997, p. 47.

Van Riper, Tom. "First Job: Gene Simmons," *Forbes*. May 23, 2006. (www.gene simmons.com)

"VH1: KISS Beyond the Makeup," Casaboontha Records & Filmworks production, 2003.

"VH1: Ultimate Albums: Kiss Alive!" Casaboontha Records & Filmworks, 2003.

WEBSITES CONSULTED

www.kissonline.com
www.genesimmons.com
www.paulstanley.com
www.namedevelopment.com

2

Highway to Heavenly Profits:
The Marriage of AC/DC and Walmart

Elizabeth Barfoot Christian

Walmart, long known for its mom-and-apple-pie family friendly appeal, announced in mid-2008 it had struck an exclusive deal with 1970s dirty-deed-doers AC/DC. While not the first big-name band to sign an exclusive contract with America's largest retailer, AC/DC was certainly the most famous and most controversial, given Walmart's track record of censoring media it chooses to sell in its nearly 8,500 retail locations and its online sites—forcing many singers to choose between censoring their CDs or not selling in the top retail market in the country—a cost to their freedom of artistic expression or their pocketbooks.

Sure, classic rockers the Eagles and Journey had already inked deals with Walmart and on independent labels. But this was AC/DC, a rock legend, on the Columbia music label. At the risk of alienating other chain stores, what was in it for Columbia and the band? And was Walmart softening its stance on music? Or was AC/DC now "tame" in the eyes of the twenty-first-century music audience?

This chapter seeks to address why iconic headbangers AC/DC would get in bed with the world's largest retailer in an exclusive relationship and how this type of music marketing is a growing trend in the twenty-first-century music industry and an increasingly profitable one for retail giants and established acts—but the cost may be to the consumer as far as censorship of content and where music may be available. Independent and corporate music/media stores are closing with increasing frequency as mega-retailers seek to control more and more areas of enterprise.

The history of both the AC/DC brand and the corporate brand of Walmart are imperative to understanding why a marriage of the two seemingly diverse images works and what it means for the future of music marketing both to retailers and to artists. Perhaps, most importantly, however, is what it means to the future of music.

AC/DC HISTORY

AC/DC, known for its power chords, big riffs and low shouting choruses, hasn't changed its formula since its beginning in the '70s. This keeps loyal fans and has been used by most of the big name bands from the '70s and '80s that remain popular. However, no AC/DC album had made a huge splash in the last two decades with the exception of AC/DC's 2000 hit album *Stiff Upper Lip* released in 2000, its last studio album before the Walmart venture in 2008. That album sold more than 1 million copies.

The alternative: appeal to aging rock fans who now do their best air guitar and karaoke while driving their children to sporting events and after-school activities, who may not be heading to a lot of concerts and clubs anymore—but who would definitely feel a pang of nostalgia at seeing a new AC/DC album or T-shirt at the local Walmart—and might pay for that pass down the memory lane of a wilder youth.

AC/DC began in Australia. Founding members, brothers Angus and Malcolm Young, spent their formative years in Scotland and later Australia, rebelling against their father's more proper desires for their futures. They were the youngest of seven brothers and an older sister, Margaret, and were both musically inclined at early ages and listened to English rockers, The Beatles, The Rolling Stones, the Yardbirds and The Who. Both were inspired by their older brother George, who had already begun his band The Easybeats, which was quite successful in Europe in the 1960s. Both younger brothers dropped out of school as teens—taking ironically apropos jobs considering the later lyrical creations of AC/DC—Malcolm working maintenance in a bra factory, and Angus as a typesetter for porn magazine, *Ribald*.[1]

By 1972, Malcolm had become interested in leaving the band he was in and forming one of his own to have more control over the musical direction. He placed an ad in the Sydney, Australia, *Sunday Morning Herald* to recruit musicians. Bassist Larry Van Kriedt, drummer Colin Burgess and vocalist Dave Evans became part of the new group. The name of the band came courtesy of the Youngs' sister, Margaret, who saw it written on the back of a sewing machine, which she later used to sew some of Angus' iconic schoolboy uniforms. The name stuck because it "suggested power and electricity."[2]

Several musicians came and went within a short amount of time. In 1974, Bon Scott—who would front the band when it came into its own—would become the lead singer, replacing Evans. While he was a perfect fit vocally,

Scott added a new troubling dynamic to the group with his excessive drug and alcohol abuse. Angus, by comparison, never took part in any vice more potent than a cigarette.

The band cuts its teeth in the tough bars in Sydney blasting deafening music from bagpipes, bass and drum with the instantly recognizable vocals of Bon Scott. Within a year of AC/DC's first album release, which topped European and U.K. charts with hits like "Hell Ain't a Bad Place to Be" and "Whole Lotta Rosie," the band's bad boy image was already setting in cement.

Right after Scott joined the band, AC/DC signed Michael Browning as its manager, and it was his leadership that catapulted the Australian sensation to superstardom. AC/DC's appeal was strongest to working-class men looking to have a good time. However, they also had a strong female and gay following, as well. The band was unlike any before it in their on-stage hi-jinks, heavy sound, and sexualized imagery and lyrics. Atlantic Records, whose acts at the time included The Rolling Stones and Led Zeppelin, saw the band in 1975 and loved the act so much the company signed them to a record contract.

The band's third album skyrocketed them to international success. *Dirty Deeds Done Dirt Cheap* included several hit songs, including the title track and explicitly sexually titled "Big Balls." The band's first U.S. release, *High Voltage*, debuted in September 1976, to little notice—even though it had been selling like crazy in Germany.[3] Even *Rolling Stone* magazine was not impressed by the Aussies. Things definitely changed, however, and as of early 2010 the band's U.S. album sales alone totaled 70 million. This makes AC/DC one of the top five grossing bands in American history.[4]

One of AC/DC's most iconic songs, "Highway to Hell," considered controversial and satanic by some fundamentalist groups on its title alone, was actually written about "being on the road for months at a time, and being squeezed into the bus with the band and the road crew," Masino said. "Angus once said, 'When you're sleeping with the lead singer's socks in your face, that's about as close to hell as you can get.' He also said the closest he ever came to being satanic was wearing a pair of black underwear once in a while."[5]

The biggest and most difficult change came to the band in February 1980 when thirty-three-year-old lead singer Bon Scott died unexpectedly from "acute alcoholic poisoning."[6] An autopsy revealed a half-bottle of whiskey in his stomach. His hard-living, risky lifestyle had cost Scott the ultimate price, and his band mates lost a family member. The band received notes of sympathy from fans and musicians from around the world.

Mourning but determined to keep the band alive, as Scott would have wanted, the members started looking for a new lead singer in late spring of

1980. Brian Johnson became the band's next lead singer, and with the direction of producer Mutt Lange the group recorded its eighth album, *Back in Black*, which would become one of AC/DC's most historic albums including the now legendary songs: "Hell's Bells," "Shoot to Thrill," "Back in Black," and "You Shook Me All Night Long," among others. For the opening track "Hell's Bells," a real church bell was used to create the mood of the song.[7]

The Back in Black tour sold out nationwide and across Europe. Fans wanted to share their mourning with the band and see if AC/DC could still rock without Scott, and they were not disappointed. In 1981 the band's 1976 album, *Dirty Deeds Done Dirt Cheap*, previously unreleased in the United States, came out and went platinum in ten weeks.[8]

By late 1981 *Kerrang!* rock music magazine listed seven AC/DC records among its All-Time Top 100 Heavy Metal Albums.[9] And its follow-up to *Back in Black*, *For Those About to Rock (We Salute You)* went platinum within weeks. The band was an international phenomenon, carrying on the legacy of the late Scott.

AC/DC was on fire, and it was teenagers who continued to fan the flames. In April 1982 *Newsweek* magazine wrote, "Middle-aged critics hate them, moms and dads blanch, the kids cheer on. AC/DC is the latest musical weapon in the war between the generations." The article went on to describe each member as the quintessential bad boy down the street and singing lyrics continually infused with off-color sexual references.[10] Sticking to what it knew best—rock and roll—Angus criticized bands he thought sold out to an image or celebrity. He said AC/DC was in it for the music—and the money—telling *Circus* magazine, "This popularity is what we wanted right from the start. We wanted to be millionaires."[11] And that, they were. By 1982's end, AC/DC had earned twenty-seven platinum and gold albums in eight countries.[12]

Then the band experienced another loss. Drummer Phil Rudd, who had never gotten over the death of Scott and had been using drugs extensively to cope, left the band in 1983. He was replaced by Simon Wright, but AC/DC sank into a lull for several years not really rising above its already established successes.

A terrible incident further attributing credibility to the satanic connection that many conservative Christian parents already feared. Serial killer Richard Ramirez was caught in California in the summer of 1983 and confessed to sixteen murders, which were inspired, he claimed, by the AC/DC *Highway to Hell* album cover and song "Night Prowler." An AC/DC ball cap was found at the scene of one of the murders, according to police reports. While since that time it has become relatively commonplace for murders to be blamed on rock music, it was not in the early '80s. The national media jumped on the bandwagon and began running stories suggesting devil worship.[13] Band members denied any dealings with the devil, but the damage was done. Cities began banning AC/DC from performing, and people picketed at concerts that were allowed to go on. Suggestions surfaced about crazy goings-on at the concerts, including damage done by the band members themselves, all of which proved unfounded. Still, damage was done to the band's reputation.

Concert sales did not increase during these years, but most of the tour dates continued to sell out. In 1990, AC/DC completed its fourteenth album, *The Razor Edge*, in only six weeks and enjoyed some of the biggest hits in years. Unfortunately, the resurgence in the band's image was again marred in January 1991 at a concert in Salt Lake City. Nearly 13,300 fans crowded into the general admission arena all vying for a place closest to the stage. Three teenagers were crushed to death in the rush to the stage, unbeknownst to AC/DC, who came out and performed the concert. The band was told immediately after the show. The tragedy was compounded by the international news that the band went on with the concert. The band was cleared of any wrongdoing, but it was devastating and still a difficult topic for the guys.

By 2000, the band released *Stiff Upper Lip*, its fifteenth album with twelve new songs. It went to Number One on *Billboard*'s Mainstream Rock Tracks chart.[14] It went Gold in the United States and Platinum in Europe within three months of release.

After three decades of non-stop rock recording and touring, AC/DC was inducted into the Rock and Roll Hall of Fame in 2003. The band has received countless awards and honors, including *Classic Rock* magazine naming the late Bon Scott tops on its 100 Greatest Front Men in history.[15] AC/DC never really lost its appeal, and even as aging rockers has had a loyal following. However, as time has moved on and technology has changed newer, younger acts more in tune with the media from which today's teens get their music. How to stay relevant well into the twenty-first century became an issue. And AC/DC, along with the world's largest retailer, had a huge response.

WALMART'S MOVE INTO MUSIC

Walmart did not start out as a major player in music marketing. Once technology started shifting music sales first from albums to cassettes in the 1980s then to CDs in the 1990s and finally to intangible digital downloads in the twenty-first century by the younger audience, it was simply a matter of time before independent and music-only retailers started closing, unable to compete with the Internet. A contender, perhaps, that music retailers didn't consider having to compete for their very existence with, however, were the mega-retailers like Walmart, who have become increasingly willing to sell hot ticket items at a loss to get customers inside the doors. According to a study by the Recording Industry of America, in 1989 record stores accounted for nearly 72 percent of music sales. By 2008, that had plummeted to just 30 percent of all music sales—just slightly higher than other stores, like Walmart and other retail giants, at 28.4 percent (a slight decrease from a high of 32.7 percent in 2006, which can be attributed to the growth in the last few years in digital downloads). During the same time period, the Internet went from nonexistent to capturing 14.6 percent of sales, while digital downloads now garner 13.5 percent of the music market.[16] Walmart, of course, has its hand in both those pockets as well. Independent and mega-record stores have been closing in droves for years; the last of Virgin Records Megastores closed in New York City in 2009. Tower Records, which still operates online and internationally, was forced to close its American retail locations in 2006 because of decreasing sales.

Perhaps the biggest problem is that these retailers are not primarily in the music business and can afford to sell music at or below cost to get shoppers into their stores for other items. This practice (referred to as predatory pricing by some of the mega-retailers it has driven out of business)[17] is now commonplace at Walmart and other large corporate retail giants.[18] However, it is doubtful Walmart would ever dare cross the line into true illegal pricing practices because it would serve the corporate leviathan no purpose. Walmart doesn't have to purposely drive competitors from the market, it is simply powerful enough to force them out from the sheer volume it is about to buy. And music sales, while growing, amount to a miniscule portion of the retailer's product.

When corporations making the decisions have no vested interest in music, they are affecting an entire industry without regard to ramifications of those decisions. When a corporation with the buying power of Walmart sets a policy, no one has the money or manpower to fight it. Mike Duke, Walmart's chief executive officer, announced the company's net sales in its 2010 Annual Report to be more than $405 billion, and more than $100 billion internationally for the first time in its history.[19] The company has 8,400 retail locations in fifteen countries, employing more than 2 million people worldwide. In 2010, Walmart was ranked number one on *Fortune* magazine's Most Admired Companies survey.[20]

In an industry now in freefall, Walmart, the world's largest company, has topped the list of music retailers for nearly fifteen years despite its refusal to carry albums with objectionable lyrics or artwork.[21] Walmart requires music to meet a stringent set of clean-cut requirements in order for the retail giant to sell it. That means bands with a penchant for profane and vulgar lyrics must clean up their act—at least for a Walmart release—or lose out on the largest retailer of music in America. CD packages contain conspicuous labeling of "edited" or "sanitized version" from artists known for a more obscene sound but who realize they can't afford not to sell to Walmart stores, which in many cases are the only retailers still carrying music in suburban and rural areas of the country.

Walmart is not the only retailer with the corporate buying power to stifle free speech and expression, as opponents have called this practice. Kmart and Blockbuster, both of which promote family values, expect the entertainment industry to cow tow to their "more decent" demands when editing movies, music and artwork for retail sale. Award-winning director Oliver Stone, who has had films banned at all three big chains, has likened it to a form of censorship.[22]

Musicians with a message about politics, race and religion are being forced to choose between being meaningful or being profitable, while large retailers make the decisions parents used to make.

Examples include:[23]

- Nirvana's song title "Rape Me" on its *In Utero* album was changed to "Waif Me" and pictures of fetuses on the cover were removed.
- John Mellencamp's CD Mr. *Happy-Go-Lucky* cover art originally depicted Jesus and the devil on either side of him in the background but were airbrushed out for Walmart.
- Rob Zombie was asked to change the cover of his group White Zombie's cover of *Superswingin' Sexy Sounds*. A bikini was painted on a nude woman lying in a hammock.

The mega-retailer refused to stock folksy rocker Sheryl Crow's self-titled album in 1996 because it disagreed with lyrics of her song "Love Is a Good Thing." In the song, which argued for stricter gun control, she suggests that American children kill one another with guns and ammunition sold at Walmart stores. (Some Walmart stores still sell guns and ammunition, though fewer than they did when Crow penned the song).[24] Crow refused to change the lyrics, and this is her only album Walmart won't carry. Censorship? You decide. Her record label, A&M said this decision cost her 10 percent of her sales.[25]

Walmart's corporate policy on Mature Merchandise: Music, Video Games and Movies states:

Walmart does not carry music that has the "parental advisory" label which warns parents about explicit lyrics. We carry some "edited" versions of music that have been provided by the artist or the music label. Walmart does not edit music. Our role is simply to provide music selections that we believe our customers want to buy.[26]

Most artists cave to Walmart's wishes, but like Crow not all see enough to lose in an industry increasingly driven by music downloads, especially among artists who appeal to a younger audience most familiar with digitized music. Green Day's 2009 release *21st Century Breakdown*, which went to No. 1 in America despite being banned from Walmart shelves because the band refused to censor content that the retailer deemed unsavory.[27]

Even as tangible music product sales, primarily CDs, have plummeted Walmart's influence has done anything but decline. The reason is two-fold: as less floor space is devoted to music, it becomes all the more important, especially for independent labels and newcomers to get promoted by the largest music retailer. Secondly, in 2007 Walmart began marketing MP3s, the latest in digital music technology, becoming an early retail contender to offer this commodity. Now only the Apple company's iTunes beats out Walmart in digital music sales.[28] According to a *USA Today* story in 2008, cheap downloads of singles are a growing challenge to the music industry that has been struggling with piracy since the software became available digitally to do it.

This makes it harder not to give in to Walmart's artistic demands, even if they appear to be a form of censorship. Some have argued that by forcing bands to alter their message and their art, Walmart is essentially setting our cultural norms.[29] Yet, it remains nearly impossible to completely shut Walmart out of a mainstream record deal—especially for newer artists because the company is so dominant in the American retail and cultural landscape.

One thing that Walmart and other large retailers like Target and Best Buy do to entice bands to sign deals with them is to market exclusive editions or bonus tracks or DVD packages.[30] Walmart has enabled established bands to cut out the middleman, or record label, and restore much of the profit to their own pockets. This has greatly benefited groups like Journey and the Eagles, previous to the AC/DC deal due to an established fan base. The record labels—what were once considered the all-powerful institutions in the music industry—are being replaced by mega-discount retailers. And Walmart is the leader of the pack. The labels just can't match the kind of marketing Walmart has the dollars to do. Hence, branding of both Walmart—as a leading music mogul—and the continued branding of individual musicians—can be achieved at a lower cost.

The downside, of course, is not a topic discussed at Walmart's annual shareholders meeting, which might be mistaken for a main street music festival. In Fayetteville, Arkansas, the 2008 meeting featured Journey, Keith Urban, Carrie Underwood and the All-American Rejects. Both Underwood and

Urban praised Walmart in their performances—Urban even changing lyrics in his song to reflect his affinity for the All-American retailer.[31]

WHY WALMART?

Even artists who haven't inked exclusive retail distributor deals realize the importance Walmart plays in moving music. Rapper Chris Brown, not necessarily known for his cool temper, wrongly accused Walmart of refusing to carry his album *Graffiti* in December of 2009 and ranted about it on the blog site Twitter. Once his rant proved erroneous, rather than apologizing, he cancelled his Twitter service.[32] The store Brown accused had actually sold out of his album, no small feat in the current state of CD sales. Many retailers report overages of albums that in times past would have sold relatively quickly—but that the younger generation prefers to download in MP3 form.

While true that there has been a steep decline over the last decade in CD sales in favor of digital downloaded tunes, some genres of music have an audience that still buys albums. Classic rock is one of the biggest—both because many of its devoted fans grew up in a different generation, are entering middle-age, and feeling nostalgic about its aging rock gods (even pushing an industry to return to pressing vinyl in many instances)—and collectors of music want something tangible to hold onto. For that reason, classic rock still sells really well because of the demographic appeal, according to Irving Azoff, chairman of Live Nation Entertainment who closed a deal for Fleetwood Mac with the retail giant.[33]

The Eagles, Journey and Garth Brooks were the largest names to sign exclusive deals with Walmart prior to the partnership with AC/DC. And it did nothing to diminish sales of their albums. *Long Road Out of Eden*, the Eagles double-disc, sold 711,000 its first week of release according to Nielsen SoundScan. Journey's *Revelation* sold 105,000 copies its first week, putting it at No. 5 on national sales charts. This was a 1,600 percent increase over first-week sales of its 2005 release *Generations*.[34] Journey guitarist Neal Schon had only praise for Walmart corporation for its in-house promotion of the band's CD.

Of course, a band with the reputation of Journey may be able to afford to make a deal that includes a 3-disc set of new and old music and a DVD of concert footage to sell for $11.88. Many artists don't have the name recognition to garner such a deal because they can't sell enough to make it profitable for either party. But these kinds of deals seem to be the current rage for veteran rockers.

BLACK ICE, GREEN CASH

In choosing to go with Walmart Corporation to the exclusion of others for its sixteenth album—its first since *Stiff Upper Lip* in 2000—AC/DC also made a conscious decision not to make its music available on the hottest tech site going, Apple's iTunes, making it one of the most famous bands to shun the site growing in popularity by the second. The band signed a deal with Verizon Wireless for the exclusive rights to its entire back catalog. Verizon to date is the only digital store to offer AC/DC music. AC/DC, unlike younger bands, has chosen not to sell individual tracks to date, preferring to sell entire albums via digital downloads. Because of its demographic appeal, it hasn't seemed to hurt the band. AC/DC is old school, and its fans are loyal and pass down that devotion to their children. By marketing the latest offering in Walmart not just through music, but a video game and T-shirts, the band is drawing in a young, new suburban and rural fan base.

Thus, a win-win pairing of *Highway to Hell* rockers and family values powerhouse was struck. It was all about how to successfully market a brand name—rather than just a band's name—which obviously Walmart does better than anyone. Rock journalist Susan Masino, who has written extensively on AC/DC, said the band's decision to sign a deal with Walmart "was purely a business decision and had nothing to do with shrinking away from their branding."[35]

But many hardcore fans of AC/DC were appalled at the pairing. After a thirty-year history of flipping its middle finger at convention and decency, how could the rockers sell out to America's retail poster child, they wondered. AC/DC fans posted to blog sites in fear that this union sounded the death knell for true rock and roll. One cringed at the thought of only being able to pick up the new AC/DC album at a store where one could also pick up a box of diapers during his shopping trip.[36] Others questioned whether the band could remain true to its rock roots with Walmart's tentacles attached. Another wrote, "This means rock-n-roll is officially dead. Someone mark the time."[37] Another pondered, perhaps more accurately, "Possibly anything that is anarchic when you're twelve, yet survives until you're forty, automatically becomes mainstream. Or was AC/DC simply mainstream all along, as neatly packaged as Pringles?"[38] So was it always about the branding? And was this just its latest smart marketing move? Or was it the money talking? The proof was in the packaging.

Black Ice debuted Oct. 17, 2008, selling 800,000 copies in its first week and more than one million within its first two weeks.[39] The album revived the aging Australian rockers' careers—but more than that served as one of the most successful examples of the new music business model—the Walmart exclusive. Building on the earlier deals with the Eagles and Journey, Walmart pre-ordered 3 million copies of *Black Ice*, and it eliminated all distribution costs, according to Masino, this was "very simple, very smart and very AC/DC. AC/DC has never made a bad business decision since the day they started playing on New Year's Eve of 1973. That is why they are one of the top five biggest selling bands in the world."[40]

Walmart went all-out for AC/DC, including promotions throughout the store. Bob Chiappardi, an independent music marketing executive, told the *Nashville Scene* that the company hung posters throughout the store, displays were placed in the CD department, the AC/DC version of the video game Rock Band was introduced, a display was placed in the men's department, and several different T-shirts were printed for *Black Ice*'s release.[41]

For AC/DC's role in promotion, the band released a video for the initial single "Rock N' Roll Train." Members did interviews and a major world tour with many sold out performances. It was quickly apparent that the exclusive with Walmart was nothing short of one of the band's best decisions ever. *Black Ice* marked the band's second time atop the music charts. The first was 1981's *For Those About to Rock We Salute You*. But this was the first time in AC/DC's 30-year history to debut at No. 1.

What makes Walmart exclusives potentially more lucrative and successful than those with other stores like Best Buy or Kmart is sheer size and volume. Because of Walmart's buying (and in-house advertising) power, it can both buy and sell at a lower price as well as afford to keep slow-moving inventory longer than smaller retailers. So music that may not sell fast—or that takes a third or fourth single to chart to start selling—doesn't hurt the company like it would a smaller chain or single music shop.

The exclusive with AC/DC is a good one for Walmart, too. The mega-chain got its first major video game exclusive as part of the deal, an AC/DC version of Rock Band, giving MTV a piece of the partnership.[42] This was the first Rock Band version to feature only the songs of an individual group.

AC/DC TOPS AT BOX OFFICE

Following the 2008 release and fanfare, AC/DC was able to cash in on its newfound younger fan base with fifteen songs on the *Iron Man 2* soundtrack. Would this have been possible without the success of the Walmart deal? *Black Ice* to date has sold more than 50 million copies, and success of *Iron Man 2* virtually ensures this number, along with the soundtrack, will go up. Director Jon Favreau told the *Los Angeles Times* it was while watching AC/DC perform its hit "Shoot to Thrill" that it dawned on him that was exactly how Iron Man would make his entrance. "I thought, 'You know this is how he should show up, right in the middle of this and take the armor off. That's the Tony Start version of doing things,'" Favreau told the newspaper.[43] AC/DC has become the signature sound of the "Iron Man" franchise, and the soundtrack to *Ironman 2*, the sequel to the 2008 blockbuster hit, includes fifteen AC/DC classics from its 1976 to 2008 albums. AC/DC had previous movie experience with Stephen King's *Maximum Overdrive*, released in 1986. King, a huge AC/DC fan approached the band about doing the soundtrack for the film he wrote based on his short story "Trucks."

WALMART'S FUTURE IN MUSIC

Following AC/DC's success with *Black Ice*, which also produced the second-highest grossing world tour of 2009 thanks in no small part to the Walmart promotions, Foreigner signed on the dotted line with Walmart a year later. The thirty year rock legend, Foreigner was looking to regain its star power that had been dimming over the last decade while the band toured in smaller venues playing its big hits that everyone recognizes like "Hot Blooded" and "I Want to Know What Love Is." The exclusive deal for a three-disc set included both classics and new songs and was released in March 2010.[44] Walmart offered the chance to reestablish the Foreigner brand marketing in a powerful new way across media platforms traditionally the mainstay of record labels but at less cost upfront to the band.

As long as Walmart, which garners 12 percent of the market share of music sales,[45]—still finds it profitable to make deals with bands, despite an industry whose consumers continue to become younger and more media and digital savvy, exclusive deals will be struck. In 2006, Walmart announced its plans to lower the cost of CDs to $10 or less.[46]

Apple's iTunes claims 28 percent of all music sales as of the summer of 2010, and Amazon.com, online retail giant, ties Walmart with 12 percent of music sales. As this chapter was completed, Apple was under investigation by the Department of Justice for allegations it "unfairly leveraged iTunes to deny exclusive music to Amazon MP3."[47] However, it may be that Walmart's role as cultural gatekeeper may be limited in the future, unless it becomes competitive in the download market, which would realistically surprise neither consumers, the music industry, nor Apple. Walmart says it bases its decisions on what its customers want. Naysayers, who think Walmart has too much control over American culture, say Walmart's only concern is the almighty dollar. Whatever the case, no one can argue that the world's largest corporation's formula for success in the music business—like its overall success—is rocking the company along now into the second decade of the twenty-first century.

NOTES

1. Susan Masino, *Let There Be Rock: The Story of AC/DC*. New York: Omnibus Press, 2006 (4).

2. Masino, 8.

3. Masino, 48.

4. Acdc.com official website. June 2010.

5. E-mail correspondence with Susan Masino, April 27, 2010.

6. Masino, 105.

7. Masino, 117.

8. Masino, 126.

9. Masino, 127.

10. Jas Obrecht, "Angus Young: Seriously, *Guitar Player,* February 1984.

11. Masino, 129.

12. Masino, 130.

13. Masino, 137.

14. Masino, 179.

15. Masino, 195.

16. The Recording Industry of America 2008 Consumer Profile, www.riaa.com. Retrieved May 17, 2010.

17. Predatory pricing is legally defined as one company selling a product at a loss with the purpose of driving competitors out of the marketplace. Once competitors have gone out of business, the company that practiced selling at a loss can then raise its costs to compensate for lost profits since it will have become a monopoly. Predatory pricing is illegal and is regulated by the Sherman Act. Walmart has not been charged in any case involving this practice.

18. Mark A. Fox, "Market Power in Music Retailing: The Case of Wal-Mart," Popular Music and Society. 28:4, 2005, (501–19) 503.

19. "Walmart Issues 2010 Annual Report to Shareholder." Press Release, April 19, 2010. Retrieved from Forbes.com.

20. *Ibid.*

21. Neil Strauss, "Wal-Mart's CD Standards Are Changing Pop Music," *The New York Times*, Nov. 12, 1996, A1.

22. Strauss.

23. Mark A. Fox, "Market Power in Music Retailing: The Case of Wal-Mart." Popular Music and Society. 28:4, October 2005, 508–9 (501–19).

24. "Walmart: Pop Culture Gatekeeper?" Aug. 20, 2004. Retrieved March 16, 2010. http://www.pbs.org/newshour/bb/business/wal-mart/impact.html

25. Strauss.

26. Walmartstores.com

27. James Montgomery, "You Won't Find Green Day's 21st Century Breakdown at Wal-Mart." May 21, 2009. Retrieved March 16, 2010 from www.mtv.com/news/articles/1611970/20090521/green_day.jhtml

28. Adam Tanner and Scott Hillis, "iTunes passes Wal-Mart as top U.S. music retailer," *USA Today*. April 3, 2008. Retrieved online April 23, 2010.

29. Fox, 512.

30. George Plasketes, "Pimp My Records: The Deluxe Dilemma and Edition Condition: Bonus, Betrayal, or Download Backlash?" *Popular Music and Society.* Vol. 31, No. 3, July 2008, (389–93) 392.

31. Robert Levine, "For Some Music, It Has to Be Wal-Mart and Nowhere Else," *The New York Times*, June 9, 2008.

32. "Chris Brown is a Twitter Quitter." EURweb, Dec. 16, 2009. Retrieved Dec. 17, 2009 www.eurweb.com/story/eur58073.cfm

33. "Wal-Mart Talks Money with AC/DC, Prepares to Slash Shelf Space Even More," June 9, 2008. Retrieved Sept. 29, 2009, from http://idolator.com

34. Geoff Boucher, "A retail 'Revelation' for Journey," *Los Angeles Times.* June 12, 2008.

35. E-mail correspondence with Susan Masino, April 27, 2010.

36. Walmartwatch.com/blog, from the Chicago Tribune Pop Machine blog, retrieved Sept. 29, 2009.

37. Walmartwatch.com/blog. From Trusty Ghetto, retrieved Sept. 29, 2009.

38. Walmartwatch.com/blog. From Kyle Smith Online, retrieved Sept. 29, 2009.

39. Chris Harris, "AC/DC's Black Ice Sells Nearly 800,000 For Year's Second-Biggest Debut," www.mtv.com, Oct. 29, 2008. Retrieved Sept. 29, 2009. Randy Lewis, "AC/DC's 'Black Ice' at No. 1 again," *Los Angeles Times* (latimesblogs.latimes.com), Nov. 5, 2009. Retrieved Sept. 29, 2009.

40. Masino, April 27, 2010.

41. Phil Freeman, "AC/DC's exclusive deal with Wal-Mart was all about the money," Jan. 29, 2009. Retrieved from www.nashvillescene.com on Sept. 29, 2009.

42. Robert Levine. "Wal-Mart Wins Deal on Album and Game," *The New York Times*, Sept. 30, 2008.

43. Geoff Boucher, "'Iron Man 2' shoots to thrill with AC/DC," *Los Angeles Times*, April 19, 2010.

44. Nekesa Mumbi Moody, "Mick Jones says he's hoping Wal-Mart deal will bring awareness to Foreigner," *Entertainment Daily*, July 30, 2009. "Foreigner Just 'Can't Slow Down,' New Album March 1st," onemetal.com, March 11, 2010.

45. Don Reisinger, "When will the music industry finally give in to iTunes?" www.ipodnn.com, May 26, 2010, retrieved June 21, 2010.

46. Ben Reid, "Wal-mart battles for $10 CDs," www.afterdawn.com. Posted Oct. 17, 2006. Retrieved June 21, 2010.

47. *Ibid.*

BIBLIOGRAPHY

Boucher, Geoff. "A retail 'Revelation' for Journey," *Los Angeles Times.* June 12, 2008.

Boucher. "'Iron Man 2' shoots to thrill with AC/DC," *Los Angeles Times.* April 19, 2010.

"Chris Brown is a Twitter Quitter," *EURweb*. Dec. 16, 2009. Retrieved Dec. 17, 2009. (www.eurweb.com/story/eur58073.cfm)

"Foreigner Just 'Can't Slow Down,' New Album March 1st," *onemetal.com*. March 11, 2010.

Fox, Mark A. "Market Power in Music Retailing: The Case of Wal-Mart," Popular Music and Society. Vol. 28, No. 4, 2005, pp. 501–19.

Freeman, Phil. "AC/DC's exclusive deal with Wal-Mart was all about the money," *Nashvillescene.com*. Jan. 29, 2009. Retrieved Sept. 29, 2009.

Harris, Chris. "AC/DC's Black Ice Sells Nearly 800,000 For Year's Second-Biggest Debut," *mtv.com*. Oct. 29, 2008. Retrieved Sept. 29, 2009.

Levine, Robert. "For Some Music, It Has to Be Wal-Mart and Nowhere Else," *The New York Times*. June 9, 2008.

Levine. "Wal-Mart Wins Deal on Album and Game," *The New York Times*. Sept. 30, 2008.

Lewis, Randy. "AC/DC's 'Black Ice' at No. 1 again," *Los Angeles Times*. Nov. 5, 2008. Retrieved Sept. 29, 2009.

Masino, Susan. *Let There Be Rock: The Story of AC/DC*. New York: Omnibus Press, 2006.

Montgomery, James. "You Won't Find Green Day's 21st Century Breakdown at Wal-Mart." Mtv.com. May 21, 2009. Retrieved March 16, 2010. (www.mtv.com/news/articles/1611970/20090521/green_day.jhtml)

Moody, Nekesa Mumbi. "Mick Jones says he's hoping Wal-Mart deal will bring awareness to Foreigner," Entertainment Daily. July 30, 2009.

Obrecht, Jas. "Angus Young: Seriously," *Guitar Player*. February 1984.

Plasketes, George. "Pimp My Records: The Deluxe Dilemma and Edition Condition: Bonus, Betrayal, or Download Backlash?" *Popular Music and Society*. Vol. 31, No. 3, July 2008, pp. 389–93.

Recording Industry of America 2008 Consumer Profile. Retrieved May 17, 2010. *(www.riaa.com)*

Reid, Ben. "Wal-mart battles for $10 CDs," *www.afterdawn.com*. Oct. 17, 2006. Retrieved June 21, 2010.

Reisinger, Don. "When will the music industry finally give in to iTunes?" www.ipodnn.com. May 26, 2010. Retrieved June 21, 2010.

Strauss, Neil. "Wal-Mart's CD Standards Are Changing Pop Music," *The New York Times*. Nov. 12, 1996, A1.

Tanner, Adam, and Scott Hillis. "iTunes passes Wal-Mart as top U.S. music retailer," *USA Today*. April 3, 2008. Retrieved April 23, 2010.

"Walmart Issues 2010 Annual Report to Shareholder," Press Release, April 19, 2010. (forbes.com)

"Walmart: Pop Culture Gatekeeper?" *PBS News-Hour*. Aug. 20, 2004. Retrieved March 16, 2010. (http://www.pbs.org/newshour/bb/business/wal-mart/impact.html)

"Wal-Mart Talks Money with AC/DC, Prepares to Slash Shelf Space Even More," *www.idolator.com*. June 9, 2008. Retrieved Sept. 29, 2009.

WEBSITES CONSULTED

www.acdc.com
www.riaa.com
www.walmartstores.com
www.walmartwatch.com/blog

NOTE: Susan Masino was a consultant for the AC/DC history portion of this chapter. For more on AC/DC please see her 2006 biography of the band, Let There Be Rock: The Story of AC/DC.

3

The Family Osbourne: A Narrative of Domesticity Tames and Enriches the Godfather of Heavy Metal

Jacqueline Lambiase

IN THE BEGINNING . . . [1]

This chapter begins as nearly all narratives of Ozzy Osbourne's life begin, with a focus on his working-class, impoverished, and abusive upbringing in rough-and-tumble Birmingham, England. Whether this story is told by *Rolling Stone* magazine,[2] by Ozzy himself in his 2009 autobiography,[3] by his wife and children,[4] or by unauthorized biographers,[5] it is this story that serves as an important part of his brand. And it is an extension of this narrative, and his identity with this narrative, that underpins his family's brand and successes.

Known as the "godfather of heavy metal" and "prince of darkness,"[6] Osbourne presides over an intangible mix of characters from past and present: an electrifying, spooky blues/rock vocalist; a badass celebrity and nearly unmanageable drug and alcohol user; and a profane but doddering father to both his own children and to legions of younger metal musicians and fans. All of these characters play important roles in Ozzy Osbourne's story. Despite the rebellion inherent in his music and its performance, Ozzy Osbourne has never turned away from these characters or his own upbringing—or at least the narrative of that upbringing—thanks to the business acumen of his then-manager, Sharon Arden. With her encouragement, Ozzy embraced the character whom he knows best: a bad-boy singer from working-class roots, searching for the next great gig.

After Ozzy's firing from Black Sabbath in 1979, Sharon Arden convinced him to front his own metal band and to retain her as his personal manager, under the structure of her father's agency.[7] This first "reinvention as himself" has led to a career as a serial collaborator with myriad bands and musicians. Yet through all of these iterations of himself, Ozzy's longest running collaborator has been Sharon Arden Osbourne, whom he married in 1982. Her involvement placed him on a pathway of steady successes in the 1980s and 1990s, especially in the heavy-metal category. Since 2000, Sharon's management has led to continued successes for Ozzy's brand, built as much on his own unbelievable life story and his family's TV-based celebrity as on his music. In the first two decades of his career, Ozzy stood alone on stage Osbourne, but now that neo-Vaudevillian stage is filled with new characters, namely his wife, Sharon, and children Kelly and Jack.[8]

BRANDING AS WRITING:
NARRATIVES, HISTORIES, AND AUTOBIOGRAPHIES

Inherent in the notion of "branding" is the act of marking, imprinting, writing, and defining. Through repetition, words and images create brand meaning for products, for organizations, and for people. Writing may be seen as definition or identification, as self-persuasion, and as transformation, according to rhetorician Kenneth Burke, who believed that in a media saturated world, identification often occurs through "trivial repetition and dull daily reinforcement."[9] Writing, and particularly writing history, then, becomes a way for people to define themselves, to "choose who they are by choosing who they were."[10] Historian/rhetorician Hans Kellner would say that writing *is* history, that these two things, one an activity and one a product of that activity, are virtually indistinguishable.[11] Writing history has become important to the Osbournes. Since 2002 when their seemingly mundane daily life was recorded for the hit MTV series *The Osbournes*, Ozzy Osbourne and his family have written at least ten books about themselves and their roles as entertainers (see Textbox 3.1). They have also participated in a documentary titled "Wreckage of My Past: The Story of Ozzy Osbourne," scheduled for release in 2010.

While Ozzy Osbourne's wife, Sharon, began to influence his career as early as 1978, it wasn't until the last decade that she has repeatedly engineered the telling of his story, and of his family story, on thousands of pages in dozens of books. It is a story that has been tested and edited for a long time, however, in mainstream media interviews. Ozzy Osbourne's music has also played a part in developing this story, in albums such as *Diary of a Madman* and on his very flesh in his many tattoos, either horrific or simplistic. That story has now shifted into digital venues and books, places in which people may write about their own lives, rather than relying on third parties to publish these stories and to represent them. In the 1970s, 1980s, and much of the 1990s, manager Sharon Osbourne had to rely on others to represent her spouse and her family; by the 2000s, she and her family had much more control over their narratives and their branding.

"GET THE STORY CROOKED"

These historical sources—media interviews, autobiographies, biographies, and the reality show *The Osbournes*—will be used both to analyze the story of Ozzy Osbourne and his family's branding. Rather than attention to "truth" or "fiction," this chapter will instead focus on the stories themselves and the ways in which they are told. This rhetorical analysis will rely on "getting the story crooked" (Kellner's term),[12] on reading stories in crooked ways to understand their construction and their conventions, their tropes and their sources. Through this deconstruction, then, will the branding be more apparent for analysis. Since branding itself is an exercise in "straightening" the story, of ensuring all parts of an entity are aligned and consistent, this deconstruction will show the parts of the Osbournes' branding strategy. One purpose of this chapter will be to collect these strategies for packaging and selling Ozzy and his family.

Most certainly, biographers of the Osbournes are trying to get the story straight in the historical tradition of collecting facts, dates, and points of view. History, however, is more than conscientious fact-checking and straight storytelling, and historiography provides a way to evaluate the ways narratives are built. Kellner asserts that "historical events do not represent themselves, they are represented; they do not speak, they are spoken for."[13] In other words, there is no straight story to tell, but simply representations created and shaped by language.

The self-labeled "unauthorized" biographers of the Osbournes, however, represent their own narratives as straight, as truth, by exploring "the true story of the Osbourne family"[14] and Sharon as "the real woman behind the relentless media circus."[15] Even the word "unauthorized" gives their narratives the appearance of "truth," a truth that perhaps the Osbournes themselves have hidden. One unauthorized Ozzy Osbourne biographer sees MTV's *The Osbournes* as a truth-telling narrative, with "Ozzy and the family . . . simply being the way they were every single day. This was them, this was their routine."[16] In a book written and published by the family in 2003, as *The Osbournes* was in production, Ozzy writes that he "didn't like the show, but I'll tell you what: The editing was fucking genius."[17] Sharon Osbourne also expresses pleasure about the editing, which made the story literally crooked, but also, straight or truthful: "Despite all the screaming and cursing that we did, I think people could see that we honestly loved one another very much."[18]

Understanding that the show's narratives were crooked, Jack Osbourne explains how the editing—or writing—worked, with himself as a character:

> Well, this is how MTV edited stuff. You know that episode where it shows a girl in my room? That was my friend Jackie. The "next morning" wasn't really the same fucking time. When they asked, "Why was your door locked, Jack?"—that was three weeks later! Then Kelly said I had a girl in the room, which I didn't that day. Plus Jackie had been sleeping on the couch.[19]

MTV producers simply found the crooked, edited narrative to be much more interesting than Jack's story (above) would have been in a more traditional, straightforward telling. In this way, then, did MTV invent a biography of everyday life for its show *The Osbournes,* which was a representation of the family, but not the Osbournes themselves. In his most recent autobiography, Ozzy Osbourne pinpoints the value of adding *The Osbournes'* narrative to his career, writing that the "power of the telly" was "a lot bigger than being the ex-lead singer of Black Sabbath"[20] and "*The Osbournes* had given me a completely new audience."[21]

NARRATIVE FORMULAS

In their own autobiographies, each of the Osbournes uses the same formulaic narratives and stock characters, laying them down in a seemingly straight, chronological fashion. First, this happened, and then, something happened next. Neil Postman would call it the "Now, This" construction of mass media,[22] putting together disparate things to create continuity and to create narrative. Ozzy and Sharon Osbourne, along with their three children (who are extensions of their family brand), conjure continuity by invoking Ozzy's tough upbringing to explain his destructive behavior as the original lead singer of Black Sabbath, as a solo artist, and as a spouse and father in his own family. The rooting of all family stories in Ozzy Osbourne's upbringing is explicit in both unauthorized biographies and family autobiographies published simultaneously with production of *The Osbournes*. This juxtaposition of texts provides a deliberate intertextuality, with the MTV series serving as an "effect," his upbringing serving as the "cause."

In their family autobiography *Ordinary People* in a chapter titled "Nativity in Black," Ozzy's three children all write about their father's upbringing on the first page:[23]

- Kelly is "sad to know how my dad was treated as a child;"
- Aimee writes that "you sense his pain. You know he's suffered a lot;" and

- Jack writes that his father "compared his upbringing to the book *Angela's Ashes*. It wasn't that bad, but he said it was close."[24]

Beyond Ozzy's upbringing, these autobiographies and biographies all repeat the usual litany of his destructive deeds (see Textbox 3.2), including biting off the head of a dove in a 1981 publicity stunt at CBS Records in Los Angeles; biting off the head of an allegedly live bat thrown on stage in January 1982 in Des Moines, Iowa; urinating on the Alamo a month later in San Antonio, Texas, while in a drug or alcohol induced stupor; and nearly strangling Sharon Osbourne in 1989 in England, for which attempted murder charges were dropped after he spent time in rehabilitation.

Two primary narratives emerge from these repetitious recitals of Ozzy Osbourne's life: a "from rags to riches" story about an underdog, and a "from addiction to redemption" story that has come forth more recently in his sobriety. Osbourne's well-known story takes on a kind of rock-styled "odyssey," a journey taken in murky, dark circumstances. Its mythical unfolding is familiar to anyone who has ever watched VH1's *Behind the Music*. All the usual plot elements are present: humble beginnings, hard work *and* luck, meteoric rise to fame, the chaos brought about by addiction, the manipulation of managers and financial advisers, disintegration. Finally redemption comes, either through more fame, a comeback, or a peaceful retirement. Historical logic like that portrayed in *Behind the Music* relies on plot and turns stories into "mythos," a metaphoric process that uses romance, tragedy, comedy, and satire.[25] All these elements appear in Ozzy Osbourne's narrative, both before and after he married Sharon Arden, and he plays stock characters fitting all of those modes. Tragedy takes the stage when his personal life is filled with addiction and abuse; comedy and satire make their entrance during his partying and performance life, when he and his band embrace over-the-top satanist personae and other attention-getting antics. Even in his pre-Black Sabbath days, Ozzy was encouraged by bandmate Tony Iommi to "do something fucking mental, to get everyone's attention" if the crowd grew bored during Star Club performances in Germany in 1969, when the band was still called Earth.[26]

Perhaps the first mode, romance, trumps all other modes in the Osbourne story. Familial love is used to conquer the chaos cycle created by addiction, abuse, and fame; emotion is valued over reason. These romantic virtues of love and emotion fill *The Osbournes*. Past tragedies may provide context. And new tragedies—Sharon's cancer diagnosis, Kelly and Jack's own addictions, Ozzy's health scares and need for sobriety, and Aimee's absence from the family narrative—may emerge in *The Osbournes*, but romance helps to polish the narrative. A biographer claims "the one thing that always was evident—indeed, it couldn't be hidden—was the love in the family."[27] Ozzy Osbourne backs up this assessment, writing that "if there's one message that gets across, it's love your family, no matter what."[28] For *The Osbournes* to remain viable for MTV and viable for the "real" family, that family's ties needed to be perceived as strong.[29] For New Year's Eve 2002, featured in an episode of *The Osbournes* titled "My Big Fat Jewish Wedding," MTV taped a party during which Ozzy and Sharon renewed their wedding vows after twenty years of marriage. Yet the episode also included footage of vintage Ozzy, heavily drinking before and after the ceremony, followed by a scene of Ozzy asleep on a couch in his hotel room, with Sharon still by his side, fully accepting him as he is, unchanged and untamed.

STEREOTYPES AND STOCK CHARACTERS

The Prince of Darkness

Ozzy Osbourne's performances and recordings as front man for Black Sabbath provided the earliest definitions of the persona he would play for audiences. He writes that he and his band mates "never took the black magic stuff seriously for one second. We just liked how theatrical it was."[30] In describing the consequences of using satanic and occult images, Osbourne writes, "I couldn't believe it when I learned that people actually 'practiced the occult.' These freaks with white makeup and black robes would come up to us after our gigs and invite us to black masses at Highgate Cemetery in London . . . The good thing about all of the satanic stuff was that it gave us endless free publicity."[31] The "satanic stuff" also sold music, with the first album, titled simply with the band's new name *Black Sabbath*, selling 5,000 copies on the first day of release in 1970.[32]

Once Ozzy Osbourne left Black Sabbath in 1979, he named himself the "prince of darkness," perhaps because it was the most obvious way to maintain his personal branding. Both Ozzy and his manager/wife Sharon, whose father performed in vaudeville, have long understood that more than the music matters in an age of images.[33] "No artist can predict, let alone control, what an audience will make of his images," writes Greil Marcus, and this matter of image vs. musician can be tricky to resolve, since a musician faces "tension between community and self reliance."[34] When a musician becomes more character than musician, then that choice will be to accept "the audience's image of himself, pretend that his audience is his shadowy ideal, and lose himself in his audience. Then he will only be able to confirm; he will never be able to create."[35] These images were important even before music videos, despite one critic's assertion that "print exposure is the least reliable of promotional tools in an aural medium."[36] Put simply, visual markers of his narrative have made a tremendous difference in Ozzy Osbourne's success as a musician-showman.

At the start of his solo career, by biting off the heads of a dove and a bat and by showering audiences in bloody mixes of raw meat, Ozzy Osbourne continued to use his "prince of darkness" character. For Live Aid, a concert to raise money and awareness about world hunger, Ozzy reunited with Black Sabbath in summer 1985, with Sharon Osbourne ensuring that "his image was exactly right for such an occasion . . . (when he) appeared from the wings in a huge purple and gold cloak, sending the audience of millions worldwide into a frenzy of excitement."[37] Just after this performance in January 1986, the family of a teenager who killed himself in California in 1984 sued Osbourne and CBS Records, since the teen had been listening to an Osbourne song titled "Suicide Solution."[38] In the language of the lawsuit, the teen's family believed in the influence of the showmanship, satanic images, and dark messages of Osbourne's narrative. Commenting on the lawsuit, a psychologist agreed with Ozzy's version of his "prince of darkness" character; the psychologist said teens enjoyed the intensity of music and images from heavy metal and did not usually "take heavy metal's satanic symbols seriously at all. To them, it's theater."[39]

For decades, fans and critics have embraced the character who plays the "godfather of heavy metal" and the "prince of darkness." (His official web site, www.ozzy.com, still used the latter term to promote his book signings in late 2009 and early 2010.) Journalists and audiences alike also played with Ozzy Osbourne's bad-boy image, writing about "bites,"[40] "the bat-snacking King of British Heavy Metal,"[41] the "Queen's original bat-man,"[42] and "ultimate rock miscreant,"[43] and continuing to throw rubber, dead and live animals on stage for years. Ozzy himself said in the 1980s that "I don't profess to be a messiah of slum people, but I was a back-street kid, and that little demon is still in there shoving hot coal in. The aggression I play is the aggression I know. And it's obviously aggression a lot of people have."[44]

The Working-Class Musician at Ozzfest

As Ozzy Osbourne continued to employ the persona of the "prince of darkness" for more than two decades, he found himself rejected by the alternative-rock festival Lollapalooza in the mid-1990s; at that time, one biographer writes, Sharon Osbourne realized "the nostalgia circuit was not for her"[45] and that "she knew she would have to work hard to change Ozzy's image."[46] Rather than contending directly with an image of an aging "prince of darkness," Sharon Osbourne, Ozzy, their family and even biographers began using the term "working-class," another aspect of Ozzy's personality that was rooted in his earliest history but still a step away from "nostalgia" and the persona of an aging rocker. Several family stories report that a rejection of Ozzy during this reinvention effort led to Ozzfest, an annual heavy metal traveling concert festival started in 1996. The "hip" Lollapalooza had rejected "hard-edged" Ozzy, so Sharon decided "what was needed was something that was not wholesome, not saving a fucking rainforest or any other charitable cause, where you didn't run the risk of any monks moaning, just hard-edged music from morning to night."[47] In her own family's autobiography, Sharon writes that "Ozzy's music is working-class music, he's a working-class hero."[48] Jack Osbourne described the genesis of Ozzfest as "we'll do it ourselves. We'll do our own tour, with our own harder-edged, working-class kind of bands, and we'll prove them wrong."[49] The working-class angle was an excellent fit for Ozzy's underdog character.

For more than a decade, Ozzfest has made millions for the Osbournes, as well as tying together at least two generations of musicians.[50] It provided a space for Ozzy Osbourne to combine the story of his upbringing and his early success, among other "working-class" bands and with a larger and younger "working-class" audience. Reflecting on his successes in an interview with *Rolling Stone*, Ozzy said, "I've done a lot for a simple working class guy."[51] Ozzy's brand connection to these younger working-class fans has been exploited in 2009 alone by performing at Blizzard Entertainment's Blizzcon (an annual gaming trade show in California), by lending his image and voice to *Brutal Legend* (a video game), and by participating in a wrestling event, World Wrestling Entertainment's *Raw*. Most work in mainstream commercials and as a celebrity endorser, however, has been in the persona of his most recent role of father, such as appearing as a spokesman for Pepsi Twist and Samsung.[52]

Doddering Dad and Powerful Mom

The opening credits of *The Osbournes* give away what it will take viewers only a short time to learn. Ozzy Osbourne is "The Dad," a new role using quote marks just like the "prince of darkness," while all his members family are playing it straight, names only, no quote marks necessary. What viewers learn is that Osbourne chaos is now generated by Sharon, Kelly, Jack, and their many pets, rather than by Ozzy. He is no more in charge of the narrative than any other television father of the 1990s and 2000s; he is not Ward Cleaver or Cliff Huxtable, but rather Homer Simpson. *TV Guide* called the show a cross between the *Simpsons* and *Spinal Tap*; one critic likens the opening music of *I Love Lucy* to *The Osbournes*, with its lounge-show version of a nearly unrecognizable Ozzy favorite, "Crazy Train."[53] While also evoking characters from *The Addams Family* and *The Munsters*, some critics believe a more accurate "metaphor to describe Ozzy would be a lumbering dazed Frankenstein monster (Sharon being Dr. Frankenstein, of course)."[54] With a dad so doddering, who is in charge? The answer to this question does recall the storyline, not just the lounge music, of *I Love Lucy*. Just as a sometimes incoherent Ricky Ricardo is sputtering in Spanish and reeling while his wife and friends create chaos, Ozzy sputters and speaks nearly incoherently much of the time. Show business is at the core of both *I Love Lucy* and *The Osbournes*; both wives have husbands who have been long-time performers, and both wives are assumed to have no talent of their own. Even though insiders knew about Sharon Osbourne's (and Lucille Ball's) management skills, that part of the Osbourne narrative was never as overtly shared until after the 2002 debut of *The Osbournes*.[55]

The trappings of a "prince of darkness" are clear: the family's new home is remodeled to include gothic features and crucifixes, boxes of "dead things" and "devil heads" are unpacked as if they came from a prior residence along with pots and pans, and Osbourne himself displays the tattooed writing of his youth. The brand marks are still present, but these now extend to his family members and their shared living space. In the first episode titled "A House Divided," Ozzy Osbourne the heavy-metal performer is escorted, made-up, and dressed before taking the stage of *The Tonight Show* with Jay Leno. Sharon and Kelly literally dust off an old costume, untangle and trim the fringe, and pack Ozzy inside. *The Tonight Show* is "too mainstream for him," says Sharon. "I make him do it." After the appearance, his children Kelly and Jack are shown fighting throughout the house, apparently tough and unruly, but the "fight club" sequence was certainly shot over many weeks and collapsed into one story segment.[56] Sharon, who is listed as co-producer of *The Osbournes*, remains almost in the background of this first episode, helping movers, working with interior decorators, and refereeing fights between her children and pets.

Photographs of the family from the autobiographies, unauthorized biographies, and opening sequences of *The Osbournes* show people who look quite different from *The Osbournes*, reality characters. While Ozzy Osbourne appears as a familiar character in *The Osbournes*, his family's looks have changed, especially his spouse. When Sharon Osbourne was "behind the music" as his manager, she dressed as a typical mother and businesswoman in the 1980s and 1990s. In a special program produced in the mid-1990s and shown on the Travel Channel in the United States, a "pre-branded" Sharon Osbourne appears wearing baggy blouses, pearls, and skirts, and she discusses their routines at two homes, one in California and one in Buckinghamshire, England.[57] Their households, decorations, and speech (except for Ozzy, who is bleeped a few times) are conventional and he says "we live quite normally" as opposed to the people's perceptions of him "hanging from the rafters" in a dungeon. "We can't get rid of that reputation," says Sharon in the program. "It precedes him." While scenes from concerts and music videos, and a photo of Ozzy holding a dove, are edited into the program, most of the time Ozzy Osbourne is represented as a wealthy English landowner, picking fruit from a tree on the vast grounds in Beverly Hills, smoking a cigar, drinking tea, making a vegetable smoothie, and enjoying his California and English mansions. The tried-and-true narrative for Ozzy, however, is present, too. The narrator says that "Ozzy has come a long way from his working-class background in Birmingham, England," and Ozzy himself says that "where I come from was very, very poor."[58] In this brief documentary from the mid-1990s, both he and Sharon recount the stock characters and storylines used time and time again: the attempted murder, the parties, and the drug and alcohol abuse, and his success despite these things.

After this special and before *The Osbournes* (and the family's appearance on MTV's *Cribs*, also a trial run for the reality series), Sharon became part of the brand herself, rather than just brand manager. Her extensive weight loss and plastic surgery since 1999 have been placed into the family narrative, along with decades-long fights with her father and extended family, so that she appears to be as "extreme" as Ozzy himself.[59] By casting herself as "extreme" and as a "survivor," as she does in her autobiographies, Sharon Osbourne plays a more fitting role opposite her leading man. Both her character and the family's must fit the overall brand of the "prince of darkness," and this characterization fit two of his teenage children, Kelly and Jack. (Aimee, his eldest child with Sharon, declares herself a non-character, not willing to write herself into the family narrative and not willing to become part of the show.[60]) As individual family members changed into characters to fit the storyline, so did Ozzy's character transform into a more fatherly "prince of darkness," named as "The Dad" to his own children and as a godfather of heavy metal for younger musicians.

A FAMILY, BRANDED

Sharon Osbourne declares the "reputation"—the character and the storyline of Ozzy Osbourne—impossible to erase. The narrative for his public life, though it may have started as an individual character who sang heavy metal music, has been built in part on his earliest family life in Birmingham, England, and the story of his upbringing. Over the past decade, that story has been synthesized with that of his more recent family life, as part of a narrative place called *The Osbournes* and through multiple autobiographies and biographies written since that show debuted.

In his most recent autobiography, Ozzy Osbourne shows readers a postmodern sensibility by writing that he does not care about his narrative's truthfulness. He writes in a footnote that "Other people's memories of the stuff in this book might not be the same as mine. I ain't gonna argue with 'em. Over the past forty years I've been loaded on booze, coke, acid . . . What you read here is what dribbled out of the jelly I call my brain when I asked it for my life story. Nothing more, nothing less . . ."[61] He disarms his readers and critics; he is simply a storyteller and a character in a story, and truth is not the point. But he is compelled, as always, to repeat that narrative, even as he undermines belief in it. One biographer says Ozzy Osbourne is "stuck in the past, to an extent."[62]

Keeping the story and the brand straight (and fresh) appears now to be the sole responsibility of Sharon Osbourne, at first locked into a role as a behind-the-scenes, long-suffering wife/manager, now more actively writing herself into a broader family narrative as a cursing but loving mother and wife, as a fighter/manager, and as an underdog herself.[63] In several books, Sharon Osbourne writes to set the record "straight." In one of her latest books, she writes that "reluctantly I have decided that, in spite of my earlier decision—and the words I have written in this book are proof of that—I must speak out. Not just for me, but for my friends, Ozzy and my children."[64] In *Survivor*, she writes to refute a news story fueled by her brother's comments after their father's death, and this same autobiography uses many "real" letters she wrote to business partners and others in her life, to refute them in short-term disputes or long-running feuds. These fights have always been prominent in the story of Ozzy's recording contracts, and Sharon Osbourne registers old and new disputes in her autobiographies, as the underdogs fight onward. Recently, she has appeared as judges and contestants on several reality shows, such as *America's Got Talent* and *The Apprentice*, where she performs in her fighter persona and mentions her spouse and children prominently. Her personal web site, www.sharonosbourne.com, calls her "the most visible representation of balls in the business."[65] Her latest book, published in March 2010 in the U.K., is called *Revenge*, one more in a long line of chances to set the record straight.

Ozzy's "prince of darkness"—and that prince's incredible story—has proven to be a perfect match for rock music, which "may matter because it is a fun, unpredictable, anarchic, a neatly packaged and amazingly intense plurality of good times and good ideas."[66] Ozzy Osbourne's character fits that prototypical anarchic rocker, creating stories in their plurality; Sharon

Osbourne, now neatly or "straightly" packaging herself as unpredictable and extreme, rearranges her family around a brand that is now as matriarchal as it is anarchic. Ozzy's match with rock music has certainly been topped by this partnership with Sharon. Their family's substantial investment in identity has extended the rocker's brand into a heavy-metal future, at least to those who will accept that narrative and play their parts.

Textbox 3.1.　Branding through Writing

These 10 books by members of the Osbourne family have been published after the debut of MTV's reality series *The Osbournes* in 2002, with at least a dozen books written by outsiders and published since 2002. (This list does not include guitar "signature licks" books published by Ozzy Osbourne and his musician partners during this time.)

Ozzy Talking: Ozzy Osbourne in His Own Words by Ozzy Osbourne and Harry Shaw (June 2002)

Bark at the Moon: The Official Osbourne Pet Book by Family Osbourne and Todd Gold (November 2002)

Officially Osbourne: Opening the Doors to the Land of Oz by Todd Gold and the Osbourne family (November 2002)

Ordinary People: Our Story by Ozzy Osbourne, Sharon Osbourne, and Aimee, Kelly and Jack with Todd Gold (July 2004)

21 Years Gone: The Autobiography by Jack Osbourne (October 2006)

Sharon Osbourne Extreme: My Autobiography by Sharon Osbourne (October 2006)

Sharon Osbourne Survivor: My Story—The Next Chapter by Sharon Osbourne (August 2009)

Fierce by Kelly Osbourne (September 2009)

I Am Ozzy by Ozzy Osbourne and Chris Ayres (U.K., November 2009; U.S. January 2010)

Revenge by Sharon Osbourne (U.K., March 2010)

SOURCE: Amazon.com and http://www.sharonosbourne.com

Textbox 3.2.　The Narrative of a Chaotic Decade

These five stories from 1979 to 1989 serve as the center of most Osbourne family autobiographies, which are always first anchored in Ozzy's tough childhood in Birmingham, England, after his birth in 1948.

1979: Ozzy Osbourne, lead singer, is fired by Black Sabbath, and he forms a partnership with Sharon Arden, who becomes his personal manager. He names himself "the prince of darkness."

1980: Ozzy bites off the head of a dove during a meeting with CBS Records in California; Sharon writes in *Extreme* that the executives needed "something to remember him by," so they bought doves from a pet shop that would be set free during the meeting.

1981: Ozzy bites off the head of a bat, allegedly alive and thrown on stage by a fan, during a concert in Des Moine, Iowa.

1982: Randy Rhoads, the lead guitarist of Ozzy Osbourne's band Blizzard of Ozz, is killed in a plane crash; a few months later, Ozzy marries Sharon Arden once his divorce from his first wife is finalized.

1989: Ozzy Osbourne attacks his wife, Sharon, and is charged with attempted murder; the charges are dropped when he agrees to rehab.

NOTES

1. The title of the first chapter of his 2009 autobiography *I Am Ozzy*, as well as, of course, the first words of the Hebrew Torah or Christian Old Testament; Ozzy Osbourne, *I Am Ozzy* (London: Sphere/Little, Brown Book Group, 2009).

2. David Fricke, "Ozzy Osbourne, July 25, 2002," *The Rolling Stone Interviews*, eds. Jann S. Wenner and Joe Levy (NY: Back Bay Books, 2007), 426–31.

3. Ozzy Osbourne, *I Am Ozzy*.

4. Jack Osbourne, *21 Years Gone: The Autobiography* (London: Macmillan, 2006); Ozzy and Sharon Osbourne, with Aimee, Kelly and Jack, *Ordinary People* (London: Pocket Books, 2003); Sharon Osbourne, *Sharon Osbourne Extreme* (NY: Springboard Press, 2005); Sharon Osbourne, *Sharon Osbourne Survivor: My Story, the Next Chapter* (London: Sphere/Little, Brown Book Group, 2007).

5. Sue Crawford, *Sharon Osbourne: Unauthorized, Uncensored—Understood* (London: Michael O'Mara Books, 2005); David Katz and Michael Robin, *The Osbournes: The Unauthorized !@#$-ing True Story of the Osbourne Family* (Kansas City: Andrews McMeel Publishing, 2002); Chris Nickson, *Ozzy Knows Best: An Unauthorized Biography* (NY: Thomas Dunne Books/St. Martin's Griffin, 2002).

6. Ozzy Osbourne, in a commercial for Blizzard Entertainment's game World of Warcraft, claims that his "prince of darkness" name goes back to 1979, after his break with Black Sabbath (accessed Dec. 1, 2009, from http://www.youtube.com/watch?v=8OgYWLSrmlI). Ozzy's autobiography and those of his family always mention Black Sabbath, but his own narrative is rarely rooted in that decade-long experience. His "godfather of heavy metal" moniker has been used for more than a decade, perhaps linked to Ozzfest, a heavy-metal festival produced by Sharon

Osbourne in 1996, and featuring Ozzy, his reunions with Black Sabbath, and up-and-coming metal bands.

7. Sharon Osbourne, *Sharon Osbourne Extreme*, 110–12; Ozzy Osbourne, *I Am Ozzy*, 195.

8. That stage was first haunted by the absence of guitarist Randy Rhoads after his death in a plane crash in 1982, and now by the absence of his living daughter, Aimee, who has refused to participate in the family's narrative, especially in its MTV show *The Osbournes*.

9. Kenneth Burke, *A Rhetoric of Motives* (Berkeley: University of California Press, 1969), 26.

10. Hans Kellner, *Language and Historical Representation: Getting the Story Crooked* (Madison: University of Wisconsin Press, 1989), 197.

11. Kellner, 208.

12. Kellner, vii

13. Kellner, 208.

14. Katz and Robin, title page.

15. Crawford, jacket cover.

16. Nickson, 167.

17. Ozzy and Sharon Osbourne, *Ordinary People*, 242.

18. Ozzy and Sharon Osbourne, 243.

19. Ozzy and Sharon Osbourne, 243.

20. Ozzy Osbourne, 342.

21. Ozzy Osbourne, 2009, 343.

22. Neil Postman, *Amusing Ourselves to Death: Public Discourse in the Age of Show Business* (NY: Penguin, 1986).

23. Ozzy and Sharon Osbourne, 13.

24. Ozzy and Sharon Osbourne, 13.

25. Kellner, 223.

26. Ozzy Osbourne, 86.

27. Nickson, 164.

28. Ozzy and Sharon Osbourne, 14.

29. If the family disintegrates, then the family-based reality show is over, as proven by *Jon & Kate Plus 8* in 2009. In Ozzy Osbourne's case, the family has become his brand in the last decade. Even Ozzy's daughter, Aimee, who did not participate in *The Osbournes*, carries the message that family is important. She believes "most people will look back on *The Osbournes* as a laugh—good entertainment. . . . I'm just glad I won't be remembered for yelling at my sister or fighting with my mother . . . I still have my *identity*" (emphasis added; Ozzy and Sharon Osbourne, 313).

30. Ozzy Osbourne, 99.

31. Ozzy Osbourne, 99–100.

32. Ozzy Osbourne, 100.

33. This is especially true of female musicians, who are nearly always branded with sexually suggestive or explicit images and placed in a kind of virtual corset by audience expectations; see Jacqueline Lambiase, "Codes of Online Sexuality: Celeb-

rity, Gender and Marketing on the Web," *Journal of Sexuality and Culture*, (Summer 2003, 7/3), 57–78.

34. Greil Marcus, *Mystery Train: Images of America in Rock 'n' Roll Music*, 3rd ed. (NY: Plume, 1990), 6.

35. Marcus, 6.

36. Robert Christgau, *Grown Up All Wrong: Great Rock and Pop Artists from Vaudeville to Techno* (Cambridge, MA: Harvard, 1998), 201.

37. Crawford, 86.

38. Bob Schwartz, "1 Dead, 3 Hurt in Violence at Rock Concerts," *The Los Angeles Times* (June 16, 1986), 3.

39. Patrick Goldstein, "Is Heavy Metal a Loaded Gun Aimed at Its Fans?" *The Los Angeles Times* (Jan. 26, 1986), 68.

40. C. Arrington, "'Man Bites Dog' Is No News When the Canine Fancier Is Voracious Rocker Ozzy Osbourne," People (Sept. 7, 1981), 57; "It Was Love at First Bite When Rocker Ozzy Osbourne Married His Manager in Hawaii," *People* (July 26, 1982), 28–29.

41. Jon Holmes, *Rock Star Babylon: Outrageous Rumors, Legends, and Raucous True Tales of Rock and Roll Icons* (NY: Plume Books, 2008), 73.

42. Bruce Pollock, *Hipper Than Our Kids: A Rock & Roll Journal of the Baby Boom Generation* (NY: Schirmer Books, 1993), 241.

43. Pollock, 138.

44. David P. Szatmary, *Rockin' in Time: A Social History of Rock-and-Roll*, 2nd ed. (Englewood Cliffs, NJ: Prentice Hall, 1991).

45. Crawford, 116.

46. Crawford, 118.

47. Sharon Osbourne, *Extreme*, 264–65.

48. Ozzy and Sharon Osbourne, 209.

49. Jack Osbourne, 42.

50. Nickson, 121.

51. Wenner and Levy, 431.

52. Many thanks to the Ozzy Work Group from JOUR 30403 at TCU (fall 2009), led by Katie Lipnick and Alicia Atwood; these undergraduate strategic communication students found many tangents of the Ozzy Osbourne story online and archived on YouTube.

53. Andrew Gumbel, "At Home with the Osbournes," *The Independent* (April 18, 2002).

54. Katz and Robin, 42–43.

55. Even after stepping on the stage of *The Osbournes* as Ozzy's hands-on manager and career partner (as well as later serving as host of her own talk show and judge for other reality competition shows), Sharon Osbourne's name appears just one time in Ozzy Osbourne's 1,500-word biography on the All American Talent & Celebrity Network, where he, not she, is credited with creating Ozzfest; Barry Weber and Greg Prato, "Biography of Ozzy Osbourne," *All American Talent & Celebrity Network* (accessed Dec. 15, 2009, from http://www.allamericanspeakers.com/speakers/Ozzy-Osbourne/2367).

56. Kelly Osbourne's own autobiography is titled *Fierce*, which fits her mother's books and their titles: *Extreme* and *Survivor*.

57. "The Osbournes Early Years, Part 1," *Travel Channel* documentary from 1997 (accessed Dec. 15, 2009, from http://www.youtube.com/watch?v=LnUA9_n-NwE).

58. "The Osbournes Early Years, Part 1."

59. Sharon Osbourne, *Extreme*, 273 and 277–79.

60. In an interview with Barbara Walters on ABC's *20/20* in 2002, after *The Osbournes* debuted, Aimee Osbourne said that in the last year, "my parents have kind of been letting it fly" in terms of cursing, and that "my family's lifestyle and attitude have changed so much in the last two years;" "Aimee Osbourne on 20/20, 2002," accessed Dec. 15, 2009, from http://www.youtube.com/watch?v=Qm05VE3fCOQ.

61. Ozzy Osbourne, *I Am Ozzy*, unnumbered page before chapter one.

62. Nickson, 192.

63. Sharon Osbourne says "We've always been sort of the underdog"; Alynda Wheat, "How to &#$@ Manage Like Sharon Osbourne," *Fortune*, May 13, 2002 (accessed Dec. 15, 2009, from http://money.cnn.com/magazines/fortune/fortune_archive/2002/05/13/322894/index.htm).

64. Sharon Osbourne, *Survivor*, 261.

65. "Biography" for Sharon Osbourne, accessed Feb. 15, 2010, from http://www.sharonosbourne.com/index.php?module=biography.

66. Marcus, 79.

BIBLIOGRAPHY

"Aimee Osbourne on *20/20*, 2002." Produced by ABC News. *20/20*. Video, 2002. http://www.youtube.com/watch?v=Qm05VE3fCOQ (accessed December 15, 2009).

Arrington, C. "'Man Bites Dog' Is No News When the Canine Fancier Is Voracious Rocker Ozzy Osbourne." *People*, September 7, 1981, 57.

"Biography." *SharonOsbourne.com*. No date. http://www.sharonosbourne.com/index.php?module=biography (accessed February 15, 2010).

Burke, Kenneth. *A Rhetoric of Motives*. Berkeley: University of California Press, 1969.

Christgau, Robert. *Grown Up All Wrong: Great Rock and Pop Artists from Vaudeville to Techno*. Cambridge, MA: Harvard, 1998.

Crawford, Sue. *Sharon Osbourne: Unauthorized, Uncensored—Understood*. London: Michael O'Mara Books, 2005.

Fricke, David. "Ozzy Osbourne, July 25, 2002." In *The Rolling Stone Interviews*. Edited by Jann S. Wenner and Joe Levy. NY: Back Bay Books, 2007, 426–31.

Goldstein, Patrick. "Is Heavy Metal a Loaded Gun Aimed at Its Fans?" *The Los Angeles Times*, January 26, 1986, 68.

Gumbel, Andrew. "At Home with the Osbournes." *The Independent*, April 18, 2002.

Holmes, Jon. *Rock Star Babylon: Outrageous Rumors, Legends, and Raucous True Tales of Rock and Roll Icons.* NY: Plume Books, 2008.

"It Was Love at First Bite When Rocker Ozzy Osbourne Married His Manager in Hawaii." *People*, July 26, 1982, 28–29.

Katz, David, and Michael Robin. *The Osbournes: The Unauthorized !@#$-ing True Story of the Osbourne Family.* Kansas City: Andrews McMeel Publishing, 2002.

Kellner, Hans. *Language and Historical Representation: Getting the Story Crooked.* Madison: University of Wisconsin Press, 1989.

Lambiase, Jacqueline, "Codes of Online Sexuality: Celebrity, Gender and Marketing on the Web." *Journal of Sexuality and Culture* 7/3 (Summer 2003): 57–78.

Marcus, Greil. *Mystery Train: Images of America in Rock 'n' Roll Music.* 3rd ed. NY: Plume, 1990.

Nickson, Chris. *Ozzy Knows Best: An Unauthorized Biography.* NY: Thomas Dunne Books/St. Martin's Griffin, 2002.

Osbourne, Jack. *21 Years Gone: The Autobiography.* London: Macmillan, 2006.

Osbourne, Kelly. *Fierce.* London: Virgin Books, 2009.

Osbourne, Ozzy. *I Am Ozzy.* London: Sphere/Little, Brown Book Group, 2009.

Osbourne, Ozzy, and Sharon Osbourne, with Aimee, Kelly and Jack. *Ordinary People.* London: Pocket Books, 2003.

Osbourne, Sharon. *Revenge.* London: Sphere, 2010.

Osbourne, Sharon. *Sharon Osbourne Extreme: My Autobiography.* NY: Springboard Press, 2006.

Osbourne, Sharon. *Sharon Osbourne Survivor: My Story, the Next Chapter.* London: Sphere/Little, Brown Book Group, 2007.

"The Osbournes Early Years, Part 1." *Travel Channel.* Video recording. 1997. http://www.youtube.com/watch?v=LnUA9_n-NwE (accessed December 15, 2009).

Pollock, Bruce. *Hipper Than Our Kids: A Rock & Roll Journal of the Baby Boom Generation.* NY: Schirmer Books, 1993.

Postman, Neil. *Amusing Ourselves to Death: Public Discourse in the Age of Show Business.* NY: Penguin, 1986.

Schwartz, Bob. "1 Dead, 3 Hurt in Violence at Rock Concerts." *The Los Angeles Times*, June 16, 1986, 3.

Szatmary, David P. *Rockin' in Time: A Social History of Rock-and-Roll.* 2nd ed. Englewood Cliffs, NJ: Prentice Hall, 1991.

Weber, Barry, and Greg Prato. "Biography of Ozzy Osbourne." *All American Talent & Celebrity Network.* http://www.allamericanspeakers.com/speakers/Ozzy -Osbourne/2367 (accessed December 15, 2009).

Wheat, Alynda. "How to &#$@ Manage Like Sharon Osbourne." *Fortune*, May 13, 2002. http://money.cnn.com/magazines/fortune/fortune_archive/2002/05/13/ 322894/index.htm (accessed December 15, 2009).

4

"Moving Her Hips, Like, Yeah": Can Miley Survive the Hannah Brand?

Deborah Clark Vance

Miley Cyrus, the wildly popular singer and star of a television show on which an average teenager secretly performs as rock singer Hannah Montana by night, has been seen posing semi-nude for an Annie Leibovitz photo in *Vanity Fair*, pole dancing at the Nickelodeon Teen Choice awards, sitting with legs spread in a "Got Milk" ad, with a tattoo, in a photo of herself in a wet T-shirt, filming a scene in *Sex and the City*: Must the Disney Corporation guard her parent-friendly brand of wholesome rocker? Or do these events indicate a natural career arc as Disney shepherds its product/employee from teen idol to sex symbol?

Music in popular culture is seldom just about the music itself, or even only about the lyrics. Rather, layers of meaning attach to the music because of its performers and their performances, and the channels through which it is mediated. When musical performers are female, more layers of meaning contribute to the mix, and when its producers are multi-national, vertically integrated corporations, a cultural critic must consider still more complexity.

To address such questions, this chapter uses a theoretical framework of critical theories, semiotics and structuralist tools to analyze the concepts of dominant culture and pop culture as well as the meanings of youth, rock music, and women in rock music; glance at the concept of teenager as it evolved through the twentieth to the twenty-first century; and examine corporate media's ability to use their many channels to sell products to children. This discussion will be applied specifically to the Disney Corporation's creation of *Hannah Montana* and its star, Miley Cyrus.

READING CULTURAL SIGNS

Understanding the meaning of a cultural product such as rock music requires analyzing the economic system in which it exists, which in the
United States is consumer capitalism. Beginning in the 1930s, critical
theorists of the Frankfurt School originating in Germany and later, the
Birmingham School in England, claimed that members of dominant culture reinforce their power by using media to circulate values and beliefs
embedded in cultural products. Adorno[1] called this process the culture
industry. While critical theorists acknowledge that corporate mass production plays a role in popular culture, they are divided about the degree to
which audiences absorb meanings rather than participate in creating them.
Roland Barthes showed how semiotics could be used to decipher the sign
systems of daily life, and Baudrillard looked at how commodities perform
as signs in capitalist consumer culture.[2] Fiske[3] claimed that it is not media
producers but audiences who create and circulate cultural meanings because creating culture is primarily a matter of meaning-making: Although
corporations can produce music, film and other products, audiences decide
how to receive it.

Cultural groups always stand in a relation of domination and subordina-
tion to one another and are locked in constant struggle.[4] Subordinate groups
compete with dominant ones for power to control the meaning of cultural
texts, as dominant culture seeks to protect itself and the status quo by taming
and subordinating symbolic meanings generated by less powerful minority
and youth cultures.[5] To tame resistance, dominant culture reframes meaning by redefining deviant behavior and converting signs—for example, the
music and clothing of subordinated groups—into consumer products; thus
subcultures become incorporated and social order repaired.[6] Although rooted
in rebellion, much rock music has become enculturated so that rather than
opposing dominant cultural values, it often upholds them. The involvement
of corporate Disney in producing a television show for children, and that
of mothers in buying Hannah Montana clothes and concert tickets for their
daughters both indicate a sanctioning of rock performer Hannah Montana/
Miley Cyrus as cultural hero, not as a countercultural icon like Elvis Presley
in the '50s or Mick Jagger in the '60s. Similarly, the rage in punk music
of the late '70s and early '80s was commodified and revived as a style in
the '90s.[7] Thus, in "The Good Life," Cyrus extols Prada shoes, Gucci bags,
Jimmy Choo, D&G, expensive restaurants, and the need for credit cards, not
the message of an oppressed underclass, but exemplification of the cultural
incorporation of rock music.

MUSIC OF THE GENERATIONS

Popular music comprises on active arena where struggle for control over meanings continuously occurs. Throughout the twentieth century, generations preferred and identified with a particular musical expression as the tastes of youth often diverges from that of their parents. While adolescents throughout time have probably disagreed with adults' stale notions to some degree, up until World War I, most U.S. youth adopted the yoke of adulthood more seamlessly than did later generations. The twentieth century saw two global wars completely change the world geopolitically from kingdoms and empires to democracies, a vast upheaval that redefined social relationships. Perhaps the generation gap first widened following that "Great War," as young men returned home to encounter an economic boom that often excluded them. Races and classes that had commingled in the army encountered each other's music and ideas, breaking down previous cultural barriers. African-American jazz appealed to white audiences, marking a departure from the middle-of-the-road music of the older dominant white, middle-class generation. The Roaring '20s represented a break with the past order that had been more stratified by class and race, less than by age cohort. Children born in that decade attained adolescence during the Great Depression in the next decade, and often had to help support their families, again aligning the interests of young and old and narrowing the gap, at least temporarily. Then World War II caused another social upheaval that put young lives on hold as men fought overseas and women worked in factories. Ears attuned to '20s and '30s jazz now listened to a bigger band jazz sound.

A burst in post-war American production output found markets among the ruins of Europe and Asia, creating unprecedented wealth that enabled large numbers to afford cars, television sets, radios, and records. Although adolescents from the mid-'50s onward experienced neither war nor depression, the world had shifted and they grew up with the consciousness of an atomic bomb that could destroy all life. Knowing they lived in an affluent world that could all disappear in an instant helped forge a psychological divide between them and their parents whom they perceived as the stewards of the corrupt world order. Psychologists labeled the discontent among youth alienation; sociologists sought to treat juvenile delinquency, another adolescent ill exacerbated during the war years when young people were left alone as their parents worked or fought overseas. The teenager was becoming recognized as a stage in human development with specific needs.

Independent music producers in the '40s and early '50s noticed the new energy in youth and released music they thought teens would buy. African

Americans had moved to cities looking for work and bringing their rhythm and blues (R&B) music.[8] Alan Freed, famous for inventing the top-40 format—a practice of radio stations featuring primarily the top-selling single records— hosted an R&B program in Cleveland in the '50s and noted its appeal to white youth. White performers watered down R&B as they transformed it to rock and roll (R&R).[9] As distinct from the middle-of-the-road music from the likes of Frank Sinatra, Doris Day, and Bing Crosby of older generations, R&R referred to here is a fusion of blues and country music. Enabling the emergence of this new sound was Broadcast Music Incorporated (BMI), a company that formed in response to the American Society of Composers, Authors, and Publishers (ASCAP)'s monopoly grip over copyright fees. Music that didn't interest ASCAP—gospel, blues, jazz and Appalachian folks songs—was available to BMI's artists[10] and these sounds influenced the development of R&R.[11]

The rhythms of R&R effused a sexuality that parents of teenagers found disturbing during the '50s and '60s.[12] R&R acquired a connotation of rebellion by the '60s and was not welcomed in public places (stores and restaurants), in advertisements, or as television theme music. Marginalizing the music of youth signaled also the marginalization of youth themselves and their interests, one of which was to end the draft. With the elimination of conscriptive military service, entering the armed forces became voluntary, and widespread youthful rage against the machine became moot. Since then, the United States has seen no overt external forces pitting the generations against each other. Most middle-class youth have enjoyed relative prosperity with little need to shoulder major family responsibilities. Marketers have steadfastly focused on acquiring some of that wealth by nurturing loyalty to particular brands among young consumers. Advertisements lure youth by colonizing media with images of themselves. One result of the preponderance of youthful images is that aging has become something to avoid to the extent that it verges on stigma. Sternbergh[13] notes the commonplace of forty-year-old adults adopting the fashions of twenty-year-olds. Generations are blurring in the other direction as well. Marketers have coined the term "kagoy" which stands for Kids Are Getting Older Younger, referring to how the same items are being sold to six- and seven-year-olds as to eleven- and twelve-year-olds.[14] The concept of cradle-to-grave marketing describes the technique of attempting to associate products with a warm, fuzzy feeling among children so that as they get older they will retain a fondness for the brand.[15] The amount of money spent on selling to children grew from $50 million in 1964 to $12 billion in 1999. Now adult products are pushed on kids.[16]

Helping to solidify the role of R&R in everyday life, music marketers constructed glamorous teen idols who served a purpose like that of the movie stars that began in the silent film era. Indeed, besides the rhythm of R&R, if not for performers' presentations, R&R music itself might not have created a sensation at all.[17] The '50s teen idol became the rock star of the '60s and beyond. In radio interviews[18] on WHYY in Philadelphia, heavy metal rock stars from Aerosmith and Metallica, Alice Cooper, and Gene Simmons of KISS, all revealed a greater concern for image—clothes, actions, connection with teen frustration, and ability to anger adults—than with music.

Teen idols and rock stars were performers above all, and if they were really famous, could also appear on television. The television, film, and music industries center around Hollywood where two powerful narratives of celebrity exist—the Romantic notion of the authentic artist with natural talent who gets discovered, and the business savvy of impresarios who construct stars out of ordinary people. These conflicting notions of art and commerce underlay the development of rock music, as authentic rock musicians tried to show their disdain for commercialism as opposed to the constructed boy bands of the '90s and '00s who acknowledge the conventions by which impresarios fashioned them.[19] In either case, audiences determine whether they can see the performer's real self through the artifice.

Because producers of media products exist in the same dominant culture as their audiences, they are aware of similar world events that ultimately shape their generation's identity. Some music production companies have been so sensitive to their times that they could understand, reflect, and influence the tastes that define their era. Such were Motown and soul music in the '60s, Def Jam and rap music in the '80s, Interscope with rap and metal in the '90s, and in the '00s Jive marketed teen pop with Britney Spears, N'Sync, and Backstreet Boys.[20] Other companies pick up and run with the trends as Disney has done with teen pop and constructed bands, categories describing Hannah Montana.

GENDER IN POP MUSIC

The twentieth century saw women challenge the feminine social identity that had been allocated to them across centuries of male domination. With the second wave of feminism reaching a pinnacle in the late '60s and early '70s, women questioned traditional sex role modeling practices for children.[21] However a backlash against feminism during the '80s is evident in popular culture texts from that time. Traditional gender socialization returned with a vengeance, thanks due in no small part to the persistence of gender role stereotyping in advertising, including an increase in gender-stereotyped ads targeted at children, and abetted by the generally conformist nature of girl culture.[22] Baker-Sperry[23] found that young girls seem concerned that others perceive them as feminine and tend not to veer from social norms.

Although women have continually been involved in R&R since the beginning, if a rock musician is a woman, this fact overshadows her role as a performer.[24] The history of R&R is often recorded in terms of commercial rather than artistic success, which causes the many women of moderate success to be overlooked; even female rock performers themselves have overlooked the long tradition of other women in R&R.[25] The rock star has generally connoted maleness while women as R&R performers have often been marginalized and welcomed only insofar as they took on a macha role. As women struggled to overcome the male dominance of rock music, they stepped into a sexualized arena. Just as when they have entered into other male-dominated fields (construction, firefighting, the military, law, medicine and engineering), women involved in playing guitars and drums, and singing R&R music had to address the meaning of femininity and womanhood. As Tannen[26] says, there is no unmarked option for women: Whatever they wear, labels them in one way or another—women cannot escape making meaning with their appearance.

Madonna, beginning as a teenybopper in the '80s, eventually cashed in on a persona that exploited female sexuality. Even while donning the corsets, heels, and makeup that in the preceding decade were considered patriarchal, Madonna claimed to liberate women because the locus of control was with the woman herself and her fans fell for it. In the context of the '80s where dress-for-success women competed with men in business and professional worlds during a socially conservative Reagan era, Madonna's hypersexuality and hyperfemininity seemed like rebellion, whereas extolling female sexuality as the primary source of women's power was a notion that previous feminists had striven to eradicate. Madonna's performances signaled that superstardom belonged to women who fit the dominant cultural notions of beauty, with sexual aggression added to the mix. The pop movement of the early '80s, typified by Madonna, has been seen as part of the backlash against feminism in that period.[27]

Women rockers reacted against the spectacle and the commodity that stars like Madonna exploited and tried to find a way to express themselves musically "without being overshadowed or scrutinized by boys."[28] The girl power movement of the '90s, for example Riot Grrls, looked back to girlhood itself for meaning. Indeed, Pipher[29] says that until they hit their teens, girls have a strong sense of themselves, their identity, and their power. The Riot Grrls asserted women's right to create and perform music in ways not defined by men, but they felt that media coverage of them attempted to impose ideals of femininity while trivializing their art.[30] The media landscape changed during the early to mid-'90s because of the multinational mergers and the Telecommunications Act of 1996. A new set of corporate values took hold and began to show a preference for women with looks rather than those with a voice. Radio, then still a primary delivery system for music, changed with the mergers: Independent stations were amassed and fashioned into national networks, Clear Channel and Infinity, whose main goal was selling airtime to advertisers. Their formats were designed as conduits for producers who wanted to sell recordings to the same target audiences, primarily youth. Dominant cultural values in media were commercial ones, with increasing emphasis on the more commercially viable sexuality of R&R and less on advertiser-unfriendly political rebellion. Arguably starting with Madonna, who released several soft-core porn music videos (*Justify My Love* in 1990, *Erotica* in 1992), pornographic images of women entered mainstream media, especially music but also music videos on cable television, such as "Uncut" on Viacom's BET network.[31] Feminism had taken on the Orwellian meaning of freedom for women to expose their bodies, equating stripping, prostitution, and porn imagery with power.[32] Moreover, pornography was becoming increasingly corporate and gaining legitimacy as a business enterprise. Major hotel chains, like the supposedly socially conservative Mormon-owned Marriott, introduced pay-per-view adult television channels, and in 1989 family-friendly Disney became the first major film company to partner with soft porn pay-per-view Viewer's Choice and its spin-off Hot Choice.[33]

Sut Jhally[34] describes how the language of music videos grew around the pornographic fantasies of the adolescent heterosexual male. In the earliest MTV music videos in the early '80s female dancers served to attract male viewers. As music videos became more competitive, they adopted an increasingly hard-core vernacular featuring a video landscape full of provocative women in a constant state of sexual arousal. *Playboy* in 1999 noted the rock-porn connection, echoed by VH1 in 2001.[35] Female artists encounter this existing language and set of narratives and have difficulty getting air play if they don't stick to the established corporate guidelines for radio and video play lists.[36] Serious musicians like Lauryn Hill, Sarah McLachlan, and Tracy Chapman who emerged during the early to mid-'90s did not conform to the porn vocabulary. Madonna who wanted to present herself as independent and powerful, Jewel who on her video for the song "Intuition" thought perhaps that she was kidding around, but could never go back; Britney Spears in 1998 released "Baby One More Time" with a "school girl in heat persona;"[37] Mariah Carey, Christina Aguilera, Jessica Simpson, and Janet Jackson all started innocently enough but all adapted to the porn vernacular.[38] Exploitation of women rockers included more than merely using their bodies: the English girl group Spice Girls was founded by three men who advertised for members in a London business paper in 1994, intending to profit by commodifying the newfound energy of the girl power movement itself.[39]

VERTICAL MONOPOLY

With the purchase of the ABC Network, Disney obtained a vertical monopoly, a situation that seems to contradict the Supreme Court's reasoning in
its 1948 decision in *The United States v. Paramount*, which broke up the monopoly of film companies over production, distribution, and exhibition. With
ABC, Disney gained control over one of the three major national networks on
which it could promote its other properties, like film productions and theme
parks. The corporate takeover of broadcasting had occurred with no public
debate, with corporate leaders promising a great diversity of consumer choice
as telephone, cable, film, and broadcast companies were allowed to enter into
each other's businesses, and broadcast networks were allowed to increase
the number of stations they owned nationwide. For example, Clear Channel bought up small local radio stations across the country where it could
target particular kinds of audiences—usually young and middle-class—and
sell air time to advertisers to reach them. The small, independent recording
companies of the '60s and '70s were engulfed by larger conglomerates that
preferred streamlining their operations by supporting a few international
mega-stars rather than a long list of performers who appeal to smaller niche
audiences. U.S. media thus largely became mere outlets for the products of
their corporate owners and able to attract exponentially increasing sums in
advertising and sales revenue.

An example of how far-reaching and powerful is the "synergy" of the vertical monopoly wielded by multinational media corporations is Harry Potter.
AOL/Time-Warner bought worldwide merchandising rights and rights to two
films, and could continually cross-promote products on its multiple media
channels—the book published, the movie made, the magazine articles extolling, the profits shared, the book and movie advertised on companies owned
by the same parent corporation. The Harry Potter character and stories fit
many stereotypes, making it compatible with various media platforms.[40] The
phenomenon of Hannah Montana/Miley Cyrus thus more resembles Harry
Potter than it does any other type of music production. When Disney began
its *Hannah Montana* sitcom, they knew their combined media outlets could
garner them a concert tour, movie, and soundtrack and enable them to cross-
promote the television show, the music and the ancillary products. Premiering
in 2006, *Hannah Montana* had become the most popular television show in
2008 with 3 million viewers per episode.[41]

Given the vastness of the Disney corporate empire, how could a viewer
escape Hannah Montana? She could appear as a product of any of Disney's
holdings, which include broadcast television network ABC and cable channels
ABC Family, ABC Kids, Disney Channel, Toon Disney, Playhouse Disney,

Disney XD, Soapnet, ESPN; production companies ABC Studios, Walt Disney Motion Pictures Group, Walt Disney Studios, Walt Disney Television Animation, Pixar, Miramax Films, Touchstone Pictures; music production companies Hollywood Records, Lyric Street Records, and Walt Disney Records; video game developers Disney Interactive and Buena Vista Games; website designers New Horizon Interactive and Disney Online Studios Canada; distribution companies Walt Disney Distribution, and Walt Disney Home Entertainment; Disney Theatrical Productions, Disney Live Family Entertainment and Disney on Ice; print divisions Walt Disney Pictures, Disney Publishing Worldwide; consumer segment includes Disney Consumer Products, Disney Store, Disney Toys, Disney Apparel, Accessories & Footwear, Disney Food, Health & Beauty, Disney Home and Disney Stationery; and the Walt Disney Parks and Resorts. Any Disney character, whether Mickey Mouse or Hannah Montana, can be streamed through any of these segments and encounter its target market not just on its many television channels or websites, not only in films and on records, but also in pictures, storybooks, toys, clothes, food, and cosmetics. Indeed, such a character would be difficult to avoid. As Disney marketing chief Adam Sanderson said, the goal of Hannah Montana was to "generate revenue across multiple products and entertainment, but also to build for the long term."[42] Thus Miley Cyrus' appearance on *Monday Night Football* was not a result of her cultural popularity, but rather because Disney owns both her contract and the ESPN sports network.

Disney has been involved in similar marketing strategies since television's early years. Originally *The Mickey Mouse Club* was conceived as a way to introduce the nation to the Disney theme parks, but also led to the production of toys, games, and comic books. The success of ancillary products released along with the opening of feature-length cartoons aimed at young children ensured an enormous revenue stream.[43] Noting Disney's long involvement with children's media and ancillaries, *Los Angeles Times* TV critic Mary McNamara said that Miley Cyrus "is the latest figurehead for a company that, if it didn't invent cold-blooded mass marketing to children, it certainly perfected it."[44]

MARKETING CULTURAL PRODUCTS TO CHILDREN

The practice of mass marketing and advertising in the United States emerged after World War I as business and political leaders took the lessons learned from wartime propaganda techniques and teamed together to forge a society based on consumerism. Because opinion leaders believed that, left to themselves buyers would not buy enough, advertising emerged as a key component in the equation. By using psychological propaganda techniques pioneered by Edward Bernays (1928/2005) and his colleagues during WWI and developed throughout the twentieth century to develop marketing campaigns that blanket the media landscape, marketers have helped shape a consumer culture.

The dominant values of U.S. culture derive from a consumerist ideology that began to flourish after World War I. Industrialization had made mass production possible, and industrialists sought ways to profit from their surplus. Advertisers stepped in to help create demand for products by using manipulative psychological techniques. Most Americans can readily see the preponderance of consumer choice in their daily lives, but less visible is how the advertising of consumer goods has helped to shape dominant cultural values. Edward Bernays, the quintessential marketer whose career spanned at least six decades, gleaned from his uncle Sigmund Freud the idea of transference, whereby associating qualities with an item, that item seems to take on those qualities.[45] An oft-used quality in advertising is youth itself. Although even Alexis deToqueville[46] in 1830s analysis of the young United States for a European audience noted the youth orientation of American culture, the value of youth to the creation and disposal of mass-produced products acquired a new dimension. Not only was youthful energy and strength necessary for factory workers, but a steady stream of youthful consumers was necessary to purchase newly fashioned goods. Products came and went as companies created and marketed new styles and made them seem necessary to potential buyers; they succeeded because of "style obsolescence."[47]

Advertisers began using psychological techniques that exploit emotions, designed to manipulate consumers, making use of radio and then television. By 1960, twelve years after the launch of consumer network television, the FCC loosened its regulations enough that ads aimed at children were commonplace. As media mergers increased through the late '80s into the '90s to the point where a handful of multinational corporations controlled most media and music production in the world, the expression of youthful rebellion against an established order was rendered more difficult, if not muted almost entirely. The PBS "Frontline" documentary *The Merchants of Cool*[48] exposes how youth find their expressions shorn of their emotion and incorporated into the hegemonic ideology of consumerism: The voice of youth overlaps with that of the corporation.

Children have been advertising targets for years, though not to the extent they are now. As long ago as 1945, *Seventeen Magazine* sent a memo to advertisers saying that their teen girl readers were copycats, and that advertising dollars in the magazine would be well spent: Sell brands to these girls and have them for life.[49] Yet, before the idea of concentrating children's television shows during Saturday mornings, advertisers hadn't grasped that children could be trained as lobbyists to annoy their parents into buying products, a practice that was the primary paradigm for marketing to children until deregulation in the '80s. Now, however, children ages two to fourteen account for more than $500 billon a year in household purchasing, with pre-adolescent girls now purchasing clothing, makeup, and other products that were formerly targeted to an older teen market.[50]

Marketers believe that advertising works best when viewers do not recognize the sales intent so they have been blurring the line between advertisement and content.[51] For example, *The Monkees* television show and records based on songs featured in the program advertised each other in the late '60s, like today's cross platform marketing.[52] However, when programs targeted young children, the Federal Communications Commission was more vigilant. At one point, they called for a clear demarcation between advertisement and program on children's shows. Also, they would not allow Kellogg's in the '60s to create a cartoon program based on its Frosted Flakes mascot, Tony the Tiger. When watchdog agencies began loosening oversight in 1979 and such regulations relaxed, children's television began broadcasting what were previously referred to as program-length commercials. Following the model of the *Star Wars* series of films where ancillaries were conceived as part of the revenue stream, television producers began aiming shows at boys—GI Joe, Transformers, GoBots, Ninja Turtles, Power Rangers, and the *Ghostbusters* film—providing a framework against which children could play with the necessary paraphernalia to reenact the fantasy they just viewed.[53] Thus, toys in the '70s were stripped of their nostalgia factor, unlike the way they had been marketed previously, by targeting children directly and omitting their parents.[54] As the female counterpart to the successful boy characters tied to TV shows, American Greeting Company along with Kenner Company created the toy and television program "Strawberry Shortcake" as a composite of elements found to appeal to girls. For example, research showed that women and girls love strawberries.[55] As with the ancillary products for the boys' programming, these toys came with pre-packaged characteristics bestowed on them by their television roles.[56]

Because children represent future customers, marketers work to instill brand loyalty, even among the very young.[57] Integrated marketing strategies now commonly use branded characters across various media, along with toys and other ancillary products: The television character SpongeBob becomes a movie character who markets Burger King products with SpongeBob premiums as rewards for product purchases.[58] Further, television networks create Internet Web sites to accompany the television programming to build their brand and develop a relationship with viewers.[59] This is one way in which corporations can create brand identity and differentiate themselves from their competition, and inspire brand loyal viewers who see themselves as members of a specific media community.

THE DISNEY BRAND OF WOMEN

Beginning in 1937 with feature length animated films, through the '50s and '60s with wholesome children's television programming, Disney's name has been associated with family entertainment and its marketers strive for consistency in presenting this brand identity.[60] In their media products, messages abound about the importance of families, which are usually shown as caring and nurturing environments where each member puts the group's well-being before his or her own.[61] Moreover, Disney symbolizes the security and romance of old-time, small town-USA where dreams come true and happiness reigns.[62] With regard to gender roles, the traditional values upon which the Disney brand rests veer toward stereotype with beautiful, dependent, and domestic women. Although Ariel in *The Little Mermaid* (1989) rebels against her father, and Pocahontas is independent, strong, and wise, female characters who look strong initially must later be rescued from even stronger men. Women also are portrayed as overly sexual with "small waists, large breasts, big eyes, and batting eyelashes."[63] By the '90s, Hollywood was shifting in its representation of women's sexuality, portraying women as both good and sexy, whereas in the past only bad girls were sexy.[64] Other negative messages for girls about the feminine gender role exist in Disney animated films; for example, Jasmine in *Aladdin*, distracts the Sultan by becoming a seductress, and Belle patiently puts up with abuse from the Beast, ultimately transforming him into a prince.[65] Further, Esmeralda in *The Hunchback of Notre Dame* also uses stereotypically feminine behavior, like pretending to cry in order to elude her pursuers.[66]

Like other Disney heroines, Hannah Montana is spunky, young, wholesome, and beautiful. The incidental adult women on *Hannah Montana* are not unlike usual adult female antagonists in Disney, a little nuts, aggressive, dim, unattractive, vengeful, and jealous of the girls.[67] Miley/Hannah appears, by contrast, as the heroine who triumphs over blundering adults. While Miley by day is the typical teen, her alter ego Hannah by night is the sexy, famous rock star. This dichotomy resembles a whole cast of Disney female protagonists who move between their mundane lives to their princess lives: Cinderella leaves a life of rags to one of great wealth, Sleeping Beauty goes from domestic servant to marrying the prince, Ariel transforms from mermaid to human, and others.

While the program is relatively free of sex and language, it does contain messages of consumerism and narcissistic attitudes[68] which may be the quintessential U.S. values of the twentieth century. Hannah sings about the fun of being famous, going to her own movie premiere, buying shoes, and seeing her face in magazines. Girls who view the program are encouraged with ancillary products to explore their own alter egos by dressing in Hannah's clothes, recreating her rock performances, wearing her blond wig, and filming themselves for YouTube videos.[69] The preteen female stereotype *Merchants of Cool* calls "the midriff"[70] is consonant with this behavior. An American Psychological Association task force argues that aggressive advertising and marketing campaigns can lead to the sexualization and exploitation of young girls[71] as well as to greater emphasis on materialism among younger children. Although Miley Cyrus is going on seventeen, many of her fans are preteens and younger, and may not be developmentally ready for Hannah Montana's clothes just as Miley herself isn't ready for pole dancing and *Sex and the City*. Still other companies participate in the trend of sexualizing teens, like Abercrombie and Fitch who told the editors of *Women's Wear Daily* that teens "love sexy bodies."[72]

CAN MILEY BE MILEY?

Disney has gained the trust of parents because they fashion their products around traditional time-tested values. Parents generally appreciate Disney Channel's predominant ideology that inspires messages like be true to yourself and express yourself as you become an ideal individual who upholds the traditional U.S. values of hard work, honesty, harmony with family and friends, and unity among children and adults.[73] Similarly, the ostensible message of *Hannah Montana* is, though you may want to be someone else, stay true to yourself to attain happiness and don't confuse fame with real life.[74] The film contained a similar message, as did the songs on the soundtrack like "The Climb" in which she's lost and trying to find direction. The acoustic track "Butterfly Fly Away" exhibits a romanticism consonant with the Disney.

Interestingly, Hannah Montana's earlier songs follow the pattern begun in the '50s of the oppressed teen ("Breakout") being told what to do, like having to go to school but wanting to be with her friends. A strong theme of girl power messages imbue the lyrics of songs like "Girls' Nite Out," where she wants to have fun with friends while keeping "him" out of her mind. Both "Good and Broken" and the September 2009 "Every Part of Me" insist she's just like us underneath, and despite all that has happened, she is still the same person inside. This adolescent rebellion and soul-searching adhere to the wholesome Disney brand. Still, on some songs, the producers seem to experiment with more adult personae, even the little moans in "True Friend" suggest an underlying sexuality not exactly aligned with the brand. Similarly, "See You Again" especially with its concert choreography, demonstrates some stripper moves.

As a producer of entertainment media, Disney creates desire for things that seem attainable because viewers see everyday people like themselves achieving it—love, fame, friendship, the perfect all-American family. They use propaganda techniques perfected throughout the twentieth century—transferring emotions onto products (girls can watch Miley and pal Lily on YouTube videos, making her seem like a friend); the bandwagon technique (everyone thinks Miley's good and so should you); glittering generalities (we're wholesome, so we won't hurt you); and filling the media landscape with Miley images so that it's encountered at every turn, made possible by Disney's holdings.

Pre-teen girls and their mothers have embraced the hegemonic Disney-brand girlhood of Hannah Montana. Women in R&R have in various ways confronted patriarchal descriptions of femininity, but *Hannah Montana* upholds and embraces patriarchy. She is groomed, tamed, packaged and sold as a model for young girls about how they can be successful as long as they behave and (increasingly for Miley) show off their bodies. The Miley Cyrus brand may differ from other young stars because of her approachability, her Southern down-home roots, or as branding expert Charlie Walk puts it, "she's aspirational yet accessible and down to earth."[75]

Miley's wholesome, pro-family Disney stamp has induced mothers to accompany their daughters to her concerts. Whereas parents previously took their children along to hear the Rolling Stones or the Grateful Dead or dropped them off at Madonna concerts, they now find themselves as fans along with their children. As the concept of youth has expanded by a few decades, it is not unusual for women twenty-five and older to strive to look and act like teenagers. Clothing, hairstyles, and entertainment seem geared toward keeping women perpetually young and thin, as well as glamorous and sexy, whether in *Desperate Housewives* or *The Real Housewives of Orange County*. As mothers look and act younger, their daughters are striving to look and act older. Carissa Rosenberg at *Seventeen* says Miley has been graduating from Disney Channel for some time, and believes that most girls would aspire to be in a movie like *Sex and the City* .[76] Growing up has come to mean sexy, and "these stars must give an image that sexy is what all innocent girls become."[77]

However, mothers who are fans of Miley are in a better position than their daughters to notice the implied career trajectory for young female pop stars that appears to consciously follow the successful path Madonna blazed across several decades: Since the '90s, this career path has been condensed so that female performers move much more quickly and less organically from young virgin to erotic vixen. Although moms may have enjoyed Miley's youthful wholesomeness and trusted the well-honed Disney brand, they should become more skeptical and teach themselves and their daughters to look beneath the surface at the interests behind mediated messages, to understand the agendas behind the promotion of particular media products. The effort to create superstars like Miley Cyrus is done for corporate profit, not to showcase the most creative musicians or to reward the wide variety of musical expression existent in the world.

Individuals form their social identities by interacting with cultural representations, including mediated ones.[78] George Gerbner,[79] well known for his longitudinal studies on the relationship between media and violent behavior, said media create a cultural environment in which certain behaviors and attitudes become tolerated because of their pervasiveness. In a media system where six multi-national corporations control most media production, distribution, and exhibition venues in the world, they claim the power to define culture, barraging audiences with commercial images and sounds intended mainly to create profits, and using all their channels to accomplish it. Audience resistance to the circulation of their messages is hampered because there are few exits out of the loop, particularly for the young who have been targeted all their lives.

Although audiences find comfort in Disney because of its tendency to portray traditional values and gender roles, some aspects of traditional gender roles serve to oppress women, especially when over-emphasizing their value as bodies rather than as complete individuals. Adolescent girls have been exploited by advertisers for years, held up as ideals of beauty in order to sell products.[80] Female bodies are used to attract attention and female characters perform roles that please male narratives. This age-old double standard of expectations for men's and women's behavior—women as the object of the male gaze—is learned by girls who by age twelve fling sexist slurs against each other[81] Women musicians experience similar pressures, as their production companies want them to act and look sexy but to be celibate.[82]

Rock music and the sexualized dance moves of its female performers have been so incorporated into dominant culture that they no longer carry an oppositional voice. Hannah Montana's provocative dance moves would have been censored on '60s *Ed Sullivan Show*, as were the moves of Elvis Presley. Indeed, viewers from the '60s transported to today would wonder that Miley/Hannah could even be perceived as wholesome. The careers of young female singers Joss Stone, Lindsay Lohan, Britney Spears, Jessica Simpson, Leanne Rimes, Mandy Moore, Christine Aguilera, Jewel, and t.A.T.u. can be examined for further evidence. Atoosa Rubenstein, editor-in-chief of *Seventeen* magazine has said that current pop stars look like porn stars, though they're all virgins.[83] Coupling a "hyper-sexed image coupled with their virginity pledges" provides much of the initial allure of the younger Britney Spears and Jessica Simpson.[84] Whether or not the Disney Corporation is directly responsible for the soft porn images surrounding the promotion of any of these young stars, the company competes in a music industry preoccupied with young female pop stars who are both innocent and sexually provocative.[85]

If American culture itself had a realistic, non-commercialized and respectful way to deal with emerging adolescent female sexuality, it could lead the way for Disney, but as long as members of dominant culture buy into the idea that adolescent bodies are our ideal and that using their bodies will lead the way to empowerment for women, exploiting young women will persist. Whatever brand Miley Cyrus eventually chooses, to the extent to which she presents herself as a marketable product, she will need to be sensitive to whether and how her fans respond to the values she embodies. As Fiske[86] says, corporations can produce images, but culture is fashioned from the bottom up, among the public at large who create and circulate meaning. No one should be so enamored of a star, or a corporation, or a brand, that they cannot abandon it when it doesn't live up to its promise.

NOTES

1. Theodor W. Adorno, *The Culture Industry*. New York: Routledge, 1991.

2. P. Gibian, *Mass Culture and Everyday Life*. New York: Routledge, 1997.

3. John Fiske, *Understanding Popular Culture*. New York: Routledge, 1989.

4. Van M. Cagle, *Reconstructing Pop/Subculture: Art, Rock and Andy Warhol*. Thousand Oaks, CA: Sage, 1995.

5. *Ibid.*

6. Dick Hebdige, *Subculture: The Meaning of Style*. New York: Routledge, 1979.

7. Tom Frank, "Alternative to What?" in *Popular Culture: Production and Consumption*, eds. C. L. Harrington and D. D. Bielby. Malden, MA: Blackwell (2001): 94–105.

8. Gillian G. Gaar, *She's a Rebel: The History of Women in Rock and Roll*. New York: Seal Press, 1992.

9. *Ibid.*

10. R. E. Rohlfing, "'Don't say Nothin' Bad About My Baby': A Re-Evaluation of Women's Roles in the Brill Building Era of Early Rock 'n' Roll." Critical Studies in Mass Communication, 13, 2. (June 1996): 93–112.

11. Harris Friedberg, "'Hang Up My Rock and Roll Shoes: The Cultural Production of Rock and Roll," in *Popular Culture: Production and Consumption*, eds. C. L. Harrington and D. D. Bielby. Malden, MA: Blackwell, (2001): 154–64.

12. Simon Reynolds and Joy Press, *The Sex Revolts: Gender, Rebellion, and Rock n' roll.* Cambridge: Harvard University Press, 1995.

13. Adam Sternbergh, "Up With Grups." *New York Times 39*, 11 (April 3, 2006): 24–130.

14. Sharon Lamb and Lyn Mikel Brown. *Packaging Girlhood: Rescuing Our Daughters from Marketers' Schemes.* New York: St. Martins Press, 2006.

15. Alyssa Quart, *Branded: The Buying and Selling of Teenagers.* New York: Basic Books, 2003.

16. *Ibid.*

17. Friedberg, op cit.

18. Terry Gross, Radio interviews on Fresh Air WHYY, Philadelphia, PA. "Alice Cooper From Ghoul-Rock to 'Golf Monster,'" May 17, 2007; "Looking Back on Metallica at a Moment of Crisis," August 29, 2007; "'Metal God' Rob Halford on Life with Judas Priest," August 29, 2007; "Aerosmith: Hard Rocking and Hard Living," August 30, 2007; "The Unpredictable Gene Simmons," Feb. 4, 2002/August 4, 2007.

19. Matthew Stahl, "Authentic Boy Bands on TV? Performers and Impresarios in *The Monkees* and *Making the Band.*" *Popular Music 21*, 3 (Oct. 2002): 307–30.

20. "Teen Idols: How Did Jive Records Make Teen Pop a Billion Dollar Business? And Will Britney, N'Sync and Co. Ever Grow Up?" *Time Europe 158,* 25 (Dec. 17, 2001): 62–64.

21. Heather Hendershot, *Saturday Morning Censors: Television Regulation Before the V-Chip.* Duke University Press, 1998.

22. Catherine Driscoll, "Girl Culture, Revenge and Global Capitalism: Cybergirls, Riot Grrls, Spice Girls." *Australian Feminist Studies 14*, 29 (Apr. 1999): 173–93.

23. Lori Baker-Sperry, "The Production of Meaning Through Peer Interaction: Children and Walt Disney's Cinderella." *Sex Roles 56* (2007): 717–27.

24. Op cit.

25. *Ibid.*

26. Deborah Tannen, "Wears Jump Suit. Sensible Shoes. Uses Husband's Last Name." *The New York Times Magazine*, June 20, 1993.

27. Susan Faludi, *Backlash: The Undeclared War Against American Women.* New York: Crown Books, 1991.

28. Reynolds and Press, op cit., p. 324.

29. Mary Pipher, *Reviving Ophelia: Saving the Selves of Adolescent Girls.* Ballantine Reader's Circle, Mass Market Paperback, 1995.

30. Reynolds and Press, op cit.

31. Meredith Levande, "Women, Pop Music, and Pornography." *Meridians: Feminism, Race Transnationalism 8*, 1 (2008): 293–321.

32. Ibid.

33. Peter Schweizer and Rochelle Schweizer. *The Mouse Betrayed: Greed, Corruption and Children at Risk.* Washington, DC: Regnery Publishing, 1998.

34. Sut Jhally, *Dreamworlds 3: Desire, Sex and Power in Music Video.* Media Education Foundation, 2007.

35. *Ibid.*

36. Gaar, p. 466.

37. *Ibid*, p. 452.

38. Jhally.

39. Gaar, op cit.

40. Anne Galligan, "Truth Is Stranger than Magic: The Marketing of Harry Potter." *Australian Screen Education 36* (Winter 2004): 38–41.

41. Magid, Jennifer. *Miley Cyrus/Hannah Montana (Today's Superstars, Entertainment)*. Gareth Stevens Publishing, 2009.

42. Joanne Ostrow. "Disney Wields Its Marketing Magic." *Denver Post*, Oct. 19, 2007.

43. Cindy L. White and Elizabeth Hall Preston. The spaces of children's programming. *Critical Studies in Media Communication 22*, 3 (Aug. 2005): 239–55.

44. E. Tiegel, *Overexposed: The Price of Fame: The Troubles of Britney, Lindsey, Paris and Nicole*. Phoenix Books. (2000): 64.

45. Edward Bernays, *Propaganda*. New York: Ig Publishing, 1928/2005.

46. Alexis deToqueville, *America*. Chicago: University of Chicago Press, 2000.

47. Stuart E. Ewen, *All Consuming Images: The Politics of Style in Contemporary Culture*, New York: Basic Books (1988): 31.

48. Rachel Dreizin, *The Merchants of Cool*. PBS Frontline, Season 19, Episode 5, Feb. 27, 2001.

49. Quart, op cit.

50. Sandra L. Calvert, "Children as Consumers: Advertising and Marketing." *The Future of Children, 18*, 1 (Spring 2008): 205–34.

51. *Ibid.*

52. Stahl, op cit.

53. Calvert, op cit.

54. Susan Gregory Thomas, *Buy Baby Buy: How Consumer Culture Manipulates Parents and Harms Young Girls*. New York: Houghton Mifflin, 2007.

55. Pat Kirkham, *The Gendered Object*. Manchester University Press, 1990; Stern and Schoenhaus, 1996.

56. Thomas, op. cit.

57. White and Preston, op cit.

58. Calvert, op cit.

59. White and Preston, op cit.

60. *Ibid.*

61. Litsa Renee Tanner et al. "Images of Couples and Families in Disney Feature-Length Animated Films." *The American Journal of Family Therapy, 31* (2003): 355–73.

62. White and Preston, op cit.

63. Towbin et al., p. 63.

64. Libe Garcia Zarranz, "Diswomen Strike Back: The Evolution of Disney's Femmes in the 1990s. *Aetnea 27*, 2 (Dec. 2007): 55–63.

65. Towbin et al., op cit.

66. Zarranz, op cit.

67. Lamb and Brown, op cit.

68. J. M. Twenge, and Campbell, W. K. *The Narcissism Epidemic: Living in the Age of Entitlement.* Free Press, 2009.

69. *Ibid.*

70. Dreizin, op cit.

71. Calvert, op cit.

72. Quart, op cit.. p. 10.

73. White and Preston, op cit.

74. Lauren Alexander, *More Mad for Miley: An Unauthorized Autobiography.* New York: Penguin, 2009.

75. Erin Carlson, "Is Miley Cyrus Too Young for Sex?" www.popeater.com/ 2009/10/21/miley-cyrus-sex-and-the-city, Oct. 21, 2009.

76. Carlson, ibid.

77. Lamb and Brown, op cit., p. 148.

78. Nicola Dibben, "Representations of Femininity in Popular Music. *Popular Music 18*, 3, (1999): 331–55.

79. George Gerbner, "A Study in Casting and Fate. Report to the Screen Actors Guild and the American Federation of Radio and TV Artists," June 1993.

80. Levande, 2008.

81. Lamb and Brown, op cit.

82. Levande, op cit.

83. Rosenbloom, op cit.

84. Levande, op cit., p. 208.

85. Levande, op cit., p. 309.

86. Fiske, op cit.

BIBLIOGRAPHY

Adorno, Theodor W. *The Culture Industry.* New York: Routledge, 1991.

Alexander, Lauren. *More Mad for Miley: An Unauthorized Autobiography.* New York: Penguin, 2009.

Baker-Sperry, Lori. "The Production of Meaning through Peer Interaction: Children and Walt Disney's Cinderella." *Sex Roles 56*: (2007): 717–27.

Bernays, Edward. *Propaganda.* New York: Ig Publishing, 1928/2005.

Cagle, Van M. *Reconstructing Pop/Subculture: Art, Rock and Andy Warhol.* Thousand Oaks, CA: Sage, 1995.

Calvert, Sandra L. "Children as Consumers: Advertising and Marketing." *The Future of Children, 18*, 1. (Spring 2008), 205–34.

Carlson, Erin. Is Miley Cyrus too young for sex? www.popeater.com/2009/10/21/ miley-cyrus-sex-and-the-city, (Oct. 21, 2009).

Chyng, Feng Sun, and Erica Scharrer. "Staying True to Disney. College women's resistance to Criticism of 'The Little Mermaid'." *The Communication Review 7* (2004): 35–55.

deToqueville, Alexis. *America.* Chicago: University of Chicago Press, 2000.

Dibben, Nicola. "Representations of Femininity in Popular Music." *Popular Music 18*, 3 (1999): 331–55.

Dreizin, Rachel. *The Merchants of Cool.* PBS Frontline, Feb. 27, (2001). season 19, episode 5.

Driscoll, Catherine. "Girl Culture, Revenge and Global Capitalism: Cybergirls, Riot Grrls, Spice Girls." *Australian Feminist Studies 14*, 29 (Apr. 1999), 173–93.

Ewen, Stuart E. (1988). *All Consuming Images: The Politics of Style in Contemporary Culture.*

Faludi, Susan. *Backlash: The Undeclared War Against American Women.* New York: Crown Books, 1991.

Fiske, John. *Understanding Popular Culture.* New York: Routledge, 1989.

Frank, Tom. "Alternative to What?" in *Popular Culture: Production and Consumption*, edited by C. L. Harrington and D. D. Bielby, 94–105. Malden, MA: Blackwell, 2001.

Friedberg, Harris "'Hang Up My Rock and Roll Shoes': The Cultural Production of Rock and Roll." In *Popular Culture: Production and Consumption,* edited by C. L. Harrington and D. D. Bielby, 154–64. Malden, MA: Blackwell, 2001.

Gaar, Gillian G. *She's a Rebel: The History of Women in Rock and Roll.* New York: Seal Press, 1992.

Gerbner, George. A study in casting and fate. Report to the Screen Actors Guild and the American Federation of Radio and TV Artists, June 1993.

Gibian, P. *Mass Culture and Everyday Life.* New York: Routledge, 1997.

Gross, Terry. Radio interviews on Fresh Air WHYY, Philadelphia, PA.: Alice Cooper, From Ghoul-Rock to 'Golf Monster' May 17, 2007; Looking Back on Metallica at a Moment of Crisis August 29, 2007; 'Metal God' Rob Halford on Life with Judas Priest August 29, 2007; Aerosmith: Hard Rocking and Hard Living August 30, 2007; The Unpredictable Gene Simmons, Feb. 4, 2002/August 4, 2007.

Harrington, C. L, and D. D. Bielby. *Popular Culture: Production and Consumption.* Malden, MA: Blackwell, 2001.

Hebdige, Dick. *Subculture: The Meaning of Style.* New York: Routledge, 1979.

Hendershot, Heather. *Saturday Morning Censors: Television Regulation before the V-Chip.* Duke University Press, 1998.

Jhally, Sut. *Dreamworlds 3: Desire, Sex and Power in Music Video.* Media Education Foundation, 2007.

Kirkham, Pat. *The Gendered Object.* Manchester University Press, 1996.

Lamb, Sharon, and Lyn Mikel Brown, *Packaging Girlhood: Rescuing Our Daughters from Marketers' Schemes.* New York: St. Martins Press, 2006.

Levande, Meredith. "Women, Pop Music, and Pornography" in *Meridians: Feminism, Race Transnationalism 8*, 1 (2008): 293–321.

Magid, Jennifer. *Miley Cyrus/Hannah Montana (Today's Superstars, Entertainment).* Gareth Stevens Publishing, 2009.

Ostrow, Joanne. "Disney Wields Its Marketing Magic." *Denver Post*, Oct. 19 2007.

Pipher, Mary. *Reviving Ophelia: Saving the Selves of Adolescent Girls.* Ballantine Reader's Circle, Mass Market Paperback, 1995.

Quart, Alyssa. *Branded: The Buying and Selling of Teenagers.* New York: Basic Books, 2003.

Reynolds, Simon, and Press, Joy. *The Sex Revolts: Gender, Rebellion, and Rock n' roll.* Cambridge: Harvard University Press, 1995.

Rohlfing, R. E. " 'Don't Say Nothin' Bad About My Baby': A Re-Evaluation of Women's Roles in the Brill Building Era of Early Rock 'n' Roll." *Critical Studies in Mass Communication, 13*, 2, (June 1996): 93–112.

Rosenbloom, Stephanie. "The Taming of the Slur." *The New York Times*, section G, (July 13, 2006): 1.

Schweizer, Peter, and Rochelle Schweizer. *The mouse betrayed: Greed, corruption and children at risk.* Washington, DC: Regnery Publishing, 1998.

Stahl, Matthew. "Authentic Boy Bands on TV? Performers and Impresarios in *The Monkees* and *Making the Band.*" *Popular Music 21*, 3 (Oct. 2002): 307–30.

Sternbergh, Adam. "Up with Grups." *New York Times 39,* 11 (April 3, 2006).: 24–130.

Tanenbaum, Leora. *Slut: Growing Up Female with a Bad Reputation.* New York: Seven Stories Press, 1999.

Tannen, Deborah. "Wears Jump Suit. Sensible Shoes. Uses Husband's Last Name." *The New York Times Magazine*, June 20, 1993.

Tanner, Litsa Renee, Shelby A. Haddock, Toni Schindler Zimmerman, and Lori K. Lund. "Images of Couples and Families in Disney Feature-Length Animated Films." *The American Journal of Family Therapy, 31* (2003): 355–73.

"Teen Idols: How Did Jive Records Make Teen Pop a Billion Dollar Business? And Will Britney, N'Sync and Co. Ever Grow Up?" *Time Europe 158*, 25 (Dec. 17, 2001): 62–64.

Thomas, Susan Gregory. *Buy Baby Buy: How Consumer Culture Manipulates Parents and Harms Young Girls.* New York: Houghton Mifflin, 2007.

Tiegel, E. *Overexposed: The Price of Fame: The Troubles of Britney, Lindsey, Paris and Nicole.* Phoenix Books, 2000.

Towbin, Mia Adessa, Shelby A. Haddock, Toni Schindler Zimmerman, Lori K Lund, and Litsa Renee Tanner. "Images of Gender, Race, Age, and Sexual Orientation in Disney Feature-Length Animated Films." *Journal of Feminist Family Therapy 15,* 4 (2003): 19–44.

Twenge, J. M., and W. K. Campbell. *The Narcissism Epidemic: Living in the Age of Entitlement.* Free Press, 2009.

White, Cindy L., and Elizabeth Hall Preston. The Spaces of Children's Programming. *Critical Studies in Media Communication 22*, 3 (Aug. 2005): 239–55.

Zarranz, Libe Garcia. "Diswomen Strike Back: The Evolution of Disney's Femmes in the 1990s." *Aetnea 27*, 2 (Dec. 2007): 55–63.

5

Birds of a Feather? Positioning Phish in Relation to the Grateful Dead in *Rolling Stone* Album Reviews

Jordan McClain

Phish has endured unlimited comparisons to the Grateful Dead throughout its career. Presumably, Phish never sought to be explicitly labeled this way, which makes the recurrence of mass media content that links the two bands especially interesting. Through an array of explanations, the band that formed in Vermont in 1983 is often connected to the band that formed in the San Francisco Bay Area in 1965.[1] The ubiquity of the Phish/Grateful Dead connection in media has fluctuated over the years, yet the connection persists.

The positioning perspective on marketing enables exploration into this topic, since it has to do with the way brands are differentiated comparatively for audiences. In a media saturated society, oversimplified messages relating the new to the old may be extremely effective in mass communication. By interpreting bands as brands, this chapter contributes a fresh application of the literature to explore how album reviews may serve to position bands.[2]

Therefore, the following study aims to systematically explore media coverage about Phish that connects the band to the Grateful Dead. The intent is much more than to verify the notion that Phish is often linked to the Grateful Dead, although a study that confirms such intuition is useful. Rather, the goal is to reveal how connections to the Grateful Dead recur and are constructed in a single source. Indications of the presence or absence of a collective view may lead to interesting future research and signal how the matter's components persist, are organized, and are made to seem salient. To begin studying these issues, this chapter includes a review of the positioning perspective, background on Phish, a content analysis performed on Phish album reviews from *Rolling Stone*, and a discussion of results.

THE POSITIONING PERSPECTIVE

In the study of marketing, many scholars have researched positioning.[3] Within this body of work, prior research is "convinced of the positive effect of positioning on firm performance."[4] Prince concluded that studies on positioning "are among the most powerful and important activities in marketing research" because they illustrate how consumers compare brands within a category and describe brand positions as perceived by the consumer.[5] The managerial and theoretical implications of these issues are considerable. Since they take into account a variety of factors, positioning studies can provide useful information about the role of marketers, media used to communicate marketing messages, and the audiences who receive those messages.

According to Al Ries and Jack Trout, most people attribute the significant birth of the positioning perspective to a series of articles the pair wrote for *Advertising Age* in the early 1970s. The authors packaged a number of perceptive fundamentals into a brief introduction on the themes that would eventually inspire their landmark text, *Positioning: The Battle for Your Mind.*[6] Fully developing their ideas on positioning, this collection of dos, don'ts, and case studies detailed what many might consider a bible on marketing strategy. The content's perspicacious logic continues to influence practical and scholarly work. Ries and Trout's positioning perspective emerged as a response to the steady increase of competing brands and communication clutter. Since there is no reason to expect a decrease in either any time soon, understanding positioning is as crucial as ever.

In attempting to define the topic of positioning in one sentence, Ries and Trout explained that it means "how you differentiate yourself in the mind of the prospect."[7] In this concise definition, "how" underscores a need for tactics and strategy. "Differentiation" stresses the need to consider competing brands and messages, and yet to utilize prior audience knowledge in the process. Finally, "the mind of the prospect" clearly reflects the emphasis that the positioning perspective assigns to consumer perceptions. Others have generally agreed that positioning is "a promotional strategy which attempts to place a brand along one or a number of dimensions relative to other brands in the same generic class."[8] Similarly, Blankson et al. conceptualized positioning "as a complex multidimensional construct that attempts to positively adjust the tangible characteristics of the offer and the intangible perceptions of the offering in the marketplace."[9]

The fundamental argument underlying the need for positioning is based on the constant increase in the volume of communication people encounter in a media saturated society. American culture is so flooded with information that the quantity of communication becomes a challenge to effectively communicate. People may be regularly exposed to media content from books, newspapers, magazines, radio, television, mobile phones, video games, or the Internet. The mind is confronted with more information than it could ever possibly retain. To this end, Ries and Trout proposed that positioning is the best way to methodically cut through the clutter.[10]

Considering the incomprehensible amount of clutter people face each day, any approach to combat a media saturated society must also consider what types of messages are most likely to cut through. Specifically, this review highlights two types that are key to the positioning process: those that capitalize on oversimplified information and those that relate new information to familiar information. In developing their approach, Ries and Trout claimed the best solution to battling overcommunication is utilizing "the oversimplified message" in the practice of positioning.[11] With a focus mostly on brand-building from a managerial view, Trout and Rivkin claimed that oversimplifying a complex issue makes it easier for people to make decisions without excessive thought. In other words, "big ideas almost always come in small words."[12]

Various modern examples effectively illustrate the use of an oversimplified message to help refine complicated ideas and position the brand. In selling cars, computers, and televisions, for instance, it is common for a technologically complex product to be reduced to a very simple positioning message. The safe car, the easy-to-use computer, and the realistic-picture TV are common oversimplified messages used to position various complex products. In this way, the oversimplified message plays a valuable role in the process of the audience learning about the brand. But what are some of the most effective approaches to crafting an oversimplified marketing message? According to Trout and Rivkin, they include: keeping ideas short, utilizing simple and familiar words over complex ones, avoiding unnecessary words, using terms that prospects can picture, and tying new ideas to the prospect's prior experience and knowledge.[13]

A second technique for effective positioning is to tie new information to familiar information to increase message efficacy and cut through competing clutter. Messages like these do not necessarily need to be complex; they are likely to be most effective when extraordinarily simple. In this sense, a key tactic in the positioning process is "to retie the connections that already exist," according to Ries and Trout.[14] The implication is that standing on the shoulders of giants allows new ideas to be generated more easily with inspiration than innovation. Thus, it makes sense that the "the basic approach of positioning is not to create something new and different. But to manipulate what's already up there in the mind."[15]

In the category of food, for instance, top competitors commonly employ this positioning technique of relating new information to relevant prior knowledge. Taco Bell's "Think outside the bun" slogan encourages the audience to consider the brand a superior alternative to popular burger-type fast food.[16] Wendy's claims that "It's waaaay better than fast food. It's Wendy's" to differentiate itself from the negative perceptions that its fast food competitors may carry.[17] DiGiorno declares, "It's not delivery. It's DiGiorno" to similarly set itself apart, implying that their pizza is as good as—yet more convenient than—the alternative.[18] All of these examples relate new concepts to familiar ones in order to position the brand in the minds of the audience.

An apparent gap in the literature is that most research on positioning addresses the topic from the brand manager's view. Studies commonly only consider what the brand manager actively controls executing (e.g., advertising messages). This raises questions about how a brand's position may emerge passively, without a master plan (e.g., in press coverage). Furthermore, discussions of brand positioning are commonly limited to traditional categories like foods, cars, electronics, service-related Internet sites, and occasionally a politician or celebrity. Positioning starts with "a piece of merchandise, a service, a company, an institution, or even a person," Ries and Trout explained.[19] This means the positioning perspective can apply to many types of brands outside the scope of conventional discussion. Therefore, this chapter assumes that the knowledge gleaned from positioning research may be applied to the uncommon realm of studying a band as a brand. If not a brand, what else is a top-grossing touring band that has made millions of dollars from merchandise, ranging from tickets and albums to socks and shot glasses, all marked with its name?

A BRIEF HISTORY OF PHISH

Phish's success is built upon a rare combination of raw talent, strategic business acumen, and various moments of rock and roll serendipity. The band—comprised of Trey Anastasio on guitar and lead vocals; Mike Gordon on bass and vocals; Page McConnell on keyboards and vocals; and Jon "Fish" Fishman on drums and vocals—formed at the University of Vermont in 1983 and became one of the most successful rock bands ever, although its music is hardly limited to the rock genre. Due to constant touring and grassroots promotion, Phish built a strong fan base through the '80s. With an independent spirit and the help of John Paluska's Dionysian Productions management team, existing to serve only Phish, the band expanded its popularity throughout the Northeast and then nationwide. By the early nineties, Phish toured more and more. The band consequently drew larger crowds to bigger shows and quickly evolved from a club and theater band to one that attracted thousands of fans and made millions of dollars. Regarded more for its concerts than studio recordings, Phish's popularity as a live band skyrocketed and the band established itself as a headlining act that continuously fills major U.S. arenas and amphitheaters.

With its first major self-produced festival, The Clifford Ball, Phish staged the largest North American concert in 1996, with about 70,000 in attendance according to *Pollstar*.[20] A few Phish-produced festivals later, the group was the sole headliner at its Big Cypress festival on New Year's Eve 1999. Playing to a crowd of 80,000, Phish celebrated the new millennium with a concert lasting from midnight until dawn at what was the "biggest money-making event in America" and the largest paid concert event in the world that night.[21] It is logical for one to consider The Clifford Ball and Big Cypress the "twin peaks" of Phish's career.[22] Certainly, these enterprising Phish fests have been an inspiration for major contemporary American music festivals, such as Bonnaroo.[23] After the career pinnacle of Big Cypress, the band went on hiatus in October 2000 and made its live return on New Year's Eve 2002. Following a few more successful tours, the band split in August 2004, with Dionysian folding as well.[24] In March 2009, the band made a triumphant live return, with Coran Capshaw's Red Light Management handling Phish's resumption as a touring phenomenon.[25]

In terms of facts and figures, Phish earned "$175,541,923 in concert grosses, with 5,842,798 tickets sold," based on reports to *Billboard* Box-score from 1989 to 2004.[26] In addition, the band "sold 7 million albums in the United States, according to Nielsen SoundScan, 2.2 million of them live sets."[27] Upon Phish's temporary 2004 retirement, *Billboard*'s Waddell described the band's career as "one of the most remarkable chapters in the history of the concert business."[28]

Elsewhere, prior works on Phish have been thorough but limited. Journalists, fans, and those who identify as both, have produced a number of books solely devoted to the topic of Phish. Budnick's *The Phishing Manual* examined the band from an early die-hard Phish fan's intellectual, cultural, and historical perspective.[29] Likewise, *The Pharmer's Almanac* and *The Phish Companion* are extensive fan-compiled tomes that similarly covered band and song histories, setlists with informative notes, show reviews, notable Phish events, interviews with Phish associates, venue details, and more.[30] Recently, Puterbaugh's *Phish: The Biography* analyzed the band's career trajectory by phases, serving as a useful Phish overview of the band's saga.[31] Moreover, Gehr's *The Phish Book*, co-authored with the band, provided expert analysis of the group's journey to that point.[32] This text offered unique insights into Phish's timeline of success and views on performance. It is, in itself, an essential part of the Phish story. These pieces, in addition to only a handful of others, represent the most significant works about Phish.[33]

PHISH IN *ROLLING STONE*

In *Rolling Stone* alone, it has been noted that Phish enjoyed "a career as the hottest cult band in America: an object of apostolic devotion from a young, neohippie congregation small enough to party happily at the fringes of the mainstream music industry but large enough to fill arenas nationwide."[34] The group's most-played live song, "You Enjoy Myself," was ranked eighty-fifth among the top one hundred guitar songs in history and Anastasio was placed seventy-third among the one hundred greatest guitarists of all time.[35] Phish has also repeatedly been given majestic titles like "apt heir to the Grateful Dead's legacy as the world's greatest jam band," "kings of the Nineties jam-band scene," and "jam-band kings in the mid-Nineties."[36] Others have said that "Phish are probably the ultimate college band" and concluded that "on the concert front, the band has become the left-field success story of the '90s."[37] Echoing this, Hendrickson momentously proclaimed that "given their sense of community, their ambition and their challenging, generous performances, Phish have become the most important band of the Nineties," a statement that has since reverberated throughout assorted media.[38] Despite such highlights, not all *Rolling Stone* coverage of Phish is so complimentary. For example, one reviewer maintained, "Phish are probably the most self-indulgent act ever to sell out New York's Madison Square Garden."[39] Like in many other sources, derision sometimes appears between accounts of the band's undeniable success. Generally, though, it seems *Rolling Stone* views Phish favorably.

THE PHISH/GRATEFUL DEAD LINK

In mass media coverage, many have connected Phish to the Grateful Dead in regard to similar attributes like improvised music, concert structure, dedicated fans and tapers, the pre- and post-show venue parking lot scene, collaboration with a lyricist, mail order ticket systems, and the independent nature of their successes. However, the extent to which the bands actually sound alike is debatable, again making the recurrence of media content that connects the two bands particularly intriguing.

From the beginning, the Grateful Dead's influence on Phish's music was clear, although arguably not much more than any other act. "Phish had covered several Dead tunes during their first couple of years together but soon dropped them to avoid the onus of being pigeonholed as yet another Dead cover band," explained Gehr.[40] On the business side, Phish drew inspiration from the Grateful Dead's approach to a career centered on the live concert experience. "Clearly, the Dead were a big influence on how we approached [Phish's] career," Paluska once explained, concluding, "I don't think we ever set out to specifically emulate the Grateful Dead, but it got into [our] blood."[41]

On August 9, 1995, the Grateful Dead's Jerry Garcia died of a heart attack, causing the band to dissolve.[42] Garcia's death led to much discussion about who would fill the cultural void left by the Grateful Dead. Journalists often directed media attention to Phish, an incredibly successful arena-sized act at that point. Such attention was manifested in catchy phrases often labeling Phish as "heir" or "new" or "next." With all this in mind, the following study investigates media content that connects Phish to the Grateful Dead.

Research Questions

The pattern of media coverage that connects Phish to the Grateful Dead remains formally unexplored. To begin systematically examining this phenomenon with a narrow focus on a single source, it is useful to learn exactly how often this pattern occurs. This raises the first of three research questions:

RQ1: How frequently is Phish connected to the Grateful Dead in *Rolling Stone* album reviews of Phish?

It is then important to analyze how such connections are specifically presented in media content. There are many ways the connection between Phish and Grateful Dead may be constructed, which raises the next research question:

RQ2: How frequently is the connection of Phish to the Grateful Dead in *Rolling Stone* album reviews of Phish constructed via different forms of links?

After asking questions about the Grateful Dead, it is also important to contemplate other musicians. Understanding connections of Phish to other musicians in media content provides valuable context for understanding the extent to which Grateful Dead references are pronounced and notable. Thus, the final research question:

RQ3: How frequently is Phish connected to musicians other than the Grateful Dead in *Rolling Stone* album reviews of Phish?

Method

The principal goal of this study was to examine *Rolling Stone* reviews of Phish albums to learn more about how connections to the Grateful Dead recur, are constructed, and are prominent. The data analyzed included all twelve Phish album reviews available on RollingStone.com, the online form of the magazine.[43] The reviews, written by eight distinct authors, span from

1995 to 2009. The analysis starts with the earliest review and ends with the most recent, as of February 2010. Hence, this study examined the following album reviews, with the year of release noted: *A Live One* (1995), *Billy Breathes* (1996), *Slip, Stitch and Pass* (1997), *The Story of the Ghost* (1998), *Farmhouse* (2000), *Round Room* (2002), *Undermind* (2004), *Live at Madison Square Garden New Year's Eve 1995* (2005), *Colorado '88* (2006), *Vegas 96* (2007), *At the Roxy* (2008), *Joy* (2009).

The chosen unit of media content was album reviews because they represent media snapshots of the band from meaningful event-to-event (i.e., album releases). Each album review may be regarded as a significant media representation of the band during a noteworthy milestone in its career. In further interpretation of band-as-brand, album reviews uniquely provide context for a commercial product in a way that everyday coverage may not. *Rolling Stone* is the chosen publication because of its reputation as the preeminent mainstream rock music magazine and because it effectively illustrates significant mainstream coverage of Phish. The bi-monthly's status as an influential chronicle of trends in rock music and popular culture—plus its deep history of Grateful Dead coverage—makes it an especially suitable source for this study.

To interpret the data, this study employed a basic content analysis on the collection of twelve reviews. The unobtrusive nature of this common and effective method makes it an appropriate tool for the study of media content in relation to brand research.[44] It is a sensible choice for such a study that asks quantitative questions about frequency and patterns of reference in media content, while also remaining interested in qualitative features of the content.

To reduce the subjective nature of the data interpretation and maximize reliable interpretation, this study utilized a coding manual for systematic measurement. The coding manual contained instructions on how to identify Grateful Dead and other references within a Phish album review, as well as space for recording the findings. The instructions contained a list of measures, the simplest being band name references like "the Grateful Dead" or "the Dead." More intricate measures included references to Grateful Dead album names, Grateful Dead song names, and Grateful Dead members. When referenced in media content, any of these examples would qualify as a link to the Grateful Dead. The coding protocol asked for examination of all twelve Phish album reviews and the use of the manual to record the presence or absence of Grateful Dead and other connections in each review. The author and two additional coders performed the content analysis on separate dates. Each coding session lasted between sixty and ninety minutes, including training. The measurement system helped supply inter-coder reliability and discover completely corresponding, consistent interpretation of the data. Overall, coding determined what reviews contained Grateful Dead references, what kinds of references each review made, and what other musicians the reviews referenced.

Results

Generally, results of the analysis revealed that most of the Phish album reviews in *Rolling Stone* connect the band to the Grateful Dead. These connections are constructed via different forms of links, as seen in table 1. Further, Phish is connected to the Grateful Dead more than any other band.

RQ1 addressed how frequently Phish is connected to the Grateful Dead in *Rolling Stone* album reviews of Phish. Eight of the twelve reviews contained at least one reference to the Grateful Dead in some form. All together, the study identified fifteen total references to the Grateful Dead in those eight reviews. The album review with the most references, *Undermind,* contained four total through various constructions. Of the eight individuals who authored the twelve reviews, six writers made Grateful Dead references in at least one review and two writers did so in two reviews.

RQ2 dealt with how frequently connections to the Grateful Dead in *Rolling Stone* album reviews of Phish are constructed via different forms of links. The analysis observed that Grateful Dead references are constructed through various forms of explicit mentions of Grateful Dead-related band names, albums, songs, and members. Overall, five reviews contained a single form of Grateful Dead reference, two contained two forms, and one contained three forms. Six album reviews contained the phrase "Grateful Dead," with one of those also mentioning "the Dead." Two reviews referenced Grateful Dead album titles, with one of the reviews citing a pair of Grateful Dead records. Likewise, two reviews referenced a specific Grateful Dead song. In terms of references to Grateful Dead-related individuals, two of the twelve reviews mentioned singer/guitarist Jerry Garcia and one of the two also cited bassist Phil Lesh.

RQ3 sought to bring context to Grateful Dead references by discovering details about references to other musicians. The analysis found that, behind the Grateful Dead, The Who is the band most frequently connected to Phish in its *Rolling Stone* album reviews. There was a total of eight connections to The Who in three reviews: three explicit references to "The Who," two references to The Who album *Quadrophenia*, two songs by The Who cited, and a single reference to bassist John Entwhistle. Beyond The Who, a handful of other artists were referenced twice out of all twelve reviews (e.g., the Beatles, Pink Floyd, Dave Matthews, Blues Traveler, John Coltrane). Notably, key Phish musical influences like Frank Zappa, Carlos Santana, Pat Metheny, and Led Zeppelin were mentioned in a single review each.

Table 5.1. Grateful Dead References in Phish Album Reviews

Phish Album (year of release)	Grateful Dead Band Name?	Grateful Dead Album?	Grateful Dead Song?	Grateful Dead Member?
A Live One (1995)	—	—	—	—
Billy Breathes (1996)	"Grateful Dead"	"Live/Dead" "Workingman's Dead"	—	—
Slip, Stitch and Pass (1997)	"Grateful Dead"	—	—	—
The Story of the Ghost (1998)	"Grateful Dead"	—	—	—
Farmhouse (2000)	—	—	—	—
Round Room (2002)	"Grateful Dead"	—	—	—
Undermind (2004)	"Grateful Dead" "the Dead"	"American Beauty"	"Box of Rain"	—
Live... New Year's Eve 1995 (2005)	—	—	—	"Jerry Garcia"
Colorado '88 (2006)	"Grateful Dead"	—	—	—
Vegas 96 (2007)	—	—	—	—
At the Roxy (2008)	—	—	—	—
Joy (2009)	—	—	"Terrapin Station"	"Phil Lesh" "Jerry Garcia"

Discussion

This study aimed to examine how *Rolling Stone* connects Phish to the Grateful Dead. The content analysis of the twelve Phish album reviews revealed a number of findings. Interesting details emerged about how frequently Phish is connected to the Grateful Dead and how these connections are constructed.

In RQ1, analysis of all units found that the majority mentions the Grateful Dead in Phish album reviews. Fifteen total references found in eight of twelve reviews is a notable pattern. The recurrence of the Phish/Grateful Dead connection shows an extreme focus on relating one band to the other. In a sense, the Grateful Dead is a subtopic often injected into the topic of Phish in *Rolling Stone*. The Grateful Dead references practically span the entire range, starting with the second (*Billy Breathes*) and ending with the most recent (*Joy*). Overall, the majority of reviews and the majority of authors that connected Phish to the Grateful Dead indicates a compelling collective view.

For RQ2, evidence showed that connections are constructed via different links and presented in a variety of forms. References to the Grateful Dead name were most common. For example, the 1997 *Slip, Stitch and Pass* review declared, "like the Grateful Dead, the eternally jamming Phish are best judged by their concerts."[45] A year later, *The Story of the Ghost* review discussed Phish in the context of "post-Grateful Dead pups."[46] Likewise, the *Round Room* review called one Phish song an "idyllic Grateful Dead-ish gospel waltz."[47]

While most reviews that contained a Grateful Dead reference had only a single mention, a few were more complex and drew deeper parallels between the two bands. For instance, the *Undermind* review conveyed that a certain Phish song "evokes 'Box of Rain,' one of the stronger tunes by Phish's obvious influence, the Grateful Dead. But *Undermind* is no vintage *American Beauty*," citing the famous Grateful Dead album.[48]

The more complex references made to Grateful Dead albums and songs illustrate a certain finesse required to draw such a layered analogy effectively. With a superior knowledge of both worlds, Gehr suggested that "if *A Live One* was Phish's variation on the Grateful Dead's *Live/Dead, Billy Breathes* is part *Workingman's Dead* and part *Abbey Road*, focused on musical essences often obscured by rock-concert spectacle."[49] In this example, the author connected the first official live Phish album to the Grateful Dead correlate, about a quarter-century its senior. He further expressed that the reviewed album resembles studio highs of both the Grateful Dead and the Beatles. Gehr's review creatively utilized the Grateful Dead analogy to deftly relay the essence of Phish without overlooking what makes the band unique.

As a whole, the pattern of connections reveals more than a direct, recurring "Recommended If You Like" reference. Rather, different forms of links introduce the Grateful Dead in various contexts throughout common Phish parlance. In addition to conveying what the music sounds like, the Phish/ Grateful Dead connection arises to help the audience understand Phish's discography, the importance of Phish's live show, who Phish may be influenced by, and Phish's career path.

This last point about the context of Phish's career is exemplified in two particular reviews. The assessment of *Live at Madison Square Garden New Year's Eve 1995* explained, in hindsight, that Phish was "affirming the strength of the jam audience in the face of Jerry Garcia's death in August" that year.[50] The review for another archival release, *Colorado '88*, stated, "long before Phish replaced the Grateful Dead as America's greatest jam band, the foursome was one goofy-ass bar act."[51] Together, the different examples of Phish/Grateful Dead connections illustrate how the media content assembles a multi-layered association between the two bands.

Meanwhile, RQ3 found that no other band is connected to Phish nearly as often as the Grateful Dead. In comparison, The Who was the second most referenced band. However, of the eight mostly objective Who references, four were about Phish covering The Who's *Quadrophenia* album on Halloween 1995, three about Phish covering The Who's songs, and one paired directly with a Grateful Dead connection: "bassist Mike Gordon, like kindred spirits Phil Lesh and John Entwhistle."[52] These results raise questions about why Phish's other key musical influences are not mentioned in closer frequency to the Grateful Dead, or why the Grateful Dead is conspicuously referenced so much more than others. It is questionable whether the frequency with which the Grateful Dead is mentioned matches the degree to which the group has influenced Phish. Overall, the examples illustrate that Grateful Dead connections are not just the most present, but are the sole pronounced recurrence. In addition, they are typically conveyed with strikingly more subjectivity and creativity than any other reference.

POSITIONING PHISH

Phish rose to the top of the jamband scene in a journey from playing small clubs to multi-night Madison Square Garden sell-outs. The band escalated above the competition of countless other improv-rocking, hippie-attracting, genre-hopping outfits. Along the way, Phish was crowned as a new Grateful Dead in various media coverage. However, Phish did not solicit this title; the band was designated as such. One might even argue that the quartet earned it. Whatever the case, Phish is often depicted in a way that lends itself remarkably well to positioning the band.

The evidence indicates a number of stimulating points in terms of positioning. The logic of positioning presupposes that a brand needs to cut through the clutter of a media saturated society by strategically differentiating itself in the mind of the right audience. One key tactic for achieving this is to consistently utilize an oversimplified message, or "sharpen your message to cut into the mind."[53] A second tactic is to relate new information to familiar information, or "retie the connections that already exist."[54] Both techniques are clearly evident throughout the *Rolling Stone* reviews, serving to position Phish. For instance, the *Joy* review stated, "on the multipart, 13-minute 'Time Turns Elastic'—Phish's own 'Terrapin Station'—there's none of the overreaching that's undercut the band's past work."[55] Here, the reviewer rendered an elaborate Phish piece into a catchy, quickly digestible form and suggested a legendary Grateful Dead epic to understand Phish's material.

Positioning Phish in relation to the Grateful Dead, the content examined from *Rolling Stone* is consistent, is oversimplified, and links the new to the old. First, it is consistent as illustrated by an overwhelming pattern revealed by the content analysis. Second, it is oversimplified in that Phish is an extremely complex phenomenon—one that spans many genres and inside jokes—whose essence is often reduced through a set of pithy descriptors characterizing them simply as Grateful Dead-like. Third, Phish is connected to the Grateful Dead in the same way that Ries and Trout advised, "the mind has no room for what's new and different unless it's related to the old."[56] To this end, the authors concluded that in a media-saturated society, brands should "[hook] your product, service or concept to what's already there."[57] Ultimately, the *Rolling Stone* content produces the message—one that is oversimplified and ties the new to the old—that Phish is a modern Grateful Dead. Thus, the pattern of media coverage that connects Phish to the Grateful Dead serves to position the former in ways that fit readily with the positioning literature.

LIMITATIONS AND FUTURE RESEARCH

In sum, this chapter sought to offer the following: a review of the positioning perspective, with emphasis on certain techniques involved in its practice; sufficient background on Phish, such as information about the band's history and accolades, prior works on Phish, background on the Phish/Grateful Dead connection; and a systematic study of Phish album reviews from *Rolling Stone* to explore content that connects the band to the Grateful Dead, including a discussion of the results.

In terms of limitations, a few components of this study should be acknowledged. Some may criticize the use of content analysis because of the interpretation required. However, the role of the researcher in this study was relatively unobtrusive and the data interpretation required little more than coders identifying easily detectable words and phrases as Grateful Dead jargon. Still, the content analysis might benefit from more detailed quantitative data interpretation and additional coders. Additionally, the earliest available *Rolling Stone* Phish album review was from 1995. This leaves a number of earlier Phish albums, dating back to the late eighties, unreviewed by the magazine. The delay to cover Phish with depth relative to its success is a common criticism of *Rolling Stone* coverage of the band. Regardless, this means that the magazine's collection of Phish album reviews does not bookend the band's output. Therefore, conclusions from this study should not be extrapolated to the band's entire career, but only applied to the meaningful range of 1995 to 2009.

Future research about similar content and issues should aim to accomplish a number of additional goals. First, studies should continue to research Phish academically. The band's cultural impact has shaped society to such an extent that much research is needed in response. The band should not be as underrepresented in academic coverage as it has been in mainstream media. Second, exploring the whole story and full context of the Phish/Grateful Dead connection in media requires a thorough account beyond the boundaries of this chapter. In the future, additional research could start by examining media coverage of Phish over an even longer range than the one available here. Third, this study does not attempt to conclude value judgments about whether media content that connects Phish to the Grateful Dead is good or bad, although this researcher is endlessly fascinated by the infinite manifestations. Some people may generalize the recurrence of Phish/Grateful Dead links in media as inimical to Phish and claim it robs the band of a unique identity. Others may suspect Phish ultimately benefited from the association or argue that a reputation as primary heir to the Grateful Dead is a precious designation that countless Phish peers would covet. However, it is difficult to deduce how much of Phish's success is because of or in spite of the Phish/Grateful Dead connection. Future research could attempt to learn more about this by investigating the views of Phish members and management, journalists who have written about Phish, or Phish's audience. Fourth, future studies should continue examining representations of Phish in media beyond album reviews or *Rolling Stone*. Additional content could be analyzed and compared to the evidence from this study. Finally, future studies should bring the issue of media framing into the discussion of Phish coverage, considering that many little stories about Phish can ultimately amount to one whole story about the band. This topic would help continue exploration into the intricate pattern of media content that emphasizes or excludes certain information in the process of constructing our social world.

NOTES

1. Parke Puterbaugh, *Phish: The Biography* (New York: De Capo Press, 2009); Dennis McNally, *A Long Strange Trip: The Inside History of the Grateful Dead* (New York: Broadway Books, 2002).

2. Roger Blackwell and Tina Stephan, *Brands that Rock: What Business Leaders Can Learn from the World of Rock and Roll* (Hoboken, New Jersey: John Wiley & Sons, Inc., 2004).

3. Eugene Anderson and Steven Shugan, "Repositioning for Changing Preferences: The Case of Beef Versus Poultry," *The Journal of Consumer Research* 18, no. 2 (1991): 219–32; Henry Assael, "Perceptual Mapping to Reposition Brands," *Journal of Advertising Research* 11, no. 1 (1971): 39–42; Charles Blankson and Stavros Kalafatis, "The Development and Validation of a Scale Measuring Consumer/ Customer-Derived Generic Typology of Positioning Strategies," *Journal of Marketing Management* 20, no. 1–2 (2004): 5–43; Charles Blankson and Stavros Kalafatis, "Congruence Between Positioning and Brand Advertising," *Journal of Advertising Research* 47, no. 1 (2007): 79–94; Charles Blankson, Stavros Kalafatis, Julian Ming-Sung Cheng, and Costas Hadjicharalambous, "Impact of Positioning Strategies on Corporate Performance," *Journal of Advertising Research* 48, no. 1 (2008): 106–22; Melvin Crask and Henry Laskey, "A Positioning-Based Decision Model for Selecting Advertising Messages," *Journal of Advertising Research* 30, no. 4 (1990): 32–38; Wayne DeSarbo, Rajdeep Grewal, and Crystal Scott, "A Clusterwise Bilinear Multidimensional Scaling Methodology for Simultaneous Segmentation and Positioning Analyses," *Journal of Marketing Research* 45, no. 3 (2008): 280–92; William Dillon, Teresa Domzal, and Thomas Madden, "Evaluating Alternative Product Positioning Strategies," *Journal of Advertising Research* 26, no. 4 (1986): 29–35; Franklin Houston and John Hanieski, "Pooled Marketing and Positioning," *Journal of Advertising* 5, no. 1 (1976): 38–39; Lynn Jaffe, "Impact of Positioning and Sex-Role Identity on Women's Response to Advertising," *Journal of Advertising Research* 31, no. 3 (1991): 57–64; Cornelia Pechmann and S. Ratneshwar, "The Use of Comparative Advertising for Brand Positioning: Association Versus Differentiation," *The Journal of Consumer Research* 18, no. 2 (1991): 145–60; Michel Pham and A. V. Muthukrishnan, "Search and Alignment in Judgment Revision: Implications for Brand Positioning," *Journal of Marketing Research* 39, no. 1 (2002): 18–30; Melvin Prince, "How Consistent Is the Information in Positioning Studies?," *Journal of Advertising Research* 30, no. 3 (1990): 25–30; Mita Sujan and James Bettman, "The Effects of Brand Positioning Strategies on Consumers' Brand and Category Perceptions: Some Insights from Schema Research," *Journal of Marketing Research* 26, no. 4 (1989): 454–67; Robert Wilkes, "Product Positioning by Multidimensional Scaling," *Journal*

of Advertising Research 17, no. 4 (1977): 15–19; Russell Winer and William Moore, "Evaluating the Effects of Marketing-Mix Variables on Brand Positioning," *Journal of Advertising Research* 29, no. 1 (1989): 39–45.

4. Blankson et al., "Impact of Positioning," 108.

5. Prince, "How Consistent," 25..

6. Al Ries and Jack Trout, *Positioning: The Battle for Your Mind* (New York: McGraw-Hill, 1981).

7. Al Ries and Jack Trout, *Positioning: The Battle for Your Mind*, 20th Anniversary ed. (New York: McGraw-Hill, 2001), 3.

8. Houston and Hanieski, "Pooled Marketing," 38.

9. Blankson et al., "Impact of Positioning," 107.

10. Ries and Trout, *Positioning* (1981).

11. *Ibid.*, 8.

12. Jack Trout and Steve Rivkin, *The Power of Simplicity: A Management Guide to Cutting Through the Nonsense and Doing Things Right* (New York: McGraw-Hill, 1999), 22.

13. *Ibid.*

14. Ries and Trout, *Positioning*, 5.

15. *Ibid.*

16. Taco Bell Corp, "Think Outside the Bun," *TacoBell.com,* 2010, http://www.tacobell.com/ (accessed February 9, 2010).

17. Wendy's, "It's waaaay better than fast food," *Wendys.com*, 2010, http://wendys.com/news_and_offers/inviteAFriend/ (accessed February 9, 2010).

18. DiGiorno, "Advertising," *KraftFoods.com*, 2010, http://brands.kraftfoods.com/Digiorno/advertising.htm (accessed February 9, 2010).

19. Ries and Trout, *Positioning*, 2.

20. As cited in Puterbaugh, *Phish: The Biography*, 11.

21. *Ibid.*, 198; Phish, "Phish Band History 1999," *Phish.com*, http://www.phish.com/bandhistory/index.php?year=1999 (accessed September 1, 2009).

22. Puterbaugh, *Phish: The Biography*, 199.

23. Ray Waddell, "On the Road: Go Phish," *Billboard*, October 18, 2008, 39, http://www.lexisnexis.com.libproxy.temple.edu/us/lnacademic/results/docview/docview.do?docLinkInd=true&risb=21_T8472570782&format=GNBFI&sort=BOOLEAN&startDocNo=1&resultsUrlKey=29_T8472570785&cisb=22_T8472570784&treeMax=true&treeWidth=0&csi=5545&docNo=17 (accessed October 1, 2009).

24. Puterbaugh, *Phish: The Biography.*

25. Red Light Management, "Phish," *RedLightManagement.com*, 2009, http://www.redlightmanagement.com/artist.php?sect=artist&num=74 (accessed September 1, 2009).

26. Waddell, "On the Road."

27. Ray Waddell, "Phish: Independent Sprits," *Billboard*, July 4, 2009, 16–19, http://www.lexisnexis.com.libproxy.temple.edu/us/lnacademic/results/docview/docview.do?docLinkInd=true&risb=21_T8472633408&format=GNBFI&sort=BOOLEAN&startDocNo=1&resultsUrlKey=29_T8472633412&cisb=22_T8472633411&treeMax=true&treeWidth=0&csi=5545&docNo=9 (accessed October 1, 2009).

28. Ray Waddell, "On the Road: Phish Manager Closes up Shop," *Bill-board*, December 11, 2004, 24, http://www.lexisnexis.com.libproxy.temple.edu/us/lnacademic/search/focusSearch.do?risb=21_T8472633408&pap=results_listview_Listview&formStateKey=29_T8472633412&format=GNBLIST&returnTo=20_T8472633410 (accessed October 1, 2009).

29. Dean Budnick, The Phishing Manual: A Compendium to the Music of Phish (New York: Hyperion, 1996).

30. Andy Bernstein, Lockhart Steele, Larry Chasnoff, and Brian Celentano, *The Pharmer's Almanac,* Vol. 5. (New York: Berkley Boulevard Books, 1998); The Mockingbird Foundation, *The Phish Companion: A Guide to the Band and Their Music,* 2nd ed. (San Francisco: Backbeat Books, 2004).

31. Puterbaugh, *Phish: The Biography.*

32. Richard Gehr and Phish, *The Phish Book* (New York: Villard, 1998).

33. Jnan Blau, "'The Trick was to Surrender to the Flow': Phish, the Phish Phenomenon, and Improvisational Performance Across Cultural and Communicative Contexts" (PhD diss., Southern Illinois University at Carbondale, 2007); Sean Gibbon, *Run Like an Antelope: On the Road with Phish* (New York: Thomas Dunne Books, 2001); Dave Thompson, *Go Phish* (New York: St. Martin's Griffin, 1997).

34. David Fricke, "Phish," *Rolling Stone,* September 30, 1999, 60, http://libproxy.temple.edu/login?url=http://search.ebscohost.com/login.aspx?direct=true&db=aph&AN=2280518&site=ehost-live&scope=site (accessed October 1, 2009).

35. Brian Hiatt, "You Enjoy Myself Phish 1988," *Rolling Stone,* June 12, 2008, 64, http://libproxy.temple.edu/login?url=http://search.ebscohost.com/login.aspx?direct=true&db=aph&AN=32517832&site=ehost-live&scope=site (accessed October 1, 2009); *Rolling Stone,* "The 100 Greatest Guitarists of All Time," *RollingStone.com,* September 18, 2003, under "73 Trey Anastasio," http://www.rollingstone.com/news/story/5937559/the_100_greatest_guitarists_of_all_time/print (accessed October 1, 2009).

36. Jenny Eliscu, "Gone Phishing," *Rolling Stone,* November 23, 2000, 35, http://libproxy.temple.edu/login?url=http://search.ebscohost.com/login.aspx?direct=true&db=aph&AN=3812935&site=ehost-live&scope=site (accessed October 1, 2009); Kevin O'Donnell, "Phish: At the Roxy," *RollingStone.com,* November 27, 2008, http://www.rollingstone.com/artists/phish/albums/album/24285555/review/24387302/at_the_roxy (accessed September 1, 2009); David Fricke, "Phish Reunite Hippie Nation," *Rolling Stone,* April 2, 2009, 13–17, http://libproxy.temple.edu/login?url=http://search.ebscohost.com/login.aspx?direct=true&db=aph&AN=37139065&site=ehost-live&scope=site (accessed October 1, 2009).

37. Parke Puterbaugh, "Phresh Phish," *Rolling Stone,* February 20, 1997, 42, http://libproxy.temple.edu/login?url=http://search.ebscohost.com/login.aspx?direct=true&db=aph&AN=9702070468&site=ehost-live&scope=site (accessed October 1, 2009).

38. Matt Hendrickson, "60,000 Fans, a Giant Elephant and Forty-Eight Hours of Psychedelic Mayhem: How Phish Staged the Summer's Most Ambitious Concert in Northern Maine," *Rolling Stone,* October 1, 1998, 20, http://libproxy.temple.edu/login?url=http://search.ebscohost.com/login.aspx?direct=true&db=aph&AN=1067752&site=ehost-live&scope=site (accessed October 1, 2009).

39. Tom Moon, "Phish: A Live One," *RollingStone.com*, August 24, 1995, http://www.rollingstone.com/artists/phish/albums/album/152796/review/5942655/a_live_one (accessed September 1, 2009).

40. Gehr, *The Phish Book*, 116.

41. As cited in Ray Waddell, "Dead Live on in Touring Legacy," *Billboard*, May 11, 2002, 69, http://www.lexisnexis.com.libproxy.temple.edu/us/lnacademic/search/focusSearch.do?risb=21_T8472570782&pap=results_listview_Listview&formStateKey=29_T8472570785&format=GNBLIST&returnTo=20_T8472570783 (accessed October 1, 2009).

42. McNally, *A Long Strange Trip.*

43. *Rolling Stone*, "Phish: Album Reviews," *RollingStone.com,* 2009, http://www.rollingstone.com/artists/phish/reviews (accessed September 1, 2009).

44. Klaus Krippendorff, *Content Analysis: An Introduction to Its Methodology*, 2nd ed. (Thousand Oaks, CA: Sage Publications, 2004); Michael Maynard and Yan Tian, "Between Global and Glocal: Content Analysis of the Chinese Web Sites of the 100 Top Global Brands," *Public Relations Review* 30 (2004): 285–91.

45. Will Hermes, "Phish: Slip Stitch and Pass," *RollingStone.com*, December 12, 1997, http://www.rollingstone.com/artists/phish/albums/album/278283/review/5940323/slip_stitch_and_pass (accessed September 1, 2009).

46. Greg Kot, "Phish: The Story of the Ghost," *RollingStone.com,* October 5, 1998, http://www.rollingstone.com/artists/phish/albums/album/105375/review/5943208/the_story_of_the_ghost (accessed September 1, 2009).

47. Tom Moon, "Phish: Round Room," *RollingStone.com*, December 30, 2002, http://www.rollingstone.com/artists/phish/albums/album/177985/review/5942496/round_room (accessed September 1, 2009).

48. Mark Kemp, "Phish: Undermind," *RollingStone.com,* June 14, 2004, http://www.rollingstone.com/artists/phish/albums/album/6115739/review/6184699/undermind (accessed September 1, 2009).

49. Richard Gehr, "Phish: Billy Breathes," *RollingStone.com*, December 9, 1996, http://www.rollingstone.com/artists/phish/albums/album/91002/review/5946698/billy_breathes (accessed September 1, 2009).

50. Kevin O'Donnell, "Phish: Live at Madison Square Garden New Year's Eve 1995," *RollingStone.com*, January 12, 2006, http://www.rollingstone.com/artists/phish/albums/album/8937556/review/9157142/live_at_madison_square_garden_new_years_eve_1995 (accessed September 1, 2009).

51. Kevin O'Donnell, "Phish: Colorado '88," *RollingStone.com*, November 29, 2006, http://www.rollingstone.com/artists/phish/albums/album/12678352/review/12684862/colorado_88 (accessed September 1, 2009).

52. Will Hermes, "Phish: Joy," *RollingStone.com*, September 8, 2009, http://www.rollingstone.com/artists/phish/albums/album/29924098/review/29951361/joy (accessed September 20, 2009).

53. Ries and Trout, *Positioning,* 8.

54. I*bid.*, 5.

55. Hermes, "Joy."

56. Ries and Trout, *Positioning,* 37.

57. *Ibid.,* 220.

BIBLIOGRAPHY

Anderson, Eugene, and Steven Shugan. "Repositioning for Changing Preferences: The Case of Beef Versus Poultry." *The Journal of Consumer Research* 18, no. 2 (1991): 219–32.

Assael, Henry. "Perceptual Mapping to Reposition Brands." *Journal of Advertising Research* 11, no. 1 (1971): 39–42.

Bernstein, Andy, Lockhart Steele, Larry Chasnoff, and Brian Celentano. *The Pharmer's Almanac.* Vol. 5. New York: Berkley Boulevard Books, 1998.

Blackwell, Roger, and Tina Stephan. *Brands that Rock: What Business Leaders Can Learn from the World of Rock and Roll.* Hoboken, New Jersey: John Wiley & Sons, Inc., 2004.

Blankson, Charles, and Stavros Kalafatis. "Congruence Between Positioning and Brand Advertising." *Journal of Advertising Research* 47, no. 1 (2007): 79–94.

———. "The Development and Validation of a Scale Measuring Consumer/Customer-Derived Generic Typology of Positioning Strategies." *Journal of Marketing Management* 20, no. 1–2 (2004): 5–43.

Blankson, Charles, Stavros Kalafatis, Julian Ming-Sung Cheng, and Costas Hadjicharalambous. "Impact of Positioning Strategies on Corporate Performance." *Journal of Advertising Research* 48, no. 1 (2008): 106–22.

Blau, Jnan. "'The Trick was to Surrender to the Flow': Phish, the Phish Phenomenon, and Improvisational Performance Across Cultural and Communicative Contexts." PhD diss., Southern Illinois University at Carbondale, 2007.

Budnick, Dean. *The Phishing Manual: A Compendium to the Music of Phish.* New York: Hyperion, 1996.

Crask, Melvin, and Henry Laskey. "A Positioning-Based Decision Model for Selecting Advertising Messages." *Journal of Advertising Research* 30, no. 4 (1990): 32–38.

DeSarbo, Wayne, Rajdeep Grewal, and Crystal Scott. "A Clusterwise Bilinear Multidimensional Scaling Methodology for Simultaneous Segmentation and Positioning Analyses." *Journal of Marketing Research* 45, no. 3 (2008): 280–92.

DiGiorno. "Advertising." *KraftFoods.com*, 2010. http://brands.kraftfoods.com/Digiorno/advertising.htm (accessed February 9, 2010).

Dillon, William, Teresa Domzal, and Thomas Madden. "Evaluating Alternative Product Positioning Strategies." *Journal of Advertising Research* 26, no. 4 (1986): 29–35.

Eliscu, Jenny. "Gone Phishing." *Rolling Stone*, November 23, 2000. http://libproxy.temple.edu/login?url=http://search.ebscohost.com/login.aspx?direct=true&db=aph&AN=3812935&site=ehost-live&scope=site (accessed October 1, 2009).

Fricke, David. "Phish." *Rolling Stone,* September 30, 1999. http://libproxy.temple.
edu/login?url=http://search.ebscohost.com/login.aspx?direct=true&db=aph&AN=
2280518&site=ehost-live&scope=site (accessed October 1, 2009).

———. "Phish Reunite Hippie Nation." *Rolling Stone*, April 2, 2009. http://libproxy.
temple.edu/login?url=http://search.ebscohost.com/login.aspx?direct=true&db=aph
&AN=37139065&site=ehost-live&scope=site (accessed October 1, 2009).

Gehr, Richard. "Phish: Billy Breathes." *RollingStone.com*, December 9, 1996. http://
www.rollingstone.com/artists/phish/albums/album/91002/review/5946698/billy_
breathes (accessed September 1, 2009).

Gehr, Richard, and Phish. *The Phish Book.* New York: Villard, 1998.

Gibbon, Sean. *Run Like an Antelope: On the Road with Phish.* New York: Thomas
Dunne Books, 2001.

Hendrickson, Matt. "60,000 Fans, a Giant Elephant and Forty-Eight Hours of Psychedelic Mayhem: How Phish Staged the Summer's Most Ambitious Concert
in Northern Maine." *Rolling Stone,* October 1, 1998. http://libproxy.temple.edu/
login?url=http://search.ebscohost.com/login.aspx?direct=true&db=aph&AN=106
7752&site=ehost-live&scope=site (accessed October 1, 2009).

Hermes, Will. "Phish: Joy." *RollingStone.com*, September 8, 2009. http://www
.rollingstone.com/artists/phish/albums/album/29924098/review/29951361/joy (accessed September 20, 2009).

———. "Phish: Slip, Stitch and Pass." *RollingStone.com*, December 12, 1997. http://
www.rollingstone.com/artists/phish/albums/album/278283/review/5940323/slip_
stitch_and_pass (accessed September 1, 2009).

Hiatt, Brian. "You Enjoy Myself Phish 1988." *Rolling Stone,* June 12, 2008. http://
libproxy.temple.edu/login?url=http://search.ebscohost.com/login.aspx?direc=
true&db=aph&AN=32517832&site=ehost-live&scope=site (accessed October 1,
2009)

Houston, Franklin, and John Hanieski. "Pooled Marketing and Positioning." *Journal
of Advertising* 5, no. 1 (1976): 38–39.

Jaffe, Lynn. "Impact of Positioning and Sex-Role Identity on Women's Response to
Advertising." *Journal of Advertising Research* 31, no. 3 (1991): 57–64.

Kemp, Mark. "Phish: Undermind." *RollingStone.com,* June 14, 2004. http://www
.rollingstone.com/artists/phish/albums/album/6115739/review/6184699/undermind
(accessed September 1, 2009).

Kot, Greg. "Phish: The Story of the Ghost." *RollingStone.com,* October 5, 1998.
http://www.rollingstone.com/artists/phish/albums/album/105375/review/5943208/
the_story_of_the_ghost (accessed September 1, 2009).

Krippendorff, Klaus. *Content Analysis: An Introduction to Its Methodology.* 2nd ed.
Thousand Oaks, CA: Sage Publications, 2004.

Maynard, Michael, and Yan Tian. "Between Global and Glocal: Content Analysis of
the Chinese Web Sites of the 100 Top Global Brands." *Public Relations Review*
30 (2004): 285–91.

McNally, Dennis. *A Long Strange Trip: The Inside History of the Grateful Dead.*
New York: Broadway Books, 2002.

Moon, Tom. "Phish: A Live One." *RollingStone.com*, August 24, 1995. http://www
.rollingstone.com/artists/phish/albums/album/152796/review/5942655/a_live_one
(accessed September 1, 2009).

———. "Phish: Round Room." *RollingStone.com*, December 30, 2002. http://www
.rollingstone.com/artists/phish/albums/album/177985/review/5942496/round_
room (accessed September 1, 2009).

O'Donnell, Kevin. "Phish: At the Roxy." *RollingStone.com*, November 27, 2008. http://
www.rollingstone.com/artists/phish/albums/album/24285555/review/24387302/
at_the_roxy (accessed September 1, 2009).

———. "Phish: Colorado '88." *RollingStone.com*, November 29, 2006. http://www
.rollingstone.com/artists/phish/albums/album/12678352/review/12684862/
colorado_88 (accessed September 1, 2009).

———. "Phish: Live at Madison Square Garden New Year's Eve 1995." *Rolling-
Stone.com*, January 12, 2006. http://www.rollingstone.com/artists/phish/albums/
album/8937556/review/9157142/live_at_madison_square_garden_new_years_
eve_1995 (accessed September 1, 2009).

Pechmann, Cornelia, and S. Ratneshwar. "The Use of Comparative Advertising for
Brand Positioning: Association Versus Differentiation." *The Journal of Consumer
Research* 18, no. 2 (1991): 145–60.

Pham, Michel, and A. V. Muthukrishnan. "Search and Alignment in Judgment Revision: Implications for Brand Positioning." *Journal of Marketing Research* 39, no.
1 (2002): 18–30.

Phish. "Phish Band History 1999." *Phish.com*, http://www.phish.com/bandhistory/
index.php?year=1999 (accessed September 1, 2009).

Prince, Melvin. "How Consistent Is the Information in Positioning Studies?" *Journal
of Advertising Research* 30, no. 3 (1990): 25–30.

Puterbaugh, Parke. *Phish: The Biography.* New York: De Capo Press, 2009.

———. "Phresh Phish." *Rolling Stone,* February 20, 1997. http://libproxy.temple.edu/
login?url=http://search.ebscohost.com/login.aspx?direct=true&db=aph&AN=970
2070468&site=ehost-live&scope=site (accessed October 1, 2009).

Red Light Management. "Phish." *RedLightManagement.com*, 2009. http://www.red
lightmanagement.com/artist.php?sect=artist&num=74 (accessed September 1, 2009).

Ries, Al, and Jack Trout. *Positioning: The Battle for Your Mind.* New York: McGraw-
Hill, 1981.

———. *Positioning: The Battle for Your Mind.* 20th Anniversary ed. New York:
McGraw-Hill, 2001.

Rolling Stone. "The 100 Greatest Guitarists of All Time." *RollingStone.com,* September 18, 2003, under "73 Trey Anastasio." http://www.rollingstone.com/news/story/
5937559/the_100_greatest_guitarists_of_all_time/print (accessed October 1, 2009).

———. "Phish: Album Reviews." *RollingStone.com,* 2009. http://www.rollingstone.
com/artists/phish/reviews (accessed September 1, 2009).

Sujan, Mita, and James Bettman. "The Effects of Brand Positioning Strategies on
Consumers' Brand and Category Perceptions: Some Insights from Schema Research." *Journal of Marketing Research* 26, no. 4 (1989): 454–67.

Taco Bell Corp. "Think Outside the Bun." *TacoBell.com,* 2010. http://www.tacobell
.com/ (accessed February 9, 2010).

The Mockingbird Foundation. *The Phish Companion: A Guide to the Band and Their
Music.* 2nd ed. San Francisco: Backbeat Books, 2004.

Thompson, Dave. *Go Phish.* New York: St. Martin's Griffin, 1997.

Trout, Jack, and Steve Rivkin. *The Power of Simplicity: A Management Guide to
Cutting Through the Nonsense and Doing Things Right.* New York: McGraw-Hill,
1999.

Waddell, Ray. "Dead Live on in Touring Legacy." *Billboard,* May 11, 2002.
http://www.lexisnexis.com.libproxy.temple.edu/us/lnacademic/search/focusSearch
.do?risb=21_T8472570782&pap=results_listview_Listview&formStateKey=29_
T8472570785&format=GNBLIST&returnTo=20_T8472570783 (accessed October 1, 2009).

———. "On the Road: Go Phish." *Billboard,* October 18, 2008. http://www
.lexisnexis.com.libproxy.temple.edu/us/lnacademic/results/docview/docview
.do?docLinkInd=true&risb=21_T8472570782&format=GNBFI&sort=BOOLEAN
&startDocNo=1&resultsUrlKey=29_T8472570785&cisb=22_T8472570784&tree
Max=true&treeWidth=0&csi=5545&docNo=17 (accessed October 1, 2009).

———. "On the Road: Phish Manager Closes up Shop." *Billboard,* December
11, 2004. http://www.lexisnexis.com.libproxy.temple.edu/us/lnacademic/search/
focusSearch.do?risb=21_T8472633408&pap=results_listview_Listview&form
StateKey=29_T8472633412&format=GNBLIST&returnTo=20_T8472633410
(accessed October 1, 2009).

———. "Phish: Independent Sprits." *Billboard,* July 4, 2009. http://www.lexisnexis
.com.libproxy.temple.edu/us/lnacademic/results/docview/docview.do?docLink
Ind=true&risb=21_T8472633408&format=GNBFI&sort=BOOLEAN&startDoc
No=1&resultsUrlKey=29_T8472633412&cisb=22_T8472633411&treeMax=true
&treeWidth=0&csi=5545&docNo=9 (accessed October 1, 2009).

Wendy's. "It's waaaay better than fast food." *Wendys.com,* 2010. http://wendys.com/
news_and_offers/inviteAFriend/ (accessed February 9, 2010).

Wilkes, Robert. "Product Positioning by Multidimensional Scaling." *Journal of Advertising Research* 17, no. 4 (1977): 15–19.

Winer, Russell, and William Moore. "Evaluating the Effects of Marketing-Mix Variables on Brand Positioning." *Journal of Advertising Research* 29, no. 1 (1989):
39–45.

6

Fandom of the Internet: Musician Communication with Fans

Daniel Cochece Davis, Bryan P. Delaney, and Heidi M. Kettler

INTRODUCTION

One major problem facing professional musicians is effectively promoting themselves to their fans. For artists with large numbers of fans to update, the difficultly can be how to accomplish this task reasonably; for artists just starting out, the challenge lies in how to build a fan base or establish a market for their music. A solution to both situations may be found in the Internet: musicians can utilize the Internet to spread their messages to fans across the world in an efficient and successful manner. Yet, doing so often amounts to an end-run around a commercial recording label's control of content, image and even legal liability associated with the musician or band.

As such, this chapter examines how the evolution of the Internet allowed musicians and their fans to come together, using messages with higher fidelity than was previously available in the commercial music industry. The success of musician websites demonstrates how attention can be garnered for musicians, while also allowing these musicians to communicate more directly with their fan base, and often market themselves until a "critical mass" of fans makes the musician/band a viable commercial interest to be signed on by a recording label (if desired). In some cases, musicians may choose to avoid commercial labels altogether, preferring to market their music directly to their fans either via the website, or through concert promotion and scheduling on the website.

Traditionally, band fans would have to rely on the band itself if they wished to receive official information not passed on through commercial press or media outlets first. In the hopes of keeping fans informed, bands have used individuals and agencies that became solely responsible for that intermediary communication.[1] There are differing opinions about the popularity and feasibility of this system. Beyond fan clubs, research exists concerning individuals' fixation upon celebrity and musicianship. Additionally, cultures have differing opinions on the roles of fans in the entertainment industry. As seen later on, the Internet directly impacted the dynamic of band-to-fan communication over the past two decades, resulting in a dramatic shift in how music can be marketed to interested consumers.

INTERNET ORIGINS AND DEVELOPMENT

The Internet itself is still a relatively new and developing area of societies across the planet: It has revolutionized not only the computer world, but also the world of communication, allowing a relatively simple, inexpensive means of global information, communication, commerce, and community operations. But what is the Internet? Where did it come from? Most Internet historians still debate its origins.[2] The Internet was originally designed as a collaborative program that would essentially be a globally interconnected set of computers, allowing government, military, and educational organizations to easily share and download information and programs.[3] Today, the Internet reaches much further than that, allowing anyone with access to a computer and minimal computer knowledge to log on and get connected to others around the globe. The original concept of the Internet can at least be traced back to a series of memos and publications between 1961 and 1968, in which scientist J.C.R. Licklider came up with the idea for a "galactic network" to which anyone could easily access data and programs from any site, and that "In a few years, men will be able to communicate more effectively through a machine than face to face."[4] This idea laid the foundation for the modern-day Internet that so many people use and are accustomed to today.[5]

DEVELOPMENT

In 1961, Leonard Kleinrock, another researcher at MIT during the same period, and receiving support from Licklider, introduced the idea and theory of "packets" that helped give new shape and realism to the idea of an Internet. This vision presented the idea that electronic communication would be more feasible if information was sent in packets, rather than in circuits, and helped researchers take great steps in computer networking. He also helped further this idea in 1965, when he connected the first wide-area network (WAN) of computers, which at the time consisted of two computers connected by a low-speed telephone line. This led to a collaboration between Kleinrock and DARPA (the Defense Advanced Research Projects Agency, also referred to as the Advanced Research Projects Agency or ARPA) in 1966; from there research and technology began to move at an incredible pace, and in the following decade successfully demonstrated what they called the "ARPAnet;" one of its "hot" applications was an idea called "e-mail."[6]

DARPA had intended for the Internet to not be solely one arbitrary design, but to be a network of multiple independent networks. DARPA introduced a number of new applications to increase collaborative productivity, including the TCP-IP system in the 1970s. The TCP-IP system allowed the reorganization of the previous TCP-only system; now it contained two separate protocols: IP for addressing and forwarding of individual packets, and TCP for service features such as flow control and recovery of lost packets.

By now, DARPA's new TCP-IP system had begun to spread, as it connected with a number of other companies and organizations, locally and around the world. As personal computers were introduced to the public during the 1980s, many believed the Internet would be too big for PCs to handle. In 1983, TCP-IP became the standard Internet protocol.[7]

GROWTH

The key to the Internet's rapid growth has always been the idea of keeping access to basic documents and specifications of protocols free and open. However, the success of the Internet is most clearly attributable to the sense of community among its members. Domain Name Servers, or DNSs, were introduced in 1984, with 1,000 individual hosts in the introduction. In the following three years, there would be more than 100 times that many hosts, with over 100,000 hosts in 1989. DARPA began a complex restructuring in 1983, introducing task forces and individual working groups, due to DARPA's decreased role and importance in funding the Internet. In 1992, the ARPAnet shut down, due to the immense size of the Internet, as well as the introduction of new commercial sponsors. DARPA could no longer compete with the larger communities that had now become the Internet's mainstream. In essence, the Internet had truly grown into a global communication medium, with communities utilizing it at local, regional, national and international levels.

In 1990, a developer named Tim Bernes-Lee developed two concepts that would revolutionize the Internet: HTML and the World Wide Web.[8] His new HyperText Transfer Protocol (http) allowed Internet users to construct documents that could now contain images, sounds, and animations, as well as text and memos. His World Wide Web (www) also allowed hosts, especially commercial and non-research or developer ones, to have a community and defined address, which today have become a part of everyday language (e.g., www.wcc.com, etc.).

By 1994, the Internet had 3.2 million hosts, as well as 3,000 websites. By late 1999, there were over 36.8 million hosts on the Internet, as well as 4.2 million websites.[9] Internet Service Providers (ISP's) such as AOL and Netscape and other companies that were based on the Internet were valued in the millions of dollars. Internet use increased at a phenomenal rate; in 1997, there were more than 41.1 million U.S. users of the Internet; of the 41.1 million, 31.3 million were 18 or older. The estimated number of persons in the U.S. with Internet access had increased to 74 million by 1999. Every hour, 760 U.S. households logged onto the Internet for the first time. World Internet users had topped 147.8 million. By 1999, 90 percent of full-time college students used the Internet regularly, with 41 percent going online for music, and 50 percent going online daily.[10]

Thus, the Internet evolved into one of today's most popular and easiest methods of communication. Although when compared to media such as the telephone, newspapers and radio it is a relatively new medium, it has also emerged as a facilitator of communication on a mass, as well as personal, scale; thereby surpassing traditional communication media in relevancy to one's life. It not only acts as a means to get information one might need, literally at one's fingertips, but also allows families and friends to maintain contact in ways never before in existence. Boundaries historically difficult to cross, due to expense, distance, and/or isolation, are now being broken down thanks to this electronic information network.

Much of the existing research on the Internet as a tool for fan communication was conducted in the relative infancy of the medium, dealing primarily with the possibilities and implications of such a medium, as well as discussing some of the early developers of web content. Additionally, the fandom and fan-fiction associated with soap operas and science fiction novels are common topics of much of the research in fan-participation on the Internet. Researchers examined soap opera fans creating their own, digital publications of scripts for scenes and scenarios that they would like to see their favorite characters act out.[11] This fan fiction also figures prominently in science fiction programs, most notably by fans of the *Star Trek* television series.[12] Researchers also looked at why females, in particular, were drawn to *Star Trek*, arguing that the diversity and overt themes of tolerance expressed on the show seemed to be factors in the show's popularity for them.[13]

Some of the first organizations to really capitalize on the Internet's potential have been from the music industry, with the Internet providing a relatively inexpensive, easily accessible medium from which to promote, market, and sell products from their respective artists, but also to introduce new record label artists for fans to communicate and get involved with, via cross-marketing of genre-specific musicians. Possibly more importantly, the Internet provides a medium where bands can now communicate easily with their fans, adding a whole new perspective and personality to the idea of "fandom."

FAN CLUBS/FANZINES

Fan clubs and magazines have been a consistent source of direct communication between both media sources (e.g., bands and personalities) and fans, as well as fan to fan, for years. The International Fan Club Organization had 340 member clubs, the most at any time in its history: "Depending on the prominence of the artist, a fan club's membership can range from a few dozen to 50,000 or more."[14]

Fan clubs and magazines have seen a significant change in their availability, with the Internet lowering production and delivery costs, and making them available 24 hours a day to all desiring access, provided they possess the necessary technology. Some have even taken the time to compile all the known fan clubs, fan mail, Internet, and e-mail addresses available in the world as a resource.[15] Simultaneously, the availability of free, public domain information from both official and unofficial media sources took away from the exclusivity of a band's direct mail communication as a source of relevant information.

GROUPIES

Groupies have long been a part of the popular culture and music scene, and the music industry has its share of fanatical followers. Some high-profile musician examples include "Deadheads," or individuals who followed The Grateful Dead band around for over three decades, and have been well documented.[16] Elvis Presley fans constituted a national phenomenon for decades during his career, were some of the earliest researched fanatics pertaining to music, and continue to be studied.[17] One particular rock groupie chronicled her life and experiences in a series of successful memoir-like accounts.[18] Others have chronicled the stories of the fan-culture associated with musical artists, focusing on females involved with the male stars of rock: girlfriends, wives, and mistresses.[19]

The near cult-status of musicians is an interesting topic that often defies explanation. In fact, the cultural context has much to do with the perceived problem or, conversely, non-issue of fanaticism. Studies in countries such as Japan concern popular musicians and their fans portrayed as an important co-dependency relationship, as opposed to the United States where, "fans are negatively viewed as passive victims of manipulation who have easily fallen prey to the seductive powers of mass media."[20] Collectively, the fans of music are often viewed as being different from sports or other entertainment followers. British fans of football ("soccer," to people in the United States), and daytime soaps or "serials" have also been examined, with the consensus in those studies being that most obsessive fan behavior, and forms of fandom, are acceptable outlets.[21]

MUSICIANS USING THE INTERNET

Still, the use of the World Wide Web as a tool for promotion and communication between bands and their fans is a fairly recent phenomenon, with little previous research conducted on the topic by the academic community. The means for a fan to directly communicate with their favorite musicians are beneficial both to the fan and the artist, by deleting a major step in the typical ladder toward commercial stardom. Record labels are still a major part of the music industry, but an analysis of trends and research shows that the Internet is an exciting new medium for musicians to gain that same stardom, without record labels interfering.

A major aspect of marketing and promotion relates to the number of fans a particular method or site, such as the Internet, can reach. *Phish*, a widely known rock band with a huge cultish following, employs an Internet manager to handle the major amounts of mail the band receives.[22] Intel's New Music Festival is an online event held to promote bands not yet signed to labels. Acts such as Bari Koral have found moderate success with online shows and may be able to thrive without any record company backing at all. One of the producers of the festival, Andrew Rasiej, states that "Bari may never have more than 20,000 fans and no record label will ever get interested in her, but if every one of those fans sends her 10 bucks a year for her albums, she's making a living."[23] Thus, new horizons can be enabled as a direct result of the popularity, widespread reach, and low cost of Internet promotion.

Other researchers have studied different methods of fan appreciation for their favorite entertainment sources.[24] For this reason, there have been attempts to profile the groups and their social conditions and habits, where researchers have been concerned with the behavior of "troubled teens" and their relationships with musical influences believed to be anti-social, such as punk rock and heavy metal bands/genres.[25] Beyond concerns for listeners' mental states, advertising and marketing interests within the music industry are interested in finding out as much as they can, regarding their audience, in order to help target needs and interests.[26]

For struggling bands looking for more thorough promotion to increase their popularity and fan base, starting a web page is a simple first step in marketing development. Services such as Geocities.com, Tripod.com and even Myspace.com offer inexpensive and easy ways for bands to get their own space on the web. One disadvantage to using these services is that they lock people into their web address, which can be hard for fans to remember. Artists can avoid this confusion by purchasing their own domain name. This solution is more costly, but much more pragmatic. Singer Donna Grayson states "Perhaps the best decision I made was to go with my own domain name and pay a little extra for it. Having my own domain name is really easy for people to remember."[27] For artists who are serious about their image, it is to their advantage to learn HTML or hire an individual to develop web content and act as the artist's "webmaster" or "webmistress." Flashy and engaging webpage designs may entice more fans to view the site and learn about the particular musician. Additionally, mailing lists are widely used by musicians to keep their fans updated. The musician can just send messages themselves, or set up the list so that fans can send messages to each other. The band Grosvenor finds that using a discussion list is very advantageous: "We've had some useful feedback from gigs," says band manager Gareth Williams. "At one gig the mix was awful, and we couldn't hear that where we were. We've also used it to find out which songs the fans like best, so we can record not just what the band wants to do but what the fans want to listen to."[28] Thus, establishing an Internet-based presence can not only allow an artist the ability to communicate with her/his fans in a higher fidelity *one-way communication mode*, but allow feedback in a *two-way communication mode*, or facilitate fan-to-fan communication about them in a third or *three-way communication mode*, as well.

It is not only unknown and/or unsigned acts who are taking advantage of thriving Internet business. Musicians such as Korn and Dave Stewart of the Eurythmics have also realized the potential of the Internet. Korn is a rock band that received little radio airplay initially, but continues to have a loyal following through their firm belief that the fans come first. Korn once updated their fans about an album via their website through a series of episodes called "Korn TV," and released the album on the Internet before it hit stores.[29] Dave Stewart has helped create and launch an online music community called Sly-Fi. Sly-Fi is basically a forum where budding musicians from all over the world can come together and experiment with their artistic expression. Stewart broke new ground on his Sly-Fi network by holding a 24-hour songwriting session with fans both in his studio and on the Internet. Fans from as far away as Japan contributed lyrics and music to the song, to which in the beginning Stewart provided only a title.[30]

The Internet not only allows artists to deal directly with their fans, and bypass the record companies, but it has also allowed them to bypass the commercial press. In the case of the Lilith Fair, an all-female music festival, rather than setting up an office to field questions it was decided to have an enlightening website that would satisfy any inquiries. Fans were able to get tickets, book hotel rooms, sign up for car pools, etc. At the height of the tour, the Lilith Fair site had more than 300,000 hits a day.[31]

Existing literature suggests that an Internet-based market presence would benefit fans the most, by allowing them immediate and constant feedback and accessibility to their favorite groups/artists. While costs in many countries are currently minimal to go online, once there, access to information and music may or may not carry additional charges. In England, a trio of female pop vocalists calling themselves Angels Online, who had yet to cut an album in a studio, got loyal fans to pay ten dollars a month to have information about the group sent to them via e-mail.[32]

Further development of the Internet as a sales and marketing tool is likely to supplant traditional commercial recording industry methods of musician product access and promotion for fans. Indeed, musician Jane Siberry's Sheeba Records is an Internet-only company and also uses the site to raise funds.[33] Thus, artists are taking steps on their own, sometimes attempting to eliminate traditional problems of dealing with recording companies and labels. This growing trend, not only in the United States, but worldwide, will change the way fans receive music and information about artists and musicians.

RESEARCH QUESTIONS

RQ1: What is the relationship between individuals using musical artist information on the Internet and their propensity to purchase an artist's music?
RQ2: What is the relationship between individuals' communication with an artist and these same individuals' likelihood to join a mailing list/fan newsletter?

Methodology

In the present study, a survey questionnaire was distributed to individuals in various buildings at a small, liberal arts college in the Northeastern United

States, during the month of April. Conducting the survey during the school week, rather than on weekend days, allowed access to both resident and commuter participants. A mixture of male (n = 56) and female (n = 44) participants were surveyed, using survey proctors who were also males and females in order to decrease the chance of participation bias across proctor category (i.e., male or female). The questionnaires were completed with anonymity.

In the survey, participants were asked twenty-five questions, including how many hours per day they listen to music, where they listen to music, their preferred format of music, as well as general demographic questions to determine age, sex, and ethnicity. Some particularly relevant questions to musical research included: how many bands participants found as a result of online searches, how often they are influenced by sound samples before deciding to purchase an artist's work, and how frequently they read album reviews before purchasing music.

Analysis

Of the one hundred surveys conducted, all were included in the research findings. This study attempted to determine the likelihood of participants signing up for an interactive mailing list/newsletter through the survey questionnaire, with the likelihood of signing up acting as the dependent variable, and the independent variable being "Favorite genre of music." Ten genres were listed and the participant was asked to select their preferred genre type. An ANOVA tested between these variables for significant differences. Pearson Product-Moment Correlation tests were also performed as exploratory analyses into the relationship between participants who were influenced by sound samples in their decision to buy music, and those who frequently read album reviews before purchasing an album.

RESULTS

The ANOVA test resulted in F 9,84 = 2.50, p=.014, eta^2=.21, indicating a statistically significant finding and 21 percent of the variance in likelihood to sign-up for a newsletter being attributable to genre choice (see Table 1 for specific means of the genres).

Correlation tests found statistically significant positive correlations between the data found for participants who were influenced by sound samples in their decision to buy music, and those who frequently read album reviews before purchasing an album (r = .286, p = .01). Results of those individuals who were asked about reading album reviews were also positively correlated with how likely they were to interact with a band member directly through e-mail communication ($r = .459$, $p = .01$). Reading album reviews was also positively correlated with how likely a participant was to sign up for a mailing list/newsletter ($r = .479$, $p = .01$). Finally, results indicated a positive correlation between those reading album reviews and how participants rated informative they found regarding artist websites ($r = .288$, $p = .01$).

In related results, participants' ratings of how likely they were to interact with a band member directly through e-mail were positively correlated with the likelihood of signing up for a mailing list/newsletter ($r = .528$, $p = .01$). Similarly, likelihood of interacting with bands through e-mail was also positively correlated with ratings of how informative they found artist websites ($r = .390$, $p = .01$).

The rating of artist website data and the data found pertaining to likelihood of signing up for a mailing list is also positively correlated data. This value, $r = .428$, is significant at the $p = .01$ level. The data pertaining to ratings of fan sights and the ratings of artist sites was positively correlated. This value, $r = .408$, was significant at the $p = .01$ level. The data pertaining to the rating of artist sites and of official record company sites was also positively correlated. This value, $r = .311$, is significant at the $p = .01$ level.

The data collected included asking how many bands the individual has learned about through online information, and this was shown to be positively correlated with that of those who were asked how frequently they read album reviews before purchasing an album. This value, $r = .378$, is significant at the $p = .01$ level. The data asking those who learned about bands through online information were also positively correlated with how likely they were to communicate with band members through e-mail. This value, $r = .439$, is significant at the $p = .01$ level. How many bands the individual learned about online was positively correlated with how likely individuals were to sign up for a mailing list/newsletter. This value, $r = .286$, is significant at the $p = .01$ level.

DISCUSSION

The present study found evidence that the Internet is an effective and viable communication tool between musical bands and their fans. Forty-eight of ninety-three participants indicated that they found information about bands of interest online, suggesting that at least a slight majority of participants found the Internet effective in this way. While at first glance this statistic may seem discouraging, the fact that so many bands have been discovered, or that information put online has been utilized by fans, is very encouraging. As recent as a few years ago, individuals would have been stifled in their attempts to learn about new music and artists, with the Internet making it possible for fans to find out more information about a favorite artist than was previously available, and helping less commercialized artists' music get heard.

The various data correlations help make some educated statements about the fans, themselves. Paramount among these findings is that certain fans are more aware and more educated about their musical choices and preferences, as seen through responses to questions dealing with likelihood to conduct research on an artist, as well as in their likelihood of listening to sound samples and reading album reviews before purchasing music. The present study also found these individuals to be more likely to be among the more active fans of a given musical artist. These fans have an increased willingness to get in personal contact with band members, as well as sign up for mailing lists and newsletters to stay informed of band activity. These active fans are also the ones who are apt to go online for their information.

The study was further able to classify the fans through the results of an ANOVA, with results able to pinpoint which musical genre's fans have been more receptive to, and empowered by, the Internet in making them more active fans. In descending order of which groups were more likely to sign up for mailing lists/newsletters, the results showed a wide range of opinions (see Table 1). Alternative fans were the most likely to e-mail band members, with a mean of 4.25 (on the seven-point scale). Rock fans were next with a mean of 3.67. Fans who selected multiple genres had a mean of 3.22, while fans choosing "other" (to represent more specialized interests) had a mean of 3.00. Rap fans were less willing to interact, with a mean of 2.078. Jazz and metal fans followed with a mean of 2.00. Pop fans, with a mean of 1.39 were found to be somewhat unresponsive to online e-mail communication, followed by classical music fans, with a mean of 1.33, and punk with a mean of "very unlikely" or 1.00. There can be many reasons for these results. Alternative fans may be very happy with how their specific interests have been catered to both online and off, and they may find it easiest to find information that fulfills their needs as fans.

The number one preference in format of choice for most participants included in the study was Compact Disks/CDs (66 percent), with mp3s coming up second (13 percent). The mp3 format is affected by availability and access to the Internet. On a college campus, with an Ethernet or other fast Internet connection, it seems that mp3s would be more popular due to the speed at which they can stream over the Internet. Those not involved with the current study may or may not have the capabilities needed to stream mp3s, resulting in lower scale ratings for mp3s.

Some groups may be underrepresented in the sample because their genre fans may be a minority on this particular campus. Rap and pop fans, the

Table 6.1.

Favorite Genre of Music	N	Mean	Std. Deviation
Alternative	8	4.25	1.98
Rock	36	3.67	1.83
Several	12	3.22	2.13
Other	5	3.00	2.45
Rap	13	2.08	1.61
Jazz	1	2.00	0.00
Metal	2	2.00	0.00
Pop	13	1.39	0.87
Classical	3	1.33	0.58
Punk	1	1.00	0.00
Total	94	2.82	1.98

groups that have the highest number of participants, seemed less willing to communicate than the alternative and rock fans, had similar numbers.

IMPLICATIONS FOR FUTURE RESEARCH

If extended in the future, this research study could be enhanced in some meaningful ways. With only one hundred students surveyed, a much broader range survey could get more accurate assessments of findings. A majority of questionnaires were conducted on students with an average age of twenty, and future research should expand to include a much more diverse population, age and otherwise. Moreover, the majority of the studies were also conducted on people from the United States. A study with global range would benefit the research greatly in that it would discover how musicians utilize the Internet across the world and how fans respond. Surveys may include musical artists themselves to gain more insight, as well as those involved in the music industry's business aspects.

NOTES

1. Edward Morris, "Membership Has Its Privileges," *Billboard*, May 8, 1993, 29.

2. For example: Michael Hauben and Ronda Hauben, *"Netizens: On the History and Impact of Usenet and the Internet,"* 1997, Wiley-IEEE Computer Society Press. Barry Leiner et al., "The Past and Future History of the Internet," *Communications of the ACM, 40*, 1997, 102–108. Christos J. P. Moschovitis, " (Oxford: ABC Clio Ltd., 1999). Stephanie Sanborn, "Internet Milestones," *InfoWorld*, October 4, 1999, 34.

3. Moschovitis, *History of the Internet.*

4. J. C. R. Licklider and Robert Taylor, "The Computer as a Communication Device," *Science and Technology, 76*, April 1968, 21.

5. Hauben and Hauben, *Netizens.*

6. Hauben and Hauben, *Netizens.*

7. Leiner et al., *The Past and Future History of the Internet.*

8. Sanborn, *Internet Milestones.*

9. Sanborn, *Internet Milestones.* W. Treese, "*The Internet Index,*" 1999, Retrieved on March 20, 2000, from the World Wide Web: http://new-website.openmarket.com/intindex.cfm.

10. Denise D. Bielby, C. Lee Harrington, and William T. Bielby, "Whose Stories Are They? Fans' Engagement with Soap Opera Narratives in Three Sites of Fan Activity," *Journal of Broadcasting & Electronic Media, 43,* 1999.

11. Camille Bacon-Smith, *Enterprising Women: Television Fandom and the Creation of Popular Myth,* (Philadelphia: University of Pennsylvania Press, 1992).

12. Bacon-Smith, *Enterprising Women.*

13. Morris, Membership Has Its Privileges, 29.

14. Patrick R. Dewey, *Fan Club Directory: Over 2400 Fan Clubs and Fan-Mail Internet and Email Addresses in the United States and Abroad* (Jefferson, NC: McFarland, 1998).

15. Examples of these works include: Carol Brightman, *Sweet Chaos: The Grateful Dead's American Adventure* (New York: Clarkson Potter, 1998). David G. Dodd, and Robert G. Weiner, *The Grateful Dead and Deadheads* (Westport, CT: Greenwood Press, 1997). Linda Kelly, *Deadheads: Stories from Fellow Artists, Friends, and Followers of The Grateful Dead,* (Secaucus, NJ: Carol Pub. Group, 1995).

16. Examples of these works include: R. Serge Denisoff, and George Plasketes, *True Disbelievers: The Elvis Contagion* (New Brunswick, NJ: Transaction Publishers, 1995). Erika Lee Doss, *Elvis Culture: Fans, Faith, and Image* (Lawrence: University Press of Kansas, 1999).

17. Pamela Des Barres, *I'm with the Band: Confessions of a Groupie* (New York: Beech Tree Books, 1987). Pamela Des Barres, *Take Another Little Piece of My Heart: A Groupie Grows Up* (New York: W. Morrow, 1992).

18. Victoria Balfour, *Rock Wives: The Hard Lives and Good Times of the Wives, Girlfriends, and Groupies of Rock & Roll* (New York: Beech Tree Books, 1986).

19. Christine Yano, "Charisma's Realm: Fandom in Japan," *Ethnology, 36,* 1997, 335.

20. Examples of these works include: D. Jary, J. Horne, and T. Bucke, "Football 'Fanzines' and Football Culture: A Case of Successful 'Cultural Contestation,'" *The Sociological Review, 39,* 1991. Glen Middleham and J. Mallory Wober, "An Anatomy of Appreciation and of Viewing Amongst a Group of Fans of the Serial, East Enders," *Journal of Broadcasting and Electronic Media, 41,* 1997.

21. Austin Bunn, "Fanning the Frame," *The Village Voice,* July 21, 1998.

22. Bunn, Fanning the Frame, 33.

23. Examples of these include: Cheryl Harris and Alison Alexander, *Theorizing Fandom. Fans, Subculture and Identity* (New Jersey: Hampton Press, 1998). Donna Gaines, *Teenage Wasteland: Suburbia's Dead End Kids* (New York: Pantheon Books,

1991). Christine Hall Hansen, and Ranald D. Hansen, "Constructing Personality and Social Reality Through Music: Individual Differences Among Fans of Punk and Heavy Metal Music," *Journal of Broadcasting and Electronic Media, 35,* 1991. Jary, Horne, and Bucke, Football Fanzines. Lisa Lewis, editor, *The Adoring Audience: Fan Culture and Popular Media* (New York: Routledge, 1992). Middleham and Wober, An Anatomy of Appreciation. Marc Peyser, "Send in the Fanatics (Fan Clubs and Devotees of Steven Sondheim)," *Newsweek,* May 25, 1998. Yano, Charisma's Realm.

24. Examples of these studies include: Gaines, *Teenage Wasteland.* Hansen and Hansen, Constructing Personality.

25. Chuck Taylor, "Modern Rock Fans Surprisingly Affluent, Study Says," *Billboard,* March 2, 1996.

26. Taylor, Modern Rock Fans Surprisingly Affluent.

27. Sean McManus, "Net Results," *Melody Maker,* September, 11, 1999, 40.

28. McManus, Net Results, 41.

29. Carrie Borzillo, "Korn Grows by Putting Fans First," *Billboard,* July 18, 1998.

30. Michel Marriott, "Log on, Rock on; Dave Stewart Sings and Writes On Line, Inviting His Audience to Collaborate," *The New York Times,* October 8, 1998.

31. For an alternative take on using this technique, read: Gerri Hirshey, *We Gotta Get Out of This Place: The True, Tough Story of Women in Rock* (New York: Grove Press, 2002).

32. Brett Atwood, "Angels Online," *Billboard,* April 10, 1999.

33. Christopher Jones, "Great Wired North: Canada Online," *Billboard,* January 10, 1998.

BIBLIOGRAPHY

Atwood, Brett. "Angels Online." *Billboard,* April 10, 1999.

Bacon-Smith, Camille. *Enterprising Women: Television Fandom and the Creation of Popular Myth.* Philadelphia: University of Pennsylvania Press, 1992.

Balfour, Victoria. *Rock Wives: The Hard Lives and Good Times of the Wives, Girlfriends, and Groupies of Rock & Roll.* New York: Beech Tree Books, 1986.

Bielby, Denise D., C. Lee Harrington, and William T. Bielby. "Whose Stories Are They? Fans' Engagement with Soap Opera Narratives in Three Sites of Fan Activity." *Journal of Broadcasting & Electronic Media* 43 (1999): 35–52.

Borzillo, Carrie. "Korn Grows by Putting Fans First." *Billboard,* July 18, 1998.

Brightman, Carol. *Sweet Chaos: The Grateful Dead's American Adventure.* New York: Clarkson Potter, 1998.

Bunn, Austin. "Fanning the Frame." *The Village Voice,* July 21, 1998.

Denisoff, R. Serge, and George Plasketes. *True Disbelievers: The Elvis Contagion.* New Brunswick, NJ: Transaction Publishers, 1995.

Des Barres, Pamela. *I'm with the Band: Confessions of a Groupie.* New York: Beech Tree Books, 1987.

Des Barres, Pamela. *Take Another Little Piece of My Heart: A Groupie Grows Up.* New York: W. Morrow, 1992.

Dewey, Patrick R. *Fan Club Directory: Over 2400 Fan Clubs and Fan-Mail Internet and Email Addresses in the United States and Abroad.* Jefferson, NC: McFarland, 1998.

Dodd, David G., and Robert G. Weiner. *The Grateful Dead and Deadheads.* Westport, CT: Greenwood Press, 1997.

Doss, Erika Lee *Elvis Culture: Fans, Faith, and Image.* Lawrence: University Press of Kansas, 1999.

Gaines, Donna. *Teenage Wasteland: Suburbia's Dead End Kids.* New York: Pantheon Books, 1991.

Hansen, Christine Hall, and Ranald D. Hansen. "Constructing Personality and Social Reality Through Music: Individual Differences Among Fans of Punk and Heavy Metal Music." *Journal of Broadcasting and Electronic Media 35* (1991): 335–50.

Harris, Cheryl, and Alison Alexander, eds. *Theorizing Fandom. Fans, Subculture and Identity.* New Jersey: Hampton Press, 1998.

Hauben, Michael, and Ronda Hauben. *Netizens: On the History and Impact of Usenet and the Internet.* Wiley-IEEE Computer Society Press, 1997.

Hirshey, Gerri. *We Gotta Get Out of This Place: The True, Tough Story of Women in Rock.* New York: Grove Press, 2002.

Jary, D., J. Horne, and T. Bucke. "Football 'Fanzines' and Football Culture: A Case of Successful 'Cultural Contestation.'" *The Sociological Review 39* (1991): 581–97.

Jones, Christopher. "Great Wired North: Canada Online." *Billboard*, January 10, 1998.

Kelly, Linda. *Deadheads: Stories from Fellow Artists, Friends, and Followers of the Grateful Dead.* Secaucus, NJ: Carol Pub. Group, 1995.

Leiner, Barry M., Vinton G. Cerf, David D. Clark, Robert E. Kahn, Leonard Kleinrock, Daniel C. Lynch, Jon Postel, Lawrence G. Roberts, and Stephen S. Wolff. "The Past and Future History of the Internet." *Communications of the ACM 40* (1997): 102–08.

Lewis, Lisa A., ed. *The Adoring Audience: Fan Culture and Popular Media.* New York: Routledge, 1992.

Licklider, J. C. R., and Robert W. Taylor. "The Computer as a Communication Device." *Science and Technology 76* (April 1968): 21–31.

Marriott, Michel. "Log On, Rock On; Dave Stewart Sings and Writes On Line, Inviting his Audience to Collaborate." *The New York Times*, October 8, 1998.

McManus, Sean. "Net Results." *Melody Maker*, September, 11, 1999.

Middleham, Glen, and J. Mallory Wober. "An Anatomy of Appreciation and of Viewing Amongst a Group of Fans of the Serial, East Enders." *Journal of Broadcasting and Electronic Media 41* (1997): 530–47.

Morris, Edward. "Membership Has Its Privileges: Country Fan Clubs Grow in Size, Status." *Billboard*, May 8, 1993.

Moschovitis, Christos J. P. . Oxford: ABC Clio Ltd, 1999.

Peyser, Marc. "Send in the Fanatics (Fan Clubs and Devotees of Steven Sondheim)." *Newsweek*, May 25, 1998.

Sanborn, Stephanie. "Internet Milestones." *InfoWorld*, October 4, 1999.

Taylor, Chuck. "Modern Rock Fans Surprisingly Affluent, Study Says." *Billboard*, March 2, 1996.

Treese, W. (1999). *The Internet Index*. Retrieved on March 20 from the World Wide
Web: http://new-website.openmarket.com/intindex.cfm.
Yano, Christine. "Charisma's Realm: Fandom in Japan." *Ethnology 36* (1997): 335–45.

*The authors wish to express their appreciation to Brian M. Johnson, Jeffrey
P. Schmitt, John H. Bryan, and John J. O'Connor for their contributions and
assistance with an earlier version of this manuscript.*

II

IMAGE IS EVERYTHING—HOW RELIGION AND POLITICS PLAY IN POP MUSIC CULTURE

I'm tired of people calling me a devil worshipper.
It's kind of pointless you know.
Because if the Devil did exist, he'd be worshipping me,
because I'm more successful than he is.

—Marilyn Manson

Different people get different things out of the images.
It doesn't matter what it's about, all that matters is how it makes you feel.

—Adam Jones

7

Manson's R + J: Shakespeare, Marilyn Manson, and the Fine Art of Scapegoating

Charles Conaway

In 2000, Marilyn Manson released *Holy Wood (In the Shadow of the Valley of Death)*, a concept album which responds to the ways in which parents, reporters, and various church and state officials scapegoated him for the 1999 Columbine High School shootings. Time after time, in response to youth violence, media reports tell us that either goth rock, movies, violent video games, rap, heavy metal, or some other seemingly frightening aspect of youth culture has motivated teens to take up arms and shoot down their peers. The reports that demonized Manson followed this by now familiar pattern. Both Manson and the goth rock subculture which he represents were pitted against mainstream culture and morality in order to mark them as degenerate. Specifically, Manson's depravity was constructed over and against Christianity and, oddly enough, the apparent epitome of elite secular culture, William Shakespeare.

On *Holy Wood*, Manson seizes the scapegoating apparatus that had been used against him after Columbine. He fashions an alter-ego, Adam Kadmon, whom he martyrs, presenting us not with a scapegoat who is so vile that he deserves his punishment, but with a scapegoat who is, perhaps, too good for this world. In appropriating and translating this art of scapegoating, Manson also seizes the cultural and moral authority of Shakespeare and Christ, turning them against the uses to which they had been put by the parents, reporters, and church and state officials who had condemned him. At the same time, he offers his fans the opportunity to share the subcultural authority of the martyr, providing them with a powerful identity category which stands in marked contrast to the ways in which, as members of the goth rock subculture, they had been defined by their parents—a definition which, according to Manson, reduces them to little more than "Disposable Teens."[1] In effect, then, Manson

119

creates an image, a brand—"the martyr"—through which he can secure the loyalty of his fans by inviting them to bond with him.

MORAL PANIC

Shortly after Columbine, the charges against Manson took a variety of forms, ranging from simple claims that the shooters, Eric Harris and Dylan Klebold, were fans of Manson to more subtle arguments such as those found in reports about the death of 17-year-old victim, Cassie Bernall. Numerous accounts of Bernall's final moments were circulating in the days and weeks after her death. Each varied slightly from the other, but as Elizabeth Renzetti notes they generally took the following shape: "On the morning of April 20 [1999], Cassie Bernall—average student, former Marilyn Manson fan and born-again Christian—was in the library at Columbine, her high school in Littleton, Colo., when two classmates burst in carrying weapons. Here, the accounts diverge: She was reading her Bible—or perhaps a volume of Shakespeare. She was standing tall in the face of evil—or perhaps cowering under a table. When the killers asked if she believed in God, she answered 'yes'; or perhaps 'Yes, I believe in God' or even 'Yes, I believe in Jesus.'"[2] Such reports suggest that Bernall did not die a meaningless death; instead, they portray her as a young woman who was martyred for her faith, killed because she said "Yes, I believe." She had been born again, we are told, and her newfound virtue is signified, in these reports, not only by the affirmation of her faith and in the presence of the Bible she might have been reading, but also by her apparent decision to leave Manson behind her. Conversely, Manson's depravity is constructed in the suggestion that he is no longer in the possession of those who have come to believe in God. Rather, he more or less remains in the hands of the killers, whom he presumably inspired.

Eventually, Bernall's mother, Misty, wrote *She Said Yes: The Unlikely Martyrdom of Cassie Bernall* (1999), a book which seemed to lend official authority to the secular sanctification of her daughter. But in his recent book, *Columbine*, Dave Cullen guides us through countless reports and representations of the activities leading up to and including the shootings at the high school in order to attempt to set the record straight. According to Cullen, for example, there is no evidence to suggest that either Harris or Klebold was a Manson fan. Cassie Bernall was not reading her Bible in the library; she was reading *Macbeth*. Furthermore, at least two eyewitnesses reported to the police that she was not standing tall in the face of evil, but, along with most other terrified students in the Columbine library, she was hiding under a table. Eric Harris did not ask her if she believed in God. Rather, he simply "slammed his hand on [the] table . . . squatted down for a look . . . [said] 'Peekaboo,'" and then brutally shot Bernall in the head with a sawed-off shotgun.[3] Cullen notes that another student in the library, Valeen Schnurr, already injured from a shotgun blast, was praying aloud when Dylan Klebold asked her if she believed in God. She replied that she did. Klebold reloaded his shotgun, but something distracted him before he pulled the trigger, and her life was spared. What interests me here is not so much Cullen's useful project of sifting through countless media reports and testimonies in order to clarify our understanding of the events, but the fact that the various and sometimes contradictory initial reports nevertheless came together in something like an erroneous consensus to locate blame for youth violence in youth culture itself—in this instance, the goth rock subculture and its figurehead, Marilyn Manson.

In *Folk Devils and Moral Panics*, Stanley Cohen argues that generation after generation, various institutions, including the mainstream media, the church, and the state, construct members of youth subcultures as "threat[s] to societal values and interests."[4] "Bishops, politicians, and other right-thinking people" join the media and hold up images of youths as distinctive social types: "folk devils," or monsters, who serve as "visible reminders of what we should not be."[5] Specifically, Cohen examines the media construction of the Mods and the Rockers, rival British subcultures whose members clashed most notoriously during the Whitsun holiday in May 1964 at seaside resorts in Brighton and Hastings. The media fanned the fires of moral outrage, inspiring panic by claiming that the riots were a kind of deviant behavior. Cohen counters that the conflicts between the Mods and the Rockers were little different from those that had erupted between members of different subcultures in previous generations. Relying on Howard S. Becker's notion that "deviance is not a quality of the act the person commits . . . [but simply a] behaviour that people so label," Cohen reveals the politics of moral panic, a politics in which the label, *deviant*, becomes "the basis for assigning social status."[6] In such a light, we might say that the purveyors of panic attempt to secure and maintain their own power. They attempt to exert social control by circulating unfounded fears about deviance in youth cultures that reinforce their own supposed normalcy and moral superiority. This is not to say that people are spreading unfounded fears about rioting itself or, in the case of Columbine, teenage violence and murder; those actions, indeed, are frightening. Rather, the point is that the moralists are generalizing, stereotyping, and spreading unfounded fears about entire subcultures that they then construct as deviant. The moralists of the mid-1960s needed to reassure themselves that they and their children were not the sort who might riot at a moment's notice: only members of a deviant subculture would do so. Likewise, in the aftermath of the Columbine tragedy, many people were so thoroughly convinced that normal teens could not do what Harris and Klebold had done, that they immediately assumed their actions resulted from membership in a youth subculture that had to be deviant.

Especially in these reports of Bernall's death, Manson's supposed deviance is constructed over and against his dissociation from God. Perhaps more surprisingly, it is also signified in his distance from William Shakespeare: both the Bible *and* the volume of Shakespeare Cassie Bernall may have been reading—was in fact reading, according to Cullen—signify her virtue and Manson's depravity. And this is not the only instance in which Shakespeare enters into discussions about youth culture and school violence. Stephen Glover writes, for example, that Virginia Tech gunman and English major Seung-Hui Cho spent his time watching "violent films, and hour upon hour of mindless television," making him only "nominally a student of English Literature" who probably never read "Shakespeare's sonnets or the novels of Charles Dickens."[7] Glover assumes that if Cho had been reading his Shakespeare rather than "playing violent video games . . . [or listening] interminably to forlorn and nihilistic music on his laptop," then he and his fellow students might still be alive. Both here and in the reports of Bernall's death, the assumption seems to be that youth culture corrupts, whereas Shakespeare does not. In fact, both Glover's article and the reports of Bernall's death summarized in Renzetti's article in the *Globe and Mail* imply that Shakespeare possesses a salvific capacity: Shakespeare can save you. In at least some segments of the popular imagination, then, Shakespeare is used as a marker in the creation and maintenance of moral panics: those who possess him, we are asked to believe, are morally superior to those who do not. Those who possess him are normal; those who do not are deviant.

I find it difficult to imagine, however, that a poem that compares a love object to a summer's day, for example, might have prevented Cho from murdering thirty-two innocent people. In fact, Cullen's book reminds us that Columbine shooter Eric Harris "enjoyed quoting Nietzsche and Shakespeare," and he reports that, in the now infamous Basement Tapes that the killers recorded in order to explain their motives, Harris more or less apologizes to his mother for what he is about to do by telling her that "Good wombs have borne bad sons"—a line Shakespeare's Miranda uses to explain the treachery of her uncle, who usurped her father's throne in *The Tempest*.[8] Exposure to Shakespeare did not prevent Eric Harris from becoming a murderer.

Likewise, exposure to or membership in a youth subculture is not necessarily going to lead to deviant or violent behavior. Media Studies scholars and Audience Studies scholars have examined this issue at great length. On the one hand, theorists like Theodor Adorno and Frederic Wertham imagine that audiences and consumers are vulnerable, passive, victimized, and enthralled by culture.[9] They assume that in the dynamic interaction between a reader and a text, power lies not in the reader but with the text. In such a light, the likes of Harris, Klebold, and Cho are seen as victims of the sometimes violent media they consume and the subcultures in which they participate. Such theorists might agree, then, with the purveyors of panic who argue that youth culture can and should be blamed for school violence. But other scholars including Michel de Certeau and John Fiske counter those arguments, claiming that readers, audiences, and members of subcultures are active and can resist the ways in which texts and cultures might attempt to hail them into violent subject positions.[10] If someone plays a violent video game, for example, he or she is not necessarily going to be conditioned or compelled to then go out and commit violent acts. In fact, readers and audiences might even develop an antipathy for violence when they consume violent texts.

Still other theorists have looked at fan cultures and concluded that some readers or audiences are not only not enthralled by the power of texts and subcultures, but they actively transform and create new subcultures that serve as bases from which they might engage with the world at large.[11] And most recently, scholars have theorized that, while readers, audiences, and members of subcultures might seem able to respond to literary and cultural texts in an infinite variety of ways, their responses are in fact limited by their own "interpretive communities" which are shaped, for example, by their class, gender, nation, and race.[12] Ultimately, then, scholars have looked at the relationships between readers and texts, audiences and texts, and young people and subcultures, from a number of perspectives and concluded that there is no simplistic or unilateral power relation between them. Certainly, there is no longer any strong sense that readers, audiences, or members of subcultures are entirely vulnerable, passive, and susceptible to complete inscription within the ideology of a subculture or a text. Such conclusions, however, are not always heard outside of academia. They do not seem to inform, for example, the moralists, from the creators of the 1936 film, *Reefer Madness*, to Tipper Gore and beyond, who continue, generation after generation, to perpetuate panic about youth subcultures.

THE FINE ART OF SCAPEGOATING

Perhaps the persistence of moral panics can be attributed to Machiavellian politics: "It is far better to be feared than loved if you cannot be both," Machiavelli infamously advised his prince, and statesmen as well as civic and religious leaders throughout history have taken his advice to heart.[13] In *The*

Culture of Fear, Barry Glassner argues that our own mainstream media perpetuates such panics because "immense power and money await those who tap into our moral insecurities."[14] Just as likely an explanation for the perseverance of moral panics, however, can be found in the psychological power of the scapegoat narrative itself. In "The Philosophy of Literary Form," Kenneth Burke argues that the scapegoat function is located in the heart of Western tragic drama. The purpose of the scapegoat narrative, he contends, is to provide catharsis by projecting blame: the scapegoat is "the 'representative' or 'vessel' of certain unwanted evils, the sacrificial animal upon whose back the burden of these evils is ritualistically loaded."[15] Despite the fact that Burke is a rhetorician and Stanley Cohen is a sociologist, I want to suggest that the discourse of moral panic is in dialogue with Burke's theory of the scapegoat function in Western tragic drama. After all, Burke claims that drama is sociological in that it expresses the logic of a society. Conversely, the discourse of moral panic is rhetorical: like some playscripts, it is a narrative that is oftentimes constructed in response to a tragedy. Likewise, a folk devil is not only an identity category that is fashioned by moralists in an effort to exert social control, but a folk devil is also a scapegoat: a "'representative' or 'vessel' of certain unwanted evils." When the moralists pointed fingers at Manson, they projected society's ills onto him precisely in order to then attempt to control the goth rock subculture and avoid any responsibility for the tragedy themselves.

According to Burke, not all scapegoats are the same. He identifies three different types, or three different logics that attempt to explain how or justify why a certain person or character can be scapegoated. The scapegoat can be defined as someone who offends "legal or moral justice" and therefore "'deserves' what he gets; alternately, he might be someone whose sacrifice is fatalistic or otherwise inevitable, "as when we so point the arrows of the plot that the audience comes to think of him as a marked man, and so prepares itself to relinquish him"; finally, a scapegoat might be someone who is, like Christ, "too good for this world."[16]

These different kinds of scapegoats, or these different kinds of scapegoating narratives, are not only found at the center of Western tragic drama, but they appear to have structured various responses to the shootings at Columbine High School. As we have seen, moralists attempted to place blame for the school violence on Manson, the goth rock shock rocker, who supposedly offends moral justice and therefore seems to get what he deserves. In *Columbine*, Cullen argues that Eric Harris was an emotionally void psychopath, a master of the false apology who only appeared to regret his actions, but cackled with glee in his journals when others swallowed his lies.[17] The conclusion here seems inevitable: Harris was going to shoot up his high school no matter what might have been done to prevent it because he was a victim of biology, fatalistically doomed because his body failed to provide him with the ability to sympathize or empathize with anyone. Finally, in the Basement Tapes documenting their reasons for the attack, Harris and Klebold attempt to set themselves up as "too good for this world" scapegoats. Cullen notes throughout his book that Harris was obsessed with his own supreme intelligence and the stupidity of everyone else around him. In his own mind, then, Harris was justified in his desire to attack the high school and end his own life in a supposed blaze of glory. As far as he was concerned, he was not responsible for actions that were criminal. Rather, the corrupt world around him was going to get what it deserved: he and Klebold were preparing to make the supreme sacrifice to redeem it—or send it to hell.

Clearly, just as playwrights have turned to scapegoating narratives to shape our understanding of the fictional tragedies they depict, journalists, moralists, and many others turn, consciously or not, to the very same kind of structuring narratives when telling us stories that attempt to explain tragic incidents in our own lives. But scapegoating narratives are as problematic as they are psychologically appealing. In a forthcoming article, Patrick Shaw notes how overwhelmingly dissatisfactory such narratives are. He rejects Virginia Tech shooter Seung-Hui Cho's Eric Harris-like attempt to fashion himself as the kind of scapegoat who is "too good for this world," noting that if we accept Cho's narrative, we "indict the victims of his bullets."[18] Indeed, all three scapegoating narratives, as they emerged in response to the Columbine tragedy, prove to be equally dissatisfactory: none of them hold Harris and Klebold accountable for their actions, and the account of the scapegoat who offends moral or legal justice—that is, Manson—like the report of the scapegoat who is supposedly too good for this world, shifts blame from the perpetrators onto the victims themselves, or at least onto the youth subcultures that some of those victims might have embraced. In his own response to the tragedy, Marilyn Manson does not call for the death of the art of scapegoating, but instead appropriates scapegoating narratives, making himself a martyr—a "too good for this world" scapegoat—and he does so in order to point out, in Shaw-like fashion, the unacceptability of the discourse of moral panic and its efforts to condemn the youth culture of his fans.

SEIZING THE APPARATUS:
HOLY WOOD, MARTYRDOM, AND "DISPOSABLE TEENS"

Holy Wood is a concept album describing, as Barry Walters writes, "how a rock star/icon can be shot down by the pressures of fame, government,

religion and greed."[19] More specifically, as April Long notes, the album "follows a character who attempts revolution through music, but ends up killing
himself when his revolution is exploited by society. It's Manson's own story,
essentially, used as a framework to indict a culture that both celebrates and
condemns violence. . . . [Manson] spotlights certain unpleasant truths—that
Christianity has justified all manner of beastly acts, and that he is not the
cause of evil in men, but rather a symptom."[20] The utter irreligiosity of our
world is proclaimed on the opening track, "Godeatgod," when the album's
protagonist, Adam Kadmon references the crucifixion of Christ and the as-
sassinations of John F. Kennedy and Martin Luther King. In a kind of letter
or prayer to god, Kadmon reminds us that if god was alive we'd kill him
too—or perhaps again. Kadmon and Manson suggest here that humanity
imagines itself as godlike, killing and devouring, say, the saints among us.
Other unpleasantries include Kadmon's claim in "The Fight Song" that, for
too many of us, the death of one person registers as a tragedy, but the death of
millions amounts to little more than a statistic. Of course, the claims are argu-
able, but Kadmon and Manson are suggesting that godlessness characterizes
our present day Christian culture. In fact, Manson's alter ego attempts to collapse the difference between Christianity and, as Long puts it, "all manner of
beastly acts," the difference between the supposedly normal and the deviant,
and such a deconstructive practice, in part, constitutes Kadmon's revolution.
The revolt is initially successful, but it is soon exploited by the media and the
music industry, and Kadmon therefore takes his own life, making himself a
"too good for this world" scapegoat: he becomes the martyr who exposes the
hypocrisies and the corrupt morals of our world and then takes his own life,
sacrificing himself in one final attempt to reveal these truths to us.

Such a martyr is depicted on the album's cover. The image, widely available on the Internet, reveals that Kadmon has been crucified. His arms are
outstretched, and he has been pierced in the chest. A thin golden halo circles
his head, and most disturbingly, his lower jaw is missing, as though it has
been ripped or hacked off, suggesting that he has been silenced by those who
usurped his revolution—except, of course, the image is anything but silent.
It signifies Kadmon's mutilation at the hands of the usurpers. He has been
crucified because he has spoken "unpleasant truths." But it's not just the alter
ego on the album cover. It is also Manson, and it signifies not only Kadmon's
mutilation but Manson's disfigurement by the rhetoric of the moralists who
emerged in the wake of Columbine. Ultimately, then, through the image of
the crucifixion, Manson aligns himself with Christ, seizing the moral authority that had been used against him in the moral panics that signified his supposed depravity. In fact, he not only turns the arguments of the moralists on
their heads, claiming moral superiority for himself, but he also more or less

accuses the moralists of perpetrating exactly the kind of brutality that they claim he incited.

Manson also appropriates Shakespeare in his effort to rehabilitate his image. On "Target Audience (Narcissus Narcosis)," the album's fifth track, he notes that, throughout time, other artists have wrongly been held accountable for society's ills. The song begins with a series of rhetorical questions wherein Kadmon wonders just how many different things he, like Manson, might be held accountable for. For what, exactly, does he need to apologize? He sarcastically queries whether or not he is even supposed to be sorry that he is alive. Should he be sorry, he asks, that the sky turned black or that John and Robert Kennedy were assassinated? The song mocks the efforts of the moralists to blame Manson for Columbine by caustically implying that there is no end to what they might blame him for.

The one thing, however, that Kadmon is genuinely sorry for is the fact that William Shakespeare was made into a scapegoat. When the album was first released, the song's lyric caused some confusion. In a posting at The Hierophant Council, a discussion forum at www.mansonusa.com, one Manson fan writes:

> I'm a bit confused on a Shakespeare reference in H W. In 'Target Audience' Manson says but I'm sorry Shakespeare was your scapegoat. The song is about Columbine and the overall tone to this song is sarcastic; no, he's not sorry because he isn't responsible, but is that particular line sarcastic in nature? A scapegoat is someone who has blame laid on them by others, however, I read somewhere (maybe several places) where Manson logically argues that 'Romeo and Juliet' is about two teenagers who kill themselves because they are misunderstood and no one *blames* this on Shakespeare the way society nowadays blames people for tragedies (ref. to Columbine). All this made sense until I thought about that phrase from Target Audience. Enlightenment, anyone??[21]

The writer recognizes the sarcastic nature of the rhetorical questions, but wonders whether or not Manson (there is no assumption of difference between Manson and the song's protagonist, here) is genuinely sorry that someone somewhere scapegoated Shakespeare.

A respondent directs the enquirer to the website of Cader Books, where an excerpt from Michael Macrone's *Naughty Shakespeare* (1997) can be found. Macrone's book is billed as "a rowdy and rollicking collection of the Bard's bawdiest blusters and steamiest scenes."[22] But the website's excerpt from Macrone's text discusses the fact that London's city fathers and religious leaders were opposed to the Renaissance stage, and it describes the function of the Master of the Revels and the potential for censorship in Shakespeare's day. Furthermore, it mentions the general bowdlerization of Shakespeare that resulted in the fact that "between about 1750 and about 1950, [people had the option of reading] either censored Shakespeare or no Shakespeare."[23] The conclusion drawn by the Manson fans at the Hierophant Council website after reading the Cader Books excerpt is that Shakespeare was just like Manson— a scapegoat of his own time and place: "Both of them have/had the same problems with censorship. . . . Shakespeare was the scapegoat of his time. . . . I believe this reference points to societies [sic] tendency to point the finger and scapegoat artists for societies actions. (Like when Manson was blamed for Columbine)."[24]

The idea that Shakespeare was scapegoated for his culture's ills may be a correct conclusion given the thread of this discussion as it follows from Manson's song, but it remains, without doubt, something of an overstatement. On the one hand, Shakespeare's works were subject to censorship at the hand of the Master of the Revels; there was a considerable amount of anti-theatricalism present during his day; and his texts were bowdlerized in *The Family Shakespeare*, published in the early nineteenth century. On the other hand, however, Shakespeare was a thriving, professional playwright who had the esteem of his peers and was in no way scapegoated for society's ills in the way that Manson was blamed for Columbine. Even though Shakespeare would have been considered as something of an early modern folk devil by the Puritan anti-theatricalists, and even though we have evidence that his play, *Richard II*, might have been censored when it was published in quarto form (though there is no critical consensus on this matter), as Cyndia Susan Clegg argues, we cannot assume that such censorship was in any way "representative of the conditions under which Shakespeare or any other imaginative writer worked."[25] "The condition of repressive writing," she concludes, "has been vastly overstated."[26]

Nevertheless, Manson implies Shakespeare's scapegoating, and his fans on the Hierophant Council website conclude that "Shakespeare was the scapegoat of his time."[27] Here, then, Manson turns Shakespeare against the uses to which he had been put by the moralists: Shakespeare had been used to demonize Manson, but Manson now aligns himself with Shakespeare, thus appropriating his cultural authority at the same time that he attacks the purveyors of panic for absurdly attempting throughout history to scapegoat artists for society's ills.

Crucially, it must be noted that while Manson's alter-ego, Kadmon, kills himself when his revolution is exploited by others, Manson does not. But Kadmon's politics are Manson's politics, and Kadmon's martyrdom is therefore Manson's martyrdom: Manson thus uses his alter-ego to fashion his own identity as the "too good for this world" scapegoat who survives. Ultimately, Manson offers that same identity of the martyred survivor to his fans. On

"Target Audience," Kadmon argues that parents attempt to hail their children into their own belief systems, but if the children decide to reject their parents' culture, if they decide, as Kadmon sings in "The Fight Song," that they do not want to be a slave to a nonexistent god and a world that doesn't care for them, then they are discarded; according to another of the album's song titles, they are regarded by their parents as "Disposable Teens." But Manson offers them a way out of such an identity category, and their avenue of escape can be found in Manson's use of Shakespeare—specifically, through his account or interpretation of *Romeo and Juliet*. As the Hierophant Council fan noted, Manson has argued "that 'Romeo and Juliet' is about two teenagers who kill themselves because they are misunderstood." More specifically, Manson had invoked Shakespeare's aid well before the Columbine shooting, when he had been treated as a kind of Stanley Cohen-esque "folk devil" by a grieving parent who testified before Congress in 1997 that Manson's music caused his teenage son to commit suicide. Manson replied that "if you want to blame music for someone hurting themselves, then you can just as easily blame Shakespeare writing 'Romeo and Juliet' which is something I was taught as a kid, and that is a story about two teenagers who killed themselves because their parents did not understand them."[28]

First of all, we should note that Manson echoes a number of similar arguments made on his behalf. Bryan Patterson contends, for example, that there is no point in blaming Manson for the Columbine shootings: "You might as well ban *Richard III* or *Hamlet*. After all, Shakespeare's tales of revenge contain several brutal murders."[29] Such arguments have also been made in defense of other notorious folk devils: in an article about the moral panic surrounding rapper Eminem, Dominik Diamond writes, "Yes [the protagonist of 'Kim,' a song from Eminem's *The Marshall Mathers LP* (2000),] kills his wife. So does Othello. King Lear wants to kill his own daughters. Hamlet wants to have sex with his mum. Should we ban Shakespeare?"[30] These counter-arguments attempt to defend the likes of Manson and Eminem by claiming that if we are going to blame youth culture for teen violence, then we should remember that the same sort of corrupting influence can and should be attributed to Shakespeare. But, of course, Manson, Patterson, and Diamond understand that when Shakespeare is set against youth culture in order to promote moral distinctions, he signifies the depravity of youth culture precisely because he is regarded as the epitome of elite culture and moral superiority. They assume, then, that only a few of us, and only those of us willing to expose ourselves to ridicule, would actually blame Shakespeare for teen suicides or school shootings. While such arguments explicitly state that both Shakespeare and youth culture are capable of producing violent teens, then, their rhetorical aim is to suggest the opposite: neither Shakespeare nor violent video games, rap, goth rock, or any other sort of youth culture should be held accountable when teens turn to violence.

Secondly, we should consider the fact that while Manson's reading of *Romeo and Juliet*—"two teenagers who killed themselves because their parents did not understand them"—might seem reductive and anachronistic, Marjorie Garber convincingly notes that throughout its history, and especially in modern popular culture, *Romeo and Juliet* has been read as a "story of a perfect love disrupted by circumstance: feud, plague, politics, parental opposition, unseemly haste, and unforeseen delay."[31] Manson's assessment of the play, then, could serve as evidence for Garber's claim: in popular culture, *Romeo and Juliet* has been received as a play which concludes with a double suicide, in part at least, because the titular characters' parents do not understand their children and oppose their marriage. Thus Romeo and Juliet might be thought of as disposable teens of their own time and place—especially, Juliet, who rejects her father's demands that she marry Paris and is told as a result that she can go "hang, beg, starve, [or] die in the street" for all her father cares."[32]

If Manson's alter ego, Kadmon, serves as the martyr who allows Manson to survive martyrdom, then in Manson's interpretation of the play—in *Manson's R + J*, we might say, altering the phrase from Baz Luhrmann's 1996 film—Romeo and Juliet might be thought of as the alter egos of his fans, as disposable teens who pay for the fact that they are too good for this all too corrupt world, but allow other teens, Manson's fans, to survive that martyrdom. Ultimately, then, we might imagine that *Holy Wood*'s cover image of the martyr includes not only Kadmon, Christ, Shakespeare, and Manson, but also, Romeo and Juliet, as well as Manson's fans—all of them too good for this world. Manson appears to have mastered the art of scapegoating. He appropriates the narrative that was used against him, seizes the moral and cultural authority of Christ and Shakespeare, and secures loyalty by offering a package, an identity category that enables his fans to see themselves in a much more favorable light than the mainstream culture's depiction of them as youths who are both disposable and responsible for society's ills.

SUBCULTURAL CAPITAL

Finally, we might note that the album's cover art must also invoke the memory of Manson's claim to be the popular "Antichrist Superstar." Manson's appropriative strategies on *Holy Wood* have been a part of his career-long deconstructive politics. He has appropriated moral panic throughout his career, and his purpose has been twofold: to reveal the hypocrisy and corruption of the so-called normal world, and to portray himself, if not always as a too good for this world martyr, then as a monstrous product of the supposedly normal—not someone who creates society's ills, but someone who is constructed by a corrupt society. In either event, that is, whether he is attempting to portray himself as a martyr or a monster, he has offered up an identity category that serves as a source of appeal to his fans.

Unquestionably, Manson was an easy target after the Columbine attacks, and perhaps he was such an easy target because, throughout his career, he has attempted to cultivate responses of shock and fear. As most people now know, Manson, born Brian Hugh Warner, created his stage name by combining the names of Marilyn Monroe and convicted murderer, Charles Manson. His band, initially called Marilyn Manson and the Spooky Kids, included Daisy Berkowitz, Olivia Newton Bundy, Madonna Wayne Gacy, and others; each band member creates a stage name by combining the name of an iconic female sex symbol with the name of a notorious mass murderer. Following in the footsteps of macabre rock and roll acts such as Alice Cooper and KISS, the band's early performances were highly theatrical. According to Greg Baker, concerts sometimes involved "naked women nailed to a cross, a child in a cage, or bloody animal body parts."[33] The members of the band sometimes performed in women's clothing, and their 1998 album, *Mechanical Animals*, drew inspiration from the glam rock androgyny of David Bowie, particularly his mid-1970s albums, *Aladdin Sane* (1973), *Pin Ups* (1973), and *Diamond Dogs* (1974). Like many rock and rollers before him, then, Manson cultivated a stage persona that attempted to shock conventional sensibilities.

In "Moral Panic, the Media and British Rave Culture," Sarah Thornton complicates Stanley Cohen's arguments by noting that youth cultures often attempt to cultivate negative press reports. Citing Malcolm McLaren's management of the Sex Pistols and Andrew Loog Oldham's promotion of the Rolling Stones as "rebellious and threatening," she argues that positive press would amount to a "kiss of death" for a youth subculture, but moral panic can "render a subculture attractively subversive as no other promotional ploy can."[34] Moral panic and negative press, then, earn a kind of "currency of the underground" which Thornton, borrowing from and amending Pierre Bourdieu, calls "subcultural capital."[35] Many youth subcultures, then, simultaneously attempt to fend off and cultivate moral panic, and Manson was no different. It was 1996's *Antichrist Superstar* that put him on the national shock rock map. Surely, a self-professed antichrist intends to inspire moral panic, and in such a light, we can see that it is no small wonder that he was targeted by the moralists. In fact, Manson basically offers that very explanation in his June 24, 1999, response to the charge that he influenced the actions of the killers in Littleton: "America loves to find an icon to hang its guilt on," he writes, implying that he had been singled out by the moralists because he had deliberately "assumed the role of Antichrist."[36]

Manson's particular brand of shock rock, however, involves considerably more than a simple, uncritical effort to set himself up as another Mick Jagger-like bad boy of rock and roll. Rather, Manson adopts a seemingly monstrous persona in order to suggest that his monstrosity is a product of mainstream culture. The liner notes for his first CD, *Portrait of an American Family* (1994), announce such an intention with the claim that "we are symptoms of your Christian America." The purpose here, as it would later be on *Holy Wood*, is to collapse the difference between the normal and the deviant. Such an effort is also evident in the mingling of opposites found in the names of the band-members' stage personas. Conjoining the names of Marilyn Monroe and Charles Manson is, of course, problematic for a number of reasons—it constructs a monstrous feminine; it glorifies and re-celebritizes a notorious mass murderer; and it shows no sensitivity whatsoever for those whose loved ones were murdered—but it also serves an important rhetorical and political purpose: "Marilyn Manson," "Madonna Wayne Gacy," and "Olivia Newton Bundy" suggest there is no difference between the beautiful and the monstrous—the normal and the deviant.

At least some of Manson's admirers are aware of such a deconstructive practice. In 1997 Manson appeared as Porno Star #1 in David Lynch's film, *Lost Highway*. Lynch is perhaps most famously known for his television series, *Twin Peaks* (1990–1991), a handful of memorable films, including *Eraserhead* (1977), *The Elephant Man* (1980), *Blue Velvet* (1986), and *Mulholland Drive* (2001), as well as the surreal or nightmarish sensibilities found in them. *Blue Velvet* more or less opens, for example, with the discovery of a severed human ear in the middle of a vacant lot in the small town of Lumberton. From its opening moments, then, Lynch's film disrupts our expectations, suggesting that somewhere in the small, middle-America town of Lumberton, we can expect to find an earless body, a knife-wielding assailant, and a subculture in which the assailant and victim circulated—a seedy underbelly of prostitution, perhaps, or drugs, or gambling. The supposed differences between the normal and the deviant are thus collapsed, and a similar sentiment is at work in the epigraph Lynch pens at the Introduction of Manson's biography, *The Long Road Out of Hell*: "Outside it was raining cats and barking dogs. / Like an egg-born offspring of collective humanity, in / sauntered Marilyn Manson. It was obvious— /he was beginning to look and sound a lot like Elvis."[37] Here, Lynch breaks down the distinctions between human and beast, suggesting that Manson is like a reptilian-human child, a hatchling of us all. And the assertion that he is beginning to look and sound like Elvis, breaks down the distinction between the epitome of mainstream rock and roll on the one hand, and the figurehead for one of its most marginalized subcultures on the other. The epigraph collapses the difference between the center and the margins.

Lynch's comment nicely fits Manson's biography because it announces a similar agenda. The first chapter of *The Long Road Out of Hell* begins with the claim that "HELL to me was my grandfather's cellar."[38] Manson recounts his early teen memories of spending time after school in what might seem to be the locus of normality: the home of the patriarch. However, like Lynch, Manson discovers for us the rotten core of the normal. "Every day," he writes, he and his 12-year-old cousin, Chad, "made new and grotesque discoveries."[39] His grandfather's cellar was "littered with empty beer cans . . . a faded red enema bag," condoms so old they'd begun to disintegrate, a "handful of the latex finger cots that doctors use for rectal exams; and a Friar Tuck that popped a boner when its head was pushed in."[40] They found 16 millimeter porno films in empty paint cans, bestiality pictures, women's clothes and wigs, and "a collection of dildoes that had suction cups on the bottom."[41] One afternoon, Manson and Chad sneak down to the cellar to discover their grandfather masturbating, and in perhaps the most disturbing disclosure in this introductory chapter, Manson tells us that when his father would come to pick him up and take him home, he would not enter the house, "as if he were afraid of reliving whatever it was he had experienced in that old house as a child."[42] While we might expect a parent to defend a child from what he himself fears, here the parent knowingly exposes the child to risk. Manson may or may not be putting us on, here, but in any event the ideological work of his biography clearly follows a process of revealing the seedy underbelly of middle America and the American family, breaking down the distinctions between what is supposed to be normal and what is supposed to be deviant. In fact, given the idea that the parent exposes the child to risk, Manson presents us with the notion that the seemingly deviant is not only a part of the seemingly normal, but that, generation after generation, the seemingly deviant is produced by the seemingly normal.

Prior to *Holy Wood*, then, Manson attempted to shock and incite panic by adopting a monstrous persona that, he claims, was a product of conservative and traditional values. In the process of securing subcultural capital for himself, he created a process and politics of identity formation that appealed to his fans, including the likes of David Lynch. On *Holy Wood*, however, Manson takes a different tack. He does not necessarily discard monstrosity—recall the image of the crucified Kadmon and the fact that his jaw has been torn away—but invests it more clearly and pointedly with virtues that surpass those of the corrupted culture that created him. He appropriates the scapegoating narrative, making a martyr of himself, while seizing the moral and cultural authority of Christ and Shakespeare. Furthermore, he invites his fans—those who are regarded by their parents as "disposable teens"—to identify with him. In so doing, Manson improves on his already effective marketing strategy. He creates a brand image for goth rock, secures the loyalty and devotion of his fans, by forging sympathetic bonds with them and offering them a share of the symbolic capital he earns by associating himself with Christ, the Antichrist, Shakespeare, and his tragic characters, Romeo and Juliet.

NOTES

1. "Disposable Teens" is the title of a song on *Holy Wood*. It's significance in Manson's appropriative and branding strategies is discussed in more detail in the following section.

2. Elizabeth Renzetti, "The Ascension of Saint Cassie: What has Happened to Cassie Bernall since her Death at Columbine High is a Study in the Inner Workings of Modern Religion; But even more Enlightening is what it Says about the Bad-girl/ Good-Girl Game that Women are Still Forced to Play," *The Globe and Mail (Canada)*, September 23, 1999.

3. Dave Cullen, *Columbine* (New York and Boston: Twelve, 2009), 222–33.

4. Stanley Cohen, *Folk Devils and Moral Panics*, 3rd ed. (London and New York: Routledge, 1972, 1987, and 2002), 1.

5. Cohen, 2.

6. Howard S. Becker. *Outsiders: Studies in the Sociology of Deviance* (New York: Free Press, 1963), 9, cited in Cohen, 4, and Cohen, 5.

7. Stephen Glover, "Guns? No, Blame the Amorality and Violence of Yankee Culture: Commentary," *Daily Mail* (London), April 20, 2007.

8. Cullen, 9 and 333, and William Shakespeare, *The Tempest*, in *The Norton Shakespeare*, ed. Stephen Greenblatt, 2nd ed. (New York and London: W. W. Norton and Company, 1997 and 2008), 1.2.119.

9. T. W. Adorno, *The Culture Industry* (London: Routledge, 1991), Fredric Wertham, *Seduction of the Innocent*. London: Museum Press, 1955, and *The Audience Studies Reader*, eds. Will Brooker and Deborah Jermyn (London and New York: Routledge, 2003).

10. Michel de Certeau, *The Practice of Everyday Life* (Minneapolis: University of Minneapolis Press, 1998) and John Fiske, *Understanding Popular Culture* (London: Routledge, 1989).

11. Henry Jenkins, "Out of the Closet and Into the Universe: Queers and *Star Trek*," in *Science Fiction Audiences: Watching Doctor Who and Star Trek*, eds. John Tulloch and Henry Jenkins (London: Routledge, 1995), Barbara Ehrenreich, Elizabeth Hess, and Gloria Jacobs, "Beatlemania: Girls Just Want To Have Fun," in *The Adoring Audience*, ed. Lisa A. Lewis (London: Routledge, 1992), and Sara Gwenllian-Jones, "Histories, Fictions and *Xena: Warrior Princess*," *Television and New Media* 1:4 (2000).

12. Ian Ang, *Living Room Wars: Rethinking Audiences for a Postmodern World* (London: Routledge, 1996), Janice Radway, *Reading the Romance: Women, Patriarchy and Popular Literature* (Chapel Hill and London: University of North Carolina Press, 1984), and Sut Jhally and Justin Lewis, *Enlightened Racism: The Cosby Show, Audiences and the Myth of the American Dream* (Oxford: Westview Press, 1992).

13. Niccoló Machiavelli, *The Prince*, Trans. George Bull (Harmondsworth, Penguin, 1961), 96.

14. Barry Glassner, *The Culture of Fear: Why Americans Are Afraid of the Wrong Things* (New York: Basic Books, 1999), xxviii.

15. Kenneth Burke, "The Philosophy of Literary Form" in *The Philosophy of Literary Form: Studies in Symbolic Action*, 3rd ed. (Berkeley and Los Angeles: University of California Press, 1973, 1967 and 1941), 39–40.

16. Burke, 40.

17. Cullen, 256–67 and 278–80.

18. Patrick Shaw, "Multiple Murders: The Virginia Tech Massacre, Multiculturalism, and the Death of Tragic Drama," *PMMLA*, forthcoming.

19. Barry Walters, "Marilyn Manson: *Holy Wood (In the Shadow of the Valley of Death)*," RollingStone.com, November 23, 2000, http://www.rollingstone.com.

20. April Long, "*Holy Wood (In the Shadow of the Valley of Death)*," NME.com, November 10, 2000, http://www.nme.com/reviews/marilyn-manson/3456.

21. The Hierophant Council, "Shakespeare," mansonusa.com, March 1, 2006, http://www.mansonusa.con/forums/archive/index.php/t-32669.html.

22. Cader Books, "Naughty Shakespeare" caderbooks.com, http://www.cader-books.com/exnshake1.html.

23. Cader Books.

24. The Hierophant Council.

25. Cyndia Susan Clegg, "'By the choise and inuitation of al the realme': *Richard II* and Elizabethan Press Censorship," *Shakespeare Quarterly* 48 (1997): 448.

26. Clegg, 448.

27. The Hierophant Council.

28. MTV.com, "Manson Rebuts Congressional Inquiry with Shakespeare," http://www.mtv.com/news/articles/1431774/19971124/marilyn_manson.jhtml.

29. Bryan Paterson, "Roots of Violence," *Sunday Tasmanian (Australia),* May 9, 1999.

30. Dominik Diamond, "The Real Slim Shady's Been Shut Up," *Daily Star,* February 3, 2001.

31. Marjorie Garber, *Shakespeare and Modern Culture* (New York: Pantheon, 2008), 56.

32. William Shakespeare, *Romeo and Juliet, The Norton Shakespeare*, 2nd Ed., Gen. Ed. Stephen Greenblatt (New York and London: W. W. Norton and Co., 2008) 3.5.192.

33. Greg Baker, "Manson Family Values: Teach Your Children Well and Accept that Heaven is Hell," *Miami New Times,* July 20, 1994.

34. Sarah Thornton, "Moral Panic, the Media and British Rave Culture," *Microphone Fiends: Youth Music and Youth Culture,* eds. Andrew Ross and Tricia Rose (New York & London: Routledge, 1994), 184.

35. Thornton, 178.

36. Marilyn Manson, "Columbine: Whose Fault Is it?" http://www.rollingstone.com/news/story/5923915/columbine_whose_fault_is_it.

37. David Lynch, "Introduction," in *The Long Hard Road Out of Hell,* by Marilyn Manson with Neil Strauss (New York: Regan Books, 1998).

38. Marilyn Manson with Neil Strauss, *The Long Hard Road Out of Hell* (New York: Regan Books, 1998), 3.

39. Manson with Strauss, 4.

40. Manson with Strauss, 3

41. Manson with Strauss, 10.

42. Manson with Strauss, 12.

BIBLIOGRAPHY

Adorno, T. W. *The Culture Industry.* London: Routledge, 1991.

Ang, Ian. *Living Room Wars: Rethinking Audiences for a Postmodern World.* London: Routledge, 1996.

Brooker, Will, and Deborah Jermyn, Eds. *The Audience Studies Reader.* London and New York: Routledge, 2003.

Burke, Kenneth. "The Philosophy of Literary Form." *The Philosophy of Literary Form: Studies in Symbolic Action.* 3rd ed. Berkeley and Los Angeles: University of California Press, 1973. (1967 and 1941). 1–137.

Cader Books. "Naughty Shakespeare." caderbooks.com. http://www.caderbooks.com/exnshake1.html.

de Certeau, Michel. *The Practice of Everyday Life.* Minneapolis: University of Minneapolis Press, 1998.

Clegg, Cyndia Susan. "'By the choise and inuitation of al the realme': *Richard II* and Elizabethan Press Censorship." *Shakespeare Quarterly* 48 (1997): 432–48.

Cohen, Stanley Cohen. *Folk Devils and Moral Panics.* 3rd ed. London and New York: Routledge, 1972, 1987, and 2002.

Cullen, Dave. *Columbine.* New York and Boston: Twelve, 2009.

Ehrenreich, Barbara, Elizabeth Hess, and Gloria Jacobs. "Beatlemania: Girls Just Want To Have Fun." *The Adoring Audience.* Ed. Lisa A. Lewis. London: Routledge, 1992.

Fiske, John. *Understanding Popular Culture.* London: Routledge, 1989.

Garber, Marjorie. *Shakespeare and Modern Culture.* New York: Pantheon, 2008.

Glassner, Barry. *The Culture of Fear: Why Americans Fear the Wrong Things.* New York: Basic Books, 1999.

Gwenllian-Jones, Sara. "Histories, Fictions and *Xena: Warrior Princess.*" *Television and New Media* 1:4 (2000).

The Hierophant Council. "Shakespeare." mansonusa.com. March 1, 2006. http://www.mansonusa.con/forums/archive/index.php/t-32669.html.

Jenkins, Henry. "Out of the Closet and Into the Universe: Queers and *Star Trek*." *Science Fiction Audiences: Watching Doctor Who and Star Trek*. Eds. John Tulloch and Henry Jenkins. London: Routledge, 1995.

Jhally, Sut, and Justin Lewis. *Enlightened Racism: The Cosby Show, Audiences and the Myth of the American Dream*. Oxford: Westview Press, 1992.

Long, April. "*Holy Wood (In the Shadow of the Valley of Death)*." NME.com. November 10, 2000. http://www.nme.com/reviews/marilyn-manson/3456.

Machiavelli, Niccoló. *The Prince*. Trans. George Bull. (Harmondsworth: Penguin, 1961).

Manson, Marilyn, with Neil Strauss. *The Long Hard Road Out of Hell*. New York: Regan Books, 1998.

Radway, Janice. *Reading the Romance: Women, Patriarchy and Popular Literature*. Chapel Hill and London: University of North Carolina Press, 1984.

Shakespeare, William. *The Tempest. The Norton Shakespeare*. Ed. Stephen Greenblatt, 2nd ed. New York and London: W. W. Norton and Company, 1997 and 2008.
———. *Romeo and Juliet. The Norton Shakespeare*. Ed. Stephen Greenblatt, 2nd ed. New York and London: W. W. Norton and Company, 1997 and 2008.

Shakespeare, William. *Romeo and Juliet. The Norton Shakespeare* 2nd Ed. Gen. Ed. Stephen Greenblatt. New York and London: W. W. Norton and Co., 2008.

Shaw, Patrick. "Multiple Murders: The Virginia Tech Massacre, Multiculturalism, and the Death of Tragic Drama." *PMMLA*, forthcoming.

Thornton, Sarah. "Moral Panic, the Media and British Rave Culture." *Microphone Fiends: Youth Music and Youth Culture*. Eds. Andrew Ross and Tricia Rose. New York & London: Routledge, 1994. 176–92.

Walters, Barry. "Marilyn Manson: *Holy Wood (In the Shadow of the Valley of Death)*." RollingStone.com. November 23, 2000. http://www.rollingstone.com.

Wertham, Fredric. *Seduction of the Innocent*. London: Museum Press, 1955.

8

Leading People to Rock: Evangelism in the Music of Bon Jovi

Mary Nash-Wood, Staci Parks, and Elizabeth Barfoot Christian

Witnessing Bon Jovi performing is an emotional experience on par with being moved by the Holy Spirit. A testament to the band's long-standing and growing fan base, it is not only the presence on the band, led by front man Jon Bon Jovi, that is so spiritual, but it is also the choice of words and phrases in the lyrics—also written primarily by Bon Jovi and lead guitarist Richie Sambora.

Like passing the offering plate at a revival meeting, multitudes of fans shell out hundreds of dollars to sit in the nosebleed sections of massive arenas and stand in line to spend fifty dollars or more on T-shirts, posters, programs and other band paraphernalia.

The choir of tens of thousands loudly belt out the Bon Jovi hymns, on their feet with arms raised in worship to their rock gods. "Living on a Prayer," "Silent Night," "Lay Your Hands on Me," "Something to Believe In," and "Hey God" are just a few of the song titles that bring to mind religious symbolism. Lyrics about curing a blind man's sight and riding with a dashboard Jesus as co-pilot strengthen the argument that the music of Bon Jovi holds strong spiritual symbolism of a Judeo-Christian tradition. In "Lost Highway," Bon Jovi calls on the patron saint of lonely souls for guidance and direction. Literally dozens of songs rely on the religious connotation to set the tone or tell a story. Bon Jovi's reappearing lyrical couple, Tommy and Gina, are "Living on a Prayer" and years and albums later living their lives without a silent prayer for their lost faith.

The running themes evident in the band's music are that faith, a good work ethic and moral living will bring happiness and success. Even the songs that discuss illicit sex, drinking and other unethical acts, describe the heartache when making the society's perceived "wrong" choices. The judgment in the lyrics is clear.

As the Bon Jovi religion is passed from generation to generation, mothers who swooned over Jon Bon Jovi and Richie Sambora, lead guitarist, as teens themselves are now introducing their own children to the rock icon famous for family values—Jon is still married to his high school sweetheart after two decades and four children. He has even referred to himself as the "poster boy for marriage" among rock stars.[1]

Why has Bon Jovi chosen to use strong religious metaphors throughout all aspects of its "branding," going so far as to be labeled a "Christian rock band"[2] by Sharon Osbourne, wife of Ozzy and a respected manager/promoter in the music industry? This chapter will primarily be a textual semiotic analysis of the band's song titles and lyrics, graphic representations for album promotions, marketing and magazine articles, performances and music videos. It will also examine interviews of the band members, the influences on their music and objectives the band is striving toward.

Semiotics is still developing as a discipline in media and the design of communication strategies assume new importance in this age of mass media. The use of semiotic methods to reveal different levels of meaning and sometimes, hidden motivations of creators of messages. One of the biggest dangers in using religious symbols in songs is that they will be missed completely or misinterpreted by the listeners.[3] This complicates the use of semiotic analysis as a legitimized field of study in this area.

ROCK MUSIC AS SACRILEGE

One can hardly disagree with the controversy that has surrounded rock music almost since its inception. From the moment Elvis Presley shook his pelvis on television, there has been an outspoken group against the "evils" inherent in the rhythm of rock. And just as long there have been multitudes of youth enamored by the music, the beat and the rock idols of the day. Rock music has "been the target of Christian crusades against the evils that allegedly threaten religion in American society. . . . Rock music appears to be the antithesis of religion, not merely an offensive art form, but a blasphemous, sacrilegious, and antireligious force in society."[4] This has been a common argument of fundamentalist groups for decades. However, a much smaller but growing constituency of popular culture scholars and more liberal theologians have begun in recent decades to recognize the power of rock music also to effect positive changes, including religiosity or spirituality.

Interestingly, many of the earliest rock and rollers who received the most criticism for playing the devil's music and for participating in hellish life-styles of drinking, cursing and fornicating are among those who have historically had the most overt relationship with religion. Elvis Presley, B.B. King, James Brown, Jerry Lee Lewis, Johnny Cash and Carl Perkins all sang both rock and gospel songs. There is no question that gospel hymns had a large influence on their musical styles and on their lives.

Jon Anderson of the rock group Yes described it this way, "Music has always been religious. Music is a passion and a vehicle for understanding of why we are here. It's a remembering of the past and of ritual."[5] Gene Simmons of KISS fame has also recognized the symbiotic relationship between religion and rock and roll. Referring to the group's live show, Simmons said, "The stage is holy ground, and what we do is electric church."[6]

This chapter will have limitations. While there are groups that actually do worship pop culture and rock music icons—like the First Church of Jesus Christ, Elvis, the First Presleyterian Church of Elvis the Divine, or the Temple of Bowie, which is devoted to rock star David Bowie—and others like the First Church of Holy Rock and Roll[7] that kind of shamanic religiosity will not be addressed. The religious and spiritual elements of this chapter will be related to the predominant accepted view of religion in the United States—those being the beliefs, ritual, symbols and experiences related to Judeo-Christian tradition. Every song on every album of music released by Bon Jovi as well as solo albums by Jon Bon Jovi and Richie Sambora were analyzed for lyrical and cover art content and symbolism.

RELIGION IN POP CULTURE

Religion can be found in all forms of popular culture, especially in the written word. Prolific horror writer Stephen King believes it is a much more common element than a lot of people realize on the surface. "Anyone who writes about hope is writing about religion," King wrote.[8] Although not Catholic, he said he finds that those raised Catholic have a richer background than most from which to draw their imagery and faith.

As mentioned earlier, there is a growing segment of the popular culture community now studying the impact both Christian rock singers and secular artists' message and lives have on the mass audience. Whereas one might expect singers who bill themselves "Christian" first and singer secondary to have as their focus leading people to Christ or explaining God's love through song and action, a religious message or influence has not been something scholars really focused on in the secular music world. A negative message has been suggested by fundamentalist groups, but this research will show it is also possible for mainstream rock groups to work toward a positive religious—or more precisely—a spiritual message through not only their music but their imagery and their actions. While the band Bon Jovi will be the primary focus of this research, literature exists showing other bands trying to incorporate a religious or spiritual calling or fervor into their work, as well.

One group that has received a lot of attention in the secular world for its spirituality is U2. In addition to the random fan blog, dozens of scholarly articles and even books have been devoted to the band's spirituality in song and deed.[9] U2's lead singer Bono is well known for his philanthropy but also has been outspoken about the spirituality of the group. Bono is rarely seen without the rosary around his neck gifted him from Pope John Paul II[10] and often speaks of the Holy Bible as the inspiration behind the song lyrics U2 sings. Through lyrics as symbols of their faith, the members express faith without verbalizing it directly. U2's hit song "Still Haven't Found What I'm Looking For" deals with his trying to come to terms with his Christian upbringing and faith and wondering what to believe.

Bono has been outspoken in interviews about the effect music and lyrics had on his own spirituality, which adds validity to the messages in his own songs. Bono wrote in the introduction to a recently released version of the *Book of Psalms*:

> "Words and music did for me what solid, even rigorous religious argument could never do, they introduced me to God, not belief in God, more an experiential sense of GOD. Over art, literature, reason, the way in to my spirit was a combination of words and music. As a result the book of *Psalms* always felt open to me and led me to the poetry of *Ecclesiastes*, the *Song of Solomon*, the book of *John* . . . [11]

Other rock artists recognized early on the power of rock music was similar to that of religion. No one can forget John Lennon's comment about the Beatles being more popular than Jesus. He also stated he didn't know which was more influential when he said, "I don't know which will go first: rock 'n' roll or Christianity."[12] That is still up for debate. Scottish musician Donovan said that pop music is a perfect vehicle for religion.

Other groups, like Bruce Springsteen and Bon Jovi, use less direct symbols to define their spirituality. Both write songs about real life, and many songs are based on situations they experienced. "I try to reflect people's lives back to them in some fashion," Springsteen wrote. "And if the show is really good, your life should flash before your eyes in some way. . . . It should be a combination of a circus, a political thing and a spiritual event."[13]

Springsteen uses many religious metaphors in his song lyrics, and it is purposeful. He had said in interviews he is not a religious person, yet he admits to having read much of the Bible and being fascinated by the stories in it.[14] "Mansion on the Hill" features lyrics that seem to come straight out of his theological knowledge—imagining what heaven might be like based on scriptures of the brightness and music surrounding God.

Springsteen and Bon Jovi share other similarities, as well. Both Springsteen and Bon Jovi members came of age in working-class New Jersey in strong Catholic traditions. This chapter will focus exclusively on Bon Jovi because research has been done by others on Springsteen's music and spirituality.

BON JOVI'S RELIGION

"Public ritual is filled with religious rhetoric, and even popular music contains religious images, "according to Conrad Ostwalt.[15] It has been socialized into American culture that U.S. society as a whole is morally superior and blessed by God. Therefore, it stands to reason that religious ritual and symbolism would touch every aspect of culture including rock music, even sometimes subconsciously on the part of both the messenger and receiver.

Every member of Bon Jovi has a Judeo-Christian religious upbringing: Jon, Tico and Richie, Catholicism; David, Judaism. Although mostly hushed when it comes to his personal life, Jon has been noted as saying he has found more strength in faith than in organized religion, adding that he does not necessarily believe in many of the rituals and practices of the Catholic religion. In several instances, he has noted that he sees God as "all around" and doesn't believe that one must rigorously attend church to reap the benefits of religion and spirituality. Aside from his work with the band, it is in Jon's solo endeavors that the strongest scripture references are visible.

The spirituality in the music has grown as the music has matured. Perhaps part of that is the inspiration Jon has drawn from Bono. "I'm Bono's biggest fan," Jon told the *Guardian*. "I love what he's doing for the world, but where he's acting locally, I act locally."[16] Jon has in recent years become very involved in fighting homelessness and poverty in the Philadelphia area, where he owns a minor-league football team, the Philadelphia Soul.

One can find few explicit religious references in *Bon Jovi* (released in 1984), and just slightly more in the second album, *7800 Degrees Fahrenheit* (1985). The popularity for the band exploded with its greater reliance on faith-filled lyrics. Bon Jovi's third album, *Slippery When Wet*, was released in late 1986. This is the first album that added famed songwriter Desmond Child to its repertoire. The spiritually titled, *Keep the Faith*, Bon Jovi's fifth studio album was released in the fall of 1992. The band's tenth album, *Lost Highway*, released in 2007, was a move toward a country/rock sound and also features distinctly introspective and religious themes, including finding lasting love in marriage and balancing real life with faith.

More significantly, Bon Jovi's music and Jon's solo creations have distinct religious themes, not commonly found in rock music. Through songs like "Living on a Prayer" and "Hey God," the listener is subconsciously shown that a good work ethic paired with living in a moral fashion will unequivocally bring happiness and personal success. On the contrary, parts of Bon Jovi's music also show how bad choices can affect one's life. Songs that discuss sex, drinking and other acts describe the heartache that comes with making the wrong choices.

Ostwalt stated that religious leaders might use pop culture to express religious lessons to the masses because of those forms abilities to get the public's attention.[17] Wouldn't that power be even greater when wielded by a rock star? In essence, through words and deeds, Bon Jovi is doing just this. While not an overt act of religion, it is more of an inner spirituality spilling out into his popular culture iconography. The effect of this cannot be discounted. Bon Jovi fans number in the tens of millions. Many of those get much more religion from the music than from the pulpit of a church. Many don't go to any organized church, and many others are young people bored or not tuned in to the sermons preached at them from ministers. Therefore, the message they get from Bon Jovi through words, deeds and symbols is significant to their spirituality. This spirituality is important to the perpetuation of religious symbols and messages.

Throughout time, humans have searched for meaning in their surroundings. Today's rock music audience is not different, nor are the artists making the music. Perhaps that is one of the main draws of certain fans to certain bands. The artist or group is speaking the language that the particular audience or fan wants to hear.

The fact is "religion is everywhere in popular music and videos, and it is not coming from religious bodies or from any recognizable religious community."[18] It's coming from secular rock stars. One must take a closer look to determine what message they are sending by examining the context. Rather than watering down accepted religious concepts and symbols, as many fundamentalist sects argue, quite possibly the effect rather is one of empowering—religion may be more potent than ever before yet without the institutional or organized religiosity[19] for which so many—especially youth—have a disdain.

Bon Jovi concerts are like religious services—church only better—to the multitudes of fans, and participation for fans is similar to reaffirming one's values, much like participation in the rituals of worship. According to *Details* magazine, "The transcendent ecstasy of a rock gig easily translates into a religious experience."[20] Tom Beaudoin writes in *Virtual Faith* that "pop music has become the amniotic fluid of contemporary society . . . the place where we work out our spirituality."[21] Andrew Greeley, a leading popular culture and religion scholar, describes pop culture as stories (or other art forms) that explain real life experiences. "A work of culture is a metaphor and a metaphor is at least potentially a story, an attempt to stretch an ordering experience from one imagination to another imagination," he wrote.[22] Greeley also suggests Catholicism is naturally disposed to search for the meaning in happenings—even if that is metaphors in popular culture. He further suggests that because the Catholic faith does not "accept the depravity of human nature" like some religious sects do that metaphors and stories within pop culture may actually reveal God to the audience.[23] At Bon Jovi concerts, one may see signs asking about Tommy and Gina, the heroes in songs on two Bon Jovi records. Their success stories are important to fans, who want to believe they too can succeed.

"Living on a Prayer," released in 1986, reached No.1 on the Billboard Hot 100, and it is also the first appearance of Tommy and Gina, tying in the band's most prominent theme of success through faith, prayer and moral living. Psalm 39:12 correlates with the song's content: "Hear my prayer, O Lord, listen to my cry for help; be not deaf to my weeping. For I dwell with you as an alien, a stranger, as all my fathers were."[24]

Both the lyrics and music video for "Thank You For Loving Me," released in 2000 on the album *Crush*, contain religious symbolism. The video begins and ends with a shot of the sky and clouds, symbolizing Heaven. One of the initial mages is that of a woman in a white wedding dress, about to attend her church-housed wedding. These images serve the importance of marriage, showing it as a holy covenant between a man and woman and God. The wedding ceremony illustrates the rituals associated with religion—historically, the lyrics of the most popular songs are anthems as important as any hymn.

Like Springsteen, Bon Jovi songs include songs of loneliness and despair and sinful love. Yet, neither chose to remain in that lonely place. There is always a sense of faith even within the questioning and doubt. And there is always a sense that one "can go home," that there is a God and that the faith, family, and hard work and friends who will pull one through the difficult times in life. Romanowski writes:

> When someone says, 'That song ministers to me,' I think they are trying to explain an artistic experience as a spiritual one. What they are describing is the experience of popular art communicating in a way that resonates with their life by affirming their beliefs and values or by presenting something in a way they

never quite thought of before. 'The line between a spiritual experience and an aesthetic one is very fine, and the two are easily confused,' scholars pointed out. 'The very feelings of tranquility and delight that art gives us can lull us into thinking that we are right with God.' Art can create a longing for God or an awareness of God . . .'[25]

It is understandable to make comparisons between religious and artistic experiences, like a hyped-up rock concert and a Saturday night revival. "The finest music 'has always pushed beyond the mundane, has always believed in a better life to come, and that in the ecstasy of the greatest musical moments we catch a glimpse of heaven.'"[26]

Still when you have artists who are clearly searching along with their audience, there is an even greater connection. In this sense Bon Jovi as "everyman." Jon Bon Jovi and Richie Sambora are like "us." One of strengths is knowing who your audience is. Unlike Sade and the Dixie Chicks, Bon Jovi members do not wear their politics—or religion—on their sleeves, but they don't back away either. Jon and Richie both wear crosses around their necks, and both have openly religious subjects in their solo albums. They have even chosen a Christian rock band, Delirious, to open for them on the *One Wild Night* Tour in the United Kingdom.[27] Scholars like David Myers believe that what popular culture, like rock music, teaches the public is far from inconsequential. Rather, those lyrics and the actions of pop stars and celebrities teach us how to behave.[28]

The visual representation of Jon's "Miracle," his second solo single released in 1990, contains what could be observed and analyzed as religious symbolism. Jon is singing about someone—possibly himself—who needs God in his or her life. Jon has done all he can to aid this person with his demons and he claims that it will take a miracle to save them this time, adding that their savior has left town. Also within the lyrics are the repetitions of the words "salvation," "savior," and "angel." He constantly sings about one "reaching for the sky." One minute and nineteen seconds into the video, crosses at a crossroad are shown as the men ride into the small village-type set. This can symbolize several religious elements, ranging from death to life after death to seeking God in times of need (a personal crossroad). Also during the course of the video, a wedding takes place, and Richie Sambora is adorned in deep purple colored shirt. Moreover, Jon rides into the small area with several other men: possibly representative of Jesus and His apostles. It seems the band is saying that sometimes we, as humans, cannot make the best decisions or get through difficult times on our own. The video obviously has religious symbols attached to it: flames at the end, the lyrics, water, splotches of white and purple and a wedding taking place. Fire and water are both classic elements and have been used in many religions. In addition to symbolizing purity, white is used to symbolize holy days in the Christian church. Purple was worn by royalty because of its scarcity and was reserved for especially important occasions.

Jon's Catholic upbringing is evident within the band's lyrics, which are fraught with the Christian teaching of "original sin."[29] "Living in Sin," a song more or less concerned with adultery, exonerates religious themes, sin and the temptation of sin, life and death, guilt, forgiveness, hope, faith and doubt. However, ending on a positive note, it shows that marriages are worked through.

Romanowski states that pop art, like rock music lyrics, can "show us the meaning of things, or their purpose in God's kingdom, by helping us articulate our experiences or by offering a deeper understanding of our own lives and the lives of others," and "can explore the heights and depths of human experience."[30] Rather than making an overt statement of the band members' beliefs, Bon Jovi has chosen to express sentiments common to humanity—and much of that is spiritual in nature. It can't be separated from others like-minded, which makes the religiosity all the more powerful.

The Bible itself included many parables—or stories told to make a spiritual or moral point. The stories—taken out of Biblical context—are often stories one might find even in secular experiences each of us may have. Therefore, they are not implicitly religious rather what the audience reads into them—or what mass communication scholars would call the "preferred reading" of the text of the story. "King of the Mountain" from the album *7800 Fahrenheit* speaks of a people crying out for a King. These souls are in need of substance. From the King James Version of the Bible, there is a similar experience in which the people of the Lord are crying out to Him—their King. The term "king of the mountain" is actually a biblical reference to God from Psalm 24:3-4, which asks: "Who may ascend the hill of the Lord? Who may stand in this holy place? He who has clean hands and a pure heart, who does not lift up his soul to an idol or swear by what is false."[31]

Bon Jovi's latest album *The Circle* is also loaded with religious connections. Jon and Richie co-wrote every track.[32] In "We Weren't Born to Follow," beginning with the first line Bon Jovi hits the ground running with the idea of mining for miracles. Now the term mining is something in itself. It indicates a hard, steadfast search for something such as a miracle. By the third line, the writer is describing both a sinner and a cynic. These are two polar ends of the spectrum with one that has made mistakes and shortfalls and someone who simply refuses to believe, maybe even in a higher power. He goes on to describe walking beside both the guilty and the innocent just as it is believed God walks beside us on our path every day or the other widely presented interpretation where he sends angels down to walk among us both to guide and protect His people. The chorus is really where the religious connotations seem to unfold. He tells listeners that they are to hold on to what they believe. What do you have other than your faith? When all is lost in the midst of the world, you must have something to hold on to and you have to have faith that brighter days will come. He also states that you must believe that both saints and sinners bleed. Pain isn't reserved solely for the nonbelievers. Both God-fearing Christians and people who do not believe in a higher power will experience turmoil in their lives. We are all born sinners, but we are also born to lead the people of this earth to a brighter day and a better world.

Although a superhero depiction is given throughout "Superman Tonight," a higher power can also be seen in a few of the lines. Furthermore, the author presents images of angels and an escape of sorts from the outside world. For many, that is how they view religion. It is a way to make it through the day to make it to a better tomorrow.

The song's author has a number of religious symbols throughout the story line in "Bullet," written by Jon and Richie. First, he picks Sunday morning, considered by many to be a day of rest and worship, to pick a violent act to occur. Amid all of this tragedy, he calls out to God asking if He is listening or if He has just given up on the world. I Peter 4:12-13 states, "Beloved, think it not strange concerning the fiery trial which is to try you, as though some strange thing happened unto you: But rejoice, inasmuch as ye are partakers of Christ's sufferings; that, when His glory shall be revealed, ye may be glad also with exceeding joy."[33] The author believes the world is in need of forgiveness and hope. He calls out to a higher power for faith, promising he will learn to pray, however, it is too late at this time.

The lyrics to "Thorn In My Side" convey that they believe there is a higher reason behind the turmoil in his life. Of course, thorns in one's side immediately draws a believer to the image of Jesus Christ on the cross, having been beaten with a thorny Cat-of-Nine Tails and then crowned with thorns. The song's words state that whether the outcome of things in this life is what one wants, he knows the one above has a greater reason in it. If he loses, it may be teaching him a life lesson. If he wins, it's the same results. One should remain true to his faith and not waiver. He holds true to what is dear to him and he knows his faith may face tests and trials, but the pride he has for himself and his religion will not be lost. In addition to the biblical character of Job, often referred to in pop culture references, scriptural basis for these lyrics include I Corinthians 10:13 which states, "No temptation has seized you except what is common to man. And God is faithful; He will not let you be tempted beyond what you can bear. But when you are tempted, He will also provide a way out so that you can stand up under it."[34]

In "Brokenpromiseland," images of a world in an apocalyptic state surround the singer. Scenes from Revelations fill the mind as angels come to earth, falling. The world is full of despair and shattered dreams and hopes and he feels the world is too far gone to be helped by prayer now.[35] Even the idea of the Promised Land has biblical connotations.[36] The Israelites searched for years for the promised land and reached it with the goal of a more religious existence. Jon says to believe in each other and get out of the rumble of this world. Have the fallen angels rise and be renewed because the people will once again break free from the world that is breaking them.

FUTURE SEMIOTIC STUDY

Bon Jovi's spiritual influences and messages are purposefully interwoven throughout their lyrics and their lives, and it is a formula that has staying power. Through semiotic analysis of the words and deeds of the band, the importance of religion in their work is clear. The signs are being received and their preferred meaning adopted by legions of fans, as well. Bon Jovi has cover bands all across the globe, including an unlikely group of Jesuit priests who lip sync and call themselves the Jon Bon Jesuits.[37] Bon Jovi headlined the 2009 Jazz Fest in New Orleans and was greeted by the International Special Sacred Shrine of Bon Jovi created by fan Tara Jill Ciccarone.[38] The altar, complete with a photograph of Jon wearing the crown of roses (not unlike artwork that has depicted Jesus Christ with a crown of thorns) from his *Keep the Faith* album, included a guest book for fans to sign, and Bon Jovi candles and crowns of roses for sale.

While this chapter focused primarily on the text of the song lyrics by the band, further research of the physical signs used in Bon Jovi's concerts and in promotional materials may lead to a greater understanding of the role the band gives religion in the work of Bon Jovi, one of the highest grossing rock bands of all time, and how they use it as a guiding force as well as a profit motif. Because semiotics is still a developing field of study, this remains open to further research as well as interpretation.

NOTES

1. Oliver Burkeman, "I'm the poster boy for marriage," *The Guardian*. May 26, 2006.

2. "Osbourne Slams 'C**P' Bon Jovi," Oct. 19, 2005, www.contactmusic.com.

3. Christian Scharen, One Step Closer: Why U2 Matters to Those Seeking God. Grand Rapids, Michigan: Brazos Press, 2006, 18.

4. David Chidester, *Authentic Fakes: Religion and American Popular Culture.* Los Angeles: University of California Press, 2005, 44.

5. Steve Turner, *Hungry for Heaven: Rock 'n' Roll and the Search for Redemption.* Downers Grove, Illinois: Intervarsity Press, 1995, 114.

6. Edna Gundersen, "With 'Sonic Boom,' Kiss will roar anew," *USA Today.* Oct. 6, 2009.

7. Chidester, 204.

8. Andrew M. Greeley, *God in Popular Culture.* Chicago: Thomas More Press, 1989, 211.

9. Scharen.

10. *Ibid.,* 16.

11. Scharen, 23.

12. Turner, 11.

13. William D. Romanowski. Eyes Wide Open: Looking for God in Popular Culture. Grand Rapids, Michigan: 2007, 142.

14. Turner, 152.

15. Conrad Ostwalt, Secular Steeples: Popular Culture and the Religious Imagination. Harrisburg, Pennsylvania: Trinity Press International, 2003, 21.

16. Burkeman.

17. Ostwalt, 31.

18. Ostwalt, 195.

19. *Ibid.*

20. Romanowski, 75.

21. Craig Detweiler and Barry Taylor, *A Matrix of Meanings: Finding God in Pop Culture.* Grand Rapids: Baker Academic, 2003, 130. Tom Beaudoin, *Virtual Faith.* Hoboken, New Jersey: Jossey-Bass, 2000.

22. Greeley, 93.

23. *Ibid.,* 94.

24. Psalms, *The Holy Bible*, New International Version.

25. Romanowski, 79.

26. Romanowski, 80.

27. Michael Swain, "Delirious? Wow Bon Jovi Fans," *Direction Magazine*, November 2001. www.delirious.org.uk

28. *Ibid.*, 141.

29. "Original Sin," *The Catholic Encyclopedia,* www.newadvent.org.

30. Greeley, 160.

31. Psalms, *The Holy Bible*, New International Version.

32. Some of the tracks also include the additional writing support of Billy Falcon, Darrell Brown, John Shanks, Desmond Child.

33. *The Holy Bible*, King James Version.

34. I Corinthians, *The Holy Bible,* New International Version.

35. Revelations 18, *The Holy Bible*, King James Version.

36. Exodus, *The Holy Bible,* King James Version.

37. Idol Chatter, Religion and Pop Culture Blog entry from November 2006, www.blog.belief.net.

38. Chris Rose, "Pilgrims flock to Bon Jovi altar outside Jazz Fest," *The Times-Picayune*, May 2, 2009.

NOTE: The music of Bon Jovi, Bruce Springsteen, and U2 were analyzed extensively for this chapter.

BIBLIOGRAPHY

Beaudoin, Tom, *Virtual Faith*. Hoboken, New Jersey: Jossey-Bass, 2000.

Burkeman, Oliver. "I'm the poster boy for marriage," *The Guardian*. May 26, 2006.

Chidester, David. *Authentic Fakes: Religion and American Popular Culture*. Los Angeles: University of California Press, 2005.

Detweiler, Craig, and Barry Taylor, *A Matrix of Meanings: Finding God in Pop Culture*. Grand Rapids: Baker Academic, 2003, 130. Greeley, Andrew M. *God in Popular Culture*. Chicago: Thomas More Press, 1989.

Gundersen, Edna. "With 'Sonic Boom,' Kiss will roar anew," *USA Today*. Oct. 6, 2009.

Idol Chatter, Religion and Pop Culture Blog entry from November 2006, (www.blog.belief.net)

"Original Sin," *The Catholic Encyclopedia*, (www.newadvent.org)

"Osbourne Slams 'C**P' Bon Jovi," *www.contactmusic.com*. Oct. 19, 2006.

Ostwalt, Conrad. *Secular Steeples: Popular Culture and the Religious Imagination*. Harrisburg, Pennsylvania: Trinity Press International, 2003.

Romanowski, William D. Eyes Wide Open: Looking for God in Popular Culture. Grand Rapids, Michigan: 2007.

Rose, Chris. "Pilgrims flock to Bon Jovi altar outside Jazz Fest," *The Times-Picayune*, May 2, 2009.

Scharen, Christian. One Step Closer: Why U2 Matters to Those Seeking God. Grand Rapids, Michigan: Brazos Press, 2006.

Swain, Michael. "Delirious? Wow Bon Jovi Fans," *Direction Magazine*, November 2001. (www.delirious.org.uk)

Turner, Steve. *Hungry for Heaven: Rock 'n' Roll and the Search for Redemption*. Downers Grove, Illinois: Intervarsity Press, 1995.

WEBSITES CONSULTED

www.bible.com

9

It's Still Rock and Roll to Me: Christian Heavy Metal and the Problem of Authenticity

Jeremy V. Adolphson

GIVE ME AN AMEN!

On a cold January 2009 night in Illinois, with temperatures barely in the teens, in a tiny bar completely surrounded by cornfields, something interesting is taking place. Two lines of people, primarily teenagers, wait, shivering, anxious to get inside, though warmth is not what will satisfy their needs. For the 500 fans waiting to gain entrance into Chubby Rain House of Tunes outside of Poplar Grove, Illinois, cold weather and bitter wind are merely minor inconveniences. On stage is a full bill of both Christian and secular heavy metal (SHM) acts, headlining the U.S. tour of the Christian heavy metal (CHM) band As I Lay Dying. The diversity of those waiting in line amazes: a predominantly underage audience consisting of an amalgam of races, ethnicities, and personalities speaks to how powerful the band's message and influence is. While not everyone present is there because it is a "Christian" show, the genre appeals to both Christian and secular "metal-heads."[1] Contemporary Christian Music (CCM) as a genre of music has commanded an audience since the late 1960s Christian youth movement. Christian music, like other genres of music today, has undergone various transformations to stay current with the changing times. Stereotypes of Christian music as traditional hymnal or gospel music have been discarded as a new wave of more mainstream friendly CCM artists such as Amy Grant and Michael W. Smith paved the way for a wider audience to participate. Watching As I Lay Dying take the stage begs the question: How does one market authenticity in Christian Heavy Metal music?

This chapter seeks to address the possibilities for the intersection of music that is authentically Christian and authentically rock, despite the seeming contradictions between these as identities or ideologies. This set of possibilities connects to the question of how CHM artists are—or can be—marketed to their audience, particularly with regards to their appearance, sound, and lyrical content. I will argue that CHM artists find the "Christian" in rock music as opposed to the "Rock" in Christian music. Given the nature of contemporary heavy metal music, CHM artists have to incorporate more than just Christian values into songs laced with metal guitar riffs, to succeed in both the sacred and the secular arenas. To find a marketable audience, these artists have to embody their message in a way that does not segregate fans and believers (when the two are mutually exclusive) and more importantly incorporate a set of meanings that can simultaneously and separately operate on two different levels, crisscrossing at different junctures both on and offstage. This delicate balancing act succeeds at multiple levels in the music operation, especially for the younger audience in the heavy metal scene that may be exposed to more than just loud indecipherable noise. The difficulty for record companies to establish a "brand name" with these CHM artists is often met with its share of criticism on whether the band is representing an authentic vessel spreading the Word across different channels, or if the artists are turning a profit and watering down Christianity. In order to recognize and/or pass judgment on these artists, critics and audiences need to be aware of these different mechanisms that CHM artists employ to spread their faith.

I will articulate two strategies used by CHM artists in expressing their faith through their music. First, I will use the metaphor of the palimpsest[2] to discuss the various layers which the religious content functions between the artist and their audience, specifically detailing how these layers bleed through onto the secular music scene. The second strategy will use J. L. Austin's[3] speech act theory to describe how CHM artists personify mortification and suffering through their double meaning and coded lyrics to explicitly witness and re-appropriate traditional views of devil imagery and rebellion as a signpost to their overarching mission as young evangelicals. CHM artists engaging in this strategy utilize the concert venue to witness their faith through a kind of "lifestyle evangelism" where the artist's onstage utterances literally embody their close relationship to God.

To simplify this analysis, I have selected two bands as representative of each strategy to exemplify different techniques to spread the Word while not alienating the surrounding secular heavy metal (SHM) community. Both bands have successfully placed in the *Billboard* music charts, selling more than 500,000 albums and earning a Gold record status. As "metal" bands, they have attained success and status; however, they also have another viable market outside of the SHM community. The first band, As I Lay Dying, is best explained by a palimpsest metaphor, since their relationship with witnessing their faith is fairly subtle and pledging allegiance to the band may or may not be equivalent to committing to Christianity. As I Lay Dying illustrates the palimpsestic metaphor which coincides with the integrational CCM typology that more readily embraces the mainstream element of Christianity, while not being overly persistent in terms of blatant religious messages. The CHM band Underoath exemplifies the separational proselytizing element of Christian music by engaging in coded lyrics through their explicit witnessing. The separational typology of Christianity is concerned with the audience's reaction not only to the lyrics, but also as an essentially active facet to attaining salvation. Both artists provide interesting opportunities to analyze not only the prevalence of religious content in American popular music, but the subtle ways that the influence of evangelicalism pervades our rhetorical discourse.

This chapter will describe the rise of CCM, paying particular attention to the mainstream success of early crossover artists during the 1980s and 1990s before turning the discussion to the rise of CHM as a distinct genre of music. CCM and CHM are rooted in American evangelicalism. In order to discuss the interconnected relationship between the secular and Christian music markets, I will use the integrational and separational typologies of CCM as elaborated by Howard and Streck[4] to illustrate CCM and CHM as a conflicted art form. Finally, I will present criticisms of the music, both Christian and secular, to suggest the prevalent amount of labor, both emotional and spiritual, needed to construct the identity of a Christian heavy metal artist.

CCM AND CHM: CHRISTIANS IN THE MAINSTREAM?

Both CCM and CHM are rooted firmly in Evangelical Protestantism whereby the emphasis is placed on preaching the Gospel to a large demographic rather than remaining so inclusive within Christianity.[5] Larry Eskridge borrowed from the British historian David Bebbington four hallmarks of evangelicalism in the twenty-first century: "conversionism, the belief that lives need to be changed; activism, the expression of the gospel in effort; Biblicism, a particular regard for the Bible; and crucicentrism, a stress on the sacrifice of Christ on the cross."[6] Evangelicals have a special connection to this world and those who feel that it is their "duty to share the Good News of the Gospel with others."[7] Evangelicalism within the United States has been quick to embrace new forms of media and technology in order to evangelize the masses.[8] However, while they may criticize popular culture in terms of morality, evangelicals have often embraced it for their own advantage by seeking "to conform public life to their own religious convictions [so] that their religious beliefs would set the agenda for the entire society, a kind of theocracy rule by religious leaders from their own traditions."[9]

Through the popular media, evangelicals could more effectively shape the national discourse. While evangelical Christians are a minority in the United States, their presence in secular culture, particularly the mass media, is substantial. Evangelicals believe that "American society as a whole has shifted away from the basic religious principles on which it was founded, and they maintain that God must be returned to a central place in American society."[10] CHM musicians promote their (Christian) message in almost every marketing venue, including merchandising and interviews, by using traditional SHM themes of power and struggle. CHM artists recapitulate these themes from a Christian perspective to increase their fan base. It is through their mission that evangelical Christians "use popular music as a way of introducing young people to their conception of morality while fulfilling youths' desire to stay abreast of contemporary music styles."[11]

Answers to questions about conversion and proselytizing depends upon the continuum by which evangelicals view "sovereignty," the contrast between the controlling influence of some external power (God) and human free will; this is the core issue of Protestant theology. The poles of the continuum are Hyper-Calvinism and Open Theism. Hyper-Calvinism suggests that individuals do not hold the power to convert or save those souls into God's elect; it is God's will that an individual should be saved or not. This perspective implies the doctrine of predestination insofar that witnessing or proselytizing to a given audience would be counterproductive, as individuals are without sufficient freedom to choose salvation (God does that choosing). Open Theism calls out for the "personal God," who through prayer, good works, or charity, will look favorably upon those seeking redemption or salvation. This perspective rejects the Hyper-Calvinists' lack of free will by arguing that God's infinite knowledge about past/future events is not contradicted by the good will and dedication by His elect. Evangelicals favoring an open theistic perspective try aggressively to save non-believers (or sometimes those from other denominations); they see proselytizing as a moral duty. Evangelicals employ a multitude of channels to spread the Word, including street corner evangelizing, popular culture, and the incorporation of new technologies to name a few. CHM artists seem to lean toward the Open Theism perspective of evangelicalism, especially with their use of and familiarity in the mainstream secular culture.

Gormly argued that evangelicals can resist the dominant secular culture by "establishing a presence through taking possession of a cultural form and redefining it as their own, hence positioning themselves as part of and, through shaping the discourse and reforming American society from within, eventually representing the mainstream."[12] Robert Walser[13] recognized that 1980s CHM group Stryper engaged in this behavior of reinterpreting the style of heavy metal through evangelicalism:

> The Christian heavy metal band Stryper demonstrates that the specific musical gestures of heavy metal operate within a code to communicate experiences of power and transcendent freedom because their attempt to appropriate the codes of metal is posited on the suitability of precisely such experiences for evangelism. The power is God's; the transcendent freedom represents the rewards of Christianity; the intensity is that of religious experience. Stryper appropriates and reinterprets the codes of heavy metal, using metal's means to produce different meanings. Stryper presents Christianity as an exciting, youth-oriented alternative; they offer their fans a chance to enjoy the pleasures of heavy metal and feel virtuous at the same time.[14]

These negotiations, while religious in nature, seek to strengthen the Christian and secular audience. CHM artists ideally want their audience to feel the energy within the concert and experience transcendence from the music. The underlying religious messages accompanying the performance serve to solidify these deep-rooted relationships between the band, the audience, and God. The rhetorical relationship surrounding whether transcendence and conversion should occur on a spiritual level would depend upon the CHM artists as evangelicals and their position along the sovereignty/free will continuum.

Contemporary Christian Music (CCM) at one time was called the "fastest growing form of popular music in the United States today."[15] CCM developed in the late 1960s during the emergence of a youth evangelical movement (the "Jesus freaks"[16]), but it was not until Larry Norman released his album *Upon This Rock* with Capitol Records when Christian music slowly expanded out from its Christian bookstore niche. As Larry Norman's song titles once commented: "Why Should the Devil Have All the Good Music."[17] As time progressed, more CCM artists began to "crossover" into the mainstream.

Perhaps no CCM artists have been more successful than Amy Grant and Michael W. Smith, who brought Christian music into popular culture not only through mainstream radio play, but also stylistically emulating the pop music sound, listened to by many youths and adults. Amy Grant established herself as a rising star in Christian music, releasing successful Christian inspired albums before gaining mainstream acceptance and airplay in the mid-1980s. With the release of her 1985 album *Unguarded* followed by her breakthrough 1991 album *Baby Baby* Grant, while retaining her Christian values in her music, realized the potential outreach her music could attract in the mainstream.

In a *Rolling Stone* interview, Grant commented on her music reaching a secular audience outside:

> Everybody wants hope . . . It's pretty bleak out there, pretty dark. The statistics are obvious from teen suicides and all the craziness. So what we're trying to do is take Christian principles and make them understandable. Even if it doesn't say Jesus, it doesn't matter. For someone whose heart is open—some kid sitting in his room at night, lonely, just thinking 'My world is bleak'—that's the time we hope this record can say something deeper.[18]

For Grant, the use of Christianity in a way that subtly infuses Christian ideas and virtues into the song lyrics without publicly condemning certain actions from a pulpit spoke to the rhetorical significance of embracing the mainstream. Michael W. Smith's 1990 album *Go West Young Man* contained the mainstream crossover hit "Place in this World" which charted at #77 on the *Billboard* Hot 100 of 1991.[19] Both artists utilized the mainstream market to get their voice and message out to a larger demographic by not being reluctant to embrace the secular audience.

CCM, according to Radwan,[20] is a "unique genre in that its primary purpose is to inspire and reinforce belief for its teen audience; it is an overtly ideological and rhetorical form of music."[21] CHM may be somewhat different. CCM artists see themselves as persuasive; they use rhetorical appeals to foster identities conducive to their own version of the Christian faith, so that fans may not be overtly aware that they are listening to Christian music. The ideal end goal for the CCM audience is to internalize the song and emulate the positive values in the lyrics. Radwan argued that the style does not always have to be a standard worship song; however, "it does have to advocate a particular way of being Christian."[22]

The success and popularity of CHM in secular markets during the twenty-first century originated as a distinct genre of religious music in 1984.[23] Historically, heavy metal as a genre of music has been interpreted as "presenting a critique of a society and culture that is viewed as false and hollow by consciously transgressing the boundaries of the socially and culturally acceptable,"[24] pretty much the opposite of the positive values of CCM. The lyrics and imagery within heavy metal music may often be extreme, which raises the shock value of the music.

During the 1980s, a California ministry known as Sanctuary International, was formed to bring CHM bands together as an "alternative church created for 'born again' Christians involved in various rock scenes as well as for the spreading of the gospel in the SHM community using metal with a Christian message."[25] This genre utilized the traditional aspects of church while allowing these musicians the freedom to play the music they were most interested in. This organization collectively gave the Christian metal community a sense of credibility and became the center where future CHM bands would get their start. By incorporating elements from the dominant secular scene while retaining their own ideological focus, Sanctuary International allowed many of these CHM bands to merge the sacred with the secular.

A possible answer to the success of these bands would be their incorporation of the secular metal sound, playing style, and imitation of what audiences want to hear from bands today. As the metal scene comprises a younger audience, CHM artists have to define who they are and who they are not. The CHM artists are able to retain their authenticity by their beliefs, but through partaking in the heavy metal scene (touring) these artists become difficult to classify in terms of a separate marketable genre. By mimicking the sound and playing style of SHM, CHM artists use this dual identity of self versus other. While SHM bands may live a lifestyle and maintain a stage persona not consistent with CHM's values and beliefs, CHM artists align themselves in the arena and mind-set of SHM music. Radwan stated, "In an oppositional sense, who and what one is *not* define who and what one is . . . [W]e enter a realm in which the 'other,' like a fictional narrative itself, stands in a metaphorical relation to the culture from which it arises."[26] CHM artists break into the mainstream using this notion of the "outsider" by sounding the same as SHM yet representing something else entirely. Echoing that CHM artists reappropriate signs and symbols within the heavy metal community, Gormly stated:

> The appropriator has embraced the language or symbols as his or her own, taking from them their originators and often facilitating the fixing of new meanings to symbols. It is this way that a group can move into and occupy a social space from which they were formerly shut out. This is especially true when occupying the cultural territory of the mainstream.[27]

It is through this involvement and success in the mainstream that CHM artists delve deeper into the blurring of the sacred and the profane.

THE PALIMPSEST:
BREAK ON THROUGH TO THE OTHER SIDE

The palimpsest provides a thorough approach to analyzing how certain CHM artists view not only their own artistic work in the mainstream but also their contribution to the breadth of Christianity in modern times. The palimpsest metaphorically picks out the laminar quality of an activity or interpretation, its layers and surfaces. The palimpsest initially was a piece of parchment that had been used and then reused by applying a fresh surface of paper (as if a kind of paint). However, upon later uses, the former layers tend to bleed through, revealing what had previously been recorded underneath; you can literally see the palimpsest (the original text) as a confusing shadow behind the current text. The palimpsest speaks not only to the construction of text and interpretation (the words that bleed through can be suggestively incorporated into the surface text), but to linkages in time, as the past and present texts partially merge. As a metaphor, the interplay of the differing layers speaks to the inherent ambiguity found in the lyrics, music, presentation, and promotion of CHM. The differing layers functioning at the SHM level may operate completely exclusive than the level of religiosity and evangelicalism. The layers conceal each other, however, sometimes these imprints are faded and hard to decipher unless the trained eye of the audience knows to recognize such subtleties. The metaphor also represents a way that people experience times, whereby individuals layer present experiences over one's faded past.

At the heart of the music lies the distinction between the core and the periphery, which is deeper than religious versus non-religious, but in fact draws the audience member to suggest a period of growth or decline from first experiencing the music to the audience member's current state. The palimpsest metaphor directly ties in with Howard and Streck's integrational typology, particularly the responsibility of the audience member to tease out the multiple layers within a song's lyrical structure. Integrational CCM, I will argue more strongly identifies with witnessing rather than proselytizing.

Integrational CCM recognizes that to be successful within popular music an artist or band must be marketable enough to impact a potential audience through various channels within the dominant discourse of the mainstream. Integrational artists do not wish to uphold the division practiced by separational CCM artists. Integrational artists view themselves as singers who happen to be of Christian faith, rather than "Christian" singers. For integrational musicians:

> The content of their live and recorded performances is intended to remain consistent with the message of the gospel, the primary purpose behind their singing and songwriting is not necessarily to proclaim God's plan for salvation through Christ, praise and worship of the Lord, or encourage Christians in their faith.[28]

Integrational CCM artists claim that while their music may be seen as a form of entertainment, they are able to reach a more diverse audience through the ambiguity in their song lyrics, rather than solely targeting the evangelical Christians that the separational artists do. The rationale behind integrational CCM artists is based in marketing and numbers; their music can reach more individuals if distributed through retail stores rather than being relegated to Christian bookstores. Integrational CCM artists find their strength by offering a wholesome alternative to contemporary popular music by articulating a Christian worldview through witnessing to record industry insiders.

Integrational artists connote commercial visibility with success, so they seek to disseminate their music to as many people as possible. This disseminative style mimics the rhetoric of Jesus' parable of the sower, where the distribution of the message is indifferent to particular receivers:

> The diverse audience members, like the varieties of soils, who hear the parable as told by the seashore are left to make of it what they will. It is a parable about the diversity of audience interpretations in settings that lack direct interaction . . . the parable of the sower celebrates broadcasting as an equitable mode of communication that leaves the harvest of meaning to the will and capacity of the recipient.[29]

As its music (as opposed to lyrics) became more extreme, CHM artists followed the trend by performing with screaming vocals and limited singing, a contrast with every gospel music tradition (except perhaps some Pentecostal services). The Christian take on extreme metal on the surface appeared allied with its non-Christian counterparts. Hearing and interpreting the message can pose a challenge: "Christian metalcore bands crank up the intensity with machine-gun drumming, churning guitars, and front men whose relentlessly fearsome screaming might get them locked up if it took place anywhere other than a concert stage."[30] The almost undecipherable lyrics may serve two purposes: appealing to the non-Christian fans in terms of sound and aesthetic value of the genre (almost impossible to tell it is not SHM by listening), and inspiring individuals to go out and purchase the CDs and read the lyrics if they wish to know more about their message. This evangelical technique of preaching at a concert and encouraging their fans/congregation to seek out their message and interpret their meaning is akin to Biblical parables where the impact of the lyrics is not always immediately felt. This more invasive method of information dissemination speaks for CHM bands' success and longevity in both secular and Christian markets.

To further exemplify this trend, let me frame the discussion of the palimpsest through the CHM band As I Lay Dying. As a band, As I Lay Dying makes use of ambiguously religious lyrics, placing greater emphasis on not overtly preaching the Word both in lyrics and on stage. The ambiguity, however, when analyzed closely, speaks not only of their Christian faith but also the community in which they live and work. As I Lay Dying does not pretend to be something that they are not. Playing to different audiences is greatly valued to integrational CCM because it can "express what they believe to that audience. It's up to the audience whether or not they look into what their beliefs are and the same thing with us."[31] Because of approach to faith and their music, As I Lay Dying has achieved an avid fan base of both Christians and non-Christians. As I Lay Dying drummer, Jordan Mancino illustrated precisely both the disseminative and palimpsest qualities of their music, particularly the band's inclusion to write songs about common problems:

> A lot of our lyrics are real-life experiences, not even like being a Christian or not. It's just real-life experiences that everybody goes through day in and day out. We want to reach people on that sort of level, and be like 'Hey, we go through this stuff like you do.'[32]

This implicit form of witnessing enacted by As I Lay Dying is a trend found within many of today's Christian heavy metal artists. The ambiguity within the lyrics acts both as a rhetorical and marketing tool by pairing up the actual song lyric and having the possibility that it can operate on different levels (layers) of meaning.

The music of As I Lay Dying, as an audience-centered evangelical tool, does not require overt proselytizing at a concert venue; rather, they engage what I might call "integrational witnessing." Because of this, As I Lay Dying finds the "Christian" in Rock Music both lyrically and stylistically. There is no need to have the lyrics double coded because the end result is that they are not trying to hide their overall mission as a musician first and Christian second. The palimpsest metaphor speaks to the different layers, not hierarchically, that they can view the band. As I Lay Dying as a band does not water down their faith, but neither do they parade it around every chance they get. The audience is left to decipher what exactly is important. Rather than explicitly proselytizing their faith door-to-door, or fan-to-fan using the stage as their pulpit, As I Lay Dying blurs the distinction between traditional notions of Christianity by illustrating their faith through their lifestyle. The disseminative quality surrounding their faith in relation to their music increases the potential marketing audience, especially since promoters do not need to sell them on the "Christian circuit." They can be "real" metal and really Christians at the same time.

Louis Althusser's concept of interpellation, or hailing, can be useful in explaining how CHM artists position both themselves and their audiences. When they interpellate or summon an audience, they indicate subject positions for the audience to listen to CHM—as "metalhead," as a Christian. This interpellation can function on different levels depending upon the motivations and roles an audience member takes on at the concert. The identifications will be layered, having a palimpsestic quality; the role of rocker and seeker may be jointly visible, yet not the same and the music may summon more easily the "metal" surface. In this sense, audience members decide whether they identify with the band through their music, their values, their personal stories, or any combination of them; they read themselves more than they read the band or its lyrics. The ambiguous lyrics can hail a Christian consciousness or could easily describe the hardships people experience in their everyday life and relationships. This rationale in terms of marketing and evangelical witnessing stands in opposition to the second approach CHM artists may use in selecting an audience.

THE SPEECH ACT OF CHRISTIAN MUSIC: ACKNOWLEDGING THE HIGHER POWER

J. L. Austin's speech act theory will function as a second approach to how Christian Heavy Metal music operates between artist and audience. The speech act in general serves to create realities in a specific context meaning. Studying and drawing meaning is paramount within a particular context, as such with the speaker/audience dichotomy prominent in the singer and concertgoer relationship. Whereas with the palimpsest, multiple meanings would occur at different levels, the messages viewed as speech acts will take a particular concept and apply it explicitly in stage presence as well as in every facet of one's life. Speech acts are important to emphasize the mission that CHM artists engage in at concerts if:

> We realize that what we have to study is not the sentence but the issuing of an utterance in a speech situation, there can hardly be any longer a possibility of not seeing that stating is performing an act.[33]

Austin differentiates between two types of utterances: constative and performative. Constative utterances are issued when making a statement that can be true or false. The performative utterances operate in a different manner altogether. Rather than describing the state of affairs of a world like constative utterances ("I believe in God"), performatives must satisfy the following conditions: "[T]hey do not 'describe' or 'report' or state anything at all, are not 'true or false;' and the uttering of the sentence is, or is a part of, the doing of an action, or as 'just,' saying something."[34] The performative element actually performs some sort of action, rather than merely stating a fact. Judging the truth or falsity in performative utterances is beside the point—a promise is not true or false. Rather, Austin gauged whether the statement was felicitous or infelicitous—"happy," or more specifically happy, appropriate, or fitting. A promise, a bet or an insult has "worked out" rather than be true; if certain conditions are met, the bet (for example) comes off properly (is "felicitous") but otherwise it misfires (suffers from "infelicity").

Austin described three components of the performative utterance: locution, illocution, and perlocution. Locutions are merely the words uttered in a sentence, phrase, or statement. What can be read into the statement comes from the illocutionary act of describing something which is actually performed by the utterance itself. Words such as "nominate" "pledge" or "promise" contain with them specific ideas about what is done by/in saying these words. The third component of the performative utterances is the perlocutionary act which is the anticipated effect of the illocutionary utterance. Austin further described:

> Saying something will often, or even normally, produce certain consequential effects upon the feelings, thoughts, or actions of the audience, or of the speaker, or of other persons: and it may be done with the design, intention, or purpose of producing them; and we may then say, thinking of this, that the speaker has performed an act in the nomenclature of which reference is made either, only obliquely, or even, not at all, to the performance of the locutionary or illocutionary act. We shall call the performance of an act of this kind the performance of a 'perlocutionary' act.[35]

Using speech act theory as a tool to explain the relationship between CHM artist and their audience illustrates a different perspective on attaining authenticity not only with the music, but also the artists' faith.

Proselytizing and witnessing function as the relevant speech acts of CHM. Crucial to illocutionary statements within these speech acts is "sincerity," especially when speaking of their own authenticity as a CHM musician who must practice what they preach. CHM artists engaging in this type of behavior are more likely to explicitly witness and proselytize their faith rather than hiding behind the layers of metaphor and ambiguity within their song lyrics. Often, bands that embody an Open Theism type of witnessing are able to embrace the dominant mainstream culture while retaining a clear-cut division and separation from it. More specifically, CHM artists take the familiar concept of devil imagery and rebellious attitude commonly associated with heavy metal culture and re-appropriate such beliefs from an evangelical position, making the terms their own. Evangelical music producers and artists "often take styles and genres that non-evangelical youth might use to articulate resistant identities and re-spin that resistance in previously unimagined ways."[36]

For example, CHM artist Steve Camp used the same rebellious attitudes made popular by non-Christian musicians (in punk rock), transforming that rebellious attitude against church and divine authority into rebellion against anyone perceived as blaspheming against Jesus Christ. This rebellion would valorize youth a more intense religious experience, personal salvation, and strict moral code; someone could be rebellious and Christian at the same time. Even more explicitly, CHM musician Michael Bloodgood vehemently announced his support of rebellion in his Christian metal by saying:

> Now I'm all for rebellion: rebellion against the world's eroding values and morals; rebellion against the violations of our fellow man's rights; rebellion against any authority who tries to suppress my freedom to worship as I choose . . . rebellion against any world system that goes against the Bible and the things of God. However, the attitude of rebellion that I'm talking about must be centered in God's love, not in uncontrolled emotionalism or with the disrespect for those who might not agree with us.[37]

This quote embodies the separational typology of CCM whereby there is a clear-cut distinction between the Christian and secular.

The separational viewpoint of CCM is closer to the evangelical tradition: it identifies a clear-cut division between good/evil, right/wrong, Christian/non-Christian. Strict adherents of this typology see no middle ground. Any ambiguity pushes one further away from the over-arching mission of CCM: spreading the word of Jesus Christ. For those who hold the separational view, "the Christian and the secular are locked in opposition, God versus the world, and accepting the one necessarily entails rejecting the other."[38] This dichotomy established by separational CCM artists as either Christian/non-Christian has been subject to problems within CCM, especially those who do not wish to further divide between the groups. Separational CCM artists who emulate non-Christian musicians can become paradoxical. Howard and Streck note that "while defining themselves exclusively in terms of their Christian faith and the principal act of their faith as proselytism, the separational artists were forced into the contradictory position of, more than any other, looking at sounding like what they claimed to eschew."[39]

These separational artists on the surface may exhibit similar fashion statements (ripped jeans, leather pants, makeup, boots, etc.), yet they are not willing to embody that particular subculture. While they may dress like band members in non-Christian acts, this dress is merely a tool to reach the youth who are immersed within the SHM lifestyle. "The clear implication was that the clothes meant nothing and that any inference about the musicians based on what they wore was an erroneous one . . . Christian artists argued that these trappings, like the music itself, carried no essential meanings."[40] What matters most to the separational artists is writing lyrics with overtly and explicit Christian messages, emphasizing the overt forms of proselytizing, as a speech act, through the vehicle of popular music. The ministry according to the separational CCM artists includes three components: evangelism, worship facilitation, and exhortation. These distinct, yet intertwined objectives help the separational artists maintain and project a Christian identity. Separational artists ideally wish to speak and convince non-Christians that they should accept Jesus Christ as their personal Savior and that through believing one can establish a personal relationship with God.

Proselytizing as a more explicit or overt form of witnessing (martyring) is the dominant mode that separational artists use to seek potential converts. Two Separational CHM artists best exemplify this overt type of witnessing through proselytizing: 1980s CHM band Stryper and the Christian metalcore outfit Underoath. During the 1980s, when much of rock music embodied glam metal, teased-out hair, and men in spandex outfits, the CHM band Stryper donned yellow and black outfits, mimicking the tendencies of secular bands such as Judas Priest and Iron Maiden. Though musically their sound may seem similar, stage antics such as tossing Bibles to their audiences were very different from their SHM counterparts W.A.S.P., who threw raw meat out to the crowd.[41] Members of Stryper were able to proselytize their faith openly not only through the locutionary and illocutionary acts of their lyrics but also the anticipated effects stemming from their stage preaching. By throwing out the Bibles during their live shows, Stryper willingly chose to display their faith unambiguously and undiluted by a multi-layered metaphor: essentially they wore their faith on their sleeves and proselytized it to the audience. With any type of perlocutionary uptake, audience members may or may not act as the speaker desired, however these actions would be felicitous, using Austin's terminology should the statements be sincere, the message was conversed in an appropriate way, the auditor/promise is actually capable of fulfilling such a promise, and finally no obligations would render the promise invalid by the time it had been made.

The CHM band Underoath embodies this explicit form of witnessing both on and offstage. During the summer of 2008, Underoath was one of the dozen or so heavy metal bands touring around amphitheaters promoting the first annual Rockstar Mayhem Festival. The band lineup consisted of various subgenres of heavy metal: death metal, shock rock, gothic, and metalcore, however Underoath was the only "Christian" act on the entire program. Prior to the headlining acts performing in the evening on the main stage, the bands throughout the afternoon performed their twenty minute set in rotation between two stages set up in adjacent parking lots. As Underoath took the stage and performed a few songs, lead singer Spencer Chamberlain approached the microphone in between songs and spoke to the audience for a minute or so. Chamberlain thanked everyone for coming out to support the Mayhem Festival and for supporting his band. He continued by stating that Underoath would not be where they are today without the unyielding love from Jesus Christ. Chamberlain acknowledged that without Jesus' everlasting sacrifice and as a source of inspiration in their music, they would not be able to do this (sing/preach/proselytize) for a living. The response to the impromptu sermon that I witnessed was met with a variety of cheers and boos. Chamberlain's felicitous comments propelled the band's lifestyle as a form of witnessing by remaining an authentically viable vessel for Christ. Underoath as a band is not relegated to Christian bookstores or playing Christian festivals, yet their Christian identity does not fade away from viewpoint both on and offstage.

As time passed, the means of communication have also expanded and CHM artists have been there. With the advent of new technologies being made available as alternative options to communicate on a national and global level, CHM artists primarily use the Internet to stay connected with fans on a more regular basis. Moberg suggested:

> A transnational level has been made possible through the development of a highly independent, and largely Internet-based, scenic infrastructure consisting of a number of central scenic institutions, including record labels, promotion and distribution channels, magazines, fanzines, online discussion forums, and festivals.[42]

Upon using the Internet as a means to stay connected with their fans, CHM bands such as Underoath have incorporated secular culture and technology but have shaped it to fit their own personal needs. CHM artists embody "metal missionaries"[43] utilizing symbols and metaphors to successfully engage in a dialogue with SHM fans in a way to attract young members into this discipline of faith.

On the band's website,[44] Underoath features a web journal where fans can check on the band's status. A unique feature from the Underoath site goes beyond tracking the band in studio and on tour. Periodically band members incorporate Christian theology in their postings, from answering questions like "What does it mean to be Christian?" or other faith-based questions that their fans inquire from the band. Other times, posts include certain religious teachings or spiritual readings that have helped the band not only find God but stay truthful and faithful while on the road. Christianity is not a selling point for bands like Underoath, it is not a façade which fades in and out of fashion once they step on/off stage. Christianity is their way of life: the double meaning and coding of the song lyrics are interpreted as Christian.

CRITICISMS OF CHM: AUTHENTICITY RENEGOTIATED

Staunch Christians and fundamentalists often point out their main concern with CCM or CHM as capitalizing on religion, or selling God.[45] Other times Christian metal has been criticized for using heavy metal in the stereotypical mentality of anything that is "loud, fast, and discordant, and its performers are aggressive, macho, antisocial, and occasionally violent."[46] Proponents of this ideology suggest that listening to heavy metal condones hypersexuality among men and disrespect toward women. CCM, like other genres of music, has the ability to reach an audience larger than its original fan base. Ideally this would be a positive attribute; however, for fundamentalists, CCM and CHM artists using inappropriate and sacrilegious music on behalf of acquiring more converts is immoral. The Rev. Jimmy Swaggart, known for his disavowal of anything related to Christian rock music, vociferously condemned CCM as a religious form of music in a 1985 interview when he stated:

> I think that the attitude, the atmosphere of trying to make a group look like a rock group . . . I don't know why anyone would want to do that. Yes, it's popular: I know a lot of young people that fall for it. Most all of them do . . . It's like giving a drug addict methadone. [The teenage rock-n-roll fan is] on drugs, so you give him methadone. You give this to kids to appease their lust for rock 'n' roll and the energy, it has great appeal to it . . . I don't feel that's leading kids to the Lord.[47]

Other criticisms stemmed directly from within the Church. CHM artists had to "worry about the pitfalls of theology and doctrine as well as the condemnations from outraged ministers who asserted that 'Christian rock' was a contradiction in terms."[48] Christian metal ran into further struggles with the Church because of the long-standing notion that rock music or heavy metal was either satanic or the devil's music.[49]

Not all criticism revolved around notions of morality and Church practices. Much research has described the inconsistencies between being a religious vehicle for Christianity on one hand yet also profiting from the success on the other. Livengood and Book[50] quoted a *Wall Street Journal* article accusing "Christian music labels of watering down their lyrics in an effort to reap more financial success."[51] CCM bands are painted as hypocritical since they "call for a simple lifestyle [by] represent[ing] a partial 'dropping out' of the capitalist system."[52] Record labels are primarily concerned with making a profit by selling CDs, and so hope to break through to the mainstream, so that they would sell more CDs. Gow noticed that while producers claimed that if more people purchased the music become converted, then ideally church attendance and offerings should likely increase. However, "the popularity of the music actually could lead to a decrease in traditional types of religious activities because Christians might be shifting expenditures of their time and money over to mediated forms of expression."[53] How then does one justify one's authenticity as a Christian while being faced with pressures from record companies who wish to market them as a commodity? The rationale behind this study has emphasized that depending on what is privileged more, the music or the mission, will determine the levels of authenticity surrounding the CHM artists.

There also remains a dual perspective between identifying band members with the Christian faith and overtly calling them a Christian band.[54] As I Lay Dying typifies this final criticism of CHM which centers on how once the label "Christian" is ascribed may impede their success or their overall publicity. Lead singer Tim Lambesis described the band's faith:

> Yeah, I mean, all five of us are Christians so I don't know if that makes us a Christian band. But at the same time, we've never been known as a band that's extremely preachy on stage. I think we intelligently represent what we believe and gain people's respect by being good musicians. You know, playing our music is the first thing that we do. When people get the chance to dig into the band and find out what we're all about, then they can learn we're behind all of our music.[55]

As I Lay Dying's willingness to let the music shine through first may represent a decrease in comfort with admitting who they are first and foremost, however, as I have argued throughout, they carefully negotiate their faith through the mainstream marketing process to establish themselves simultaneously as Christians not overtly proselytizing their faith, yet still remaining authentic to anyone who knows their work and their message. Not all bands however are as comfortable accepting or rejecting the "Christian" label. Labeling a band as "Christian" may cause tension and detrimental effects between members. For example, Sinai Beach's lead vocalist, CJ Alderson, stated, "We're angry. We're rebelling against the people that make us look bad. We rebel against the stigma that we have to fight every single time we go on tour with another band, and they're like, 'Oh crap, they're a Christian band'."[56]

The label carries a stigma that many artists and bands are not willing to embrace. Contemporary bands such as Switchfoot and Red both tour the Christian circuit, yet they seem more comfortable referring to themselves as 'Christians who play in a rock band' rather than pigeonholing themselves into the Christian rock genre."[57] The lead vocalist of Switchfoot, Jon Foreman, was hesitant in fully embracing the label of being in a Christian band:

> That's the thing. If we're going to stay out of the box, we're gonna have to be very conscientious of what everything is saying. Even opening up for Kid Rock says something. Like everything in life, any relationship is a compromise. But where we're at right now we're fortunate enough to pick the shots, and this is one of the festivals [Cornerstone Music Festival] that, for the most part, it's actually a lot of people that are, you know, searching spiritually. It's a bunch

of people that want to see the world change for the better. I don't know. That's
just important to me.[58]

It is this stigma that brings up the important notion of how these bands are
presented and the rhetorical techniques for why CHM bands should embrace
this non-Christian culture.

> As much as bands defined themselves against secular bands in terms of morality
> and discipline, they strive to emulate secular metal in sound quality, live per-
> formance, and appearance, and felt compelled to explain why these similarities
> were necessary for evangelical success. There was a simple division in Christian
> thought: that is, Christian artists and fans disagreed whether metal music should
> be a lifestyle or tool. Metal as a lifestyle presented Christians with a broad set
> of problems, as it suggested that personal preference took precedence over faith.
> On the other hand, if metal was a tool, Christians could clothe themselves in
> culture's accoutrements because it aided their goals as missionaries who sought
> to bring glory to God.[59]

Luhr relegated heavy metal music to a tool rather than a lifestyle. CHM artists
therefore could fashion this tool within the secular culture by seeking to shape
change from within, rather than remaining on the fringe.

CARRY ON MY WAYWARD SON

What then is the future for Christian Heavy Metal? As a genre of music there
seems to be a constant renegotiation of being religious yet ambiguous enough
not to eliminate a potential fan base that enjoys heavy metal music. Brandon
Ebel, president of the CCM/CHM label Tooth & Nail records, once declared,
"There's no such thing as Christian music."[60] Taken literally, the statement
seems preposterous, however, what Ebel likely was referring to is the unclear
distinction between Christian and secular music. It becomes difficult for the
casual fan listening to a song on the radio or on a CD, to tell whether the song
has Christian roots in the lyrics. In some ways, sound and style outshine the
religious content for those fans already tuned in to that particular genre of
music. Christian record labels such as Tooth & Nail are no longer relegated
to evangelical bookstores: they are everywhere, from promotional materials
to being advertised in popular music magazines. The branding of CHM constructs an interesting ideology not only with the artist but also their influence
and interaction with the audience. Bands such as Underoath are signed to
Christian label imprints, while groups such as As I Lay Dying are signed to
Metal Blade Records, a SHM imprint that distributes music from secular acts

such as Cannibal Corpse, Behemoth, GWAR, Mercyful Fate, and others. If it is about reaching as many people as possible with their music, CHM artists have successfully invaded the mainstream at a much greater success rate than Amy Grant, Jars of Clay, or Michael W. Smith.

Evangelicalism in CHM takes two dominant forms: the first involves witnessing performed by CHM artists who rely upon explicit proselytizing occurring both onstage as well as offstage through the speech act and the perlocutionary reactions of the audience members. The second, more implicit form of witnessing used by CHM artists infuses prevalent aspects of ambiguity into metaphorical layers similar to the palimpsest by disseminating their mission and lyrics to an audience who may or may not associate with the religious content.

These two perspectives of witnessing and proselytizing fit nicely by categorizing them according to the integrational and separational perspectives, however, as elements of CHM bleed into SHM, and vice versa, so, too, do these perspectives fluctuate between themselves. These two terms should not be taken as mutually exclusive; hearing and doing can go hand in hand, especially with the relationship between artist and audience. Branding CHM to an audience requires more than merely targeting an evangelical population. As a metaphorical tool, the palimpsest can be applied to the artist who beneath the long hair and tattoos an evangelical presence is waiting to be unleashed. It is important to note that no longer are the lines between Rock-n-Roll and Christian music so clear-cut. The New Wave of American Heavy Metal interacts and encompasses a growing surge of young evangelicals using the genre of heavy metal to seek out potential converts. Though not as overt, the "Christian" message, once unveiled, pervades much of contemporary popular culture.

NOTES

1. Metalheads is a popular term with the heavy metal subculture that describes a devoted and dedicated fan of heavy metal music. The term can also carry with it a pejorative sense of someone who is strongly masculine, short-tempered, and predisposed to alcoholism. Within the heavy metal subculture one attains metalhead status by embracing the lifestyle, purchasing heavy metal music, attending metal concerts, and emulating the style of heavy metal musicians: black T-shirts, tattoos, long hair, and leather jackets, to name a few. For more information on metalheads and authenticity see: Jeffrey Arnett. *Metalheads: Heavy Metal and Adolescent Alienation* (Boulder, CO: Westview Press, 1996).

2. A palimpsest is a type of writing material, often parchment that has been used multiple times after the text has been erased. Reusing the material causes different layers to appear, sometimes faint, while other times more pronounced. Using the

palimpsestic metaphor describing Christian heavy metal provides a useful tool in describing one approach to address questions of authenticity within the CHM community.

3. J. L. Austin was a British philosopher credited with inventing the speech act theory which stressed the performative quality of words. Austin went beyond thinking that words represent things, rather, he emphasized what one can do with words: commanding, promising, insulting, and praising. See: J. L. Austin. *How to Do Things with Words*, 2nd ed. (Cambridge, MA: Harvard University Press, 1975).

4. Jay R. Howard and John M. Streck. *Apostles of Rock: The Splintered World of Contemporary Christian Music* (Lexington: The University Press of Kentucky, 1999).

5. Marcus Moberg. "The Internet and the Construction of a Transnational Christian Metal Music Scene," *Culture and Religion* 9 (2008): 1, 81–99.

6. Larry Eskridge. "Defining the Term in Contemporary Times," *Institute for the Study of American Evangelicals* (1995), http://www.isae.wheaton.edu/defining -evangelicalism/defining-the-term-in-contemporary-times

7. Heather Hendershot. *Shaking the World for Jesus* (Chicago: The University of Chicago Press, 2004), 52.

8. Eric Gormly. "Evangelizing through Appropriation: Toward a Cultural Theory on the Growth of Contemporary Christian Music," *Journal of Popular Film and Television* 2 (2003): 4, 251-265.

9. *Ibid.*

10. *Ibid.*, 259.

11. Eileen Luhr. "Metal Missionaries to the Nation: Christian Heavy Metal Music, 'Family Values,' and Youth Culture, 1984-1994," *American Quarterly* 57 (2005): 104.

12. Gormly, "Evangelizing through Appropriation," 263.

13. Robert Walser. *Running with the Devil: Power, Gender, and Madness in Heavy Metal Music* (Middletown, CT: Wesleyan University Press, 1993).

14. *Ibid.*, 55.

15. Joe Gow. "Saving Souls and Selling CDs," *Journal of Popular Film and Television* 25 (1998): 183.

16. A "Jesus freak" initially was a pejorative term used to describe members of the Jesus Movement during the 1960s and 1970s. The term became embraced by the movement. For a more detailed look at this phenomenon, see: Preston Shires. *Hippies of the Religious Right* (Waco, TX: Baylor University Press, 2007).

17. Michael J. Gilmour. *Gods and Guitars: Seeking the Sacred in Post-1960s Popular Music* (Waco, TX: Baylor University Press, 2009), 39.

18. Michael Goldberg. "Amy Grant Wants to Put God on the Charts," *Rolling Stone*, 6 June 1985, 9–10.

19. The Longbored Surfer. "Billboard Top 100–1991," 2009, http://www.long boredsurfer.com/charts/1991.php

20. Jon Radwan. "Music and Mediated Religious Identity: 'Jesus Freak'," *Journal of Media and Religion* 5 (2006) 1–23.

21. *Ibid.*, 2.

22. *Ibid.*, 20.

23. Johannes Jonsson. "Christian Metal History," 2009, http://www.metalforjesus .org/history.htm

24. Moberg, "Transnational Christian Metal Music Scene," 87.

25. Ibid., 90.

26. Radwan, "Music and Mediated Religious Identity," 3.

27. Gormly, "Evangelizing through Appropriation," 261.

28. Howard and Streck, *Apostles of Rock*, 81.

29. John Durham Peters. *Speaking into the Air: A History of the Idea of Communication* (Chicago: The University of Chicago Press, 1999), 51-52.

30. M. Doherty. "An Almighty Sound: A Growing Number of Young Christian Bands are Finding Success with their Own Brand of Hardcore Heavenly Metal," *National Post*, 18 August 2005, AL1.

31. WayTooLoud. "As I Lay Dying—Jordan Mancino," 2008, http://www.way tooloud.com/2008/06/07/as-i-lay-dying-jordan-mancino/.

32. *Score!* Music Magazine. "Interview with As I Lay Dying," 2005, http://www scoremusicmagazine/scorerocks/112005/asilaydying.

33. Austin, *How to Do Things with Words*, 139.

34. *Ibid.*, 5.

35. *Ibid.*, 101.

36. Hendershot, *Shaking the World for Jesus*, 28.

37. Luhr, "Metal Missionaries," 119.

38. Howard and Streck, *Apostles of Rock*, 49.

39. *Ibid.,* 51.

40. *Ibid.,* 52.

41. Luhr, "Metal Missionaries," 112.

42. Marcus Moberg. "The Transnational Christian Metal Scene Expressing Alternative Christian Identity through a Form of Popular Music," *Advanced Cultural Studies Institute of Sweden* (2007): 429.

43. Luhr, "Metal Missionaries."

44. Underoath. "Homepage," 2009, http://www.underoath777.com

45. Harold Perkins. "American Fundamentalism and the Selling of God," *Political Quarterly* 71 (2000): 79–89.

46. Christine Hall Hansen and Ronald D. Hansen. "Constructing Personality and Social Reality through Music: Individual Differences among Fans of Punk and Heavy Metal Music," *Journal of Broadcasting and Electronic Media* 35 (1991): 336.

47. Hendershot, *Shaking the World for Jesus*, 37.

48. Luhr, "Metal Missionaries," 120.

49. Moberg, "The Transnational Christian Metal Scene," 427.

50. Megan Livengood and Connie Ledoux Book. "Watering Down Christianity? An Examination of the Use of Theological Words in Christian Music," *Journal of Media and Religion* 3 (2004): 119–29.

51. *Ibid.*, 120.

52. Jay R. Howard. "Contemporary Christian Music: Where Rock Meets Religion," *Journal of Popular Culture* 26 (1992): 126.

53. Gow, "Saving Souls and Selling CDs," 7.
54. Jonathan Dueck. "Crossing the Street: Velour 100 and Christian Rock," *Popular Music and Society* 24 (2000): 127–48.
55. MetalUnderground. "Interview with Tim Lambesis from As I Lay Dying," 2005, http://www.metalunderground.com/interviews/details.cfm?newsid=12929.
56. Doherty, "An Almighty Sound," AL1.
57. David Nantais. "What Would Jesus Listen To?" *America* 196 (21 May 2007): 23.
58. Andrew Beaujon. *Body Piercing Saved My Life: Inside the Phenomenon of Christian Rock* (Cambridge, MA: Da Capo Press, 2006), 12.
59. Luhr, "Metal Missionaries," 121.
60. Dueck, "Crossing the Street," 136

BIBLIOGRAPHY

Austin, J. L. 1975. *How to Do Things with Words*. Cambridge: Harvard University Press.

Beaujon, Andrew. 2006. *Body Piercing Saved My Life: Inside the Phenomenon of Christian Rock*. Cambridge: Da Capo Press.

Doherty, Michael. "An Almighty Sound: A Growing Number of Young Christian Bands are Finding Success with their Own Brand of Hardcore Heavenly Metal." *National Post*, August 18, 2005.

Dueck, Jonathan. "Crossing the Street: Velour 100 and Christian Rock." *Popular Music and Society* 24 (2000): 127–148.

Eskridge, Larry. "Defining the Term in Contemporary Times." Institute for the Study of American Evangelicals. http://isae.wheaton.edu/defining-evangelicalism/defining-the-term-in-contemporary-times (accessed December 18, 2009).

Gilmour, Michael J. 2009. *Gods and Guitars: Seeking the Sacred in Post-1960s Popular Music*. Waco: Baylor University Press.

Goldberg, Michael. "Amy Grant Wants to Put God on the Charts." *Rolling Stone*, June 6, 1985.

Gormly, Eric. "Evangelizing through Appropriation: Toward a Cultural Theory on the Growth of Contemporary Christian Music." *Journal of Media and Religion* 2 (2003): 251–265.

Gow, Joe. "Saving Souls and Selling CDs." *Journal of Popular Film and Television* 25 (1998): 183–188.

Hansen, Christian Hall, and Ronald D. Hansen. "Constructing Personality and Social Reality through Music: Individual Differences among Fans of Punk and Heavy Metal Music." *Journal of Broadcasting and Electronic Media* 35 (1991): 335–350.

Hendershot, Heather. *Shaking the World for Jesus*. Chicago: University of Chicago Press.

Howard, Jay R. "Contemporary Christian Music: Where Rock Meets Religion." *Journal of Popular Culture* 26 (1992): 123–130.

Howard, Jay R., and John M. Streck. 1999. *Apostles of Rock: The Splintered World of Contemporary Christian Music.* Lexington: The University Press of Kentucky.

Jonsson, Johannes. "Christian Metal History." http://www.metalforjesus.org/history.htm (accessed December 18, 2009).

Livengood, Megan, and Connie Ledoux Book. "Watering Down Christianity? An Examination of the Use of Theological Words in Christian Music." *Journal of Media and Religion* 3 (2004): 119–129.

Lurh, Eileen. "Metal Missionaries to the Nation: Christian Heavy Metal Music, Family Values, and Youth Culture." *American Quarterly* 57 (2005): 103–128.

MetalUndrground. "Interview with Tim Lambesis from As I Lay Dying." http://www.metalunderground.com/interviews/details.cfm?newsid=12929 (accessed December 19, 2009).

Moberg, Marcus. "The Transnational Christian Metal Scene Expressing Alternative Christian Identity through a Form of Popular Music." Paper presented at a symposium conducted by the Advanced Cultural Studies Institute of Sweden, Norrkoping, Sweden, June 2007.

Moberg, Marcus. "The Internet and the Construction of a Transnational Christian Metal Music Scene." *Culture and Religion: An Interdisciplinary Journal* 9 (2008): 81–99.

Nantais, David. "What Would Jesus Listen To?" *America* 196 (2007): 22–24.

Perkins, Harold. "American Fundamentalism and the Selling of God." *The Political Quarterly* 71 (2000): 79–89.

Peters, John Durham. 1999. *Speaking into the Air: A History of the Idea of Communication.* Chicago: The University of Chicago Press.

Radwan, Jon. "Music and Mediated Religious Identity: 'Jesus Freak'." *Journal of Media and Religion* 5 (2006): 1–23.

Score! Music Magazine. "Interview with As I Lay Dying." http://www.scoremusic-magazine/scorerocks/112005/asilaydying (accessed December 18, 2009).

The Longbored Surfer. "Billboard Top 100—1991." http://longboredsurfer.com/charts.php?year=1991 (accessed December 18, 2009).

Underoath, "Homepage." http://www.underoath777.com (accessed December 18, 2009).

Walser, Robert. 1993. *Running with the Devil: Power, Gender, and Madness in Heavy Metal Music.* Middletown: Wesleyan University Press.

WayTooLoud. "As I Lay Dying—Jordan Mancino." http://www.waytooloud.com/2008/06/07/as-i-lay-dying-jordan-mancino/ (accessed December 18, 2009).

NOTE: The author wishes to thank William Keith for his guidance and support throughout the numerous drafts and to Nathan England for his insight into the evangelical Christian movement.

10

Sight and Sound: How a Louis Vuitton Advertisement Defines Rock and Roll

Heather Pinson

When sixty-four-year-old Keith Richards modeled for Louis Vuitton's "Core Values" campaign in March of 2008, the result was an estranged-looking man, alone in his luxury hotel room cradling his guitar in the name of fashion instead of the name "the Rolling Stones." The tagline states simply: "Some journeys cannot be put into words. New York. 3 am. Blues in C." Famed photographer Annie Leibovitz captures the rocker in as much detail as possible in order to echo Richards's cratered face with designer Louis Vuitton's custom made guitar case appearing as second fiddle to Richards on the bed.[1] What makes this photograph initially shocking is the jolting transition from Richards's image of hard-edged rocker to modeled softy, peddling handbags, clutches, shoes, sunglasses, and other fashionable items by merely posing in a picture as a representative. Here, image becomes the agent of change.

"I think I am going to change my research topic to Britney Spears," said one of my female students who was responding to my question on each student's choice for their final research paper for my Rock and Rhetoric course. The class examines the ideologies of popular music and lyrics through hermeneutics and communication theories. The entire class paused for a moment and then simultaneously leapt into laughter, until they realized, as I did, that she was serious.[2] Due to the impossibility of covering every musician or even every decade of popular music in a fifteen-week course, Spears was not included as a focus of study. In a class filled with students who had Jay-Z cell phone ring tones or wearing Linkin Park 2009–2010 touring schedule tee shirts, Britney Spears was interpreted by most students as too mainstream, too pop, pulled by the puppet strings of Hollywood glitz and glam and considered an upgraded, grown up version of Disney marketeering. Her image does not fit with the edgy, antiauthoritarian status inhabited by many of her Goth

Figure 10.1.
© Annie Leibovitz/Contact Press Images, for LVMH (original in color) used with permission of the artist.

coated contemporaries, yet she remains at the forefront of popularity in pop culture. Therefore, my students interpreted Britney Spears as an entertainer, unworthy to include in a final research paper even if the university course did cover rock and roll history.

These two examples create several key questions: How can musical taste be determined by an image? What effect does the image of a popular style of music have on the music itself? How can the popularity of a band or musician grow depending on a collective "mental picture," since, as David Ake states, "we 'see' music as well as hear it?"[3] The popularity of a band depends on a particular set of circumstances that involve concentrated mass marketing tactics and the assumption that the audience will embrace these tactics eventually. In pop culture, the image of a band becomes a marketable and profitable object which, through repetition, manages our society's collective musical taste. In turn, the public identifies first with the image of a band, then with their sound. Since the image is an information-carrying entity, as indicated by Ferdinand de Saussure's theory of semiotics, it can take the form of a sign, word, association, photograph, article of clothing, or sound which construct a relationship to the receiver of the image/sign.[4] This chapter takes a philosophical rather than sociological approach to the influence of the popular music image, as seen in the Vuitton advertisement featuring guitarist Keith Richards, and examines our captivation with the image of popular music possibly circumventing the music itself. Thus, as a marketable and profitable inspiration of counterculture, the image homogenizes our collective musical taste into something that is perceived socially and culturally as "cool."

EXPLANATION OF THE POPULAR MUSIC IMAGE

We visualize what a musical genre sounds like based on how this genre is marketed or simply how the genre is presented in society, whether through peers and education or advertising and entertainment. With classical music, one generally envisions an instrument indicative of classical music, such as a flute or violin, and then recalls the sounds of a symphony orchestra and place such as a concert hall. With an image of classical music in mind, one may imagine the thunderous rhythms of Beethoven or the scene of Mozart at the clavichord in the movie *Amadeus* whereas with popular music, one mentally conjures up the facial makeup of KISS or The Beatles' album covers or jeans, a cowboy hat, and an acoustic guitar with country. Dreadlocks immediately connects us with Bob Marley and Rastafarian reggae sounds, while an image of a saxophone in a nightclub takes us to jazz. Instrumentation also garners a strong relationship to a style of music: violin in classical versus fiddle in bluegrass or country; upright bass with straight ahead jazz versus the electric bass for fusion. The African instrument of the banjo is now synced with bluegrass, and the tin whistle is linked to the rolling country land of Ireland.

By repeating certain visual icons alongside of music, we begin to associate a style of music to a particular object, emotion, place, experience, smell, or even taste. Together with various modes of social and cultural behavior, an image of popular music is created through the perception and understanding of what constitutes as the norms for that particular style. For instance, country music contains an image of American history, regional locations with Appalachia and the American West, ruggedness, the working class, honor, story telling, patriotism. In the music itself, there are also stylistic tendencies that lean toward a previously established homogenization of country music; for instance, the instrumentation of a steel guitar, the emphasis on the lyrics as a narrative, lyrical singing, and tone of the voice—all contribute to a timbral canon. The repetition of this sound within the oeuvre of country music artists is accumulated and feeds back to the next generation of rising young stars.

Of course, these associations do not adhere to every song classified as "country," yet there are some stigmas both positive and negative that each popular style contains. It is up to the musician whether to normalize, push, or even break these labels; however, the labels are created by the repetition of certain images that fit the sound and understanding of country music. Both the listeners and the performers of country choose this style of music because of how it sounds and the messages it carries through its amalgamated image. The cultivation of these labels infiltrate pop culture over a period of several decades resulting in the establishment of an image of country music as it is understood by both the average listener and the expert.

While the continued existence of country music appearing as a singing cowboy still lingers in our current American culture (even with acts such as the Dixie Chicks), what is not apparent is how the image of country music has essentially become a simulacrum for the sound of country. The term "image" as used here refers to a particular aural, visual, social, and cultural understanding of a music style.[5] An image is a composite of one's individual experiences (including peers' tastes), upbringing, and education combined with the social and cultural forces to create one's own mental picture to represent the physical manifestations of a musical genre. The popular music image, as with any other presupposition, contains stereotypes that break down or summarize the entire history of a musical genre in a single visual picture. One image, such as a photograph or video, can be repeated over and over in society, thus solidifying, for better or worse, the musical genre with that image. For instance, hard rock can be identified through a picture of KISS in make-up, which is coveted in one short sound clip, "Rock and Roll All Nite," just as Southern rock is identified with Lynard Skynard's "Sweet Home Alabama." This is, of course, coupled with the physical image of the musician, the visual presentation of the band and other pop culture commercialization such as music videos, album covers, fashion, accessories, and streamlined marketing procedures.

The word "image" can be illusive and loaded with multiple meanings, but for the purposes of this paper, it not only means a concrete visual depiction, but also a mental picture or collective understanding of something. Visual culture, as Nicholas Mirzoeff states, "does not depend on the pictures themselves but the modern tendency to picture or visualize something."[6] Hence, when studying the role popular music plays in one's society, we must examine the process of visualizing popular music. Of course, images are not limited to popular music alone, but by definition, popular music maintains its "popularity" by participating in the modern process of image-making, ranging from the evolving romantic relationships of musicians to material on their album covers. All of the material that is processed daily becomes a format for identifying a particular genre of popular music. Thus, if one can determine the relationship of an image as it functions in society, one may gain further insight into how we function in society.

ANALYSIS OF THE LOUIS VUITTON ADVERTISEMENT

A single image can mean several things to many different people, but when perceptions reach some general agreement, we then claim them as standards of judgment.[7] Roland Barthes was successful in expanding Saussure's idea of the signified (or the mental image of an object) by examining the composite of several variables that are found in one single picture, specifically by focusing on nonverbal signs as they are used in society. Barthes traces the word "image" from "imitari," which indicates a reproduction, imitation, appearance, copy, or a mental picture of something: a conception, idea, or impression. He concludes that an image contains several signs that create a chain reaction in our brain, instilling more codes and more signifiers and more signifieds.[8] Hence, images play a large role in our society since we rely on them to communicate, and the repeated occurrence of images, signs, and objects are further evidence of society's desire to communicate efficiently.

Let us now examine the specific meaning found in an image of popular music such as the photograph of Keith Richards taken by Annie Leibovitz. The photograph according to Barthes, contains two things: (1) a denoted message, which is the subject in the photograph itself, and (2) a connoted message, which is either the viewer's interpretation of the photograph, a coded message, a visual metaphor, or how that subject is presented. The denotation is what is being photographed. Initially, the advertisement is a denoted message by the fact that this is presented as an advertisement, but simultaneously, the name "Louis Vuitton," as the French lineage of luxury handbags and luggage, establishes a connoted sense of luxury. The hotel room setting itself is a denoted message, taken literally, while the process of interpreting the setting is a connoted message. The interpretation of the photograph then lies through the analysis of connotation through particular signified messages found in the photograph.

With fashion brazenly linked with the high-end status of the people involved in the photograph, Barthes would conclude that fashion, as a coded sign, represents luxury and fame. The "A" listers appearing in these advertisements constitutes an image of celebrity stardom that is intoxicating. One assumes that the amount of money involved to have the right people staged to be in the right place must be astounding. The blatant use of familiar names in the photograph establishes a direct connection between the luxury items (Vuitton custom made guitar case and guitar) and the lavish personalities hired to stand next to them (Keith Richards and Annie Leibovitz). Celebrity status becomes a repeated message throughout other Vuitton ads shot by Annie Leibovitz which included such icons as Mikhail Gorbachev and others

Figure 10.2.
© Annie Leibovitz/Contact Press Images, for LVMH (original in color) used with permission of the artist.

with Catherine Deneuve "sitting on a Vuitton trunk in a film-set train station, and tennis champions Andre Agassi and Steffi Graf cuddling on a couch near their luggage."[9]

More recent photos feature Francis Ford Coppola and daughter Coppola lounging in the countryside outside Buenos Aires, Sean Connery barefoot and reclining on a deck on a beach, and finally astronauts Buzz Aldrin, Sally Ride, and Jim Lovell looking toward the moon in tow with a Vuitton $1,530 "ICare" travel bag named for fellow Greek mythical traveler, Icarus. Besides the designer product and the celebrities themselves is the name of *Vanity Fair* contributor and greatly acclaimed photographer, Annie Leibovitz. Leibovitz shoots the Richards photo with the same panache as her earlier modeling acolytes. Finally, celebrity status is subtly configured with the surprise guest of the Gibson ES-355, a guitar of its own ranking since it was played by B.B. King among others and held by Richards in the photograph.

With Annie Leibovitz working behind the camera (and in front of the computer screen to make any needed adjustments), the photograph becomes an amalgam of realism mixed with fantasy: realism which is found in the elaborate detailing of the hotel room makes it seem as if the viewer was casually asked to join in a jam session, and fantasy with Richards himself moving from guitarist to fashion icon. This dichotomy is echoed by the odd juxtaposition between the careless nature of Richards's expression and the purposeful arrangement of objects around him. The photogenia or techniques of lighting, exposure, and printing become clear representatives of artful qualities tied in with commercialism. Richards looks to the left, and with this act, points the viewer to the left as well toward the trim but slightly worn guitar case. Richards shares the bed with the case, but the flatness of it allows the viewer to gaze around the hotel room. The objects around the room provide a feeling of "highly polished fashion meets vintage classic" with items such as a Victorian style tea service, the spyglass sitting vertically on the table, the magnifying glass on the book, and the room's decor, which is also Victorian (curtains, picture, chair, and bedding fabric). The room is framed by two lamps covered by black scarves containing the same skull that Richards wears as a ring and found on the nightstand on the right.

Two compositional elements, texture and light, clearly establish a painterly feel in Leibovitz's photograph. One of the most striking features is its crispness, exhibiting each granulated surface from the texture of the cloth chairs, to the leather of Richards's jacket, to the murky, Metamucil-like orange drink on the table. With the viewer's freedom to gaze about the room, we become mesmerized by the surfaces presented to us, which is typical of other advertisements in the core values campaign. The denoted setting includes the slick black guitar face which swirls like oil beneath Richards's fingers, and the reflection of light bounces off of his bracelet and cup and saucer. Light also flutters between the back lit door and the two lamp shades which emit a late night glow echoed by the pulled drapes in the background to keep out the sun or other harsh luminaries. Richards's haunting eyes with black eyeliner are reminiscent of the Looney Tunes's Wile E. Coyote, as he loosely shifts his gaze to the direction of the case. This draws the viewer's eye toward the case, since the neck of the guitar is leading the eye away. Richards's finger position on the neck of the guitar (noted by guitar players to be a C chord) helps point the viewer back to the center of the photograph, in addition to the door in the background which brings the viewer back to Richards's face.

The color seems muted, almost monochromatic, which is atypical in fashion photography. Usually magazine and Internet advertisements contain large print and bright colors that push through to the viewer. Other photographs must make an impression while the viewer pauses briefly to examine the advertisement and moves on. On the contrary, here Leibovitz creates a more subtle and richly detailed environment indicating that the viewer is invited to stay and linger. Thus, the arranged objects connote time and preservation in accordance with the time-honored individuals and materials in the photograph that need to be regarded and observed.

It continues to adhere, however, to the conventions of fashion photography by focusing on all of the objects in the image except the one it is advertising. One must disengage with Richards momentarily in order to locate the product he is marketing. When we do find the guitar case, it becomes apparent that

Richards's face is the visual connection to the patterned product. His face signifies life of the road which makes the viewer think of travel. With the caption "New York. 3 am," one can conclude that travel is the established theme and connoted message while Richards returning to his New York hotel room after a gig is the denoted message. He is living the rock and roll lifestyle on the road, as indicated by the words, "Some journeys cannot be put into words." Richards's face is as telling as an autobiography and one is able to see that his personal journey is beyond description. So, one may conclude that even Richards when traveling takes his custom made Vuitton guitar case, and if we want to live the life of a rock star, then so should we.

Even though his brief appearance in the Vuitton photograph appears to be a striking juxtaposition of a rock musician's role into the second decade of the twenty-first century, it is surprisingly similar to what musicians have been doing for decades. Musicians must act as their own agents, often touting a double-edged sword in order to keep their fame intact. One must move with agility across various social-scapes ranging from the financial and entrepreneurial encounters at high-end parties and promotional set-ups to colleagues at recording sessions, service workers preparing on stage strategies, and finally appealing to the ardent fan as if he or she is one of them. Popular musicians and entertainers must act as if they live the same daily life as everyone else, but their life is full of expectations, pressure, and tabloids ready to mark their every whim, change of dress, weight loss or gain, and mood swings. Musicians must guard themselves and their image constantly because that is what ensures their place at the top of the charts. They must not alter the perception of themselves for fear of ridicule and reduced popularity. In addition, they must interact with fans more and hone networking skills such as mastering the blog post, the casual street photo, the not too overtly promotional self-promotion, the sudden personal revelation, and the witty Tweet and Facebook exclamation.

Richards has been in the business long enough to know how to play the game. He has been able to market successfully his sound, songs, guitars, face, and now his image through the unreleased documentary, Cocksucker Blues, by Robert Frank and vicious happenings at the Altamont Speedway Free Festival. His cameo appearance as Jack Sparrow's father, Captain Teague, in Walt Disney's *Pirates of the Caribbean: At World's End*, remains one of the first comical encounters that poked fun at Richards's wrinkly face, since he resembles a pirate already. Even Depp acknowledges that he used Richards as a model for the creation of Jack Sparrow.[10] Similar to the character of a pirate, Richards's face becomes the link between his music and the texture of the suitcase he is modeling.

In society, just as our minds are overwhelmed by the constant sight of celebrities; so do our ears become saturated with the sounds of popular music heard in pop culture. One advantage of images is that they do not have to occur linearly. They can occur as they appear, without provocation, and appear in the mind as a response to and stimulation from the music. For example, when we see Keith Richards, we think Rolling Stones, guitar, 1960s, drugs, touring, amps, blues, Mick Jagger's lips; and each sign leads to the next with no particular narrative in mind. He becomes what Barthes would describe as a sign that, once identified, creates a chain reaction in the viewer's brain. Richards is the causality of these images, all of which are mental projections that occur in the mind of the viewer depending on their previous knowledge and musical taste. His physical embodiment, as a member of the Rolling Stones, channels the music, albums, and band history into the photograph merely by his presence.

He also provides us with a mental picture of rock and roll musicians from the past since he is identified with the unexpected marriage between American R&B and blues-based British rock etched into history like the lines in his face. As a musical hero in pop culture, he stands for bluesy guitar riffs and on stage swagger which has accumulated in various photo montages depicting Richards and/or the Stones over the decades.[11] This example of a popular music image is specific to the blues that influenced British rock of the 1960s. The Rolling Stones had already been immortalized in pop culture as one of the most famous bands of all time, but now the band has reached even further acclaim through longevity, since one wonders how the musicians are able to keep playing, touring, recording, and singing as a band for more than forty years. This is unheard of due to the rigorous, stressful, and often deadly lifestyle of a touring musician. Richards's face acts as a testament to the difficulties of life on the road.

Even with the legendary status that comes with being a member of the Rolling Stones, Keith Richards remains a king in a world among men. His prowess on the guitar and his on stage flair remains respectable marks of the trade among rock stars. Although he has drank, smoked, and partied like a rock star, he is not physically abusive toward others, at least not in public, and his romantic relationships have not been controversial enough to distort his image. He remains a constant and irrefutable source of rock and roll history. As recorded on Bloomberg.com, Antoine Arnault, Vuitton's head of communications, said Louis Vuitton is choosing "achievers who changed things," and Rita Clifton said Keith Richards is "timeless and ageless." As Clifton, who heads the UK division of brand consultant Interbrand, said "He's lived his life on the edge, but he's not a sleaze bag. He's lean and mean and he's still current."[12] Arnault and Clifton reaffirm that Richards was asked to be in the photo based on his reputation and personality although he is known to throw temper tantrums. In other words, he may not be a sleaze bag, but he is also no Taylor Swift.

It is therefore easy to see why Louis Vuitton consultants chose Keith Richards for the advertisement because he resonates with pop culture and is not typically fashionable. He has persevered through a forty-year career in the limelight of rock and roll while maintaining his tough image throughout. As lead guitarist for the Rolling Stones, Richards physically embodies the Baby Boomer icon and lifestyle of a rock musician: late nights, touring, hotel rooms, drugs, alcohol, women, guitars, money, fame, and glory. His leather jacket and shiny black guitar also aid in the identification of rock. Hence, he becomes the ideal character for high-end fashion because, as a rebel, Richards personifies those who would not be interested in fashion. But even Richards must succumb to Vuitton's allure. By his facial expression and weathered skin, Richards looks as if he has been through all his forty years and then some. His history as a touring musician, his haggard physical look, and his association with a well-known band solidifies his image as a rebellious artist, even when approaching his seventies.

With all of the signs pointing to the sounds of blues and early rock, popular music literally becomes the mental soundtrack for the viewer when examining the photograph, "[t]hat is to say, the connotative qualities of the music complement the denotative qualities of the words and pictures. Or to put it another way, the music interprets the words and pictures."[13] For example, the subtext of "Blues in C" and Gibson ES-355 provide the viewer with a specific genre of popular music to go with the photograph. The gritty sound of the blues found in the picture of the guitar acts as a direct musical link between the musical blues heroes of the past and present. In the making of the photograph, Robert Johnson's "Crossroad Blues" is heard in the background, possibly played for inspiration for Richards and crew to replicate a bluesy feeling.[14] Richards, himself a blues musician, invokes the masters of the past by his wrinkled and storied face, indicative of his lifestyle. The guitar, clothing, person, and musical style as given by the subtext are all signs that create a dialogue between the photograph and the viewer.

According to art critic Joanna Lowry, "The act of taking a photograph is a communicative act in itself which exposes the social dynamic through which identities (both of the photographer and of the subject) are formed."[15] Similarly, music is situated in a particular social and historical context, a context that includes the location at which music production occurs, the prior musical experiences of both performers and audience, as well as their expectations and prejudices. Therefore, music as a communicative art form constructs a dialogue between the musician and the audience. This dialogue is initiated from Richards's appearance in the photograph. Then, other items become recognized as connoted messages which are the interpretations found within the photograph, or as Barthes says, "the manner in which the society to a certain extent communicates what it [society] thinks of it [the photograph]."[16] Such a relationship between the viewer and advertisement begins when the viewer attempts to subjectively view the object, and in the process of reading an image, the viewer gains analytic and creative power over the stationary, non-responsive image that cannot explain itself. And through the exchange of information and ultimately power, the image or advertisement acquires significance and value in society. What is important is not the photograph itself, but rather the relationship between the image, its meaning in society, and its meaning in the mind of the receiver. As a process of communication, signs are exchanged, ideologies are created, and power is transferred.[17]

However, in the circuitous dialogue between musician, photographer, and viewer, the musician has the last word through the additional association of sound to the image. Music often evokes images merely through the style of music itself. The genre of music, stimulated by the denoted and connoted signs in an image, strikes a chord with the viewer who, even after looking away from the photograph, can remember the sound of the Rolling Stones. The listener is reminded of both sound and sight through the Stones' music and physical appearance; however, the viewer is "not just remembering but reliving" past aural experiences with the Stones or Keith Richards's guitar riffs.[18] The sound of the Stones which is stimulated by the visual image creates an aural memory peg in the viewer's mind. Because the viewer has been exposed in some form to blues and rock prior to seeing Richards in the photograph, the viewer projects their own set of preconceived values onto the image, and in so doing, perpetuate and determine social values. Louis Althusser argues that "the image can be seen as the inscription of those values and beliefs…but [the visual is also] a mechanism that produces as well as represents culture to itself, constituting its relations of power and difference."[19]

FINDINGS

Music, as a finite temporal event, is extended and reverberated through the fixed, but longer lived, visual image. The visual image acts as a conduit to music; however, listeners are not purely attracted to the style of music exhibited by a photograph. Instead, they are attracted to what the music represents, since popular music is as much of a social construct as it is a musical one. Nicholas Cook states,

> As Derrida and de Man have shown, music may give the appearance of going directly from the heart to the heart, to borrow Beethoven's famous words, but in reality no musical style is unmediated. To put it another way, music is the discourse that passes itself off as nature; it participates in the construction of meaning, but disguises its meanings as effects. Here is the source of its singular efficacy as a hidden persuader.[20]

Therefore, music is stimulation. We understand popular music as a style of music that links masses of people to certain visual, social, ideological, political, or musical attributes that each audience member believes to find in the music and/or image of the band. We project our own influences onto the band or artist and identify with their music that fits our personalities and upbringing. It is our infatuation or fetishization with what the style of music, band, or musicians, represent to us personally that affects our musical taste.

The public asserts value to certain styles of music over others because it, and other works of art for that matter, present a greater potential for interpretation, uniqueness, or creativity. By interpreting the sound of a band, the viewers impose a subjective view onto material that is presented to them and is not their own. This process of interpretation enables viewers to speculate, judge, recommend, or dissuade others on the importance of the image, thus projecting an agency over the artist. Because of its accessibility through technology and visual media, the public seems to be even more scrupulous with musicians than, say, with painters. This distribution of power from the artwork to the patron is a main factor in the discernment of taste. If more people can debate the intended smile of the "Mona Lisa," then more people will become informed of Da Vinci's painting, and more people will contribute to the celebrated status of the painting. Similarly, popular music has continually included an image that runs counter to the supposed mainstream with songs like Chuck Berry's "Roll Over Beethoven" to the Vivienne Westwood and Malcolm McLaren designed attire worn by the Sex Pistols that inspired the British punk scene. If a rock song seems to comply with the majority or to reinforce accepted behavior, then it is not seen as "cool." Keith Richards's presence makes Annie Leibovitz's photo "cool," not vice versa. The meaning of the Vuitton advertisement would change if Pat Boone was used as the model for Vuitton. Our collective tastes determine much of what we listen to as seen when a Pandora user was shocked to find that he actually liked Celine Dion, someone that culturally is not seen as cool.[21]

In an age where a four-second sound bite could be the next big hit, marketing companies have had to adjust quickly to stay afloat in a competitive environment. Yet, as seen with Keith Richards's modeling for a Louis Vuitton advertisement, one thing remains clear: we consume the image of music in addition to the sound of music. Thousands of messages are displayed every-day in some multi-media method that includes popular music as a message to promote a product.[22] Popular music itself acts as an image, a visual represen-tation of the sound of the music as it is heard in the mind of the listener.[23] In this case, the image is not necessarily an exact representation of the person, since no popular musician wants to be photographed or portrayed exactly as he or she looks in day-to-day life. Instead, the image represents the idealiza-tion of a band or musician. As a composite of our individual experiences, upbringing, and education combined with the social and cultural forces, the musical image represents the physical manifestations of a musical genre. We visualize what a musical genre sounds like based on how this genre is marketed to us.

NOTES

1. Richards donated the fee for his involvement to The Climate Project, an organi-zation for raising environmental awareness.

2. The reason the students laughed with the idea of Spears as a source for serious study lies in the cultural preponderance of her music: she is popular but not seen as "cool" when in comparison, as my class had done, to Pink Floyd, Chuck Berry, Cream, Led Zeppelin, and Jimi Hendricks.

3. David Ake, *Jazz Cultures* (Berkeley: University of California Press, 2005) 159.

4. In his book entitled *Representations,* Stuart Hall suggests that our theory of representation has been changed to include three methods of interpretation: (1) the *reflective* or *mimetic* approach proposes a direct relationship of imitation or reflection between words as signs and things, (2) the *intentional* theory reduces representation to the intentions of its author or subject, (3) the *constructionist* theory proposes a mediated relationship between things in the world, our concepts in thought and lan-guage. All three of these approaches are used in the study of semiotics. Stuart Hall, ed. *Representation: Cultural Representations and Signifying Practices* (London: Sage, 1998) 35.

5. For more information on image as that which defines a style of music, see Heather K. Pinson, *The Jazz Image: Seeing Music Through Herman Leonard's Pho-tography* (Jackson: University Press of Mississippi, 2010.)

6. Nicholas Mirzoeff, *An Introduction to Visual Culture* (New York: Routledge, 1999) 5.

7. There are many theories, ideologies, and philosophies aided by a myriad of rhetorical conjectures that grapple with images as they function in society. In terms of theoreticians, there are Ferdinand de Saussure, *Course in General Linguistics*

trans. Wade Baskin, (New York: McGraw-Hill, 1969); Michel Foucault, *The Order of Things: An Archaeology of the Human Sciences*. A Translation of *Les Mots et les choses* (New York: Vintage Books, 1970); Michel Foucault, *Language, Counter-Memory, Practice; Selected Essays and Interviews* (Ithaca: Cornell University Press, 1977); Michel Foucault, *This is Not a Pipe* trans. and ed. James Harkness (Berkeley: University of California Press, 1983); Hans-Georg Gadamer, *Philosophical Herme-neutics* trans. and ed. David E. Linge, (Berkeley: University of California Press, 1976); Roland Barthes, *Image, Music, Text* Trans. Stephen Heath (New York: Hill and Wang, 1977), Roland Barthes, *S/Z* Trans. Richard Miller (New York: Hill and Wang, 1974), and Roland Barthes, *Camera Lucida: Reflections on Photography* (New York: Hill and Wang, 1981). Many of these theorists find new meanings for images, and in turn, disassemble age-old views on truth and reality, as they have been understood from the Enlightenment until the twentieth-century. Many of these scholars feel terms such as truth, reality, image, icon, subject, history, identity, code, and sign need to be re-evaluated. Through an expanding sense of self-consciousness and social construction, these theorists explore identification and representation in society.

8. If (sign= signified / signifier) or (n=d/r), then [(n=d/r) + (x= d/n) + (y= d/x) + (z= d/y), etc…]. This post-structuralist process can be repeated endlessly, building a layered discourse of an image. Signs that are repeated so extensively that they lose their meaning as a highly conventionalized sign are called codes. The visual image, in general, is layered with coded messages.

9. Sara Gay Forden, "Keith Richards Is New Face of Vuitton as LVMH Promotes Luggage" *Bloomberg News,* 5 March 2008. Accessed 9 January 2010 http://www .bloomberg.com/apps/news?pid=newsarchive&sid=aFGtAVSoFBAw.

10. David Wild, "Johnny Depp & Keith Richards: *Pirates of the Caribbean*'s Blood Brothers" *Rolling Stone*, 31 May 2007. Accessed 10 January 2010 http://www .rollingstone.com/news/coverstory/johnny_depp__keith_richards_ipirates_of_the_ caribbeanis_blood_brothers.

11. See Keith Richards's homepage for examples http://www.keithrichards.com/ index_flash.html.

12. Forden, "Keith Richards Is New Face of Vuitton as LVMH Promotes Lug-gage," *Bloomberg News.*

13. Nicholas Cook, "Music and Meaning in the Commercials" *Popular Music*, Vol. 13, No. 1 (Jan. 1994): 39.

14. This is heard in a youtube clip entitled, "Making of video Louis Vuitton Keith Richards" posted May 06, 2008 by urbansteel, The UrbanSteel You Tube Rolling Stones Channel. Accessed 10 January 2010 http://www.youtube.com/ watch?v=XuZc1_gI4vE.

15. Joanna Lowry, "Negotiating Power," from Mark Durden and Craig Richard-son, eds., *Face On: Photography as Social Exchange* (London: Black Dog Publish-ing, 2000) 13.

16. Barthes, *Image, Music, Text*, 17.

17. The "sign," according to Vincent M. Colapietro's *Glossary of Semiotics*, is a term traditionally defined as "aliquid stat pro aliquo" or something that stands for

something else. Sign is used alongside of other terms with similar meanings such as "symbols," "icons," and "myths." (New York: Paragon House, 1993) 179–180. Charles S. Peirce specified three types of signs according to the relationship between the sign and the object. The grouping of three types of signs or Trichotomy includes: the icon, index, and symbol. The icon designates a sign that specifically resembles the object or produces a mental image of the object such as a map that represents a region or territory. If the sign that points to something, indicates it, or directly relates to an object by physical or actual connection as smoke escaping from a fire, then the sign is called an index or indexical sign. If a sign stands in place of an object like a single red rose as the symbol for affection, then it is a symbol. For further information see Colapietro, *Glossary of Semiotics* (New York: Paragon House, 1993), Max H. Fisch, *Pierce, Semiotic, and Pragmatism* eds. Kenneth Laine Ketner and Christian J. W. Kloesel, (Bloomington: Indiana University Press, 1986), and C. M. Smith, "The Aesthetics of Charles S. Peirce" *The Journal of Aesthetics and Art Criticism* 31.1 (Fall, 1972): 21–29.

18. Arnheim, 103.

19. Louis Altusser, "Ideology and Ideological State Apparatuses," *Lenin and Philosophy and Other Essays* trans. Ben Brewster (London: Monthly Review Press, 1977) 11, quoted in Julia Thomas, ed. *Reading Images* (New York: Palgrave, 2000): 7.

20. Cook, "Music in Commercials," 38.

21. A Pandora user e-mailed creator Tim Westergren to make a complaint about Pandora. The user claimed that he provided a song by Sarah McLachlan on his personalized radio station and one of the songs that were suggested was by Celine Dion. Westergren asked the user if it was a malfunction in the system to which the user replied no, but he was shocked to see Celine Dion offered as a selection by Pandora. Dion is not positioned as culturally cool or hip, singing for the *Titanic* soundtrack and occasionally Las Vegas. The user was conditioned not to like her, but after seeing a computer system unaffected by tastes of popular culture post Dion in the same channel as McLachlan, he realized that they were similar stylistically. He had to throw off his cultural aversion to Dion and grew to like listening to her. Rob Walker, "The Song Decoders" *New York Times Magazine,* 18 October 2009: 48–53.

22. When hearing "1901" by Phoenix in a Cadillac commercial, the listener connects the sound of the song with the moving pictures of the car. In the short span of a commercial, "One or two notes in a distinctive musical style are sufficient to target a specific social and demographic group, and to associate a whole nexus of social and cultural values with the product." Cook, *Music and Commercials,* 35. Sometimes we are consciously aware of these audio-visual outlets that occur in rapid fire as they constantly join sound and picture with our eyes and ears. Other times we are able to bypass music and the image associated with it as background noise. Thus, once these images are shown in a film or commercial, the listeners are primed to recall specific images from the film or commercial when they hear the music. Outside of the audio-visual realm, popular music can become culturally "assigned" to an event or image of an event. As in sports, "Welcome to the Jungle" by Guns N' Roses is commonly used at the beginning or during a game, as is "Crazy Train" by Ozzy Osbourne and "Rock and Roll, Pt. 2" by Gary Glitter. Such songs are used to excite fans and encourage the

sportsmanship of the game. Thus, specific songs can be attributed to a visual event (NFL opening kickoff) that happens at a specific time and place. In other instances, images surrounding a particular tune can be stimulated by the time (Bob Marley's "What's Going On?") or place (John Denver's song "West Virginia").

23. There are constant streams of visual associations with popular music as seen through commercials, film, music videos, movies, album covers, the web, television, sporting events, cell phones, and digital devices, not to mention the social means of sharing music and images together through Facebook, Myspace, Hallmark cards that play a pop song when opened. Popular music has various roles in film and entertainment ranging from background music, diegetic or non-diegetic to some character association with the actors themselves. Of course, the most common examples occur in a multi-media format in which some form of popular music is specifically assigned to the visual image that it accompanies. For a summary on the history of music and narrative or music and video in particular see, Alf Bjornberg, "Structural Relationships of Music and Images in Music Video" *Popular Music* 13. 1 (Jan 1994): 51–74.

BIBLIOGRAPHY

Ake, David. *Jazz Cultures.* Berkeley: University of California Press, 2005.

Altusser, Louis. "Ideology and Ideological State Apparatuses," *Lenin and Philosophy and Other Essays* trans. Ben Brewster (London: Monthly Review Press, 1977) 11, quoted in Julia Thomas, ed. *Reading Images* (New York: Palgrave, 2000): 7.

Barthes, Roland. *Camera Lucida: Reflections on Photography.* New York: Hill and Wang, 1981.

Barthes, *Image, Music, Text* Trans. Stephen Heath. New York: Hill and Wang, 1977.

Barthes, *S/Z* Trans. Richard Miller. New York: Hill and Wang, 1974.

Bjornberg, Alf. "Structural Relationships of Music and Images in Music Video" *Popular Music* 13. 1 (Jan. 1994): 51–74.

Colapietro, Vincent M. *Glossary of Semiotics.* New York: Paragon House, 1993.

Cook, Nicholas. "Music and Meaning in the Commercials" *Popular Music*, Vol. 13, No. 1 (Jan. 1994): 39.

de Saussure, Ferdinand. *Course in General Linguistics* trans. Wade Baskin, (New York: McGraw-Hill, 1969.

Fisch, Max H. *Pierce, Semiotic, and Pragmatism* eds. Kenneth Laine Ketner and Christian J. W. Kloesel. Bloomington: Indiana University Press, 1986.

Forden, Sara Gay. "Keith Richards Is New Face of Vuitton as LVMH Promotes Luggage" *Bloomberg News,* 5 March 2008. Accessed 9 January 2010 http://www.bloomberg.com/apps/news?pid=newsarchive&sid=aFGtAVSoFBAw.

Foucault, Michel. *Language, Counter-Memory, Practice; Selected Essays and Interviews.* Ithaca: Cornell University Press, 1977.

Foucault. *The Order of Things: An Archaeology of the Human Sciences.* A Translation of *Les Mots et les choses.* New York: Vintage Books, 1970.

Foucault, *This is Not a Pipe* trans. and ed. James Harkness. Berkeley: University of California Press, 1983.

Gadamer, Hans-Georg. *Philosophical Hermeneutics* trans. and ed. David E. Linge. Berkeley: University of California Press, 1976.

Hall, Stuart, ed. *Representation: Cultural Representations and Signifying Practices.* London: Sage, 1998.

Lowry, Joanna. "Negotiating Power," from Mark Durden and Craig Richardson, eds., *Face On: Photography as Social Exchange.* London: Black Dog Publishing, 2000.

Mirzoeff, Nicholas. *An Introduction to Visual Culture.* New York: Routledge, 1999.

Pinson, Heather K. *The Jazz Image: Seeing Music Through Herman Leonard's Photography.* Jackson: University Press of Mississippi, 2010.

Smith, C. M. "The Aesthetics of Charles S. Peirce" *The Journal of Aesthetics and Art Criticism* 31.1 (Fall, 1972): 21–29.

Walker, Rob. "The Song Decoders" *New York Times Magazine,* 18 October 2009: 48–53.

Wild, David. "Johnny Depp & Keith Richards: *Pirates of the Caribbean*'s Blood Brothers" *Rolling Stone*, 31 May 2007. Accessed 10 January 2010 http://www .rollingstone.com/news/coverstory/johnny_depp__keith_richards_ipirates_of_the_ caribbeanis_blood_brothers.

11

Kanye West: A Critical Analysis of Mass Media's Representation of a Cultural Icon's Rhetoric and Celebrity

Hazel James Cole

"[President] George Bush doesn't care about black people."[1]

—*Kanye West (2005)*

The above quote catapulted superstar rapper Kanye West into the spotlight—not as the multiple Grammy Award–winning rapper—but, as an instant celebrity politician bringing awareness to the plight of African Americans in the wake of the deadly Hurricane Katrina. At least for a little while.

When Hurricane Katrina, a deadly Category 5 storm, ravaged New Orleans, Louisiana, and the Mississippi Gulf Coast in August 2005, no one could have expected the bureaucratic insanity that would follow for New Orleanians. While the world viewed shocking images of stranded, hungry, sick and many dead African Americans on national television, Kanye West shocked the world with seven words.

Nonetheless, the national media for several weeks broadcasted the black faces of New Orleanians as hopeless and helpless, without proper food and care for what seemed like an eternity. Mainstream media soon began to refer to the victims of Katrina as refugees instead of evacuees, contributing to the notion that the New Orleans' blacks were un-American and unimportant. A cynic might wonder why these "refugees" did not seek cover and that their failure to evacuate in a timely manner resulted in their own demise. The reality is that poor planning on local government's behalf and the lack of federal resources and information contributed to the bureaucratic failures, which cast a long shadow on the Bush administration. That long shadow would lead to an opportunity for the twenty-something-year-old Kanye West to voice his discontent about the documented slow government response under President George W. Bush's administration. Kanye was one of several celebrities participating in a live telethon and concert produced by NBC News titled "A Concert for Hurricane Relief." He was not scheduled to perform, however. Kanye was paired with comedian Mike Myers and read from a prepared script. The segment began with Myers speaking about the devastation of Hurricane Katrina in New Orleans and the Mississippi Gulf Coast. In an instant, Kanye took the opportunity to depart from the script to criticize the leader of the free world by calling him a racist on national television. He said:

> I hate the way they portray us in the media. If you see a black family, it says they're looting. See a white family, it says they're looking for food. And you know that it's been five days, because most of the people are black. And even for me to complain about it, I would be a hypocrite because I've tried to turn away from the TV, because it's too hard to watch. We already realize a lot of people that could help are at war right now, fighting another way, and they have given them permission to go down and shoot us . . . George Bush doesn't care about black people.[2]

That rallying cry was heard verbatim in some markets. *The New York Times* writer Sean Alfano wrote, "The show, simulcast from New York on NBC, MSNBC, CNBC and Pax, was aired live to the East Coast, enabling the Grammy-winning rapper's outburst to go out uncensored."[3]

Kanye's words echoed perhaps what many people were thinking. His declaration would, in essence, become his political moment for "representing" for African Americans, not as a rapper but as an American citizen.

Issues of race and poverty would become mainstream topics of discussion for months to come. Public intellectual Dr. Michael Eric Dyson chronicled the African American suffering in his book, *Come Hell or High Water: Hurricane Katrina and the Color of Disaster.* Dyson poignantly explains that President George Bush and a white-run system of bureaucracy had failed the minority citizens of New Orleans. He stated:

> But Hurricane Katrina's violent winds and killing waters swept into the mainstream a stark realization: the poor had been abandoned by society and its institutions, and sometimes by their well-off brothers and sisters, long before the storm. We are immediately confronted with another unsavory truth: it is the exposure of the extremes, not their existence that stumps our national sense of decency.[4]

Dyson's explanation mirrors Kanye's seven words depicting President Bush's perceived lack of humanity toward ethnic minority groups as revealed through mass media's 24-hour media coverage of the Katrina disaster. Cultural critic Mark Anthony Neal (2006) notes that rappers are not known for garnering national publicity for something they said. He determined that Kanye West's magnificent power in the media is generally unheard of:

> West . . . has made his impact on the level of discourse—when was the last time a "rapper" drew attention to herself because of what he or she said? Despite the fact that many believe that hip-hop's importance resides in its rhetorical power, there are relatively few examples of hip-hop artists drawing mainstream attention for the content of their rhetoric—not as popular musicians—but as citizens providing social commentary.[5]

RAP AND IDEOLOGICAL HEGEMONY

In hip hop culture, most rappers come from urban settings where poverty and violence are commonplace. In many cases, their rap lyrics express anger about these types of conditions. Kanye West does not come from "the streets" as many of his counterparts but enjoyed a middle-class upbringing. However, as a rapper he uses his celebrity and music to connect with audiences about his own politics and creativity. In that context, rap music serves as a mechanism to express discontent about society's social ills and resistance to ideological hegemony and the "establishment." Ideology sets the dominant cultural norms and ideas in hip hop culture.

In this chapter I analyze the social aspects of ideology, including the role of Kanye West as a *conscious* rapper and cultural icon, representing the minority voice of the marginalized as it relates to the Hurricane Katrina disaster. French sociologist Pierre Bourdieu suggests that knowledge has tremendous power in our society.[6] In that vein, Kanye West, as a cultural icon, uses his music, knowledge, public relations skills and finesse, in tandem with mass media, to reach key audiences in an effort to educate, empower and attract mainstream audiences. His use of mass media as a communications vehicle, either through coverage of his public outbursts, public appearances or published documentation of his music sales, is necessary in creating and maintaining his image.

With rappers in general, music is a powerful way to communicate messages of political, economic and social conditions in society. Kanye's political rhetoric is juxtaposed with his on-stage antics and need for media exposure, paired with his obsession with publicity, is one way he employs public relations strategies to garner favorable publicity or at best, any publicity.

In her book, *Black Noise: Rap Music and Black Culture in Contemporary America*, hip hop scholar Tricia Rose suggests that rap music "takes place under intense public surveillance, similar contradictions regarding class, gender, and race are highlighted, decontextualized, and manipulated so as to destabilize rap's resistive elements."[7] In the context of consumer culture and freedom of expression, Rose points out that "rapper's speech acts are also heavily shaped by music industry demands, sanctions, and prerogatives."[8] That is to say that rap music's social critiques from within the industry are influenced by hegemonic forces that control the medium and essentially the social argument or ideological message. In that context, it may explain why Kanye seized the moment to "perform" an extemporaneous political act during a live broadcast where network censorship would be almost impossible. Whether planned or spontaneous, Kanye had opportunity, target audience, key message on an emotional topic, and the brilliance to spread his political rhetoric at the television network's expense.

Kanye's rant and resistance to the "establishment" contributed to his celebrity iconic status by positioning him as a temporary legitimate voice of the African American community during the Katrina disaster. Kanye is the type of rapper that falls into Antonio Gramsci's ideology of "organic intellectuals" and his position as a rapper/producer is further reinforced by his mainstream acceptance. Nathan Abrams extends his ideas of Gramscian thought to "those rappers who consciously and explicitly claim to speak for their communities."[9] Historian George Lipsitz explained Gramsci's ideology of traditional intellectuals as "experts in legitimation" and "organic intellectuals" serve to "give voice to the repressed needs and aspirations of oppressed groups."[10] In a culture of access, "organic intellectuals" (rap musicians) give us instant gratifications such as rebellion and freedom of expression. They also have the platform (mass media) to express what others might be thinking. The question becomes, "How often do we hear the minority voice in media?" The implication is that media are powerful in that they help us interpret our existence. Rappers use media as a filter to provide information and insight into the political consciousness of the rap artist by connecting people to cultural differences and social disturbances, as cultural studies scholar Stuart Hall describes as "partial synchronization, of engagement across cultural boundaries, of the confluence of more than one cultural tradition, of the negotiations of dominant and subordinate positions," meaning rap's place in history transcends boundaries and culture. [11] It is important to mention that there are other "cultural producers" of resistance music who operate independently as "underground" artists who resist hegemonic oppression in the music industry and in society and have not quite achieved mainstream favor like Kanye has. An example of these underground artists (dead prez, Talib Kweli, and numerous others) often rap about the oppression of the marginalized.

Hip hop, as a capitalistic culture also falls in line with Gramsci's concept of hegemony, where power is in the hands of the elite or ruling class in society (e.g., the owners of mass media).[12] Hip hop's success is perpetuated by white media institutions who determine what music will be produced, how it is disseminated and what images (mainly negative ones in hip hop) are mediated to consumer audiences. Fiske proclaims that "ideological forces of domination are at work in all products of patriarchal consumer capitalism."[13] When it comes to hegemonic capitalistic ideologies, it can be inferred that rappers are victims being part of their own victimization. I argue that the hegemonic power structure is only part of the problem. Contributing to the hegemonic dynamic, rappers are compliant in creating music to achieve economic outcomes. In the end, the creation of and the production and dissemination of negative rap music essentially achieves hegemonic ends. *TIME* writer Christopher John Farley wrote, "Hip-hop is perhaps the only art form that celebrates capitalism openly. . . .Rap's unabashed materialism distinguishes it sharply from some of the dominant musical genres of the past century."[14] Roger Simon notes that hegemony "gains the consent of other classes and social forces through creating and maintaining a system of alliances by means of political and ideological struggle."[15] As Lipsitz noted, those in power "must make their triumphs appear legitimate and necessary in the eyes of the vanquished. "[16] Under this view, White suggests:

> Social and cultural conflict is expressed as a struggle for hegemony, a struggle over which ideas are recognized as the prevailing, commonsense view for the majority of social participants. Hegemony appears to be spontaneous, even natural, but it is the historical result of the prestige enjoyed by the ruling class by virtue of their position and function in the world of production.[17]

In essence, hip hop is important for a number of reasons as it relates to ideology. First, rappers are able to relate to large and diverse audiences in some way; whether it's a personal struggle or political preference, their relationship to their listeners is essential. Second, hip hop is important because of capitalism. In order to make a living and gain notoriety, most rappers succumb to those in power to create music that is cloaked in misogyny and materialism.

KANYE WEST: CELEBRITY AND CONTROVERSY AS BRANDING STRATEGIES

A celebrity can be defined as an individual that is known for being well known and occupies space in the public spotlight.[18] Kanye's controversies perhaps have been a strategy to assist in the development of his own brand—the outspoken hip hop creative genius with a flair for couture. Branding is defined as "the promise, the big idea, and the expectations that reside in each customer's mind about a product, service or company."[19] That brand reinforces his celebrity. Whether in music, sports, film, television or any medium, celebrities are held in high regard. Kanye's trajectory as a celebrity or media figure was evident with his commercially successful debut album *College Dropout*, which earned ten nominations at the 47th annual Grammy Awards in 2004. *Billboard* reported that Kanye's first album won multiple Grammy Awards including: Best Rap Album for *The College Dropout*; Best Rap Song for "Jesus Walks" and a songwriting credit on "You Don't Know My Name" by Alicia Keys and Harold Lily. His sophomore album *Late Registration* won the coveted "Album of the Year" award at the 2005 Grammy Award ceremonies.[20]

His distinctive image is often noted and his look and style demands attention. His savvy eye for fashion and his ultra-casual high fashion attire are frequently talked about in entertainment and fashion magazines. In 1999, *TIME* reported on how corporations were taking note of hip hop's influence on the fashion industry and culture, noting that Madison Avenue recognized rap's entrepreneurial spirit: "Tommy Hilfiger has positioned his apparel company as the clothier of the hip-hop set, and he now does a billion dollars a year in oversize shirts, loose jeans, and so on."[21] Celebrities influence our thoughts about fashion and the image we want to create. For example, Kanye's designer clothes and bright smile are distinct signs of his trademark image. Kanye is so popular that his image has been commodified and he has made appearances in national commercials for Pepsi and other companies. According to Ian Crystal, brand director with Absolut Vodka, West was featured in a 2008 Absolut Vodka ad titled "Be Kanye in an Absolut World." Crystal said of the Kanye West-Absolut partnership:

> Absolut has a long history of working with engaging artists, beginning with Andy Warhol and continuing over the last 27 years. As we usher in a new creative era with our 'In An Absolut World' advertising campaign, we want to work with artists who spark dialogue and inspire people in the 21st century. . . . This collaboration with Kanye West, whose creative talents extend far beyond his musical career, will use our collective voice to bring style and excitement to our consumers.[22]

Kanye is an exemplary example of a black man that mainstream America finds palatable, considering the gangsta and/or criminal image is perhaps the most mediated image in popular culture. *Rolling Stone* writer Lola Ogunnaike (2006) states, "West is one of the most popular and polarizing artists in music today. And while he's sold more than 4 million albums to date, he is known for his outspokenness as he is for his hitmaking ability . . . not since Tupac Shakur has a rapper been so compelling, so ridiculously brash, so irresistibly entertaining."[23]

USA Today writer Jenny Eliscu in her article "Genius is as Genius Does" expounds on West's genius possibility:

A multi-platinum rapper and producer who is, some say, his generation's most prodigiously gifted hip-hop artist, West has a theory or two about genius and expounds on them with a mixture of enthusiasm and bravado that hints at why critics tend to call him arrogant. West, however, insists that he's just telling things like they are. And, when it comes to the topic of genius, he sees it like this: Anybody can have isolated strokes of genius, but if someone keeps having them, it's fair to say that the person actually is a genius.[24]

Kanye is the exception to the rule when it comes to dark-skinned black men and the stereotypical images portrayed on television, in music videos or in film. He serves as a cultural signifier who represents the social significance of "black" success and he is an example of mainstream's social acceptance of the minimal amount of "good" that rap music can represent. As a polysemic signifier, Kanye represents many fantasies for black male youth. For instance, his race is a signifier, his creativity is unmatched in the music industry, he is a mentor and role model for young black males, and he's rich (in assets and in creativity). Even with his admitted transgressions (his views on gay relationships, his over-the-top egotistical antics on stage), the media are somehow turned on by his rebellious behavior. Furthermore, he delivers on his promise of creating great music that crosses the boundaries into mainstream arenas. Thus, when Kanye seeks attention, the media play into it. That media attention translates to what Douglas Kellner refers to as "media spectacle." Kellner notes that media culture contributes to the fantasy world of celebrity. He writes, "Media culture not only takes up always-expanding amounts of time and energy, but also provides ever more material for fantasy, dreaming, modeling thought and behavior, and identities."[25]

Celebrities embody the spectacle that we (as a society) seem to aspire to become. America's youth are in tune with celebrities and their interests, whether it is their occupation, political viewpoint or, in Kanye West's case, the widely reported death of his mother in 2007. A celebrity's influence also helps the fan base identify with what's relevant to them personally. For instance, West's outrage against President George W. Bush could be viewed as a single event. Yet when the controversy exploded, the outburst took on the liveliness of an intertextual media event. Whether he planned the "spectacle" or acted spontaneously on live television, it became fare for all media. The Bush criticism by a black man was speculated about across the media: in newspapers and magazines, on the Internet, and on televised national news programs such as "Larry King Live" on CNN. Black Entertainment Television (BET) hosted programs to openly discuss race and politics in the aftermath of Hurricane Katrina and the bureaucratic nightmare that led to minorities being treated as what the national news media called "refugees" or second-class citizens in America. Further, Kanye's criticism of this country's most powerful leader received national media attention and created a platform for open dialogue in the mass media on how this country has historically failed its minority citizens. Mass media outlets are the places where the public gains access to celebrities. For Kanye, mass media serve as an open door into every household that has some form of technology—whether it is the Internet, television, radio, iTunes downloads or other technological advances that make media accessible.

There are important implications in the discussion of Kanye West as a cultural icon and celebrity. If you take his philanthropic work, his creative genius in the music industry, his high-fashion style and the work he is doing as an activist, he becomes this multi-faceted person that can relate to many people on many levels. Interest in West is then extended beyond his familiar musical persona and parlance. He becomes more of a "real" person, which authenticates him in the eyes of minority groups and his rhetoric filters into mainstream media attracting broader audiences. This connection is powerful because West is elevated to what anthropologist Christine Yano calls "commodified identity," which explains how images are cultivated and perpetuated.[26] Just as the American flag can serve as the primary symbol of freedom and pride, Kanye's role as a cultural icon is symbolic in that he represents one dimension of the *black* American dream. He represents "the dream" that the Rev. Dr. Martin Luther King spoke about in civil rights speeches. He represents hope and prosperity in a capitalistic culture, serving as a symbol of wealth and enterprise, which is fascinating to both black and white folks in America. Another dimension he adds to his iconic status is that white folks are not only buying his music in record numbers, contributing to his financial success, but his image has been branded in advertising campaigns. He takes advantage of the fact that white teenagers are buying his music and are enthralled by hip hop. They not only buy his music, they also attend his concerts with a heightened expectation of what *The Seattle Times* writer Patrick Mac-Donald calls a "good performance." MacDonald said of West's August 2008 concert at KeyArena in Seattle that "it's the biggest rap show to ever play Seattle." He expounds on West's media hype and his braggadocios behavior:

> It's comical sometimes, the way West needs to brag that he's the greatest. He's so sensitive about it that he gets easily offended when reminded that maybe he's not as talented as he thinks. The way he keeps harping on himself, you figure he must have to constantly stroke his own ego just to stay in the game . . . But in reality he doesn't have to say a thing. The boasts are unnecessary. All he has

to do is get on stage and *show* us how great he is. A good performance is worth a thousand boasts.[27]

Over the past few years, West has used his celebrity to garner favorable publicity by making the cover of mainstream news publications such as *TIME,* high-end male fashion magazines such as *GQ* and entertainment publications such as *Rolling Stone.* No stranger to controversy, West's portrayal as Jesus Christ with a crown of thorns on his head on the February 9, 2006, cover of *Rolling Stone* stirred emotions from religious groups and drew criticism from major news outlets and others. "The Passion of Kanye West" cover is a paradoxical reference to the box office smash "The Passion of The Christ," a Mel Gibson film about the last twelve hours of Jesus of Nazareth's life.

At the time Kanye graced the covers of this entertainment publication, he was a 27-year-old rapper/producer who had been nominated for eight Grammy awards, including album of the year for his sophomore album *Late Registration.*[28] Offended Christian organizations such as the Catholic League for Religious and Civil Rights criticized West and *Rolling Stone.* The Catholic League's president, William Donahue, took issue with both West and the magazine, calling the publication "racist" for not publishing a similar submitted photograph of radio shock jock Howard Stern years earlier. On the organization's website, Donahue's disapproving comments were perhaps indicative of what many Christian white readers felt:

> If it is true that West is a morally confused black young man, it is also true that Rolling Stone is staffed by morally challenged white veterans: they are to West what white boxing agents in the 20th century were to black boxers—rip-off artists. It is not for nothing that West poses as a Christ-like figure on a magazine geared to whites. To top it off, the white readership is bound to get a kick out of knowing that the 'The Passion of Kanye West' is the rapper's self-confessed passion for pornography.[29]

Adding fuel to the flame, Christian writers Jason Barnes and Jim Meyers in their article "Christians Angered by Kanye West Mockery" posted on the religious Web site also expressed outrage over West's photograph, stating that offended Christian groups have called the cover image "sacrilegious" and "an insult to Christians."[30] Charnaine Yoest, vice president of the Family Research Council concurred with the Christian criticism of West stating, "I think Kanye West is a distraction from the real story. . . . The real story is *Rolling Stone* mocking millions of Christians in this country and worldwide who believe in Jesus Christ. . . . This is an issue of corporate responsibility."[31]

The reaction to West's controversial cover is an example of the white-privileged religious ideology in this country and the juxtaposition of a young black man portraying the "son of God." How dare a rapper portray such a sacred image in a hegemonic and patriarchal culture where the worldview of Jesus is associated with purity and the "white" race? For Kanye, I argue that he used the controversial magazine cover and article to shock people into learning more about his religious and personal politics by presenting an image of "I'm equal to Jesus Christ," which resulted in mainstream publications, religious organizations and others expressing criticism across media outlets, contributing to the discourse surrounding rap music. It also garnered intense publicity for Kanye, if only for a little while. The very idea of his self-critique coupled with his large ego elevates him to a level where he, for a moment, had the world stage to showcase the power of his celebrity. That world stage is the paradoxical fine line where West makes his comparison to Jesus Christ—through words and actions which are compelling and cause for intellectual examination. It is not important whether West thinks of himself as Christ. It's obvious the spectacle he creates when he pushes the envelope to gain media attention, which results in dialogue associated with social attitudes about his controversies. I argue that Kanye is what Gramsci refers to as an "organic intellectual" to one group, a creative musical genius to another, a superstar or cultural icon to a large segment of the population. Kanye also diverted attention from the type of publicity generally associated with hip hop—a misogynistic, materialistic, women-bashing culture of disrespect—to the polar opposite of mainstream rapper whose persona is elevated to a divine state.

Kanye does more than create good music. He has the power to make mainstream audiences and media institutions pay attention to what he has to say, even if the content and context is controversial. He cannot be discounted in popular culture because his relationship with his audience members and mass media together ultimately contribute to his popularity. Even *TIME,* one of America's top mainstream news magazines recognized Kanye's star power and genius characteristics. He has achieved what no other black male hip hop artist has accomplished thus far in the history of *TIME* magazine—making the cover of the August 29, 2005, issue.[32] Only one other hip hop artist has experienced this milestone; singer-actress, Lauryn Hill, was the first hip hop artist (male or female) to make the historic front cover on February 8, 1999.[33]

Kanye's heightened celebrity led to more front cover exposure and in-depth coverage with mainstream entertainment publications like *Entertainment Weekly* and African-American targeted publications such as *VIBE, Source* and others.

In addition, many of Kanye's song lyrics address his stance on political issues and his views on media ownership and hegemonic challenges. Jason Birchmeier (2008) with *Billboard* confirms Kanye's crossover appeal to mainstream audiences and his iconic status. He states:

It's worth noting how West shattered certain stereotypes about rappers. Whether it was his appearance or his rhetoric, or even just his music, this young man became a superstar on his own terms, and his singularity no doubt is part of his appeal to a great many people, especially those who don't generally consider themselves rap listeners.[34]

Kanye reached No. 1 on the *Billboard* charts with his inaugural album *The College Dropout* in 2004 on Roc-A-Fella Records. This album won the Grammy Award for Best Rap Album. The song "Jesus Walks" won for the Best Rap Song. His sophomore album in 2005 titled *Late Registration* won Album of the Year.[35]

Throughout the narrative in West's songs, he articulates the plight of blacks and his music represents various contradictions in black life and expresses his anti-establishment ideology in many of his songs.

West's success in music and his politics are interrelated. While West maximizes his fame by appearing in mass media in multiple forms (rapper, philanthropist, activist), he certainly fits the definition of what Boorstin refers to as "celebrity" who is "known for well-known"[36] regardless of "whether that eminence derives from the entertainment field, medicine, science, politics, religion, sports, or close association with other celebrities."[37] His celebrity status continues to evolve. Whether he sets a trend in fashion, criticizes the president of the United States, loses a parent, or makes unwelcomed appearances on stage to interrupt the spotlight for another celebrity, he garners publicity in mass media.

As a culture, we try to make sense of the world around us. We try to understand popular culture without considerations of global exploitation and capitalist injustices. Our ever-increasing demand for more celebrity, more mediated reality, more status and more information contributes to the continued growth of a culture of access and a culture of excess. Within that culture of access and excess is celebrity worship and heroism. Boorstin explained celebrities are different from heroes. He posits that the "hero created himself; the celebrity is created by the media. The hero was a big man, the celebrity a big name."[38] Kanye blurs the line between commodification and his self-righteous rhetoric with the branding of his image. He bragged about his designer clothes; when he didn't win music awards, he loudly showed his discontent; yet he consistently cranked out hits. In media saturated countries such as the United States, celebrities can have an enormous impact on the social behavior of their followers. As a celebrity, Kanye has tremendous influence because his fans can be forgiving of his controversial actions. The music industry rewards him with nominations and awards for his music; he garners publicity via mass media, thereby reaching broader segments of the population. In that vein, when

Kanye's mother, Dr. Donda West, passed away in 2007, his fans could relate to losing a parent or loved one. When Kanye called President George Bush a racist on national television, his African American fan base applauded his reaction to the "establishment's" bureaucratic failure. When he disappeared from the spotlight to grieve his mother's death and to reflect on past mistakes, his public persona would remain and his creative genius would continue to flourish. An example of Kanye's impact on popular culture would become more evident when he not only appeared on Fox's *American Idol*, but one of the final two contestants would perform his hit song "Heartless." According to *American Idol*'s Web site, Kris Allen performed the song in a final pairing with Adam Lambert and a "record-setting number of votes were cast, with nearly 100 million votes cast on Tuesday night, and a total of 624 million votes cast this season alone."[39] It is not certain what, if any, impact Kanye West's appearance and performance on *American Idol* had on the viewing and voting public. What we know is that Allen's performance and his winning the coveted title as the Season 8 winner cannot be ignored. The connection between a cultural icon's appearance on the show, a contestant's performance of the icon's popular song, and the enormous number of votes cast demonstrates Kanye's ability to create dialogue among followers and non-followers and move people to action or perhaps reaction.

Although he has moved on past his much-publicized Hurricane Katrina emotional outburst in 2005 where he was deemed a temporary "hero," opportunity for other on-stage antics would continue. One rant in particular was the 2009 MTV Video Music Awards (VMAs) held at Radio City Music Hall. The award-winning rapper stormed the stage in protest just after the first award for Best Female Video was presented to the teen country/pop music sensation Taylor Swift. Apparently, Kanye thought Beyoncé Knowles was deserving of the honor. [40] According to *The New York Times*, "Ms. Swift had her microphone taken by Mr. West, who told the audience that Beyonce's video in the same category was "one of the best of all time" and should have won the award instead. A stunned Ms. Swift stood by in shocked silence, unable to continue her acceptance speech."[41] Once again, an apology followed, which doesn't excuse his behavior. However, apologizing is necessary to demonstrate some level of remorse.

It wouldn't be long before Kanye would once again garner national media coverage with six Grammy Awards nominations in 2010. Ironically, Kanye would be absent from the 52nd annual Grammy Awards held in February, and according to MTV the hip-hop superstar "was not only missing from the performance of "Forever" (which also features Drake, Lil Wayne and Eminem) but also missed out on collecting a pair of awards—Best Rap Song and Best Rap/Sung Collaboration, both for his team-up with Jay-Z and Rihanna on "Run This Town.""[42] Perhaps his action to not make an appearance was part of his strategy for managing his image amid the recent Taylor Swift controversy. Whatever the rationale, his absence was as controversial as his presence at events, garnering media attention once again.

The New York Times writer Jon Caramanica offers clarity to some of Kanye's actions throughout the new millennium,

> These moments were blasts of arrogance, sure, but also showed the raw pain of rejection laid bare. In an era where micro-confession became the main form of communication, and where masquerade was rewarded with scrutiny and dismantling, Mr. West helped set the tone. Important moments and insignificant ones tend to have the same value in his world. His mother dies, he assaults a paparazzo, President Obama calls him "a jackass:" it's all just more data for the live stream.[43]

Kanye's musical success and his politics are interrelated. His reputation as a venter is solid. While he maximizes his fame by appearing in mass media in multiple forms (rapper, philanthropist, activist, troublemaker), he certainly fits the definition of what Boorstin refers to as "celebrity" who is "known for well-known"[44] regardless of "whether that eminence derives from the entertainment field, medicine, science, politics, religion, sports, or close association with other celebrities."[45] Like him, love him, or hate him, Kanye's brand is fueled by creative genius, controversy and high fashion in a global, media saturated society.

NOTES

1. Alfano, Sean. 2005. Rapper blasts Bush over Katrina: Kanye West says Bush 'Doesn't care about black people' on telethon, September 3, http://www.cbsnews.com/stories/2005/09/03/katrina/main814636.shtml (accessed January 23, 2010).

2. Goodman, A. 2007. Kanye West: "George Bush doesn't care about black people." http://www.democracynow.org/2005/9/6/kanye_west_bush_doesnt_care_about (accessed August 30, 2008).

3. Alfano, September 3, 2005.

4. Dyson, Michael Eric, *Come hell or high water: Hurricane Katrina and the color of disaster*, p. 2.

5. Neal, Mark Anthony. Kanye walks, http://www.seeingblack.com/printer_10.shtml, accessed July 31, 2008.

6. Bourdieu, Pierre. 1980. The aristocracy of culture, *Media, Culture and Society*, 2, 225–54.

7. Rose, Tricia. *Black Noise: Rap music and black culture in contemporary America.* Hanover: University Press of New England, 104.

8. Rose, 104.

9. Abrams, Nathan. 1992. Antonio's B-boys: Rap, rappers and Gramsci's intellectuals. *Popular Music and Society*, 16(3), p. 1.

10. Lipsitz, George. 1988. The struggle for hegemony, *Journal of American History* 75(1), 146.

11. Hall, Stuart, *Representation, meaning and language.* In *Representation: Culture representations and signifying practices,* ed. Stuart Hall, 28–29. Thousand Oaks: Sage.

12. Gramsci, Antonio. 1983. *Selection from the prison* notebooks, ed. Quintin Hoare and Geoffrey Nowell-Smith. New York: International Publishers.

13. Fiske, John. 1989. *Reading the popular.* London: Routledge.

14. Farley, Christopher John. 1999. Hip-hop nation. February 8. *TIME.* http://www.time.com/time/printout/0,8816,990164,00.html (accessed August 3, 2008).

15. Simon, Roger. 1991. *Gramsci's political thought.* New York: Lawrence & Wishart.

16. Lipsitz, 147.

17. White, 167.

18. Boorstin, Daniel J. 1961. *The image: A guide to pseudo-events in America,* New York: Harper and Row. Gamson, J.1992. The assembly line of greatness: Celebrity in the twentieth century America, *Critical Studies in Mass Communication,* 9: 1–24.

19. Wheeler, Alina. 2006. *Designing brand identity: A complete guide to creating, building, and maintaining strong brands.* Hoboken: John Wiley & Sons.

20. Birchmeier, Jason. 2008. Kanye West biography, August 12, http://www.billboard.com/bbcom/bio/index.jsp?pid=322005 (accessed August 12, 2008).

21. Farley, n.p.

22. Crystal, Ian. 2008. *Absolut partners with Kanye West.* http://www.beverage world.com/content/view/34806/ accessed October 28, 2008 quoted in concluding paragraph.

23. Ogunnaike, L. 2006. Kanye West world: A nerdy Midwestern kid braces to become America's most provocative pop star, February 9. http://www.rollingstone.com/news/story/9183008/cover_story_kanye_west_world/print (accessed July 31, 2008).

24. Eliscu, J. 2007. Genius is as genius does, *USA Weekend,* August 19. http://www.usaweekend.com/07_issues/070819/070819kanye_west.html (accessed August 3, 2008).

25. Kellner, Douglas. 2003. Media spectacle. New York: Routledge.

26. Yano, Christine. Intervening selves: Images and image-making in a Japanese popular music genre. *Journal of Popular Culture* 31(2): 125.

27. MacDonald, Patrick. 2008. Kanye West gets a chance to put his money where his mouth is at Key Arena. The Seattle Times, April 11., n.p. http://seattletimes.nwsource.com/html/musicnightlife/2004340276_kanye110.html (accessed July 31, 2008).

28. MSNBC. 2006. Kanye West plays Jesus on Rolling Stone: Rapper poses with a crown of thorns atop his head. http://www.msnbc.msn.com/id/11009059/from/RSS/ (accessed July 28, 2008).

29. Donahue, William.2008. Is Rolling Stone racist? Catholic League for Religious and Civil Rights. http://www.catholicleague.org/catalyst.php?year=2006& month=March&read=2005 (assessed July 31, 2008).

30. Barnes, Jason, and Jim Meyers. Christians angered by Kanye West mockery. http://archive.newsmax.com/archives/articles/2006/1/25/180150.shtml?s=rss (accessed July 31, 2008).

31. Yoest, Charnaine. 2006. This quote is taken from Jason Barnes and Jim Meyers' article "Christians angered by Kanye West Mockery" found at http://archive .newsmax.com/archives/articles/2006/1/25/180150.shtml?s=rss (accessed July 31, 2008).

32. *TIME*, August 29, 2005. Kanye West graced the cover of this news magazine as the first African-American hip hop male rapper in the magazine's history.

33. *TIME*. February 8, 1999. Singer-actress, Lauryn Hill, was the first hip hop artist (male or female) to make the historic front cover on February 8, 1999.

34. Birchmeier, n.p.

35. Birchmeier, n.p.

36. Boorstin, Daniel. 1961. *The image: A guide to pseudo-events in America.* New York: Harper and Row.

37. McCutcheon, L., R. Lange and J. Houran. 2002. Conceptualization and measurement of celebrity worship. *British Journal of Psychology* 13: 67–87.

38. Boorstin, 61.

39. Congratulations, Kris Allen! May 21, 2009, http://americanidol.com/news/ view/pid/1739/ (accessed May 24, 2010). Kris Allen was crowned the Season 8 winner, beating Adam Lambert for the coveted title.

40. Rodriguez, Jason (with additional reporting by Montgomery, James and Reid, Shaheem). Kanye West crashes VMA stage during Taylor Swift's award speech: Kanye continues his history of onstage award-show rants. May 4, http://www.mtv .com/news/articles/1621389/20090913/west_kanye.jhtml (accessed May 24, 2010).

41. Kanye West, September 15, 2009. Retrieved from http://topics.nytimes.com/top/ reference/timestopics/people/w/kanye_west/index.html?scp=1-spot&sq=kanye%20 west%20&st=cse (accessed July 1, 2010).

42. Anderson, Kyle. Grammy No-Show Kanye West Is 'Doing Really Good,' Common Says (February 1, 2010). Retrieved from http://www.mtv.com/news/ articles/1630920/20100201/west_kanye.jhtml, (accessed July 4, 2010).

43. Caramanica, Jon. 2009. Creativity and chaos, served in equal measure. *The New York Times*, December 30, Music section, http://www.nytimes .com/2010/01/03/arts/music/03kanye.html, accessed January 26, 2010. Also, in the September 14, 2009 edition of the *The Los Angeles Times,* writer Andrew Malcolm reported that an ABC reporter Twittered to a million or so folks that President Obama unofficially called Kanye West a "jackass," for his outburst at the Video Music Awards after country music star Taylor Swift beat out hip hop star Beyonce for the top award.

44. Boorstin, 1961, p. 57.

45. McCutcheon, Lange & Houran, 2002, p. 67.

BIBLIOGRAPHY

Abrams, Nathan. Antonio's B-boys: Rap, rappers and Gramsci's intellectuals. *Popular Music and Society*, 16(3), 1992.

Alfano, Sean. Rapper blasts Bush over Katrina: Kanye West says Bush 'Doesn't care about black people' on telethon, September 3, 2005. http://www.cbsnews.com/stories/2005/09/03/katrina/main814636.shtml (accessed January 23, 2010).

Anderson, Kyle. "Grammy No-Show Kanye West Is 'Doing Really Good,' Common Says," Feb. 1, 2010. Retrieved from http://www.mtv.com/news/articles/1630920/20100201/west_kanye.jhtml, (accessed July 4, 2010).

Barnes, Jason, and Jim Meyers. "Christians angered by Kanye West mockery." http://archive.newsmax.com/archives/articles/2006/1/25/180150.shtml?s=rss (accessed July 31, 2008).

Birchmeier, Jason. Kanye West biography, August 12, 2008. http://www.billboard.com/bbcom/bio/index.jsp?pid=322005 (accessed August 12, 2008).

Boorstin, Daniel J. *The image: A guide to pseudo-events in America*, New York: Harper and Row, 1961.

Bourdieu, Pierre. "The aristocracy of culture," *Media, Culture and Society, 2*, 225–254, 1980.

Caramanica, Jon. Creativity and chaos, served in equal measure. *The New York Times*, December 30, 2009. Music section, http://www.nytimes.com/2010/01/03/arts/music/03kanye.html, accessed January 26, 2010.

Congratulations, Kris Allen! May 21, 2009, http://americanidol.com/news/view/pid/1739/ (accessed May 24, 2010).

Crystal, Ian. *Absolut partners with Kanye West*. 2008. http://www.beverageworld.com/content/view/34806/ accessed October 28, 2008 quoted in concluding paragraph.

Donahue, William. "Is Rolling Stone racist?" Catholic League for Religious and Civil Rights. http://www.catholicleague.org/catalyst.php?year=2006&month=March&read=2005 (accessed July 31, 2008).

Dyson, Michael Eric, *Come hell or high water: Hurricane Katrina and the color of disaster*.

Eliscu, J. "Genius is as genius does," *USA Weekend*, August 19, 2007. http://www.usawekend.com/07_issues/070819/070819kanye_west.html (accessed August 3, 2008).

Farley, Christopher John. "Hip-hop nation." *TIME*. February 8, 1999. http://www.time.com/time/printout/0,8816,990164,00.html (accessed August 3, 2008).

Fiske, John. *Reading the popular*. London: Routledge, 1989.

Gamson, J. "The assembly line of greatness: Celebrity in the twentieth century America," *Critical Studies in Mass Communication, 9*: 1–24, 1992.

Goodman, A. Kanye West: "George Bush doesn't care about black people." 2007. http://www.democracynow.org/2005/9/6/kanye_west_bush_doesnt_care_about

Gramsci, Antonio. *Selection from the prison notebooks*, ed. Quintin Hoare and Geoffrey Nowell-Smith. New York: International Publishers, 1983.

Hall, Stuart, *Representation, meaning and language.* In *Representation: Culture representations and signifying practices,* ed. Stuart Hall, 28–29. Thousand Oaks: Sage.

Kanye West, September 15, 2009. Retrieved from http://topics.nytimes.com/top/reference/timestopics/people/w/kanye_west/index.html?scp=1-spot&sq=kanye%20west%20&st=cse (accessed July 1, 2010).

Kellner, Douglas. Media spectacle. New York: Routledge, 2003.

Lipsitz, George. "The struggle for hegemony," *Journal of American History* 75(1), 1988.

MacDonald, Patrick. "Kanye West gets a chance to put his money where his mouth is at Key Arena," *The Seattle Times,* April 11, 2008, n.p. http://seattletimes.nwsource.com/html/musicnightlife/2004340276_kanye110.html (accessed July 31, 2008).

McCutcheon, L., R. Lange and J. Houran. Conceptualization and measurement of celebrity worship. *British Journal of Psychology* 13: 67–87, 2002.

MSNBC. Kanye West plays Jesus on Rolling Stone: Rapper poses with a crown of thorns atop his head. 2006. http://www.msnbc.msn.com/id/11009059/from/RSS/ (accessed July 28, 2008).

Neal, Mark Anthony. Kanye walks, http://www.seeingblack.com/printer_10.shtml, accessed July 31, 2008.

Ogunnaike, L. Kanye West world: A nerdy Midwestern kid braces to become America's most provocative pop star, February 9, 2006. http://www.rollingstone.com/news/story/9183008/cover_story_kanye_west_world/print (accessed July 31, 2008).

Rodriguez, Jason (with additional reporting by Montgomery, James and Reid, Shaheem). Kanye West crashes VMA stage during Taylor Swift's award speech: Kanye continues his history of onstage award-show rants. May 4, 2009, http://www.mtv.com/news/articles/1621389/20090913/west_kanye.jhtml (accessed May 24, 2010).

Rose, Tricia. *Black Noise: Rap music and black culture in contemporary America.* Hanover: University Press of New England,

Simon, Roger. *Gramsci's political thought.* New York: Lawrence & Wishart, 1991.

TIME. February 8, 1999.

TIME, August 29, 2005.

Wheeler, Alina. *Designing brand identity: A complete guide to creating, building, and maintaining strong brands.* Hoboken: John Wiley & Sons, 2006.

Yano, Christine. Intervening selves: Images and image-making in a Japanese popular music genre. *Journal of Popular Culture* 31(2): 125.

12

Country Crooners and FOX News: Country Music and the FOX Brand

Dave Robinson

Ever since FOX News Channel's launch, its primetime roster has been spearheaded by two avid country music fans. Whilst best known for expounding uncompromisingly conservative opinions on their nightly political talk shows, both Bill O'Reilly and Sean Hannity wear their love of country music boldly on their sleeves. Examples of their own public involvement in country music include O'Reilly appearing as a guest presenter at the 2009 CMT Awards, and Hannity presenting a series of Freedom Concerts featuring country artists since 2003.[1] From the outset, FOX has included more entertainment in its programming than either of its main cable rivals, CNN or MSNBC, and it would be reasonable to conclude that the influence of stalwarts O'Reilly and Hannity may in itself account for the proliferation of country music stars appearing as both performers and interview guests on the channel. In fact, country music is a pervasive ingredient of FOX News programming, with, for example, weekdays morning show *Fox and Friends* regularly including performances by country artists, and Glenn Beck, the recently added program host, featuring appearances from country singers with a political angle. Over at FOX News Radio, reporter Todd Starnes carries the torch for country music, whilst a number of FOX affiliate stations give country music a high profile accordant on local markets. In short, country music has come to be identifiable with the FOX brand, and this chapter attempts to provide an explanation of how and why this should be so.

Rupert Murdoch, chairman of parent organization News Corporation, launched FOX News in October 1996 as a direct competitor with Ted Turner's CNN cable news channel, as well as MSNBC. At the time, there was much debate among journalists as to whether the new channel was intended as a platform for Murdoch's own conservative political views, or whether it was primarily intended to exploit a perceived gap in the market.[2] Perhaps conscious of the former perception, the slogan "fair and balanced" was adopted from the outset in respect of FOX News Channel's reporting ethos, and Murdoch himself was at pains to stress that the distinction between reporting and opinion should be clearly labeled in the programming. Nevertheless, the suspicions of many were reinforced by the appointment of Roger Ailes as head of FOX News Channel.[3] Ailes joined FOX from being president of CNBC (NBC's cable business channel), but he was best known as a heavy-weight Republican political strategist and media consultant, credited with having helped George H. W. Bush to victory over Michael Dukakis in the 1988 presidential election. With the notable exceptions of Geraldo Rivera, Juan Williams and Alan Colmes, most of the political contributors on FOX News are, and have been, right of center. Newt Gingrich joined the network in 1999, and, in more recent times, Karl Rove has come on board, and Mike Huckabee has been given his own show. In a contemporary context, the latest recruit, Sarah Palin, is the most high-profile contributor of them all.

Market research consistently shows the regular FOX News audience to be more Republican than Democrat (the reverse being the case for both CNN and MSNBC), and regular viewers of *Hannity* and *The O'Reilly Factor* in particular, as being overwhelmingly Republican.[4] However, there is a strong argument that the FOX News product is as much based around appealing to conservative lifestyle norms and values as it is about communicating party political opinion, and I would argue that the dual commercial and ideological motivations behind the brand are each served in different ways by the channel's country music content.

As a political strategist since the 1960s, Roger Ailes would have been well aware of the role that country music has played as a vehicle for expressing political opinion and reinforcing conservative values at particular moments in time. From Jimmie Davis, "the singing governor'" of Louisiana, and George Wallace's mobilization of a "Nashville command post" during the civil rights era, through to Merle Haggard's anti-protest anthem "Okie From Muskogee" at the height of the Vietnam War, country music has been used to convey "traditional" rural American values, and continues to do so today. At the same time, and in contrast to artists in most other popular music genres, commercial country singers are marketed for their girl (or boy) next door appeal. Whereas rock stars tend to present themselves to their audiences like alien deities—unreachable, unfathomable, and assuming the right to expound wisdom on a range of issues on the basis of their creative talent, country singers generally have a closer affinity with their audiences, who tend to perceive them as people just like themselves. More so that country music has a history of what has been described as "participatory commercialism," and still hosts events such as the annual Fan Fair in Nashville where fans can go along and meet up with their favorite stars.[5] Invariably, country singers will seek to up-play whatever working-class and small town connections they can lay claim to, and in doing so, they continue to encourage the idea of the American dream, as portrayed through their own success stories. An area in which FOX News has been particularly successful in contrast to its cable rivals has been in building a loyal base of viewers for particular programs, what are known as *appointment viewers*, and I suggest that the feelings of familiarity, comfort, and hope generated by regular appearances of girl/boy next door style country stars are some of the ingredients that have continued to attract this loyalty.

While the average FOX viewer described himself ideologically as a conservative and the average CNN viewer described himself as a moderate in a 2006 survey, it may be significant that between 2000 and 2006 Democrats' trust in both news sources declined, whilst during the same period Republicans' trust in FOX News increased but their trust in CNN declined.[6] Given that the same survey shows that growth in FOX News overall audience figures had leveled out by 2006, the data strongly suggests that whilst FOX was no longer gaining significant numbers of new converts, the network had substantially succeeded in strengthening its ideological ties with its core audience. In considering how country music may have played a part in cementing these network-audience ties, both in broadly ideological and overtly party political frameworks, I have chosen to examine a number of examples of country singers appearing on FOX News and the contexts of the moment at which these appearances took place. I will also be examining the ways in which individual FOX presenters have built country music associations into their own public personas.

As well as this, I will be looking at how commercial country music as an industry, and some of its prominent stars, stand to gain from the media exposure derived from cable television during a period in which new technology has put the traditional main revenue source of recording sales under threat.

THEM AND US

On May 9, 2007, Muslim country singer Kareem Salama was interviewed live on the FOX News' *Your World* program by anchorman Neil Cavuto. During a segment on terrorist profiling, captioned as *Good v Evil*, the son of Egyptian immigrants, who was born and raised in small town Oklahoma, provided balanced and moderated responses to questions from Cavuto about his views on Muslim terrorists and the consequences of terrorism for himself as an American Muslim. The young Salama, who is also a law school graduate, had recently released a CD entitled *Generous Peace* on an independent label, but had not enjoyed the level of commercial success that might be expected in order to warrant a live interview on FOX. Neither was Salama a vocal activist on political, racial or religious matters. During the interview, Cavuto referred to Salama having the same "racial profile" as Islamic terrorists, but also referred to the "anomaly" of being both Muslim and a country singer. The way that Salama reconciled this, essentially by emphasizing what people have in common rather than what divides them, appears to be what made Salama's profile worthy of interest for the FOX network.[7]

What might be considered a moment of multicultural enlightenment, however, appears in stark contrast with the appearance of aging satirical pop-country singer Ray Stevens, during a feature about healthcare reform on FOX News' top-rating primetime slot *The O'Reilly Factor*, on January 15, 2010. Bill O'Reilly introduced a clip from the video of Stevens' new song "We, The People," a comic ditty protesting President Obama's healthcare reforms ("Obamacare"), in which "we" are likened to "Joe the Plumber," and in which "this O'Reilly fellow on FOX," and other FOX News personalities "Hannity" and "Beck" (as well as "Limbaugh") are held up as people to whom "we" listen. This was followed by a brief discussion with Stevens, after which O'Reilly introduced a video clip of a song recorded in 1962 by Ray Stevens titled "Ahab the Arab," a song that had subsequently led to "Ahab" being regarded as a racial slur by many. Whilst "We, The People" is a topical song, the relevance of playing the "Ahab the Arab" clip is not in any way clear, other than to enable O'Reilly to bemoan the way in which political correctness has changed America.[8]

Two such varying examples of country singers featuring on FOX News provide an interesting counterpoint, and the respective moments in time may be relevant. In May 2007, whilst fear and anger about terrorism remained strong, particularly in light of the discovery of a terrorist plot against the Fort Dix military base in New Jersey, prevailing sentiments toward Muslims in general had softened considerably since the terrorist attacks of September 11, 2001, and the invasions of Afghanistan and Iraq. So too, the Hurricane Katrina disaster, which had itself produced the biggest spike in cable news viewing figures since the invasion of Iraq, had led to increasing sensitivity and concern on issues of race. By January 2010, a year into Barack Obama's presidency, and with healthcare reform established as the central issue in the "big government—small government" debate, culture-war rhetoric had been cranked up once again to pre-2004 election levels.

However, each of the above FOX News appearances provide evidence of the polemic nature of cable network news, in which issues are reduced to point and counterpoint and in which the middle ground is most often lost.[9]

The feature that Kareem Salama is brought in on is captioned *Good v Evil*, and during the interview Salama is invited to condemn terrorists as "evil," which he does, whilst in the background, moving images of Muslim's at prayer are interspersed with an image of Salama himself at a gas station wearing a cowboy hat. Although Salama attempts to explain the things that people of different cultures share in common, the dominant image of the piece is one of the perpetrators of terrorism being identified with Islamic culture, and being condemned as "wretched" by a Muslim man who himself propounds the values of country music. In the case of Ray Stevens' appearance on *The O'Reilly Factor*, the ideological ties between host and guest were pointed with O'Reilly asking Stevens whether he is a conservative, and Stevens affirming to being so. The lyrics to Stevens' new song also appear to be clearly written with a FOX audience in mind. The rightful masters who constitute the "we" in "We, The People" appear to be a specific "we" who identify with Joe the Plumber and listen to Rush Limbaugh rather than the inclusive "we" for whom Abraham Lincoln was speaking. This piece was presented at a light-entertainment level, but it does appear to be setting up and exploiting a tribalist media construct of two Americas.

SHOCK AND ANGER

While country music has been an associated feature in Fox News branding since the channel's launch, it is in post 9/11 America that the full value of that brand association has been realized. In a world where "you're either with us or against us," the things that differentiate "us" from the otherness that constitutes "them," rapidly took on heightened significance. The point about my previous examples of country singers on FOX is that the channel's country music content in recent times may continue to be influenced by the cultural references taken up in the channel's branding in the wake of the 9/11 attacks.

There are few more powerful American icons than the cowboy, and the large number of "hat acts" that were around in country music at the time of 9/11 made the music's association with the idealized all-American hero all the more clear. Just as blue-collar television viewers could identify with the figure of the New York firefighter, so too could they identify with the emotional expression of bewilderment in Alan Jackson's song "Where Were You (When The World Stopped Turning)," released in November 2001, and later anger, in Toby Keith's "Courtesy of the Red, White and Blue (The Angry American)," both of which topped the *Billboard* country singles chart.[10] Rockers and rappers were generally slow off the mark in positioning their responses to the 9/11 attacks, perhaps, in some cases, due to the wide ideological gap between themselves and the Bush administration. Stetson-wearing country singers, on the other hand, were already saddling up and galloping to the aid of a nation in crisis. As had happened through the songs of country artists such as Merle Haggard at the height of the Vietnam War, country music once again served as the voice of many ordinary Americans at this moment of national crisis. Written and delivered from an honest, unsophisticated working-class perspective, Jackson's "Where Were You" remains perhaps the most immediately identifiable song about the 9/11 attacks, but at the same time Johnny Cash's 1974 album *Ragged Old Flag* was being hurriedly reissued to coincide with the pervasive nationalist fervor of the moment.[11] Ethnomusicologist Aaron Fox links this outburst of nationalism with one of cultural nostalgia in the wake of the 9/11 attacks, and, I suggest, these are both sentiments that FOX News picked up on in the ways that the channel subsequently incorporated country music in its broadcasting.[12]

WAR AND DISCORD

In the words of his song, Alan Jackson claimed to watch CNN, but fellow country singers such as Darryl Worley and Martina McBride have formed a close relationship with FOX News, and with Sean Hannity in particular. Worley is most widely known for the song "Have You Forgotten," which was released on the eve of the invasion of Iraq and appeared to many to be making a connection between Saddam Hussein and Al Qaeda terrorists, although Worley insisted that the song was written after visiting troops in Afghanistan months earlier.[13] It has been claimed that some radio stations refused to play "Have You Forgotten" on account of its pro-war message, but FOX News embraced Worley's song with open arms, providing appearances on both *Hannity and Colmes* and *FOX and Friends* within weeks of its release. Alongside Worley, another *Hannity and Colmes* guest and FOX News favorite, Martina McBride, took part in the first series of the Sean Hannity organized Freedom Concerts in 2003, which raise scholarship funds for the children of military personnel killed in action. McBride's hit song "Independence Day" also provides the theme song for Hannity's radio show, and this song later came to be used to introduce Sarah Palin at a rally during the 2008 presidential election campaign.[14]

Although there was a dramatic spike in cable news viewing following the 9/11 attacks, the highest cable audience figures achieved over the last decade were at the start of the Iraq War, in March and April 2003.[15] For many, an abiding memory of the first Gulf War in 1991 will have been CNN's eye-witness pictures from the rooftops of Baghdad showing American cruise missiles being directed toward their targets. CNN had been the only major Western broadcaster allowed to remain in Baghdad, and although the reports Peter Arnett sent back were censored, the moment signified a cable news coup for Ted Turner's network.[16] In 2003, by contrast, the abiding memory for many people will have been of the debate on the eve of war over whether or not the invasion of Iraq could be justified on either moral or security grounds, and this proved to be a coup for Rupert Murdoch's FOX News Channel. As reported on BBC Business News in August of that year, "Fox News' diet of conservative commentators and unashamedly patriotic frontline reports from Iraq was a real ratings winner." FOX News increased its viewers by 300 percent to some 3.3 million at the height of the conflict, and saw its profits double as viewers switched en masse from other channels.[17] Backing up FOX News patriotic frontline reports were the patriotic voices of Toby Keith and Darryl Worley on the home front—Keith's jingoistic lyrics spurring on support for the troops and Worley's song title perhaps inaccurately reminding the folks at home why "we" were there in the first place.

But if country music was to be showcased as America's patriotic music, the one significant fly in the ointment that needed to be dealt with was Natalie Maines of the Dixie Chicks, whose off-the-cuff disparaging remark about President George W. Bush while on stage in London on March 10, 2003, just ten days before the invasion of Iraq began, had been turned into an act of near treason by some sections of the media once the story reached American shores. For FOX News' inquisitor-in-chief Bill O'Reilly to slam the Dixie Chicks for Natalie Maines' remark was simply not sufficient.[18] The rebuke needed to come from among her peers, and on the March 18 edition of *The O'Reilly Factor*, fellow country singer Travis Tritt, who shared the same record label and public relations management as the Chicks, duly obliged. Tritt castigated Natalie Maines and the Chicks on the highest rating cable show in the country for having behaved in a cowardly fashion by making the remarks while overseas, and suggested they should volunteer to perform at a military base if they were really sorry.[19] Blacklisting of the Chicks took place across many country radio stations, and in some cases, it was claimed, as a result of audience pressure. Tritt's *O'Reilly Factor* denouncement of their actions is useful in understanding why their remarks led to such a strong reaction. To country fans, the Dixie Chicks were seen as three wholesome Texas girls whose vocal and instrumental talents belonged among the rich traditions of southern folk music. Not only were they country music stars but they were "authentic," and with that authenticity went an expectation of them sharing the same values as the people who listened to their songs. At a moment in time when many of these ordinary folks might be anticipating their sons or daughters being shipped off to war, Natalie Maines anti-war, anti-Bush remarks were seen as a betrayal by those who had previously identified the Chicks' music with the very values that Americans would be fighting for. Travis Tritt no doubt felt an earnest need to make his rebuke, whilst FOX News had (if nothing else) a perceived commercial need to ensure that they maintained the cultural purity of country music as a united voice for patriotism and comfort across the homeland. This was very much a "with us or against us" incident in which the Dixie Chicks were given no other choices than to either apologize unreservedly and do penance, or be cast out and no longer be one of "us folks." This incident, on its own, can be seen placing another brick in the wall that separates "us" from "them," and further reducing civil discourse to the rhetoric of two opposing camps, whilst sections of the mass media watch over and direct as the gatekeepers of their consumers' values.

COUNTRY MUSIC AND THE COMMON MAN

Of all the FOX News presenters, Sean Hannity is the one who most identifies with country music. He is also second only to Bill O'Reilly in prime-time ratings across all cable news channels, and it is worthy of note that when Hannity's liberal counter-balance, Alan Colmes, left the *Hannity and Colmes* show at the end of 2008, the solo *Hannity* show was launched in its place, and has continued to attract the same level of audience figures since.[20] Joining FOX News from CNN in January 2009, the same month in which Hannity went solo, Glenn Beck quickly established himself as the third most viewed show host on all cable news networks. In Beck, FOX News had found yet another opinionated right-wing voice with a similarly confrontational style to that of Hannity and O'Reilly, but with a more manic delivery. From the start, Beck invited country singers onto his show, and country singers who had something to say about the predicament that America currently found itself in at that time. Trace Adkins had offered up his credentials as redneck philosopher in his 2007 book *A Personal Stand*, and had already been interviewed on both *Hannity and Colmes* and *The O'Reilly Factor* since its publication.[21]

On Adkins' February 23, 2009, appearance on *Glenn Beck*, Beck made reference to Thomas Jefferson's remark that he would rather be judged by a farmer than by any learned man, and posed Adkins the question as to what the problem facing America was. Adkins struggled to identify just what the problem was or how to fix it, other than acknowledging that it was "huge." He then went on to perform his song "Muddy Water," about a man returning to his hometown and seeking forgiveness at the local church for the bad life he had been living, presumably in an urban environment full of sin and temptation. In spite of Adkins having already published his own opinions on subjects ranging from organized labor to illegal immigration, the received message from the piece is that it is the responsibility of the president and politicians to decide and do what is right by the common man, who himself can only be kept clean of corruption and wrongdoing by adherence to or by return to the Christian values of small town life.[22] Originally from a small town in northern Louisiana, Trace Adkins, who once entered an alcohol rehabilitation program in Nashville, and who also has something of a love-hate relationship with tractors,[23] is projected to the FOX News audience as both Jefferson's farmer and the seeker of redemption in "Muddy Water." As more appearances by Adkins on the network follow, identification with his figure of a flawed but morally aware, common-sense speaking, small town, conservative, is reinforced among core FOX viewers. Adkins, 6'6'' tall and wearing a hat, looks like an "American" (icon) and talks like an "American." In his 2007 book, *The Neglected Voter*, David Paul Kuhn refers to Ronald Reagan's capacity to focus on "the big thing," and "his willingness to speak in the language of right and wrong," as attributes that endeared him to the white male voter.[24] In the post-9/11 era, I suggest that the core FOX News audience recognized similar attributes, not only in President George W. Bush, but also in country singers like Trace Adkins.

With George W. Bush out of office, it suddenly became much easier for conservatives to distance themselves from what had gone wrong in Washington and on Wall Street during the latter part of his presidency. As the effects of the economic recession hit hard in middle-America during early 2009, and anger over the bankers' bailout spread, country singer and John McCain supporter John Rich appeared on FOX News screens to point the finger of blame, not only at the wheeler-dealers on Wall Street but at Capitol Hill as well. Released during the first week of February 2009, Rich's "Shuttin' Detroit Down" was described in *The New York Times* as "the first great song of the bailout era." In the song and during his appearance on *Glenn Beck* on March 25, Rich protests at how the bosses are being paid bonuses and Washington is bailing out the banks while factories are closing and farmers are auctioning off their land. "Shuttin' Detroit Down" is a populist conservative anthem in the mold of Merle Haggard's "Okie From Muskogee," forty years earlier, and it is clear how Glenn Beck believes it will hit a chord with his audience as he introduces the song with the question "tell me if you don't feel like this?"[25] This is perhaps as good an example as any of FOX News saying to its core audience "we understand how you feel—we feel the same—and we have someone here who can express how we all feel in a song."

FOX News coverage has continued to clearly identify an externalized enemy in the form of middle-Eastern terrorism since 9/11, and the Iraq War enabled FOX to extend the notion of enemies of the nation to all those effete liberals from New York to Hollywood who opposed the war. At the same time, the recession and bailout has internalized the polemic further by adding economic class-consciousness into the media's culture war arena. Country music had already assisted FOX News in portraying liberals as the enemy of true Americans—the outpourings of Charlie Daniels, as regularly posted on the "Soapbox" section of the singer's website, being a good example.[26] In "Shuttin' Detroit Down," corporate capitalists are also identified as the enemy of the honest, hardworking American. The fact that Rich appears on FOX News, itself part of a global media empire, to publicize the song's message, perhaps holds a certain irony. FOX News has always been careful not to alienate audience on grounds of religious belief, but there is an implied adherence to Christian belief and principles in much of the output. John Rich explains that Detroit is "emblematic of hard working America," and also points out that he himself grew up in a trailer park and that his dad is a smalltown preacher. With the assistance of the show's host, Rich, like Adkins, puts himself across to FOX News viewers as being one of "us folks;" and by mentioning along the way that he comes from west Texas, he perhaps draws a distinction between coming from there and coming from a more liberal community such as West Hollywood, for example. Just as George W. Bush gained re-election in 2004 partly because ordinary Americans identified with him more than with John Kerry; so too, FOX News appears to be continuing to win the cable ratings war through its use of faces and voices that identify with that group who were once upon a time described as the "silent majority."

ELECTIONS, ISSUES, AND IDENTITY

When it comes to elections, and particularly presidential elections, where the character of the candidates takes primacy of place to conservative-minded voters, the FOX-country music coalition goes into overdrive. In 2004, George W. Bush played the role of the down-to-earth regular American guy through his further cultivation of the Texas rancher image; and the entertainment at the Republican National Convention was headlined by country stars Brooks & Dunn and Lee Ann Womack and backed up by other country and Christian acts. In his study of country music radio and voting behavior in the 2004 election, David Firestein postulated that country music radio helped to reinforce conservative values among the "red state" voters, and concluded that the 2004 election was "less about values than it was about identity." According to Firestein, the Bush campaign succeeded among "red state" voters in 2004 by tapping into the "code and symbolism" of country music at an intuitive level.[27] For the tele-visual media, the images were there on a plate, and all FOX News needed to do was to pick up on them at campaign events and transport them to the living rooms of their core audience. Simply by screening country music imagery on a regular basis, FOX News was reinforcing audience identity with Bush.

FOX News Radio, launched in 2003, and Texas-based media conglom-erate Clear Channel Communications, provide another link between FOX News and country music. In 2004, Clear Channel owned 1,250 radio stations, including more country music stations than any other provider. Reportedly having business links with George W. Bush, Clear Channel came under fire through accusations of corporate blacklisting during the Dixie Chicks controversy, although was later exonerated of any corporate interference.[28] Through a reciprocal deal, Clear Channel stations carry FOX News Radio newscasts, and FOX Radio News picks up news content from Clear Chan-nel. Premiere Radio Networks, a wholly owned subsidiary of Clear Channel, syndicates many of the top-rated talk radio shows, including *The Glenn Beck Program* and handles distribution of *The Sean Hannity Show*. In other words, the branding that FOX News provides for conservative cable news viewers is effectively replicated through the FOX-Clear Channel association on radio.

Following Firestein's reasoning that the 2004 election was won on the basis of voters identifying with the candidate, it is worth looking at how FOX News Radio builds identification with listeners into its branding. In an article posted on the FOX News Radio website, titled "Country Music, Whoopie Pie and Barbecue," news anchor Todd Starnes described his thoughts as he stopped off in Manchester, New Hampshire, days before the 2008 presidential primary. Contemplating what it was that made the United States the greatest nation on earth, Starnes narrowed it down to five reasons: "Freedom, Our Military, Barbecue, Guns, and Country Music." This list, like much of the devoutly Christian Todd Starnes' media output, was no doubt intended to entertain in a tongue-in-cheek style, but not without a point. Explaining why country music was one of the five things that made America great, Starnes points out that "country singers look like real folks," and that "the women look like women and the men act like men." He finished his piece by quoting some poignantly patriotic lines from country singer Lee Greenwood's "God Bless The USA," and in a short article in which he managed to make reference to cheeseburger, root beer, high school football, church on Sunday, and NASCAR racing, Todd Starnes has summarized an America that many can identity with.[29]

Unlike 2004, the 2008 presidential election turned out to be more about is-sues than identity, although if Mike Huckabee had won the Republican nomi-nation, the campaign for the country music vote might have been somewhat different. However, the 2008 campaign demonstrated that country music can be utilized to promote issues as well as reinforce identity. An example of this can be seen in the form of the recession-linked American Solutions "Drill Here, Drill Now, Pay Less" petition, which inspired country music star Aaron Tippin's song "Drill Here, Drill Now." Released as a single, Tippin premiered the song on September 9, 2008, on Sean Hannity's radio show during an interview with American Solutions chairman Newt Gingrich.[30] On October 9 Tippin performed the song on *FOX and Friends*, and then October 18 he guested on the new *Huckabee* show, performing together with Mike Huckabee in the regular live music segment of the show.[31]

In between these appearances, Tippin was also performing the song live at several Sarah Palin campaign rallies, which themselves became regular viewing on FOX News during the lead up to election day. Whilst other country singers including Gretchen Wilson and Hank Williams Jr. appeared at Palin rallies and were shown on FOX News doing so, the particular point of interest about the "Drill Here, Drill Now" example is that it begs the question: Who is exploiting who? Through Aaron Tippin's song, Newt Gingrich and American Solutions were able to get invaluable exposure for their cause on cable network news, and also directly raise the profile of the American-made energy issue in the presidential campaign. FOX News can be seen to be broadly manipulating country music for the purpose of brand reinforcement, but there would also appear to be a flip side to this coin involving political interest groups use of FOX News as a vehicle for promoting specific causes.

At the same time, by releasing a song about an issue of such popular concern during an election year, Aaron Tippin, however earnest in his cause, provided his career with a tremendous boost. Similarly, by releasing a bailout song at the beginning of 2009, John Rich had a sure-fire way of achieving media exposure on FOX News; and, according to the transcript of the *Glenn Beck* show of March 25, it was Rich who had initially approached Beck with the song.[32] These can both be seen as examples of country singers with a good understanding of their markets, in a way that the Dixie Chicks did not. In the case of the Dixie Chicks, the publicity surrounding "the incident" ultimately led them to spread their wings to the much wider adult-oriented rock market, and to achieve recognition from the more liberal-minded National Academy of Recording Arts and Sciences in the form of Grammy Awards.

FOX, THE MUSIC BUSINESS, AND COUNTRY VALUES

The country music business is corporately controlled within tightly regulated parameters, and in terms of its target market, has a great deal in common with FOX News Channel. Technological innovations, enabling Internet news sourcing and digital downloading have put both cable news organizations and record companies under increasing commercial pressures over the last few years. FOX News Channel achieved impressive audience growth over its first eight years, after which audience figures leveled out. In 2009, however, FOX News again showed significant audience growth, in part due to the success of the newly launched *Glenn Beck* show, and largely through gaining increased market share at the expense of its cable news rivals (CNN in particular).[33] Nevertheless, cable news channels continue to compete for share within a market that shows little further growth potential. At the same time, sales of country music CDs (as with sales of all recorded music) have fallen dramatically, and there are no signs that this is likely to improve in the near future. Both industries need to consolidate their market position and tap into new revenue streams where possible. In the country music business, which is almost entirely based in Nashville, one of the ways this may happen is through inclusive deals between the artist and their record company or management (sometimes described as 360 deals), which incorporate all revenue generated by the artist.[34] In these circumstances, the country music business has every incentive to seek to promote its product through FOX News Channel.

Some artists already mentioned help to reinforce the FOX brand in an ideological way, and there has been something of a clamor to get exposure for the current country music chart-toppers on FOX News in recent times. One of the biggest-selling country artists for the last five years is Carrie Underwood, who personifies the girl-next-door image, and is one of the most familiar faces across FOX broadcasting networks—what might be described as a "FOX favorite." In December 2009, for example, Underwood hosted an "All Star Holiday Special" for FOX Network, and duly undertook the promotional rounds, appearing on FOX affiliate stations such as FOX 26 News—Houston.[35] Her initial success came about through winning the FOX show *American Idol* in 2005, and she is by far the most successful winner of that show to date.

Although branded as a country singer, Underwood's meteoric rise to fame through *American Idol* gave her the best of opportunities for pop-crossover success from the outset, and each of her three albums so far has reached number one on the country charts. Her two most recent albums have also reached number one on the all-genre *Billboard* 200 Chart.[36] The careful cultivation of Carrie Underwood's wholesome role-model image has maximized her merchandising potential to the benefit of both FOX, and her record label, Arista Nashville.

As music CD sales have plummeted across all genres, and record companies increasingly look out for new talent with "crossover appeal," anyone watching recent music awards ceremonies might conclude that there is something of a "genre war" taking place in the music business. Market conditions have led to increased importance being attached to winning the main all-genre categories at events such as the Grammy and MTV awards. Pitting R&B singer Beyonce Knowles against country singer Taylor Swift in a number of categories at the 2009 MTV Video Music Awards produced even more theatre than anticipated when rap artist Kanye West interrupted Swift's acceptance speech to protest the superiority of Beyonce's work. This incident provided a whole lot of fun for the press, and led to the January 2010 Grammy Awards being billed as something akin to a rematch between Beyonce and Taylor Swift. Two months after the MTV VMA Awards, the Country Music Association (CMA) Awards took place in Nashville, at which Carrie Underwood and fellow country star Brad Paisley had some fun at Kanye West's expense by rebuking his lack of manners in song. Interestingly, the following day the clip of this was shown on FOX News on both *The O'Reilly Factor*'s "Pinheads and Patriots" feature, and on *Hannity's America*. Bill O'Reilly awarded Underwood and Paisley the accolade of "patriots" for defending Taylor Swift, and Sean Hannity described their tuneful rebuke of Kanye as "great advice from two great country superstars." While Underwood, Paisley, O'Reilly and Hannity all presented this prank as a bit of lighthearted "payback," it is interesting to note that both O'Reilly and Hannity specifically refer to Kanye West as a "rapper" and Paisley sings "Cuz cowboys have manners. They don't interrupt."[37] The labeling of Kanye West as a "rapper," appears to be being used here to imply difference, and, perhaps, to imply a different set of behavioral norms to the description "cowboy." Or, to put it another way, is Kanye West's rude behavior being explained on the basis of him being a "rapper" rather than a "cowboy?" There is, I suggest, a contrived separation that FOX News seeks to exploit between which product is regarded as "wholesome" and which is regarded as "unwholesome" by their core audience, and labeling music genres as either one or the other further reinforces audience identification with the FOX brand. Taylor Swift is the new Carrie Underwood, and drawing attention to her mistreatment by someone of an alien genre only works to strengthen her wholesome virtue in the eyes of the FOX faithful.

IDENTITY AND BRAND LOYALTY

Retaining faith with its core audience has been the key to success for FOX News Channel. While the network is frequently discredited for pedaling right-wing bias, it is essentially a populist media format which came into being at a time when the main cable news channel, CNN, had no serious competitor, and when America was increasingly being split into two ideologically, largely through the organized efforts of conservative-minded people. Similarly, country music is an essentially populist music format, which celebrates its lack of sophistication and embraces the conventions of tradition. As such, dominant themes in country music have always included family, God, self-reliance, and love of country. These themes alone could go a long way to forming a social conservative agenda for the George W. Bush era. No doubt, FOX executives realized from the outset that the political middle ground was disappearing fast and that success relied on positioning FOX News clearly on one side of the divide.

In order for FOX News to achieve rapid growth in viewing figures strong branding was necessary, and the iconic all-American imagery surrounding country music provided one of the ways of achieving this. Boosts in ratings during the "War on Terror" and the Iraq War significantly helped FOX to consolidate its growth, and even by 2002 it had moved ahead of CNN in popularity. It was during this period that the channel's relationship with country music was solidified. This is a relationship that continues to benefit both parties. Country music helps to place a relatively new, foreign owned, cable television channel at the heart of the nation's identity, whilst FOX News takes what was once regarded as "hick" music into suburban living rooms across the country. One is rusticating its brand image, whilst the other is becoming almost cosmopolitan. For all the issues songs and political statements made by country singers on FOX News, the main reason for country singers being there is to remind viewers that FOX is their kind of television channel.

NOTES

1. Christian Grantham, "Bill O'Reilly to present award at the CMT Awards," *Nashville is Talking*, June 8, 2009. http://www.nashvilleistalking.com/2009/06/ (accessed January 26, 2010).

2. Lawrie Mifflin, "At the new Fox News Channel, the buzzword is fairness, separating news from bias," *New York Times*, October 7, 1996. nytimes.com (accessed August 8, 2009).

3. Ronald Grover, "The Importance of being Ailes," *Bloomberg Business Week*, September 15th 2009. Bloomberg.com. http://www.businessweek.com/innovate/FineOnMedia/archives/2009/09/ (accessed January 26, 2010).

4. *The State of the News Media 2009* (PEW Project for Excellence in Journalism, 2009). http://www.stateofthemedia.org/2009/narrative_cabletv_audience (accessed January 31, 2010).

5. For "participatory commercialism": see Diane Pecknold, *The Selling Sound: The Rise of the Country Music Industry* (Durham, NC, Duke University Press, 2007) 124–32.

6. "Cable News Believability," *The State of the News Media 2007* (Project for Excellence in Journalism, 2007). http://www.stateofthemedia.org/2007/narrative_cabletv_publicattitudes (accessed January 31, 2010).

7. *Your World,* Presented by Neil Cavuto, FOX News (TV broadcast), May 9, 2007. At http://www.thefilter.com (accessed February 8, 2010).

8. *O'Reilly Factor,* Presented by Bill O'Reilly, FOX News (TV broadcast), January 15, 2010. http://billoreilly.com/show (accessed February 2, 2010).

9. David Paul Kuhn, *The Neglected Voter: White Men and the Democratic Dilemma* (New York, Palgrave Macmillan, 2007) 133.

10. Chart positions accessed at "Chart Archives" at Billboard.com. http://www.billboard.com/charts/country-songs#/charts/country-songs (accessed February 2, 2010).

11. Anthony DeCurtis, "An American Original Returns," *New York Times*, February 24, 2002. http://www.nytimes.com/2002/02/24/arts/music-an-american-original-returns (accessed January 31, 2010).

12. Aaron Fox, "Alternative to What? O Brother, September 11, and the Politics of Country Music," in *Country Music Goes to War*, ed. Charles K. Wolfe and James E. Akenson (Lexington: University of Kentucky Press, 2005)172–173: Account of the resurrection of the blue-collar hero in the aftermath of 9/11, and the *obvious outburst of nationalism and cultural nostalgia that followed the attack.* Cites Alan Jackson's "Where Were You" as the most successful song to deal specifically with the 9/11 attacks, and also refers to the hurried re-issue of Johnny Cash's "Ragged Old Flag."

13. Chris Wilman, *Rednecks and Bluenecks* (New York, The New Press, 2005) 15. Re: Darryl Worley – "Have You Forgotten."

14. James Hirsen, *Nashville Dems Take on Sean Hannity.* NewsMax.com, May 3, 2004. http://archive.newsmax.com/archives/articles/2004 (accessed January 31, 2010). Ironically, "Independence Day" is actually about domestic abuse rather than 4th of July.

15. Iraq War cable ratings: "Cable News Primetime Audience during Big Events 1998–2007," *The State of the News Media 2008* (Project for Excellence in Journalism, 2009). http://www.stateofthemedia.org/2008/chartland.php (accessed January 31, 2010).

16. CNN, Gulf War 1: Phil Harding, *Reflections* (BBC College of Journalism, 2009) http://www.bbc.co.uk/journalism/blog/2009/08/cnn-reporting-from-baghdad-gul.shtml (accessed February 2, 2010)

17. *War coverage lifts News Corp,* BBC Business News, August 13, 2003. http://news.bbc.co.uk/1/hi/business/3148015.stm (accessed January 30, 2010).

18. Soon after Natalie Maines made her remark about President George W. Bush while on stage in London, Bill O'Reilly referred to the Dixie Chicks on *The O'Reilly Factor* as "callow, foolish women who deserve to be slapped around." See *Shut Up & Sing.* Barbara Kopple and Cecilia Peck, directors (Weinstein Company 79929DVD1, 2006).

19. Travis Tritt on *The O'Reilly Factor*, March 18, 2003. Taken from: Randy Rudder, "In Whose Name? Country Artists Speak Out on Gulf War II," in *Country Music*

Goes To War, ed. Charles K. Wolfe and James E. Akenson (Lexington: University Press of Kentucky, 2005).

20. *Hannitty* ratings: data by Nielsen Media Research at http://www.mediabistro .com/TVNewser/Ratings/ (accessed February 1, 2010).

21. Trace Adkins, *A Personal Stand: Observations and Opinions from a Free-thinking Roughneck* (New York, Random House, 2007).

22. Trace Adkins on *Glenn Beck*, FOX News (TV broadcast), February 23, 2009. Transcript at http://www.foxnews.com/story/0,2933,499545,00.html (accessed January 28, 2010).

23. Trace Adkins' involvement in a tractor accident and his voluntary attendance on an alcohol rehabilitation program were both reported at CMT News on October 9, 2002, and January 21, 2003, respectively. See http://www.cmt.com/news/country -music/1458040/trace-adkins-injured-in-farm-accident.jhtml, and, http://www.cmt .com/news/news-in-brief/1459611/trace-adkins-completes-rehab-program.jhtml (accessed January 28, 2010).

24. David Paul Kuhn, "The Measure of the Man: The Politics of Personal Manhood," in *The Neglected Voter: White Men and the Democratic Dilemma* (New York: Palgrave Macmillan, 2007) 72–73.

25. John Rich on *Glenn Beck*, FOX News (TV broadcast), March 26, 2009. Transcript at http://www.foxnews.com/story/0,2933,510758,00.html (accessed January 28, 2010).

26. See http://www.charliedaniels.com/soapbox.htm (accessed March 4, 2010).

27. David J. Firestein, "The Honky Tonk Gap: Country Music, Red State Identity, and the Election of 2004," in *Vital Speeches of the Day*, 72.3 (2006) 83–88.

28. Randy Rudder, "In Whose Name? Country Artists Speak Out on Gulf War II," in *Country Music Goes To War*, ed. Charles K. Wolfe and James K. Akenson (Lexington: University of Kentucky Press, 2005) 212–13.

29. Todd Starnes, *Country Music, Whoopie Pie and Barbecue*, foxnewsradio.com, July 3, 2008. http://www.foxnewsradio.com/2008/07/03/country-music-whoopie-pie -and-barbecue (accessed January 31, 2010).

30. Aaron Tippin on *The Sean Hannity Show*: "Country Star Aaron Tippin Debuts New Single 'Drill Here, Drill Now' On The Sean Hannity Show," *Music Industry Today*, September 9, 2008. http://music.einnews.com (accessed September 27, 2008).

31. Aaron Tippin on *Huckabee*, FOX News (TV broadcast), October 18, 2008. Sourced at *E&P* Magazine. http://blogs.epmag.com/judy/2008/10/20/drill-here-drill -now/ (accessed January 31, 2010).

32. John Rich on *Glenn Beck*, FOX News (TV broadcast), March 26, 2009. Transcript at http://www.foxnews.com/story/0,2933,510758,00.html (accessed January 28, 2010).

33. Marisa Guthrie, "Cable News Ratings: Fox News Has Highest Rated Year In Network History," *Broadcasting & Cable*, December 16, 2009. Broadcastingcable. com. http://www.broadcastingcable.com/article/440766 (accessed March 10, 2010).

34. The "multiple rights" or "360" deal came about in response to falling record company revenues resulting from the worldwide increase in digital downloading

since the millennium. These deals give record companies or management organizations rights over different aspects of the artist's product, including live performances, television and radio appearances, and merchandising, as well as recording rights. Proponents of such agreements argue that by signing artists to deals that include a share of the income from all sources, record companies can develop longer-term marketing strategies that are mutually beneficial. For a detailed report on the development of 360 deals see: Jeff Leeds, "The New Deal: Band as Brand," *New York Times*, November 11, 2007. http://www.nytimes.com/2007/11/11/arts/music/11leed.html (accessed March 5, 2010).

35. FOX 26 News – Houston, morning show featuring Carrie Underwood, December 4, 2009 at http://www.myfoxhouston.com/dpp/entertainment/ (accessed February 2, 2010).

36. Carrie Underwood: Billboard 200 / Country album chart positions accessed at http://www.billboard.com (accessed February 2, 2010).

37. *O'Reilly Factor – Pinheads and Patriots*, Brad Paisley and Carrie Underwood feature, FOX News (TV broadcast), November 12, 2009. http://www.foxnews.com/search-results/m/27378596/pinheads-patriots (accessed January 31, 2010); and, *Hannity – Hannity's America*, Taylor Swift, Brad Paisley and Carrie Underwood feature, FOX News (TV broadcast), November12, 2009. http://www.foxnews.com/search-results/m/27378593/hannity-s-america (accessed January 31, 2010).

BIBLIOGRAPHY

"Aaron Tippin on The Sean Hannity Show: Country Star Aaron Tippin Debuts New Single 'Drill Here, Drill Now' On *The Sean Hannity Show*," *Music Industry Today*, September 9, 2008. http://music.einnews.com (accessed September 27, 2008).

Adkins, Trace. *A Personal Stand: Observations and Opinions from a Freethinking Roughneck*. New York: Random House, 2007.

"CNN, Gulf War 1: Phil Harding," *Reflections*. (BBC College of Journalism, 2009) http://www.bbc.co.uk/journalism/blog/2009/08/cnn-reporting-from-baghdad-gul.shtml (accessed February 2, 2010).

DeCurtis, Anthony. "An American Original Returns," *The New York Times*. February 24, 2002. http://www.nytimes.com/2002/02/24/arts/music-an-american-original-returns (accessed January 31, 2010).

Firestein, David J. "The Honky Tonk Gap: Country Music, Red State Identity, and the Election of 2004," in *Vital Speeches of the Day*, 72.3 (2006) 83–88.

Fox, Aaron. "Alternative to What? O Brother, September 11, and the Politics of Country Music," in *Country Music Goes to War*, ed. Charles K. Wolfe and James E. Akenson. Lexington: University of Kentucky Press, 2005.

FOX 26 News – Houston, morning show featuring Carrie Underwood, December 4, 2009. at http://www.myfoxhouston.com/dpp/entertainment/ (accessed February 2, 2010).

"Glenn Beck," FOX News, (TV broadcast). February 23, 2009. Transcript at http://www.foxnews.com/story/0,2933,499545,00.html (accessed January 28, 2010).

"Glenn Beck," FOX News, (TV broadcast). March 26, 2009. Transcript at http://www.foxnews.com/story/0,2933,510758,00.html (accessed January 28, 2010).

Grantham, Christian. "Bill O'Reilly to present award at the CMT Awards," *Nashville is Talking*, June 8, 2009. http://www.nashvilleistalking.com/2009/06/ (accessed January 26, 2010).

Grover, Ronald. "The Importance of being Ailes," *Bloomberg Business Week*, September 15th 2009. http://www.businessweek.com/innovate/FineOnMedia/archives/2009/09/ (accessed January 26, 2010).

Guthrie, Marisa, "Cable News Ratings: Fox News Has Highest Rated Year In Network History," *Broadcasting & Cable,* December 16, 2009. Broadcastingcable.com. http://www.broadcastingcable.com/article/440766 (accessed March 10, 2010).

"Hannity" FOX News, (TV broadcast). November12, 2009. http://www.foxnews.com/search-results/m/27378593/hannity-s-america (accessed January 31, 2010).

Hirsen, James. "Nashville Dems Take on Sean Hannity," NewsMax.com, May 3, 2004. http://archive.newsmax.com/archives/articles/2004 (accessed January 31, 2010).

"Huckabee," FOX News (TV broadcast), October 18, 2008. Sourced at *E&P* Magazine. http://blogs.epmag.com/judy/2008/10/20/drill-here-drill-now/ (accessed January 31, 2010).

Kuhn, David Paul. *The Neglected Voter: White Men and the Democratic Dilemma.* New York: Palgrave Macmillan, 2007.

Leeds, Jeff. "The New Deal: Band as Brand," *The New York Times*, November 11, 2007. http://www.nytimes.com/2007/11/11/arts/music/11leed.html (accessed March 5, 2010).

Mifflin, Lawrie. "At the new Fox News Channel, the buzzword is fairness, separating news from bias," *The New York Times*, October 7, 1996. nytimes.com (accessed August 8, 2009).

"The O'Reilly Factor." FOX News (TV broadcast), January 15, 2010. http://billoreilly.com/show (accessed February 2, 2010).

"The O'Reilly Factor." Brad Paisley and Carrie Underwood feature, FOX News (TV broadcast), November 12, 2009. http://www.foxnews.com/search-results/m/27378596/pinheads-patriots (accessed January 31, 2010).

Pecknold, Diane. *The Selling Sound: The Rise of the Country Music Industry* (Durham, NC: Duke University Press, 2007) 124–32.

"Shut Up & Sing," Barbara Kopple and Cecilia Peck, directors (Weinstein Company 79929DVD1, 2006).

Starnes, Todd. *Country Music, Whoopie Pie and Barbecue*, foxnewsradio.com, July 3, 2008. http://www.foxnewsradio.com/2008/07/03/country-music-whoopie-pie-and-barbecue (accessed January 31, 2010).

The State of the News Media 2008 (Project for Excellence in Journalism, 2009). http://www.stateofthemedia.org/2008/chartland.php (accessed January 31, 2010).

The State of the News Media 2009 (PEW Project for Excellence in Journalism, 2009). http://www.stateofthemedia.org/2009/narrative_cabletv_audience (accessed January 31, 2010).

"War coverage lifts News Corp," BBC Business News, August 13, 2003. http://news
.bbc.co.uk/1/hi/business/3148015.stm (accessed January 30, 2010).

Wilman, Chris. *Rednecks and Bluenecks*. New York: The New Press, 2005.

Wolfe, Charles K., and James E. Akenson, eds. *Country Music Goes To War*. Lexington: University Press of Kentucky, 2005.

"Your World," Presented by Neil Cavuto, FOX News (TV broadcast), May 9, 2007.
At http://www.thefilter.com (accessed February 8, 2010).

III

OUTLASTING YOUR 15 MINUTES— MAKING THE MEDIUM WORK FOR YOU IN LIFE AND DEATH

"I don't know anything about music. In my line, you don't have to."

—Elvis Presley, 1935–1977

"Without marketing plans, the greatest music in the whole world don't mean shit."

—Christopher Knab, FourFront Media and Marketing

13

"If You Catch Me at the Border I Got Visas in My Name": Borders, Boundaries, and the Production of M.I.A.

Mary Beth Ray

As digital technology evolves, society is continually offered new means to produce and consume musical media. This evolution allows for the creation of hybrid musical styles that defy traditional cultural, technological, and generic boundaries. This chapter explores this issue by examining the case of musician M.I.A. What makes M.I.A. a significant case is that she could not have successfully existed twenty years ago. Today, however, as a result of the evolution of digital technology, boundary-breaking artists like M.I.A., as well as others who approach production in an unconventional, forward-thinking manner, do exist. This exploratory chapter argues M.I.A. represents the direction the music industry and culture is taking. Her case highlights not only where the relationship between artist and audience is headed, but also what it means to be a musical artist in global, digital times. The reason is connected to a number of interrelated concepts including globalization, hybridity, popular music and digital communication technology.

Globalization and hybridity are key concepts that need to be understood to make sense of who M.I.A. is as a musical artist. How M.I.A. acts out her identity and how she is marketed as a musician, cannot be discussed without foundational knowledge on both concepts. Concurrently, digital communication technology, as well as its relationship with music, also brings up a number of issues that need to be addressed to unpack M.I.A. as a musical artist, because so much of who she is stems from collaborative and interactive media.

Recording technology has produced a powerful media industry, which is able to convey messages from producer to consumer and generate billions of dollars in annual sales. However, traditional avenues of industry revenue are changing as a result of digital technology and subsequent Web 2.0 phenomenon. Three major music studios closed in 2005: Muscle Shoals, Cello, and the Hit Factory. These closings highlight the significance of changing production practices and are indicative of the shift that the music industry is experiencing. Not only is a new breed of musical work being created but also new business strategies and new ways of consuming are emerging as a part of the evolution of digital technology. New media technologies influence how music is distributed, rendered, purchased, organized, shared, chosen, listened to, interacted with, and repurposed. As a result, new music listening practices emerge from new social spaces and change the way people interact with music. As each of the aforementioned concepts comes together, we can begin to understand how M.I.A. markets herself as a musical artist in our contemporary media saturated society. The following paragraphs lay the foundation for this chapter by providing background information on these concepts.

GLOBALIZATION AND HYBRIDITY

Globalization and hybridity are concepts key to M.I.A.'s identity as a musical artist. Globalization, in its most basic characterization refers to things that were once local phenomena, be they food, music, media, or style, that are now global phenomena. When conceptualizing globalization many people have different characterizations causing conflict within the scholarly community.[1] As such, conceptualizations of globalization have changed over time. On the one hand, globalization is sometimes seen as the emergence of a global culture.[2] Conversely, it is also characterized as the domination of Western culture over third world cultures.[3] Nederveen Pieterse charts this change in the concept's characterization over time from "cultural clash," to "McDonalization," to "hybridization" and argues that globalization does not equal homogenization but hybridization, by placing emphasis on the multiple processes that inform the concept.[4] These three stages can be understood as globalization's evolution from Western homogenization to a concept better characterized by its complexities.[5] As Lull states, "What many contemporary observers conclude is that the global circulation of images, ideologies, and cultural styles; actually fuels symbolic creativity, lessens homogeneity, and increases cultural diversity."[6] Appadurai agrees, arguing that the two polarized readings oversimplify the relationship between first and third world cultures.[7] However, at the same time, Lull acknowledges that dominant Western influences "unquestionably introduce and reinforce certain standardizing values and practices."[8] Overall, globalization is a challenge to define because we are in the middle of it unfolding so it is important to acknowledge process as a key character trait.[9]

Digital communication technology facilitates global cultural exchange by exposing various cultures to Western media. Flew and McElhinney suggest three dimensions to the media's role in the globalization process.[10] First, they note that media are the main platforms that spread information; second, media industries are major proponents of global expansion; and third, media provides information people use to situate themselves in the world where they live.[11] Similarly, Castells argues that globalization is driven by communication technologies through the ubiquity of media in everyday social interaction, networking based social systems, and convergence of media technologies.[12]

By acknowledging the heterogeneous nature of culture and that cultural interaction leads to change for groups involved brings us to hybridity. At its simplest, hybridity refers to a blending of identity and culture, but also entails taking into consideration what that means for those involved. It is often seen as an effect of globalization, as is evident in the merging of various cultures. As Lull states, "The typical result of global cultural interaction is the creation of hybrid forms."[13] However, defining hybridity is often a challenge and as such, many scholars present varied descriptions. In the past, the concept has been used as a tool for a variety of scholarly agendas, with some characterizations drawing criticism for being overly celebratory and not fully acknowledging the processes that inform the concept.[14]

In response, Kraidy proposes a framework to better understand hybridity called critical transculturalism.[15] It addresses the various conceptualizations inherent in hybridity's varying characterizations. Critical transculturalism posits that hybridity must be understood historically, rhetorically and empirically in order to work toward a more in-depth understanding of the concept.[16] Kraidy argues that hybridity is in essence the "cultural logic" that informs globalization.[17] Similarly, Brah and Coombes argue that work on hybridity calls for consideration of social, cultural, historical and political practices within which the concept is situated.[18] Nederveen Pieterse also concentrates on the multi-level processes that inform the concept stating, "hybridity denotes a wide resister of multiple identity, crossover, cut'n'mix, experience, and styles, matching a world of growing migration and diaspora lives, intensive intercultural communication, everyday multiculturalism, and erosion of boundaries."[19]

When considering hybridity specifically in reference to media production and audience consumption Kraidy states:

> Hybrid media texts have the intertextual traces of an increasingly standardized global media industry where successful formats are adapted ad infinitum, hybridized to cater to the proclivities of one audience after another, but always remaining firmly grounded in the same commercial logic where hybrid texts are instruments finely tuned in the pursuit of profit.[20]

In other words, contemporary media products often reflect hybrid style that is both profitable and attractive to media audiences. Likewise, Nederveen Pieterse reflects on the nature of contemporary media consumption and explains, "A major terrain of newly emerging mixtures is the new middle classes and their cultural and social practices arising in the context of migration and diaspora and the new modernities of the emerging markets."[21]

When examining Maronite culture Kraidy found consumption of non-traditional, hybrid media texts "can, in some cases, subvert the politico-economic context in which it occurs."[22] He also found that the younger population "drew on a variety of texts, many outside their ascribed cultural space, to articulate their hybrid identities."[23] Lastly, he found negotiation of media consumption involved a combination of media texts "selectively unearthed from the remembered past and integrated in an unstable present to make better sense of that present."[24] These three aspects of media consumption highlight the uses and appeals of hybrid media content.

Hybridity and globalization have consequences for the concept of genre, particularly in a media saturated society. Genre has always been a traditional way of defining a musical work. Genre can be defined by a work's technical, semiotic, behavioral, ideological, and commercial roles. However, as time has passed scholars have broadened the definition to account for new generic categories. Frith argues that while the aforementioned areas begin to define genre, it is not a clearly defined concept but one that is constantly changing.[25] Indeed, the importance lies in the connection between the musical and the ideological. Genre is in part determined by audience perception of style and meaning, which is framed by the culture's dominant ideology. Once classified, musical work is then turned into a profitable commodity by the music industry. For example, Pearl Jam was packaged and sold as grunge, the Dixie Chicks as country, and Britney Spears as pop. By compartmentalizing an artist into a particular genre, record companies can instantly know what the artist sounds like and which consumer group will purchase their work. Frith explains, "In deciding to label a music or a musician in a particular way record companies are saying something about both what people like and why they like it; the musical label acts as a condensed sociological and ideological argument."[26] As digital technology makes hybridity more palpable in contemporary media content an ideological shift becomes apparent in the music industry.

MUSIC AND DIGITAL TECHNOLOGY

Music plays an important role in many people's lives. It lets us explore emotions, experiences, and can provide us with pleasurable connections to moments in time, objects, friends, or family.[27] Music has the ability to accomplish this through its use of recording technology. As Katz states, "Our very notions of musical beauty and of what constitutes a musical life have changed with the presence of recording."[28] As digital technology continues to change the nature of recording, the public is offered new and varying means to consume musical media. Recording technology allows people to hear and experience music that not only extends beyond their own cultural constraints, but also beyond generational constraints. Americans can listen to Chennai Gaana or Trinidadian Soca and contemporary teens can listen to the Zombies or Chet Baker.

While some tend to think of technology as simply a machine or something invented to serve a practical purpose, Shuker argues we need to think in terms of actual practice by considering the uses to which people put technology, in this case compact discs or mp3s, etc., and the devices that play back those recordings.[29] As time goes on, technological advances have provided society with multiple formats that enable us to hear sounds. These formats include the wax cylinder, the 78, 45, 33 1/3, cassette tapes, compact discs, and digital mp3 files. Changes in format influence popular music culture because each time a new technology is introduced to the public it changes the way we experience music and therefore changes how we relate to and consume music. As Shuker explains, "New markets are created as older consumers upgrade both their hardware and their record collections."[30] O'Hara and Brown concur, suggesting that digital technology has "disrupted existing music practices and created new social phenomena around music."[31] One outcome of digital technology is that consumers discover a significant amount of new music online.[32]

Indeed, technology has not only significantly influenced media audiences, but also the music industry, leading to major structural and promotional reconsiderations for record companies and their artists. The traditional music-marketing environment has changed with the rise of the online market. New business strategies and new ways of consuming emerge in relation to our continually growing, digitally saturated environment. Most notable is how the Internet allows artists to become producers and distributors of their own product, which leaves technology savvy consumers with expectations that differ from the more traditional audiences.[33] Tech savvy consumers discover most of their music online and encounter such issues as, which music player is platform compatible and which connection is fast enough to download without any hassle. It is important to note as Jones explains, "The movement of people, however, is not in the music industry's control, and so at the very least the industry needs to be immediately responsive to audience and place."[34]

In the beginning of the decade the music industry panicked because downloading contributed to notable profit loss.[35] News headlines at the time included, "Thousands of Jobs at Risk from Net Piracy"[36] and "Online Piracy Plagues Music Industry."[37] *The Independent* stated, "Downloading music from the Internet has become so common it is seriously affecting CD sales—which dropped worldwide by 5 percent in 2001 from the previous year."[38] *The Financial Times* concurred, "Music piracy poses a greater threat to the international music industry than at any other time in its history!"[39] In response to the panic concerning technology's influence on music consumption, Jones sought to understand cultural processes through an examination of production, distribution, and consumption of music as influenced by emerging technologies.[40] Jones argued that digital technology creates "new territorizations of space and of affect" as consumers download digital music rather than purchase physical media.[41]

However, by 2005 music downloading had decreased from 32 percent to 22 percent.[42] Around this time, scholars started publishing work that revealed findings contrary to the industry's original expectations. For example, La Rose et al. sought to understand downloading behavior through a social cognitive framework and found that file sharing becomes a mindless habit, "with files accumulating on college students computers that they may never even open or listen to."[43] O'Hara and Brown's examination of iPod use found that people cannot process the sheer volume of music they carry around with them resulting in changed listening behavior characterized by focus on a select few musical artists.[44]

Tanaka describes how new "technological infrastructures for creating, rendering, and distributing music change the way that music can be consumed and appreciated."[45] As some consumers mindlessly continue to download music, others consciously choose to purchase physical media. For example, Brown and Sellen found that "physical objects are more suitable for collecting and that current digital files do not support all the subtle activities involved in collecting."[46] Similarly, Katz found that people prefer CDs because of the physicality, performance, visual aspects, convenience, enhancement, and the fact that the purchase supports musicians.[47]

These viewpoints are indicative of the challenges consumers face as they negotiate the contemporary media saturated environment. Accordingly, Thornton explains the discourse surrounding music and technology embraces conflicting views about creativity and musicianship, artistic freedom, and property rights.[48] More specifically:

> New technologies are variously seen as democratizing or consolidating established music industry hierarchies; rationalizing or disruptive of distribution processes; confirming or challenging legal definitions of music as property; and inhibiting or enabling of new creativities and sites of authorship.[49]

Economic and bureaucratic corporate forces within the music industry favor a shift toward proficient practices of music production. This is driven primarily by economic, profit-based considerations. In other words, the need to bring order and cost-effectiveness to musical production has overridden concerns with the creative act of performing music.[50] On the other hand, audiences grapple with the freedom digital consumption offers. This tension reflects the nature of the current music industry. As explained by Beer, "Social networking sites have caused a rapid and radical reconfiguration of the relations between performers and their respective audiences. It is this reconfiguration that, considering the significant and rapidly escalating number of users, requires urgent and critical inquiry."[51] Overall, digital technology's influence on music production and consumption is transforming contemporary popular music culture.

BACKGROUND: WHO IS M.I.A.?

Maya Arulpragasam, also known as M.I.A., is a New York City and London-based singer, songwriter, producer, and visual artist. *Time* magazine included M.I.A in the 2009 *TIME* 100 list of "World's Most Influential People" for having "global influence across many genres."[52] However, her musical career began in 2003 when Showbiz records released a limited pressing of her track "Galang." It generated a massive buzz on the Internet and led M.I.A to sign with a major label, XL Recordings. In 2004, by remixing, sampling and mashing-up tracks, which would end up on her first album, M.I.A. created the digital mix tape *Piracy Funds Terrorism*. The mix tape was distributed at live shows and also released through the website Turntable.com. *Piracy Funds Terrorism* furthered M.I.A's popularity, and stirred a good deal of anticipation for her debut album *Arular*, released in early 2005; *Arular* was nominated for the Mercury Music Prize,[53] a yearly award for best album in the United Kingdom and Ireland, as well as the Shortlist Music Prize,[54] a yearly award for the best U.S. album selling fewer than 500,000 copies. She released her second album, *Kala*, in August 2007. It reached No. 22 on the United World Chart and was named album of the year by *Rolling Stone* and *Blender* magazines.[55] In February 2008 M.I.A. digitally released "Paper Planes - Homeland Security Remixes," the third single off *Kala*. More recently, she contributed music to two feature films, including *Pineapple Express* (2009) and the Academy Award–winning Best Picture for 2008 *Slumdog Millionaire*.

REDEFINING MUSICAL ARTISTS: M.I.A.'S BLOG

M.I.A.'s hybrid style addresses a number of social and political issues including power, violence, identity, and survival in a globalized world. She engages
these concepts in a variety of ways, including in her music, her use of social
media, and finally in her interaction with the press. In each avenue we can
see how M.I.A. challenges traditional definitions of what it means to be a
contemporary musical artist. The following paragraphs specifically explore
highlights of her blog in order to provide an overview of what has influenced
her work and shaped her identity as a musical artist. When choosing these
posts my aim was to include those that highlight key themes related to her
identity, as well as reference the previously noted literature concerning globalization, hybridity, and digital technology. Particularly, the posts chosen
include her most recent post this year, her very first post made in 2005, as
well as a number of posts written during the recording of *Kala*, including her
report on her trip to Liberia.

Her most recent post focused on attending the *TIME* Top 100 Most Fascinating People event.[56] She writes:

> SHE (Oprah) SAID SHE LIKED MY JACKET FROM THE MAGAZINE
> (THE ONE MY BROTHER GOT FOR ME FROM THE SIDE OF THE
> STREET AT SXSW 09) SHE SQUEEEEZED MY HAND SO HARD, I WAS
> CONVINCED SHE CARED. MICHELLE OBAMA GAVE A SPEECH AND
> THERE WAS MAD SECRET SERVICE IN THE AIR SO I DIDNT GET TO
> THROW A PAPER PLANE AT HER SAYING "STOP THE BOMBING OF
> THE TAMILS IN SRI LANKA."[57]

Here, emphasis is on the jacket that originated from the side of the street, as
opposed to being purchased in an expensive store, which is reminiscent of
the third world refugees she so often speaks of receiving aid from first world
countries. The plight of the Third World again surfaces when she mentions
wanting to send the first lady a message about the current situation in Sri
Lanka. Her plan involves throwing a paper plane, the title of one of her more
popular songs off *Kala*, at Michelle Obama in order to get her message across.

In another post where M.I.A. reflects on the abrupt explosion of popularity
surrounding the Grammies, she addresses how she is going to use that popularity to highlight a large part of her identity. She writes:

> I want you to know that, everyone has been asking me on the shows to talk about
> the sudden popularity im experiencing, the babies, the grammies the oscars etc
> and i want you to know that this has been part of the plan from day 1. this is the

only opportunity i have had to do something about the genocide in Sri Lanka and im seizing that opportunity so for a lil while im gonna go from being M.I.A. TO I. Y. F. IN YA FACE!!!!!!!!!!!![58]

There is obvious importance placed on using the digital media that has been integrated into her life and, in essence, become her life. She brings together two aspects of her persona through media attention. In other words, she is drawing attention to herself as a person and Sri Lankan, with what originally got her attention, primarily digital distribution, as a musical artist.

While recording *Kala* she took what seems to be a very influential trip to Liberia. Her blog post after returning from her trip is one of the longest and heaviest posts in the entire blog and, as with other posts, reflects her passion for the third world's plight. The following includes excerpts from that post. She states:

I HAD A GUCCI SWEATER ON, AND THEY ASKED ME IF IT WAS REAL, I SAID NO AND THE MEN WERE LIKE OHHH SORRY IT WOULDA BEEN NICE IF U HAD THE REAL AUTHENTIC THING, AND I TOLD EM I WASNT SAD AT ALL. I JUS RATHER HAVE MY MONEY GO TO SOME POOR DUDE MAKIN EM IN CHINA OR AFRICA THEN THE POWER HOUSES IN THE WEST, THEN THEY GAVE ME THE LIBERIAN HIGH FIVE; THIS ISNT AFRICA AGAINST THE WORLD THING MAYBE NOT EVEN RICH / POOR THING WAR THINGITS 1ST WORLD. . . . MEDIA VS 3 WORLD MESSAGE THING. "I NEED TOOLS SHOW ME HOW TO USE TOOLS ILL DO IT MY FUCKIN SELF AND SELL IT TO YOU!!"[59]

Her attitude questions traditional definitions of authenticity and embraces bric-a-brac, DIY (do-it-yourself) culture. Items that could be characterized as hybrid are positioned as more authentic. The blog entry evokes Jenkins' work on convergence culture calling for the convergence of the media producer and consumer, as well as the convergence of grassroots and corporate media.[60] In another post and in a similar vein she again touches on the convergence of both corporate and grassroots media, as well as the intersecting power of the media producer and consumer. She writes:

IM ABOUT TO PUT A SONG UP HERE CALLED "BIRD FLU"!!!
AND THE PHOTOS ON MY PAGE ARE FROM THE VIDEO I DID OUT THERE IN A FISHING VILLAGE IN SOUTH COAST OF INDIA; WE DIS-COVERED AN AMAZING BOY WHO CAN OUT DANCE ANYTHING I VE ever SEEN. HE INVENTED ME THE BIRD FLU DANCE. I CALLED THIS BIRD FLU BECAUSE THIS BEAT GON KILL EVERYONE!![61]

The community that she inhabits heavily influences much of her music, in both sound and visual form. For example, this post mentions the integration of an Indian village into the music video for the song "Bird Flu," which features a dance by a local boy. She has also done music videos in other locations representative of her community such as southern Indian, urban Britain, and Brooklyn, New York; all areas where she at one time lived.

Finally, her very first blog post works to make sense of who she is and will become as a musical artist in contemporary digitally mediated culture. She writes:

> The first thing thats important to me right now is my space, so I'm trying to get one on the planet, at the moment its where ever I lay my phone that's home. It has become more and more clear that I am a citizen of the world, and I can't quite seckel . . . I'm really excited by the amount of true freedom my work and music has bought me and you guyz are smart! I'm thinking everyday of how best to communicate the things . . . I will try and give you the most realistic insight into what is going on with me. Watch this space and I will write and show you photos. Tell me what you want to see! [away] M.I.A.[62]

The beginning of her blog post acknowledges her global quality and highlights the importance of the global connections made possible with digital media. The importance of the connections afforded lie in the fact that she has the power to incorporate her community into her work and into her identity as a musical artist.

BREAKING BORDERS AND BOUNDARIES: LEVELS OF IMPACT

M.I.A.'s musical work is reflective of globalization's influence at three levels: cultural, technological and political. First, on a cultural level M.I.A. articulates her hybrid identity by drawing from "a variety of texts" often outside her "ascribed cultural space."[63] Her work encompasses multiple styles and genres ranging from hip-hop, punk rock, dancehall, Indian pop, as well as the traditional music of Ghana and Trinidad, which creates a musical product best characterized by cultural hybridity. And, it can be argued that she creates this hybrid work to reflect her identity as a musical artist, which in turn, facilitates a better understanding of the contemporary cultural climate.[64]

Second, on a technological level, her music integrates original work with samples of other musicians' work from past decades. M.I.A. also makes full use of digital technology in terms of musical distribution by releasing, for example, both traditional physical albums, such as *Arluar* and *Kala*, and also digital albums/mix-tapes, such as *Piracy Funds Terrorism*. Third, it is political, as she often positions herself as a voice for the third world in Western-dominated global society. M.I.A. creates and consumes hybrid texts to "subvert the politico-economic context in which it occurs."[65] In other words, she uses her work to draw attention to Third World dilemmas while encouraging others to do the same.

As previously mentioned, Lull explains that globalization fuels creativity and that is something explicitly seen in M.I.A.[66] As Brah and Coombes argue "music is one of the more productive sites for hybrid interactions which could be described as both cultural exchange and commodification without being reduced to either one or the other."[67] Concurrently, M.I.A. embodies Clothier's argument that the Internet is a key factor in manufacturing hybrid cultural identities.[68] *Piracy Funds Terrorism* challenges First World culture's dominant ideology with its themes of political power and Third World empowerment. Similarly, her first album *Arular*, named for her father who was a founding member of the Eelam Revolutionary Organization of Students (EROS) a militant Tamil group, also challenges hegemonic positions. M.I.A.'s personal style itself mocks dominant ideological values with its mish mash of East and West, old and new, and high and low cultures.

Beer and Sandywell argue that "the hyper-commodification of popular cultural forms has accelerated the transmutation of genres in the digital age."[69] The reaction to this hyper-commodification, which is seen in M.I.A., leads to the accelerated transmutation of genres that she embodies. Technology that enables such remixes, samples and mash-ups is M.I.A.'s tool to create a product reflective of a hybrid style that allows her to produce work that is not classifiable by any one genre. Clothier explains, "Hybrid cultures are antagonistic to standing authority and cultural hegemony – hybridization engenders diversity and heterogeneity, which was once framed as bastardization."[70] In essence, convergence culture generates an environment that allows her hybrid cultural identity and style to thrive.

Convergence culture enables this specific, globally characterized musical artist. As Jenkins explains, "Convergence culture alters the relationship between existing technologies, industries, markets, genres, and audiences" and involves a number of intersections that M.I.A. embodies.[71] The first intersection is between old and new media, which is seen in her use of online mix tapes. The second intersection, between grassroots and corporate media, is seen in her use of Aboriginal children rapping on a verse of her song released on a major label. In this case a traditionally marginalized population becomes a part of a corporate commodity. Finally, the intersection between media producer and consumer is also evident in her work. M.I.A. aims to break down the traditional barriers between the two by encouraging her audience to not merely consume, but also produce. She also does this by involving those in her community into the production of herself as an artist, which she accomplishes by incorporating them into music videos and songs.

This concept of creatively empowering the audience, for M.I.A, is about empowering herself as a voice for the Third World. Throughout her blog she often challenges the notion of authenticity. In many cases, the traditional version of a product is seen as less authentic than the "remixed" product. She leads by example through repurposing and remixing to create globally relevant discourse through her music. As evident in her blog posts, she openly encourages others to repurpose and remix as well, in order to create unique cultural representations from the empty commodities that are so often sought after. In essence, M.I.A. attempts to overcome negative effects of globalization through the empowering facets of sociable media, often dubbed Web 2.0. As Beer and Burrows explain, "The key-defining feature of web 2.0 is that users are involved in processes of production and consumption as they generate and browse online content, as they tag and blog, post and share. This has seen the 'consumer' taking an increasingly active role in the 'production' of commodities."[72] Both, convergence culture and the web 2.0 phenomenon go hand in hand to highlight the collaborative and creative enabling of the audience.

On her blog M.I.A. writes that she is going to go from being M.I.A. to IYF, or in your face. Digital technology enables her to do so and being named one of *Time's* Top 100 Most Fascinating People supports that fact. However, she is only one voice existing within the media clutter. We must wonder how in your face one can be when they are one blog post or one Tweet in a million. While M.I.A. is enabled through digital technology on some levels, that same technology that enables also constrains. It is important to note that while she is in essence adding another level to the branded identity that is M.I.A. the musician, it is not necessarily going to be heard louder than work that traditionally goes into making and marketing an artist. Regardless, having a dedicated digital space is key for a musical artist in a time period so heavily characterized by digital media. To not include this aspect of musician branding would be imprudent at a time when society is so taken with sociable media. Having that digital aspect, in this case her blog, integrated into M.I.A.'s identity as an artist, along with integrating into that digital aspect a point of sale is a key to being a successful musical artist. The musician becomes the point of sale. We cannot think of the artist and point of sale as two separate entities. Everything is integrated due to the decentralized nature of the Internet and artist success depends on a fully integrated digital identity. M.I.A. addresses a key component of selling sound in digitally mediated culture: she sells her own sound.

M.I.A. IN A MEDIA SATURATED SOCIETY

Coombes and Brah, as well as Kraidy, point out that in order to truly understand hybrid texts they must be examined culturally, socially, historically and politically.[73] [74] This exploration of M.I.A.'s brand is far from complete and would benefit from the inclusion of research addressing these other levels, for example the deeply embedded political context surrounding her identity as a musical artist. While a number of topics apparent in her blog are explored in this chapter, a notable amount of M.I.A.'s blog content focuses on the political context of the third world. This work would serve to gain from continued exploration and a close reading of the issues surrounding this concept, as well as more in-depth research into the social and historical aspects in order to round out the groundwork started here. Also, continued building on the foundational connections between globalization, hybridity and digital technology, as well as the varying characterizations of identity, to fully explicate the concepts would be beneficial in order to further expand on what it means to be a contemporary musical artist in a media saturated society.

Throughout history, whenever technology impacts music production and distribution it influences popular music culture. Today, many people have the ability to download, burn, create, remix, redistribute and reinvent sound. This is in contrast with the traditional ideals on which the music industry functions. In industry terms, the pursuit of profit dictates the form of the work. In other words, popular music is art being produced for profit and that determines what type of music will be made. Standardizing music into a profitable type is part of what links the music industry with the dominant cultural ideology. That ideology is worked into the social practice surrounding the music industry. In other words, it is manifest in the relationship between the music, creativity, the industry and its publics.

However, digital technology's influence on popular music production, as evident in M.I.A.'s work, seems to represent a restructuring of popular communication and, in turn, a reconfiguration of the traditional process of marketing a musician. A strong identity, complete with digital components is a key characteristic of this reconfiguration. As previously mentioned, M.I.A. represents the direction the music industry and music culture is headed. As explained by Elberse, "A strong artist representation helps to curb the negative impact of unbundling."[75] Unbundling is just one of the many issues digital technologies have brought to the music industry.

On the whole, there is a palpable exchange between musical artists, their listeners and the global community. In a sense, the audience creates the artist with each exchange, creation, and download of information. On the other hand, the artist does his or her part by not only providing the audience with the material with which to work, but also by incorporating them into the material itself. Overall, this occurs contextually within the contemporary cultural climate. The relationship goes beyond the traditional, unidirectional relationship between artists and their audiences. What we see in the case of M.I.A. is a multi-faceted exchange between the musician, technology, and global society, which reflects her identity as a contemporary musical artist.

NOTES

1. Marwan Kraidy. *Hybridity, or the cultural logic of globalization*. Philadelphia: Temple University, 2005.

2. James Lull. *Media, communication, culture: A global approach*. NY: Columbia University, 2000.

3. *Ibid.*

4. Jan Nederveen Pieterse. *Globalization and culture: Global melange*. Lanham, Maryland: Rowman & Littlefield, 2004.

5. Valur Ingimundarson, Kristin Loftsdottir and Irma Erlingsdottir, Eds. *Topographies of globalization: Politics, culture, language*. Reykjavik: University of Iceland, 2004.

6. James Lull. *Media, communication, culture: A global approach*. NY: Columbia University, 2000, 232.

7. Arjun Appadurai. "Disjuncture and difference in the global cultural economy." *Theory, Culture and Society* no. 7 (1990): 295–310.

8. James Lull. *Media, communication, culture: A global approach*. NY: Columbia University, 2000, 233.

9. Frank Lechner. *Globalization: The making of world society*. Malden, MA: Wiley Blackwell, 2009.

10. Terry Flew and Stephen McElhinney. "Globalization and the structure of new media industries." In *The Handbook of New Media*, edited by Sonia Livingston and Leah Lievrouw, 287–306. London: Sage, 2006.

11. *Ibid.*

12. Manuel Castells. *The rise of the network society*. Oxford, UK: Blackwell, 2000.

13. James Lull. *Media, communication, culture: A global approach*. NY: Columbia University, 2000, 230.

14. Marwan Kraidy. *Hybridity, or the cultural logic of globalization*. Philadelphia: Temple University, 2005.

15. *Ibid.*

16. *Ibid.*

17. *Ibid.*

18. Avtar Brah and Annie Coombes. Eds. *Hybridity and its discontents: Politics, science, culture*. New York: Routledge, 2000.

19. Jan Nederveen Pieterse. *Globalization and culture: Global melange.* Lanham, Maryland: Rowman & Littlefield, 2004, 87.

20. Marwan Kraidy. *Hybridity, or the cultural logic of globalization.* Philadelphia: Temple University, 2005, 115.

21. Jan Nederveen Pieterse. *Globalization and culture: Global melange.* Lanham, Maryland: Rowman & Littlefield, 2004, 88.

22. Marwan Kraidy. *Hybridity, or the cultural logic of globalization.* Philadelphia: Temple University, 2005, 145.

23. *Ibid.,* 146.

24. *Ibid.,* 146.

25. Simon Frith. *Performing Rites: On the value of popular music.* Cambridge, MA: Harvard University, 1998.

26. *Ibid.,* 86.

27. Tia DeNora. "Music and emotion in real time." In *Consuming music together,* edited by Barry Brown and Kenton O'Hara, 19–33. The Netherlands: Springer, 2006.

28. Mark Katz. *Capturing sound: How technology has changed music.* Berkeley: University of California, 2004, 189.

29. Roy Shuker. *Understanding popular music culture.* London: Routledge, 2008.

30. *Ibid.,* 38.

31. Kenton O'Hara and Barry Brown, eds. Consuming music together: Social and collaborative aspects of music consumption technologies. The Netherlands: Springer, 2006, 4.

32. Adam Webb. "Technology: How to get music to our ears." *The Guardian,* December 14, 2006.

33. Paula Swatman, Krueger C., and K. van der Beek. "The changing digital content landscape: An evaluation of e-business model development in European online news and music." *Internet Research* 16, no. 1(2006): 53–80. Swatman, P., and C. Krueger. *The Impact of Internet Technology on the Online Content Sector: Value Webs in online news and music.* Presentation CollECTeR LatAm: Building Society through E-Commerce, Talca, Chile, October 3–5, 2005.

34. Steve Jones. "Music that moves: Popular music, distribution, and network technologies." *Cultural Studies* 16, no. 2(2002): 213–12, 213.

35. Clinton Heylin. *Bootleg! The rise and fall of the secret recording industry.* NewYork: Omnibus Press, 2003. Steve Knopper. *Appetite for self-destruction: The spectacular crash of the record industry in the digital age.* New York: Free Press, 2009.

36. A. O'Connor "Online piracy plagues music industry." *The Financial Times,* June 13, 2001.

37. Leyla Linton. "Thousands of jobs at risk from net piracy." *The Independent,* July 11, 2002.

38. *Ibid.,* 11.

39. A. O'Connor "Online piracy plagues music industry." *The Financial Times,* June 13, 2001, 12.

40. Steve Jones. "Music that moves: Popular music, distribution, and network technologies." *Cultural Studies* 16, no. 2(2002): 212–13.

41. Steve Jones. "Music that moves: Popular music, distribution, and network technologies." *Cultural Studies* 16, no. 2(2002): 212–13, 213.

42. Mary Madden and Lee Rainie, "Music and video downloading moves beyond P2P" *Pew Internet & American Life Project*, 2005, http://www.pewinternet.org/.

43. Robert LaRose, Ying-Ju Lai, Ryan Lange, Bradley Love, and Yuehua Wu. "Sharing or piracy? An exploration of downloading behavior." *Journal of Computer-Mediated Communication* 11, no. 1 (2005), article 1, Discussion Section.

44. Kenton O'Hara and Barry Brown, eds. *Consuming music together: Social and collaborative aspects of music consumption technologies*. The Netherlands: Springer, 2006.

45. *Ibid.*, 14.

46. Barry Brown and Abigail Sellen. "Sharing and listening to music." In *Consuming music together*, edited by Barry Brown and Kenton O'Hara, 37–54. The Netherlands: Springer, 2006, 47.

47. Mark Katz. *Capturing sound: How technology has changed music*. Berkeley: University of California, 2004.

48. Roy Shuker. *Understanding popular music culture*. London: Routledge, 2008.

49. *Ibid.*, 45.

50. *Ibid.*

51. David Beer. "The pop-pickers have picked decentralised media: The fall of top of the pops and the rise of the second media age." *Sociological Research Online* 11, no. 3 (2006), 3.8.

52. Staff. "The 2009 TIME 100 finalists." *Time*, April 27, 2009, http://www.time.com/time/specials/packages/0,28757,1894410,00.html

53. Mercury Music Prize http://www.mercuryprize.com/

54. Shortlist Music Prize http://www.shortlistofmusic.com/

55. Metacritic http://www.metacritic.com/music/artists/mia/kala

56. Staff. "The 2009 TIME 100 finalists." *Time*, April 27, 2009, http://www.time.com/time/specials/packages/0,28757,1894410,00.html

57. Maya Arulpragasam. "M.I.A.'s Blog" *MySpace Music*, May 6th, 2009, http://www.myspace.com/miauk/

58. *Ibid.*, January 28, 2009.

59. *Ibid.*, December 12, 2006.

60. Henry Jenkins. *Convergence culture*. New York: NYU Press, 2006.

61. Maya Arulpragasam. "M.I.A.'s Blog" *MySpace Music*, August 18, 2006, http://www.myspace.com/miauk/

62. *Ibid.*, November 17, 2005.

63. Marwan Kraidy. *Hybridity, or the cultural logic of globalization*. Philadelphia: Temple University, 2005, 146.

64. *Ibid.*

65. *Ibid.*, 145.

66. James Lull. *Media, communication, culture: A global approach*. NY: Columbia University, 2000.

67. Avtar Brah and Annie Coombes, eds. *Hybridity and its discontents: Politics, science, culture*. New York: Routledge, 2000, 1.

68. Ian Clothier. "Created identities: Hybrid cultures and the Internet." *Convergence* 11, no. 4(2005): 44–59.

69. David Beer and Barry Sandywell. "Stylistic morphing: Notes on the digitization of contemporary music culture." *Convergence* 11, no. 4(2005): 106–205, 107.

70. Ian Clothier. "Created identities: Hybrid cultures and the Internet." *Convergence* 11, no. 4(2005): 44–59, 44.

71. Henry Jenkins. *Convergence culture.* New York: NYU Press, 2006, 15.

72. David Beer and Roger Burrows. "Sociology and, of and in Web 2.0: Some initial considerations." *Sociological Research Online* 12, no. 5 (2007), 3.1.

73. Avtar Brah and Annie Coombes, eds. *Hybridity and its discontents: Politics, science, culture.* New York: Routledge, 2000.

74. Marwan Kraidy. *Hybridity, or the cultural logic of globalization.* Philadelphia: Temple University, 2005.

75. Sean Silverthorne. "Tracks of my tears: Reconstructing digital music." *Working Knowledge*, November 30, 2009, http://hbswk.hbs.edu/item/6312.html/.

BIBLIOGRAPHY

Appadurai, Arjun. "Disjuncture and difference in the global cultural economy." *Theory, Culture and Society* no. 7 (1990): 295–310.

Arulpragasam, Maya, "M.I.A.'s Blog" *MySpace Music*, 2010 http://www.myspace.com/miauk/.

Beer, David, and Roger Burrows. "Sociology and, of and in Web 2.0: Some initial considerations." *Sociological Research Online* 12, no. 5 (2007).

Beer. "The pop-pickers have picked decentralised media: The fall of top of the pops and the rise of the second media age." *Sociological Research Online* 11, no. 3 (2006).

Beer, and Barry Sandywell. "Stylistic morphing: Notes on the digitization of contemporary music culture." *Convergence* 11, no. 4(2005): 106–205.

Beer. "Reflecting on the digit(al)isation of music." *First Monday* 10, no. 2(2005).

Brah, Avtar and Annie Coombes, eds. *Hybridity and its discontents: Politics, science, culture.* New York: Routledge, 2000.

Brown, Barry, and Abigail Sellen. "Sharing and listening to music." In *Consuming music together*, edited by Barry Brown and Kenton O'Hara, 37–54. The Netherlands: Springer, 2006.

Castells, Manuel. *The rise of the network society.* Oxford, UK: Blackwell, 2000.

Clothier, Ian. "Created identities: Hybrid cultures and the Internet." *Convergence.* 11, no. 4(2005): 44–59.

DeNora, Tia. "Music and emotion in real time." In *Consuming music together*, edited by Barry Brown and Kenton O'Hara, 19–33. The Netherlands: Springer, 2006.

Flew, Terry, and Stephen McElhinney. "Globalization and the structure of new media industries." In *The Handbook of New Media*, edited by Sonia Livingston and Leah Lievrouw, 287–306. London, UK: Sage, 2006.

Frith, Simon. *Performing Rites: On the value of popular music*. Cambridge, MA: Harvard University, 1998.

Heylin, Clinton. *Bootleg! The rise and fall of the secret recording industry*. New York: Omnibus Press, 2003.

Ingimundarson, Valur, Kristin Loftsdottir and Irma Erlingsdottir, eds. *Topographies of globalization: Politics, culture, language*. Reykjavik: University of Iceland, 2004.

Jenkins, Henry. *Convergence culture*. New York: NYU Press, 2006.

Jones, Steve. "Music that moves: Popular music, distribution, and network technologies." *Cultural Studies* 16, no. 2(2002): 213–212.

Katz, Mark. *Capturing sound: How technology has changed music*. Berkeley: University of California, 2004.

Knopper, Steve. *Appetite for self-destruction: The spectacular crash of the record industry in the digital age*. New York, NY: Free Press, 2009.

Kraidy, Marwan. *Hybridity, or the cultural logic of globalization*. Philadelphia: Temple University, 2005.

LaRose, Robert, Ying-Ju Lai, Ryan Lange, Bradley Love, and Yuehua Wu. "Sharing or piracy? An exploration of downloading behavior." *Journal of Computer-Mediated Communication* 11, no. 1 (2005), article 1.

Lechner, Frank. *Globalization: The making of world society*. Malden, MA: Wiley Blackwell, 2009.

Linton, Leyla. "Thousands of jobs at risk from net piracy." *The Independent*, July 11, 2002.

Lull, James. *Media, communication, culture: A global approach*. NY: Columbia University, 2000.

Madden, Mary, and Lee Rainie, "Music and video downloading moves beyond P2P" *Pew Internet & American Life Project*, 2005, http://www.pewinternet.org/.

Mercury Music Prize http://www.mercuryprize.com/

Metacritic http://www.metacritic.com/music/artists/mia/kala

Nederveen Pieterse, Jan. *Globalization and culture: Global melange*. Lanham, Maryland: Rowman & Littlefield, 2004.

O'Connor, A. "Online piracy plagues music industry." *The Financial Times,* June 13, 2001.

O'Hara, Kenton, and Barry Brown, eds. *Consuming music together: Social and collaborative aspects of music consumption technologies*. The Netherlands: Springer, 2006.

Shortlist Music Prize http://www.shortlistofmusic.com/

Shuker, Roy. *Understanding popular music culture*. London: Routledge, 2008.

Silverthorne, Sean. "Tracks of my tears: Reconstructing digital music." *Working Knowledge*, November 30, 2009, http://hbswk.hbs.edu/item/6312.html/.

Staff. "The 2009 TIME 100 finalists." *Time*, April 27, 2009, http://www.time.com/time/specials/packages/0,28757,1894410,00.html

Swatman, P., Krueger C., and K. van der Beek. "The changing digital content landscape: An evaluation of e-business model development in European online news and music." *Internet Research* 16, no. 1(2006): 53–80.

Swatman and Krueger. *The Impact of Internet Technology on the Online Content Sector: Value Webs in online news and music.* Presentation CollECTeR LatAm: Building Society through E-Commerce, Talca, Chile, October 3–5, 2005.

Tanaka, Atau. "Interaction, experience, and the future of music." In *Consuming music together*, edited by Barry Brown and Kenton O'Hara, 267–286. The Netherlands: Springer, 2006.

Webb, Adam. "Technology: How to get music to our ears." *The Guardian*, December 14, 2006.

14

Your "American Idol": The Intersection Between Reality Television, Ideology and the Music Industry in Popular Culture

Alison Slade

Branding is what Fuller is all about. He redefines the role of manager for the 21ˢᵗ century. He treats pop acts as brands, to be exploited over as different media, rather than performers who make money selling records and playing concerts. He's a genius—he makes everyone else look like complete amateurs.—Eric Olsen[1]

American Idol: The Search for a Superstar debuted in June 2002 as a summer replacement program on the Fox network. Creator Simon Fuller, borrowing from Great Britain's reality show *Pop Idol*, introduced the competition for a new solo musical act in which contestants vocally battled for the ultimate title of "American Idol," with the winner receiving a recording contract under the parent companies of 19 Management and FremantleMedia. Initially rejected by Fox and Rupert Murdoch, the hesitantly accepted first fledgling season of *American Idol* arrived on the reality television scene with little fanfare. Amazingly, the season one finale drew more than 22 million viewers.[2] Since 2002, the program has continued a steady rise in popularity, consistently earning the number one spot in ratings from 2003 to 2009 and causing rival television networks to refer to *Idol* as the "Death Star."[3]

Over eight seasons, *Idol* has seen its fair share of rock stars and rock flops. Aspiring singers from around the United States wait for auditions in lines upward of the tens of thousands to get a chance to sing for the judges and a slot on one of reality television's greatest hits. The impact of reality television on this ideology driven sound, then, lies within its ability to transform music from merely aural entertainment on the afternoon drive or a summer concert in the city, to one of capitalistic enterprise in which the voting audience has a seemingly direct impact on the outcome of the program and the path of the rising star. Meyrowitz asserts as changes in society occur, television programming evolves to mirror those changes.[4] Viewers have the opportunity to observe ideological representations that may be challenging to their own ideological views as well as views that challenge societal views as a whole. Reality television, specifically *American Idol*, offers a means of disseminating musical artists and their individual brands to the masses with the bottom line of making money and reshaping the capitalist enterprise in the music industry. According to Fairchild, "the main goal of *Idol*'s producers is to build affective investment in contestants and gradually shift that investment to the narrative and drama of the program itself."[5] *American Idol* is a capitalistic venture at its very core, a new means to cultivate and integrate new musical talent into mainstream popular culture. Even those who are not fans of the actual program will find themselves exposed to *American Idol* talent after the program; often, the actual *American Idol* artist who won the program is not the object being thrust upon the cultural landscape (e.g., Jennifer Hudson, Chris Daughtry). The intersection between the capitalist ideologies of *American Idol* and the ideologies within reality television programming have combined to create a powerful cultural force in the formation of musical artists' brands. The ideology within *American Idol* is not limited to capitalism, but also embraces and conveys messages concerning celebrity, patriotism and the American Dream.

This chapter seeks to examine the following questions: What is the power of reality television as a cultural force and image creator within our society? What is the power of reality television to shape and market the next greatest musical artist in our society? What ideologies are evident within *American Idol?* How has capitalism surrounding music and music culture changed since the advent of reality television, if at all? What, if any measure can be determined, is the success of the *American Idol* finalist dependent upon within society? Is the creation of music artists and branding changed forever due to reality television and the vote of the American population?

DEFINING REALITY TELEVISION

Due to the lower production costs and high ratings, reality television programming began flooding the television line-up after the swift rise in popularity of *Survivor* in the summer of 2000. Today, there are as many as 200 reality programs available for viewing on network and cable channels. There are three cable networks devoted entirely to reality programming (e.g., Fox Reality Channel, developed in 2006). However, it is important to note reality television programming is not a new phenomenon in the viewing landscape.

The roots of reality television can actually be linked to the beginnings of television programming. Early television programs, such as *I'd Like to See*, *Candid Camera*, or *Queen For A Day*, placed real people in dramatic situations. Ouelette and Murray note "the landmark cinema verite series, *An American Family* . . . is often cited as the first reality television program."[6] According to McCarthy the "first-wave of reality television" began in 1948 with the release of *Candid Camera*, with host and creator Allen Funt often hailed as "reality television's creative ancestor."[7] Programs such as *Star Search* and *America's Funniest Home Videos* can also be considered a part of reality television history for their portrayal of amateur talent and mundane activities. However, the first modern network to push the limits of realism through programming was the Fox network production of *America's Most Wanted* and *Cops*.

When Fox debuted in 1986, the network struggled to gain momentum into competition with the three main broadcasting networks of NBC, ABC, and CBS. Therefore, Abelman notes, Fox was "most successful in establishing itself in this highly competitive industry by pushing actualism—drama presented realistically—to its limits of realism."[8] By the time *The Real World* debuted on MTV in 1991, the groundwork for the exciting narratives and cultural conflicts that are the hallmark of the reality format were already in place.

The definitions of reality television appear in a variety of scholarship, ranging from reality television being characterized as the careful video construction displaying "the 'lives' of ordinary people engaged in sometimes extraordinary events,"[9] or as Ouelette and Murray explain reality television as "an unabashedly commercial genre united less by aesthetic rules or certainties than by the fusion of popular entertainment with a self-conscious claim to the discourse of the real."[10] Reality television is a means by which television programmers attempt to portray a constructed "reality" that will gratify the needs of the audience, a similar goal of much, if not all, of the programming found on television.

Fiske and Hartley assert the more "realistic a program is thought to be, the more trusted, enjoyable—and therefore the more popular—it becomes."[11] Also, Gitlin notes that the "most popular shows are those that succeed in speaking simultaneously to audiences that diverge in social class, race, gender, region, and ideology . . . appealing to a multiplicity of social types at once" in order to satisfy market demands.[12] Thus, the diverse audience and the depiction of realistic events have caused reality television to enjoy an enduring popularity. For example, the realistic portrayal of average citizens engaged in auditions and/or competition for a place in music history draws a large viewing audience in each season of *American Idol*.

REALITY TELEVISION AND IDEOLOGY

According to Blumler and Katz mass media are cultural institutions serving social and psychological functions and can evoke longitudinal effects on participants or viewers.[13] Nelson notes television is a strong socialization agent, capable of stimulating broad questions of public values by conveying a sense of reality and personal involvement.[14] Further, Haque notes a basic function of the mass media is to reinforce existing cultural values, through a combination of "themes, characters, and personalities in fictional and reality-based media content."[15] The longevity of reality television suggests this programming has the potential to enact long-term value and attitude change, as well as reinforce pre-existing ideological viewpoints within culture and society. Specifically, long-running reality television programs have hit upon the necessary formula to garner continued audience support, some actually gaining larger fan bases over time, by promoting certain ideological positions in each broadcast.

Television programming in and of itself is situated in a position of power within our culture, one of the most visible forms of cultural transmission. Barker asserts ideology as seen in television formats is not the simple transmission or injection of dominant ideas into audience members, but rather the ideological representations found within television programming present a preferred meaning for readers.[16] According to Fiske, television works "ideologically to promote and prefer certain meanings of the world, to circulate some meanings rather than others, and to serve some social interests better than others."[17]

In the most recent use of the term in media studies, ideology refers to a system of beliefs, values and behaviors that have a dominant position in society.[18] The Marxist concept of ideology is a system of illusory beliefs, also referred to as a "false consciousness."[19] The ideas of the dominant class are viewed and accepted as natural and normal, and the ruling class is the dominant producer of ideas, as well as the main distributor of those dominant ideas and concepts. Marxist ideology perpetuates the notion knowledge is class based, with lower or working classes receiving less information than higher classes. Further, the information is limited to those views the dominant class disseminates within the media or along other channels. This dissemination is based on the Marxist concept of production within a given culture.

According to Marx, the core elements of a culture are determined by the modes of production within that society.[20] All society's institutions, whether political, educational, legal or cultural, can be placed with the base/superstructure model. The base consists of the modes and means of production, whereas the superstructure contains the ideas and values of the culture. The base can significantly impact the superstructure, as changes within the base "affect all other changes in society, the entire culture, above all, of the ideas, institutions, values, religion."[21] For example, media are dependent upon the context of production, and thus are considered part of the superstructure. Television programming in the 1950s (e.g., *The Donna Reed Show*) was indicative of a particular era in society. As the basic modes of production within society changed (i.e., women entering the workforce in record numbers), the face of programming also began to shift. By the 1970s, the ideologies of some network programs were becoming more focused on the independence of women (e.g., *Maude*).

Real culture within capitalist societies was replaced with a "false" sense of culture, vulgar commodities created to "ideologically ensnare and hypnotize the masses."[22] Further, some scholars extended this argument, noting, in true Marxist fashion, "the mass media are a powerful ideological weapon for holding the mass people in voluntary submission to capitalism.[23] Many scholars supported this definition of ideology, however, some questioned the authenticity of an argument that virtually ignored the individual member of society, or in the case of the media, the individual audience member.

Italian Marxist Antonio Gramsci further expanded upon the concept of ideology by developing the idea of hegemony. Hegemony is the mechanism by which the dominant class maintains control in society by propagating news and ideas on society and society accepting them. Corcoran asserts "hegemony implies the active engagement of individuals with the ideology of the dominant sectors of society and therefore active cooperation in their own domination."[24] The hegemony model views media and culture as a terrain of an ever-shifting and evolving hegemony in which consensus is forged around competing ruling-class political positions, values and views of the world.[25] This version of the media allows other views the opportunity to be presented, however, the dominant perspectives will win out the majority of the time in media decisions. Hegemonic relationships are based on class, and therefore based on culture. Without culture, there are no class relationships and, therefore, no grounds for contesting, negotiating, or resisting hegemony. According to Hall, ideology and hegemony do not imply a single dominant ideology, but "a complex field of competing ideas which have points of separation and break as well as those of juncture; in short, an ideological complex, ensemble or discursive formation."[26] For example, successful television programming must accomplish two goals concurrently: win support from the audience and propose ideological views which do not threaten the status quo.[27]

THE IDEOLOGIES OF *AMERICAN IDOL*

Reality television programming, taken as a whole, can be analyzed from a variety of ideological positions.[28] By viewing *American Idol* with the ideological lens, three distinct dominant positions can be determined: capitalism, the value of celebrity and fame and the hegemonic relationships between the audience, capitalism and *American Idol*.

Capitalism. Reality television is a reflection of the concept of culture as commodity. Over the course of the past few decades, capitalism has shifted from the industrial production of goods and services to the production of culture. Culture has become a commodity, up for sale to any consumer willing to pay top dollar not only for products, but also for experiences. According to Fiske and Hartley "television is one of the most highly centralized institutions within our culture" due to commercialism, government control and the need for a common center in a highly fragmented society.[29] Berger notes "capitalism, from the perspective of consumer culture theorists, is not simply an economic system, but a kind of culture in which almost everything is subordinated to consumption."[30] The main source of this new trend in capitalism: technology. According to Bogart, "new technology [has] added more than 50[percent] to the consumer's entertainment and information budget."[31] The digital channel is the method of dissemination to the masses.[32]

The marketing of these programs allows viewers to purchase items or souvenirs from the programs; specifically, *American Idol* branded products come in the form of T-shirts, song releases and downloads, temporary tattoos, video games (across four different gaming platforms), posters, commercials, concert tours, films, as well as "The American Idol Experience," a new attraction at Walt Disney World Resort in Orlando, Florida.[33] The Internet is the most common source of merchandise, as this new medium provides a means of instant gratification (e.g., ordering the products immediately). *American Idol* host Ryan Seacrest does a majority of the program's marketing within the actual broadcasts, directing the viewer on how to access the items for purchase. It is important to note reality programs have been criticized for depicting "marketing as a bunch of hyperbolic nonsense brainstormed into existence by teams of cutthroat opportunists who understand the brands they work on only as a means to win the game."[34] The capitalistic tendencies to market the *American Idol* brand are not limited to the actual program, but are extended to the contestants through the branding of the individual artists.

Much like television programming, the ideology of music within culture is reflective of the time in which it was produced. Generation after generation has relied upon cultural influence and values to create musical artistry indicative of a specific period in cultural history. From the lilting jazz of the 1920s to the 1950s birth of rockabilly and the rise of Elvis Presley with vulgar hip moves, music, on the whole, has maintained the same sense of ideological surge toward freedom of expression, freedom of ideas, and representative of the youthful generational push toward independence and occasionally self-indulgence, most notably culminating in the Woodstock concert of 1969. Also, we cannot ignore the influence of the rock members of the British Invasion, although scholars have noted the reciprocal cultural relationship between the United States and Great Britain in regard to the music industry.[35] Reality television, specifically *American Idol*, has not lessened the ideological impact of music. Rather, the format of reality television has forever changed this traditional approach to the creation of not only the music, but also the brand of the artists themselves.

Historically, musical artists had to work to define themselves in the industry, either independently or through an agency. Branding of the individual artist within the larger fabric of music culture was cultivated over time with careful construction of identity and connections with the audience. Reality television has allowed this process to significantly speed up. Specifically, *American Idol* methodically creates the brand of the contestant by "acting within a rule-bound series of media events, through which the larger values of the music industry are made comprehensible and material."[36]

Inevitably, the branding of the idol hopeful comes at the forefront of the program. In the early audition weeks of *American Idol*, the judges are often quick to label the potential artist as pop, country, or rhythm and blues, thus compartmentalizing contestants in their tryouts. This branding possibly allows the potential artists to fill a niche from the beginning. By labeling Carrie Underwood (the winner of season four in 2005) at the outset of the audition portion of the season, the viewing audience is inclined to file Underwood away as country.

One of the potential problems of branding the artist up front is it becomes increasingly difficult to remove the label over the course of the program. Viewers could potentially become dismissive of the country star remade into the pop star after winning the competition, or even after being voted off the program. However, the producers of *American Idol* will go to great lengths to ensure their vision of the artist remains intact throughout the program in an attempt to ensure potential future success. Clay Aiken, the eventual runner-up on season two (2002), was initially dismissed by judge Simon Cowell for not having the image, or look, of a pop music star. Aiken was transformed week by week from a goofy, yet lovable, geek to being a more sexual, admirable figure in order to boost sales. His transformation via reality television programming played out for all to see, and the branding of Clay Aiken, the superstar followed by the self-proclaimed Claymates, helped propel Aiken to outsell season two winner Reuben Studdard. By the end of each season of *American Idol*, a majority of the contestants, whether winner or not, have been molded into a specific brand and market image in order to maximize sales and profit.

However, the true illustration of consumer culture and capitalism occurs in reality programming with the reason many viewers are drawn to the genre: to view the interaction between contestants and watch their experiences. As viewers of reality programming, we buy into the idea that we can live vicariously through the participants; we thrive on knowing every detail of contestants' experiences, creativity, and imagination. Recent scholarship has focused on these consumer culture aspects of reality television, investigating not only consumer practices as related to reality television, but also the culture of surveillance and voyeurism.[37]

According to Rifkin, we live in the age of access, in which the consumer is constantly searching for the right to view, own, or experience as much of culture as quickly as possible.[38] Reality television allows viewers to experience or access the lives of others, a "real-life soap opera."[39] Admittedly, *American Idol* is not plagued by the often-tedious interactions and game-play seen on other reality television programs. However, there have been peripheral events surrounding the show which makes the participants more real to the audience. In 2005, two contestants were eliminated from the competition for reasons not associated with the voting: Corey Clark, a top twelve finalist, was removed from the program for not disclosing a prior police record, and Frenchie Davis was not allowed to compete after nude photographs surfaced on the Internet. In an unprecedented move for reality television programming, Davis' photographic mishap prompted producers to enlist the aid of a faith-based marketing team to ensure the program's image with religious-minded viewers.[40]

Additionally, reality programming illustrates access by the method in which viewers receive instant gratification from these programs. Jagodozinki notes reality television has a "particular flavor of 'presence,' of the here and now."[41] Reality television exists in a post-modern society, where television is written in "present tense . . . everything is always happening right now."[42] Gone are the days of waiting patiently for satisfaction on the tube. Viewers want to know what is happening at any given moment. Viewers can now download musical performances on the same night as they are broadcast, and host Ryan Seacrest reminds the audience of this possibility numerous times during each segment. Also, although voters for *American Idol* contestants have a limited time to phone in votes for their favorite artists, they must only wait 24 hours for the results. Furthermore, *American Idol* producers utilize the results show to increase marketing tactics for both the program band and more in-depth conversations with the potential artists, highlighting personal information and messages from *Idol* hopefuls in efforts to increase connections with the fan base.

Celebrity

There is no doubt regarding the security of reality television in American programming. There is always doubt and uncertainty in the world of celebrity, as fame and fortune can come and go as quickly as the next big product on the market. In the world of reality television, the possibilities of future stardom after the show seem endless.

A celebrity can be defined as an individual distinguished by image, a product of the media pushing him or herself into the public spotlight.[43] In today's society, celebrities are held in high regard, as viewers look to celebrities for guidance on such topics as fashion or relationships. American viewers are generally preoccupied with celebrities, where they are, how much they spend, who they are dating or divorcing. Campbell asserted society seems to worship celebrities, as people seek to be known and enjoy name and fame themselves.[44] Thompson asserts that as Americans, we place a "large degree of value and power on celebrity," and Americans have an obsession with their moment in the proverbial media spotlight.[45] Warhol's notation of everyone getting fifteen minutes of fame in his lifetime proved remarkably accurate two decades later. Thus, it is no surprise that reality programs featuring access to celebrity culture are fairly popular. The ideology of celebrity and fame is imprinted on American culture with such ferocity, that even in the wake of global disaster or politics, it the American celebrity who first takes center stage in response. For the winners and losers of *American Idol*, celebrity has various forms.

American Idol is specifically designed to create, brand and market a celebrity. The numbers for previous *Idol* participants are an impressive illustration. Kelly Clarkson, the winner of season one, saw her first album debut double-platinum, while her second studio release hit platinum six times. Clarkson, who has also won two Grammy awards, saw her most recent disc hit No. 1 on the *Billboard* charts. Carrie Underwood is the highest selling *Idol* champion, with 11.5 million in sales, in addition to five Grammy awards and two Academy of Country Music Entertainer of the Year awards.[46] Chris Daughtry, lead singer of Daughtry, has also enjoyed a skyrocket to fame after his *American Idol* appearance in 2006. Although Daughtry did not win season five of *Idol*, he has enjoyed perhaps more success than some winners, boasting two number one albums, several top 40 singles, and an American Music Award. Jennifer Hudson is another *Idol* castoff (season four, 2005) that has enjoyed great success, including a Broadway run in "Dreamgirls," which led to a role in the Hollywood production of the same name and earning Hudson an Academy Award.

In addition to *American Idol*'s development of celebrity in the more traditional sense, it must be noted that prior to attaining celebrity status, these contestants are still merely characters in a reality television program. According to Chesebro, mythical characters are perceived as god-like, other-worldly, and heroic because of inhuman and special abilities in dealing with situations.[47] *American Idol* does not offer representations of the mythical character in the sense of the traditional superhero; however, the ability of these characters to become celebrities or begin as celebrities, as the case may be, can be considered a mythical quality as the audience views celebrities as larger than life. Further, these characters are indicative of the ideology Himmelstein identified as the celebration of celebrity, where "those who have achieved media exposure are, in turn, given greater access to the media exposure because of their celebrity."[48] Thus, those characters on reality television programs who endure continued media exposure after the program has ended could be considered as mythical characters. However, it is important to note since the viewer has no way of predicting which characters can achieve greater success, the participants of reality programming in some sense are all mythical.

Reality television has transformed the way characters are not only introduced, but also the way the viewing audience relates to the characters. It is assumed by many the characters of reality television programs are real; however, the patterns these characters follow may not be as real as they appear. Reality television offers scripted scenario programming, in which writers skillfully craft situations for the performers to follow. On *American Idol*, this can be seen in a number of ways. First, on a majority of the programs, contestants are allowed, and often encouraged, to choose songs to reflect their personality, backgrounds and personal experiences. One of the critiques offered most often by Simon Cowell is the contestant lacks personality or that "it" factor that it takes to make a star. When the producers of *American Idol* choose the songs for performance, the producers are then guiding in a sense the direction of the contestant in the program. One wrong choice by the producers can cause elimination of the contestant. In the spirit of Marxist theory, this is a classic example of the base being directly affected by the superstructure. The production of the musical selection impacts the worker. Secondly, from early on in the competition, viewers identify with specific contestants and thus increases their chance to vote for their favorite, perhaps even having to choose a new favorite if their original choice did not secure enough votes to stay in the competition.

Finally, a powerful element of television programming in the lives of viewers can be classified as performing parasocial functions, a process in which the television characters replace real social relationships. [49] As the performers of reality television come into the homes of millions of Americans per week, the audience forms relationships with the characters. It is these relationships and the possibility of continued perceived interactions with their favorite performers that serves as partial motivation for voting repeatedly for their favorite musician to carry on through the competition.

Hegemony

Reality television often mirrors and reflects the values and basic belief systems within a culture. [50] As Corcoran implied, we are all active participants and willing participants in a culture of domination, where the dominating ideas of what is normal or correct is imposed through our exposures to selected media. The selected media are, by and large, the personal choice of the individual audience member, and a reflection of individual belief systems through those choices. Thus, we actively seek our programming aligned with our own moral compass or view of the world. Further, Abelman notes the underlying assumption of ideological analysis is the "television industry as a whole or individual artists within the industry embrace a particular political position which, in turn, is reflected incidentally or intentionally in the programming." [51] The struggle between dominant positions and those of the individual voice is indicative of the varying hegemonic relationships existent throughout society. *American Idol* is chosen by millions of viewers each season, and the program does not fail to present examples of hegemonic relationships at work.

Although one of the most blatant hegemonic messages within *Idol* relates to image, or the idea of what a pop star in our culture should embody physically and aurally, we cannot ignore the values and belief systems of the artists individually. The artists who unsuccessfully attempt to subvert the dominant paradigm are indicative of the presence of hegemony within the *Idol* programs. An example of this hegemonic tension within the audience can be seen in the 2009 season of *Idol*, and the different ideologies and values represented by the two finalists, Adam Lambert and Kris Allen. Openly homosexual, Adam Lambert was representative of a minority class within society. Though Lambert was praised more often by the judges for his superior talent, with Simon Cowell picking Lambert as the contestant to beat as early as week three, it was soft spoken and more conservative Allen who would win the 2009 *Idol* crown. The competing ideologies embodied by Lambert and Allen is indicative of the struggles within our society to accept different as normal or mainstream. Berger further argues audience members traditionally seek "reinforcement" in the media for their basic beliefs and values and wish to avoid cognitive dissonance. [52] Television programming can tailor messages in the narrative to suit political cultures, as well as reflect the beliefs and values of these groups. Thus, it can be argued the success of the *Idol* contestant within the competition is somewhat dependent upon the contestant's ability to resonate with the dominant values and beliefs in society.

American Idol has come under fire in the 2010 season with the replacement of fan favorite judge Paula Abdul with comedienne Ellen DeGeneres. Further, the 2010 season of *Idol* saw the end of an era with the departure of judge Simon Cowell. However, the strength of *Idol* to weather the storm and survive into another season lies within the cultural power of the program to transmit the values and ideologies of mainstream society. *Idol* is now a veteran in the programming tactics of reality television as a cultural force. Since 2000, reality television programming has enjoyed an increasing power in our culture. The transmission of dominant ideological views can be seen across the genre, imbuing culture with a multitude of messages about values, beliefs and attitudes. *American Idol* emerged as a reality program consistent with the perpetuation of the dominant ideology.

NOTES

1. Eric Olsen, "Slaves of Celebrity," *National Geographic Channel* (18 Sept. 2002), online, 30 January 2010 http://www.salon.com/ent/feature/2002/09/18/idol_contract.

2. Steve Rogers, "Ratings: ABC's 'Dancing with The Stars' finale hits summer highs not seen since 'Idol'" *Reality TV World* (10 July 2005), online, 30 January 2010 http://www.realitytvworld.com/news/ratings-abc-dancing-with-stars-finale-hits-summer-highs-not-seen-since-idol-3598.php

3. Carter, Bill, "For Fox's Rivals, 'American Idol' Remains a 'Schoolyard Bully'." *The New York Times.* Feb. 20, 2007.

4. J. Meyrowitz, *No Sense of Place: The Impact of Electronic Media on Social Behavior.* New York: Oxford University Press, 1985.

5. Charles Fairchild, "Building the Authentic Celebrity: The "Idol" Phenomenon in the Attention Economy," *Popular Music and Society* 30 (2007): 355–75.

6. L. Ouelette and S. Murray, "Reality TV: Remaking Television Culture." New York: New York University Press, 2004.

7. A. McCarthy, "Stanley Milgram, Allen Funt, and Me: Postwar Social Science and the "First Wave" of Reality TV," in *Reality TV: Remaking Television Culture,* eds. L. Oulette and S. Murray (New York: New York University Press, 2004), 19–40.

8. Rob Abelman, "Reaching a Critical Mass: A Critical Analysis of Television Entertainment." (Mahwah, New Jersey: Lawrence Erlbaum Associates, 1998).

9. J. Jagodozinki, "The Perversity of (Real)ity TV: A Symptom of Our Times." *Journal for the Psychoanalysis of Culture and Society* 8 (2003): 320–332.

10. Ouelette and Murray, p. 2.

11. John Fiske and John Hartley, "Reading Television," (London: Methuen, 1978).

12. Todd Gitlin, "Television's Screens: Hegemony in Transition," In *American Media and Mass Culture*, ed. D. Lazere (Berkeley: University of California Press, 1982).

13. Joseph G. Blumler and Elihu Katz, "The Uses of Mass Communication," (Beverly Hills, CA: Sage Publications, 1974).

14. J. L. Nelson, "Values and Society," (Rochelle, New York: Hayden Books, 1975).

15. S. Mazharul Haque, "Cultural Values and Mass Communications," *Encyclopedia of International Media and Communication* 1 (2003): 369–80.

16. C. Barker, "Television, Globalization, and Cultural Identities," (Buckingham: Open University Press, 1999).

17. John Fiske, "Television Culture," (London: Methuen, 1987).

18. B. Casey et al., "Television Studies: The Key Concepts," (New York: Routledge, 2002).

19. Haque, 2003.

20. Casey et al., 2002.

21. F. Gross, "Ideologies, Goals, and Values," (Westport, Connecticut: Greenwood Press, 1985).

22. Casey et al., 130.

23. For further analysis of capitalism and ideology, see Robert Milibrand, "The State in Capitalist Society," (London: Weidenfeld and Nicolson, 1969); Dennis McQuail, "The Influence and Effects of Mass Media," In *Mass Communication and Society*, eds. J.Curran, M. Gurevitch, and J. Woollacott, (Beverly Hills: Sage Publications, 1977): 70–94; Herbert Marcuse, "One Dimension Man," (New York: Routledge, 1964).

24. Frank Corcoran. "Television as Ideological Apparatus: The Power and the Pleasure." In *Television: The Critical View*, ed. Horace Newcomb, pp. 533–52.

25. M. White, "Ideological Analysis and Television." In *Channels of Discourse, Reassembled*, ed. Robert Allen, (Chapel Hill: University of North Carolina Press, 1992).

26. Stuart Hall. "Gramsci's Relevance for the Study of Race and Ethnicity." In *Stuart Hall*, eds. D. Morley and D-K Chen, (London: Routledge, 1996).

27. Casey et al., 2002

28. Alison Miller, "Cultural Values, Narratives and Myth in Reality Television," doctoral dissertation, 2007.

29. Fiske and Hartley, 86.

30. Arthur Asa Berger, "Cultural Criticism," (Thousand Oaks: Sage Publications, 1995).

31. L. Bogart, "Commercial Culture," (New York: Oxford University Press, 1995).

32. J. Rifkin. "The Age of Access: The New Culture of Hypercapitalism Where All of Life is a Paid-For Experience," (New York: Tarcher/Putnam, 2000).

33. Travis Reed, AP. "Become an American Idol, Ride the Mantas and More at New Theme Park Attractions." *Travel, MSN.* http://travel.msn.com/Guides/article. aspx?cp-documentid=1054824&GT1=41000. Retrieved 2010-01-24.

34. J. Hardison, Confessions of an 'Apprentice' insider. *Brandweek*, 46, 2005: 18.

35. For a more detailed analysis of the recording industry and the relationships between the United States and Great Britain, see Laura E. Cooper and B. Lee Cooper, "The Pendulum of Cultural Imperialism: Popular Music Interchanges Between the United States and Great Britain, 1943–1967," *Journal of Popular Culture* and Alan Wells, "The British Invasion of American Popular Music: What Is It and Who Pays?" *Popular Music and Society* 11 (1987): 65–78.

36. Fairchild, 356.

37. For more analysis regarding consumerism and reality television, see A. J. Frutkin, "Reality Formula on Notice," *MediaWeek*, 15, 2005: 6–8; J. Hardison, "Confessions of an 'Apprentice' insider." *Brandweek*, 46, 2005: 18; R. L. Rose and S. L.Wood, "Paradox and the Consumption of Authenticity Through Reality Television," *Journal of Consumer Research*, 32, 2005: 284–297. For more information on reality television, voyeurism and surveillance, see V. Pecora, "The Culture of Surveillance," *Qualitative Sociology*, 25, 2002: 345–358; K. LeBesco, "Reality TV: The Work of being watched (book)," *Journal of Popular Culture*, 38, 2005: 1116–1118; J. Jagodozinki, "The Perversity of (Real)ity TV: A Symptom of Our Times," *Journal for the Psychoanalysis of Culture and Society* 8 (2003): 320–332; M. Jonathan, "From scopophilia to Survivor: a brief history of voyeurism," *Textual Practice*, 18, 2004: 415–35.

38. Rifkin, 2.

39. C. Littleton, "Reality television: keeping the heat on." *Broadcasting & Cable*, 126, 1996: 24–27.

40. Carter, 2007.

41. Jagodozinki, 322.

42. Todd Gitlin, "Postmodernism and Beyond," *Utne Reader*, 1989: 51–67.

43. For more reading on celebrity and image, see Daniel J. Boorstin, "The image: A guide to pseudo-events in America." (New York: Harper and Row, 1961); Joseph Campbell, "The Power of Myth." (New York: Doubleday, 1988); J. Gamson, "The Assembly Line of Greatness: Celebrity in the Twentieth Century America. *Critical Studies in Mass Communication*, 9, 1992: 1–24.

44. Campbell, 1988.

45. R. Thompson, "Reality and the Future of Television." *Television Quarterly*, 31, 2001: 20–25.

46. Eric Ditzian, "'American Idol Winners' Careers Give Clues to Lee DeWyze's Future," 27 May 2010 http://www.mtv.com/news/articles/1640184/00527/ clarkson_kelly.jhtml?mobile=true.

47. James Chesebro, "Communication, Values, and Popular Television Series: A 25 Year Assessment and Final Conclusions." *Communication Quarterly*, 51, 2003: 367–418.

48. Hal Himmelstein, "Television Myth and the American Mind." (New York: Sage Publications, 1994).

49. Leah Vande Berg, and Bruce Gronbeck, "Critical Approaches to Television." (Boston: Houghton Mifflin Co., 2004).

50. Miller, 2007.

51. Abelman, 1998.

52. Berger, 1995.

BIBLIOGRAPHY

Abelman, Rob. "Reaching a Critical Mass: A Critical Analysis of Television Entertainment." (Mahwah, New Jersey: Lawrence Erlbaum Associates, 1998).

Barker, C. "Television, Globalization, and Cultural Identities," (Buckingham: Open University Press, 1999).

Berger, Arthur Asa. *Cultural Criticism.* (Thousand Oaks: Sage Publications, 1995).

Blumler, Joseph G., and Elihu Katz, "The Uses of Mass Communication," (Beverly Hills, CA: Sage Publications, 1974).

Bogart, L. *Commercial Culture.* (New York: Oxford University Press, 1995).

Boorstin, Daniel J. "The image: A guide to pseudo-events in America." (New York: Harper and Row, 1961).

Campbell, Joseph. "The Power of Myth." (New York: Doubleday, 1988).

Carter, Bill, "For Fox's Rivals, 'American Idol' Remains a 'Schoolyard Bully'." *The New York Times.* Feb. 20, 2007.

Casey, B. et al. *Television Studies: The Key Concepts.* (New York: Routledge, 2002).

Chesebro, James. "Communication, Values, and Popular Television Series: A 25 Year Assessment and Final Conclusions." *Communication Quarterly*, 51, 2003: 367–418.

Cooper, Laura E., and B. Lee Cooper, "The Pendulum of Cultural Imperialism: Popular Music Interchanges Between the United States and Great Britain, 1943–1967," *Journal of Popular Culture.*

Corcoran, Frank. "Television as Ideological Apparatus: The Power and the Pleasure." In *Television: The Critical View*, ed. Horace Newcomb, pp. 533–552.

Ditzian, Eric. "'American Idol Winners' Careers Give Clues to Lee DeWyze's Future," 27 May 2010 http://www.mtv.com/news/articles/1640184/00527/clarkson_kelly.jhtml?mobile=true.

Fairchild, Charles. "Building the Authentic Celebrity: The "Idol" Phenomenon in the Attention Economy," *Popular Music and Society* 30 (2007): 355–75.

Fiske, John. *Television Culture.* (London: Methuen, 1987).

Fiske, John, and John Hartley. "Reading Television," (London: Methuen, 1978). Jagodozinki, J. "The Perversity of (Real)ity TV: A Symptom of Our Times." *Journal for the Psychoanalysis of Culture and Society* 8 (2003): 320–32.

Frutkin, A. J. "Reality Formula on Notice," *MediaWeek*, 15, 2005: 6–8.

Gamson, J. "The Assembly Line of Greatness: Celebrity in the Twentieth Century America. *Critical Studies in Mass Communication*, 9, 1992: 1–24.

Gitlin, Todd. "Postmodernism and Beyond," *Utne Reader*, 1989: 51–67.

Gitlin, Todd. "Television's Screens: Hegemony in Transition," In *American Media and Mass Culture*, ed. D. Lazere (Berkeley: University of California Press, 1982).

Gross, F. "Ideologies, Goals, and Values," (Westport, Connecticut: Greenwood Press, 1985).

Hall, Stuart. "Gramsci's Relevance for the Study of Race and Ethnicity." In *Stuart Hall*, eds. D. Morley and D-K Chen, (London: Routledge, 1996).

Haque, S. Mazharul. "Cultural Values and Mass Communications," *Encyclopedia of International Media and Communication* 1 (2003): 369–80.

Hardison, J. "Confessions of an 'Apprentice' insider." *Brandweek*, 46, 2005, p. 18.

Himmelstein, Hal. "Television Myth and the American Mind." (New York: Sage Publications, 1994).

Jagodozinki, J. "The Perversity of (Real)ity TV: A Symptom of Our Times," *Journal for the Psychoanalysis of Culture and Society* 8 (2003): 320–32.

Jonathan, M. "From scopophilia to Survivor: a brief history of voyeurism," *Textual Practice*, 18, 2004: 415–35.

LeBesco, K. "Reality TV: The Work of being watched (book)," *Journal of Popular Culture*, 38, 2005: 1116–18.

Littleton, C. "Reality television: keeping the heat on." *Broadcasting & Cable*, 126, 1996: 24–27.

Marcuse, Herbert. *One Dimension Man*. (New York: Routledge, 1964).

McCarthy, A. "Stanley Milgram, Allen Funt, and Me: Postwar Social Science and the "First Wave" of Reality TV," in *Reality TV: Remaking Television Culture,* eds. L. Oulette and S. Murray (New York: New York University Press, 2004), 19–40.

McQuail, Dennis. "The Influence and Effects of Mass Media," In *Mass Communication and Society*, eds. J.Curran, M. Gurevitch, and J. Woollacott, (Beverly Hills: Sage Publications, 1977).

Meyrowitz, J. *No Sense of Place: The Impact of Electronic Media on Social Behavior*. New York: Oxford University Press, 1985.

Milibrand, Robert. *The State in Capitalist Society*. (London: Weidenfeld and Nicolson, 1969).

Miller, Alison. *Cultural Values, Narratives and Myth in Reality Television*, doctoral dissertation, 2007.

Nelson, J. L. *Values and Society*. (Rochelle, New York: Hayden Books, 1975).

Olsen, Eric. "Slaves of Celebrity," *National Geographic Channel* (18 Sept. 2002), online, 30 January 2010 http://www.salon.com/ent/feature/2002/09/18/idol_contract.

Ouelette, L., and S. Murray, "Reality TV: Remaking Television Culture." New York: New York University Press, 2004.

Pecora, V. "The Culture of Surveillance," *Qualitative Sociology*, 25, 2002: 345–358.

Reed, Travis. "Become an American Idol, Ride the Mantas and More at New Theme Park Attractions". *Travel, MSN*. http://travel.msn.com/Guides/article.aspx?cp-documentid=1054824&GT1=41000. Retrieved 2010-01-24.

Rifkin, J. *The Age of Access: The New Culture of Hypercapitalism Where All of Life is a Paid-For Experience.* (New York: Tarcher/Putnam, 2000).

Rogers, Steve. "Ratings: ABC's 'Dancing with the Stars' finale hits summer highs not seen since 'Idol'" *Reality TV World* (10 July 2005), online, 30 January 2010 http://www.realitytvworld.com/news/ratings-abc-dancing-with-stars-finale-hits -summer-highs-not-seen-since-idol-3598.php

Rose, R. L., and S. L.Wood, "Paradox and the Consumption of Authenticity Through Reality Television," *Journal of Consumer Research*, 32, 2005: 284–297.

Thompson, R. "Reality and the Future of Television." *Television Quarterly*, 31, 2001: 20–25.

Vande Berg, Leah., and Bruce Gronbeck. "Critical Approaches to Television." (Boston: Houghton Mifflin Co., 2004).

Wells, Alan."The British Invasion of American Popular Music: What Is It and Who Pays?" *Popular Music and Society* 11 (1987): 65–78.

White, M. "Ideological Analysis and Television." In *Channels of Discourse, Reassembled*, ed. Robert Allen, (Chapel Hill: University of North Carolina Press, 1992).

15

Gaming the Guitar: Aerosmith, Metallica, The Beatles, and the Music Video Game Revolution

Bob Batchelor

High atop the Mount Olympus of rock music strides its guitar gods, a small band of brothers with the uncanny ability to make the guitar sing. From early luminaries such as Jimi Hendrix, Eric Clapton, and Keith Richards to modern virtuosos like Eddie Van Halen and Slash, these guitar masters earn their fans through flying finger work and uncanny skills. While an adoring public benefits from their expertise, there is something greater on display. As listeners and enthusiasts we understand the basic fact that playing guitar is hard work, necessitating years of endless practice and determination. Unlike sports or academics, mastering the guitar is not a talent that one acquires through great genetics or casual play. While many people learn the rudimentary bass riff opening Deep Purple's "Smoke on the Water" or pick through "Mary Had A Little Lamb," few gain an even cursory ability to play anything else.

Given this scenario, imagine, then, the euphoria unleashed in late 2005 when video game developer Harmonix teamed with publisher Red Octane to release *Guitar Hero*, a single-player music game that enabled regular people to almost instantly become rock gods. Using a plastic guitar with color-coded buttons on the fret, players jammed to tunes from Queen, Pantera, Black Sabbath, Stevie Ray Vaughn, ZZ Top, and many others. Suddenly, anyone could become a worshiped axe man, grinding through classic rock songs. For the countless millions who had ever dreamed of playing guitar, or powered through a face-melting solo "air guitar" style, the dream of shredding became a ("virtual") reality.

What transformed *Guitar Hero* from a big video game release to an iconic piece of popular culture history is that Harmonix developed the game to be ultra user-friendly. With a little practice, mere mortals could unchain their inner Jimi Hendrix, jamming to classic rock standards with heavy infusions of guitar. The game required that players use the guitar-controller in a fashion similar to the real thing. Chris Roper, an early reviewer, discussed the link between real and virtual strumming, saying, "Hammer-ons, pull-offs and up-down strumming all work with this device, making the transition from the real thing to the *Guitar Hero* SG as minor as moving from strings to buttons . . . Note and chord progression is essentially as accurate and true-to-life as it could possibly be on a guitar with only five buttons."[1] Clearly, *Guitar Hero's* playability spurred its popularity among both hardcore gamers and casual users. Fans flocked to the game, with reports of all-night, marathon gaming sessions and *Guitar Hero* contests across the nation. More than 2.3 million copies of *Guitar Hero* sold in the 18 months after its release.[2]

From a cultural perspective, *Guitar Hero* hit the market at an interesting time in American pop culture history, since several interlocking influences converged to propel its success. Technologically, *Guitar Hero* benefited from a long line of interactive games that pulled users up off the sofa. The pioneering global hit *Dance Dance Revolution* (*DDR*) made exercise-based (exergames) cool. While *DDR* featured a much greater full-body workout, the transition from couch potato, handheld controller to pseudo-guitar eased the way for *Guitar Hero* fanatics to rock.

Another essential aspect of the *Guitar Hero's* early success centered on the ubiquity of video games in people's lives. Web-based technological innovations, such as the ability to play with others in real-time, added fuel to the growing popularity of video consoles and games. Two decades ago, an enthusiast might have been embarrassed by the title "Gamer," but in the contemporary world, the moniker is worn with pride. The top video game players in the world even turned professional, playing in video game leagues globally. While critics bemoan the physical and psychological detriments of extended video game play, the nation's young people have turned the video game industry into a big business that routinely generates more revenue than the movie business.

Finally, *Guitar Hero* came about in an era marked by intense celebrity obsession. The game offered players the opportunity to not only embody the iconic avatar on the screen, but also show themselves off based on their playing skills. The modern technological age dominated by Facebook, MySpace, and other social networking sites makes users comfortable in presenting a created self in those illusionary environments, essentially hiding behind virtual selves.

Guitar Hero and other music-based games gives players the (electronic) chance to enter the realm of celebrity icon without leaving their own (physical) space in a multi-layered amalgamation of celebrity, opponent, created self, and physical self.[3] *Guitar Hero* enables users to transcend their own identities on one hand through the guise of a rock music legend, while simultaneously offering individuality via playing ability in a competitive setting.

The physical self that embodies the onscreen avatar also contends with the real life persona of the rock hero, thus adding an additional layer to the dichotomy. When a player embodies a real person via the avatar, it is a different experience than if playing an anonymous or fictional character in traditional video games. *Guitar Hero* and *Rock Band* feature celebrities who have their own inimitable personalities and lifestyles. At the same time, the rock gods also exist as individuals that ordinary people aspire to be or emulate. In many cases, the player knows quite a bit about the person he is imitating on the screen, through books, magazine articles, interviews, movies, and televised stories that make up the person's celebrity character.

Divergent forces compete with each CD release, new video generated, or ring tone created—media convergence and the white noise produced in a culture that churns on and on nonstop. The idea behind convergence is that lines between media channels no longer exist. For instance, where does viral marketing for a new band begin and how does that intersect with traditional forms of advertising? Guitar- and music-based video games have developed into an essential marketing tool. The deeper connection with performers and music fuels the kind of tie between fans and bands in a way marketers dream about. A person can love a new song, buy a ringtone, and even see the performer on tour, but *Guitar Hero* and *Rock Band* take the bond much further by actually enabling the fan to become the musician.

The virtual embodiment of a rock god via the video game takes the notion of marketing to another level, allowing the consumer to become a version of the product. As a result, consumers are creating a more intimate relationship with the product that encompasses physical, mental, and creative spaces. People consume many brands that they cherish, though even the sipping of a Diet Coke or eating a donut from Dunkin Donuts does not approach the level of personifying an iconic figure in a music-based video game. One might enjoy the taste or feel of a particular brand, but one does not actually ingest the company the brand symbolizes. In *Rock Band* and *Guitar Hero*, the performer is captured in a deeper manner.

THE MUSIC INDUSTRY IN THE TWENTY-FIRST CENTURY

From Thomas Edison's invention of the wax cylinder phonograph in 1877 to the latest Web-based innovations, technology is at the heart of the music industry. Technological innovation and change go so completely hand-in-hand that one can practically chart the direct evolution over time from records and phonographs to mp3s. Each subsequent invention builds on its predecessor and subsequently revolutionizes music performance and consumer response. The intersection of performance (the music itself) and consumer response (people listening and/or purchasing) defines the music business.

The popularity of music video games is tightly linked to the current state of the music industry. The interactivity of *Guitar Hero* and *Rock Band*, combined with the rush to put out competing titles with various rock groups that feature new music and downloads specifically designed for the video game experience further blur the lines between consumer desire, marketing, and celebrity influence. While *Guitar Hero* briefly had the market to itself, the increased competition with *Rock Band*, a competing title in the rock game genre, has made the genre more aggressive. A new CD release, for example, is no longer a single incident or merely followed up by the band touring. Instead, the release means availability through traditional purchasing and online availability. The release also coincides with the guitar game version of the band itself or new downloads made specifically for the game console. Many bands are even releasing new music simultaneously with the release of one of the guitar games or making songs directly for the video games. The band is getting a desired product into consumer hands, but from another viewpoint the video game is merely an additional tool to profit from the music, which the music business sorely needs given the pervasiveness of online music swapping and resulting decline in CD sales.[4]

For the music business, convergence provides greater opportunities for artists and management to compete in the battle for consumers across all mediums. However, the sheer volume of messages produced in a converged society also leads to information overload, or a seemingly endless cloud of marketing, advertising, sales, and informational touch points demanding something from consumers—their attention, money, memory, or actions. Therefore, every artist in a converged culture operates in a setting that enables constant interaction with consumers across numerous media outlets, but the idea that everyone is always adding to the system creates a crisis situation in which people cannot decipher or distinguish the messages.

The search for a footing in the slippery, converged world really defines what popular culture is all about in the new millennium. For most artists and the corporate marketing efforts supporting them, convergence leads to a blockbuster mentality, or an all-out strategic plan designed to create huge release day sales that will then lead to greater exposure, thus greasing the marketing gears that keep the pop culture industry churning.

Pulling the fans into the creative process and then giving them a chance to interact with their submissions plays on the general narcissism of Americans today. With outlets such as online video site YouTube, people know that they can create their own version of their favorite songs. As a result, record companies and artists attempt to bring them into the process sooner.

YouTube adds an additional dimension as well. Players all over the world post videos of themselves playing the guitar game, which gives others the ability to post comments and reactions to the actual play. This idea of a "virtual scoreboard" built around music gamesmanship serves as a marketing opportunity for the real live band and music behind the games and for the video games as separate entities. A recent search for "guitar hero" on YouTube, for example, resulted in 316,000 videos, ranging from instructional pieces teaching newcomers certain solos or riffs to the 2008 world record score achieved by teenager Chris Chike.

A constant yearning for fame—almost a feeling of being entitled to it— gripped the nation as social media blossomed. As a result, young people would do just about anything to have their moment in the public eye. For a tiny minority, the payoff takes place, but the vast majority either never achieves his or her bit of fame or washes up on the wreckage that is a natural by-product of the reality industry.

The popularity of *Guitar Hero* is tied to two previous influences: the development of mp3 music files and the ability of users to easily download these packets (legally or illegally). The rise of the web in the mid-to-late 1990s led to the popularity of the mp3, a new kind of compressed music file condensed enough that it could be swapped online. Although compressing the file reduced the sound quality, manageability trumped the aesthetics. For the most part, only true aficionados could tell the difference between an mp3 file and audio CD track. Depending on a person's computer modem speed, an mp3 could be downloaded in minutes or as quickly as a couple seconds.[5]

The ability to trade music over the Internet had a mushrooming effect culturally. First, users essentially violated copyright rules when swapping music online. Then, as is typical of a capitalist system, innovation runs with money-making potential. A number of file-sharing companies formed, the most infamous being Shawn Fanning's Napster, which became synonymous with free downloading. Soon, however, consumers seemed to believe that the ease of downloading music from Internet sites somehow made the music "free."

In the early days of file-sharing, most users stored the music on their computer hard drives, either using their computers as a sound system or burning the files onto CDs to play on the go. Later, with the rise of portable MP3 players, most notably the iPod, people uploaded the files to the device directly.

Despite rampant file-sharing and the music industry's weak initial reaction, the courts eventually caught up with Napster. In 2001, the U.S. Supreme

Court ruled against the company, declaring free music swapping illegal and in violation of music copyrights.[6] Although the music industry shut down Napster as an illegal file-sharing site, others such as KaZaA and Limewire used a new innovation, called peer-to-peer (P2P) networking, to continue the practice. P2P is a decentralized file-swapping service that enables users to download from computer to computer without housing music or video centrally.

These services—whether the downloader understands them to be legal or illegal—ushered in an era that placed music at the center of people's lives, thus making it easier to capitalize on video game innovations. Combining the enjoyment of gaming and music made the guitar games more enjoyable for the user, while simultaneously providing a much-needed revenue boost for rock bands and music companies.

THE PERVASIVENESS OF VIDEO GAMES

The ever-increasing popularity of video games, bolstered by the union of technology and culture, has significant consequences, from changing the nature of leisure time for young people to transforming and creating entire industries, such as mobile gaming and interactive play. Many young people would much rather spend their days playing games online or via the hottest video console in front of the television or computer screen, rather than go outside to play or physically engage in a sport. Although the growing presence of music video games arguably leads to more youngsters desiring to pick up a real instrument, it is impossible to imagine that most *Rock Band* and *Guitar Hero* enthusiasts want to spend the time devoted to the guitar, drums, or bass to master them.

Although critics bemoan video games for contributing to childhood obesity and diverting young people's attention away from schoolwork, the gaming industry is big business. Journalist Laura M. Holson reported on the growth of video games versus movies based on 2004 revenue totals, stating, "Video games are among the fastest-growing, most profitable businesses in the entertainment world. In the United States, domestic sales of video games and consoles generated $10 billion in revenue, compared with movie ticket sales of $9.4 billion."[7] Some critics shrug off the video game industry as if it were merely pimply-faced kids sitting in a basement playing pong. The reality is that gaming is big business and a major player in the worlds of technology, consumer goods, and entertainment. The industry has morphed from a niche category into an $18 billion enterprise. The names that dominate the field include a who's who of global corporations, including Microsoft and Sony, as well as divisions of all the major film studios.

The next wave in video game development centers on making games more accessible to a wider audience. Teenage boys, while still important to the overall picture, are no longer the only market. Games like *Guitar Hero* and *DDR* prove that video game companies are designing games that appeal to people of both sexes and all ages. According to journalist Seth Shiesel, "Companies that are making games more accessible are growing like gangbusters, while traditional powerhouses with a traditionally limited strategy of building around the same old (if you will) young male audience have stagnated, both creatively and on the bottom line."[8] The move is toward social gaming, where people interact with each other in front of the television. Then, gaming develops into a party atmosphere, a big hit with college students and players in their twenties, who want the social along with the online experience. Nintendo's Wii console is a prime example of this trend, as is *Guitar Hero*. For example, in its first several years of release, Nintendo could not keep up with Wii demand, shipping 1.8 million units a month globally.

Clearly, social gaming is driven by technological innovations and a more robust broadband network, which reveals the tight relationship between culture and technology. Online PC games, for example, allow people to interact on the screen, eliminating physical distances, but necessitate high-speed Internet connections and souped up computer graphics and processors, necessitating faster, more powerful computing systems. While these systems still appeal primarily to lone gamers, the numbers of subscribers are in the tens of millions.[9]

Concurrently, an even faster segment of the market is enabling interaction in front of the screen and bringing in families, older users, and females. Wii symbolizes this revolution, outselling more advanced systems, such as Microsoft's Xbox 360 and Sony's PlayStation 3. *Wii Play* ranked number two on 2007's bestselling video games. The game enabled interactive, yet simple, play among people using the system, which appealed to those not interested in learning codes or pressing multiple buttons in some arcane sequential order to win. "If new acceptance by the masses is one pillar of gaming's future, gaming's emergence as a social phenomenon is the other," explains Schiesel. "Hard-core gamers are still willing to spend 30 hours playing along through a single-player story line, but most people want more human contact in their entertainment."[10] In the 2009 holiday season, shoppers could find the *Wii Fit* system offered in sales fliers for months, tempting users to employ the video game and its accessories as a means of exercise and weight management.

MARKETING AND ECONOMICS

The incredible success of the *Guitar Hero*—with *Guitar Hero* I and *II* grossing $360 million between 2005 and 2007—made the franchise an important powerbroker in the music industry. As a matter of fact, according to *Rolling Stone*'s Hiatt, the total revenue of the first two iterations of *Guitar Hero* swamped any album released in the same time frame. Ultimately, however, the success of *Guitar Hero* led to the breakup of the original team that developed the game. MTV purchased Harmonix for $175 million in 2006, later followed by long-time gaming company Activision buying RedOctane for $99.9 million. While the latter retained the *Guitar Hero* name, the MTV/ Harmonix partnership teamed to release its own music video game—*Rock Band*—which upped the ante by including vocals, drums, and bass lines to the original idea.[11]

On one hand, the rivalry between the competing companies sparked interest in the music game genre, forcing each to introduce new innovations and artists into the mix. The warfare also swelled marketing and advertising budgets. The companies relied on traditional advertising based on TV and print channels and built state-of-the-art Web sites to give the user a feel for the games themselves. Live events also generated consumer interest. For example, the release of *Guitar Hero III* included the launch of 20,000 kiosks in retail stores like Best Buy and Toys R Us where consumers could test it for themselves. MTV used its multichannel resources to market *Rock Band*, including a 27-city tour in late 2007 and Beatles documentary specials to coincide with the release of that game.[12]

For many rock bands—particularly legendary groups that rely heavily on their iconic status to fuel current revenue—the guitar-based video games propelled them back into the limelight, while simultaneously introducing or reintroducing their music to younger audiences. Certainly the fact that guitar-based, classic rock dominated the early iterations of the video games caused young fans to reinvestigate their ties to iconic music. Yet, at this time, no one is sure if the "discovery" of early Van Halen by a young Millennial actually led to more money in the pockets of the record company or group itself. Virgin's Joshua Freni explains, "[The games] exposes bands to a great new young demographic, who hopefully will love playing the song and will pick up the new and old albums."[13] As a result, many indie, cult, and once-popular bands are finding their way into the guitar game universe, such as Credence Clearwater Revival, the Stooges, and the Ramones.

There are bands whose brand grew more popular based on the strength of music video games, while others are still up in the air. Aerosmith, for example, capitalized on its resurgent popularity based on *Guitar Hero* to not only fuel a world tour, but also to become the face of a new roller coaster at Disney's Hollywood Studios. Becoming one of the park's main attractions, riders endure long lines for the high-speed thrill, while listening to Aerosmith's music.

The marriage of online, offline, and video game platforms creates a legacy for the 40-year-old band that perpetually creates new fans and rewards long-time supporters. Brian Hiatt of *Rolling Stone* reports that the group sold more than 567,000 copies of *Guitar Hero: Aerosmith* in its first week, grossing more than $25 million. In contrast, the band's last studio album, *Honkin' on Bobo*, released in 2004, which sold 160,500 copies in its first week, grossing about $2 million.[14]

According to journalist Beth Snyder Bulik, many bands saw digital single sales skyrocket based on inclusion in one of the guitar music games. In December 2007, Aerosmith's 1974 song "Same Old Song and Dance" sold greater than 2,000 digital copies, up 446 percent over the previous week. Similarly, Alice Cooper's "School's Out" (1972) reached 12,000 copies, an increase of 453 percent and Kiss hit 18,500 with "Rock and Roll All Nite" (1975), a 485 percent jump. She reports that sales sixty-two out of sixty-three songs on *Guitar Hero III* experienced an increase of greater than 100 percent that week. "The teaming up of the music industry and the video-game industry has been a match made in heaven," explains NPD analyst David Riley. "For the music industry, it's a great way to promote new bands and revive old bands while introducing them to entirely new, younger audiences. For the video-game industry, titles such as '*Guitar Hero: Aerosmith*' can help to introduce gaming to entirely new audiences, especially aging baby boomers and the Gen X group."[15]

In contrast, industry insiders expected *The Beatles: Rock Band* video game to enjoy unprecedented sales, given the band's status as the greatest rock and roll group in history. However, sales figures are mixed, despite the simultaneous release of the entire Beatles music catalog in remastered format. According to MTV's Scott Guthrie the video game has sold 1.7 million copies worldwide, and "more than 1 million" Beatles songs have been downloaded. Journalist Luke Plunkett surmises that, "Since they're most likely including albums sales in that number, however (which will bloat the figures), it shows most people picking the game up either aren't aware of, or are simply not interested in, downloadable content."[16]

The Beatles: Rock Band game serves as a kind of bellwether for the industry, which has some commentators fearful that the guitar game market is oversaturated. Market research firm NPD Group, for instance, released a January 2010 report on the 2009 holiday sales season. While the gaming industry reported its best month ever in December 2009, selling $5.5 billion, the sales for music-based games paled in comparison. NPD Group reveals that *Rock Band 2* sold as many copies as *The Beatles: Rock Band* in its first four months after release, while *Guitar Hero: World Tour* dwarfed both selling 3.4 units over the same period. Certainly the release of the video game has not hurt The Beatles as a brand, but sales have not lived up to expectations based on the global marketing campaign to launch the game.[17]

Ben Fritz of the *Los Angeles Times* reports the 2009 music video games sales dropped 46 percent to $1.06 billion. He concludes, "It was the largest decline of any genre, indicating that the once red-hot music gaming trend, which took off with the original *Guitar Hero* in 2005, is losing steam. Part of that drop, however, is because in 2008 more music games were sold with pricey instrument controllers than last year."[18] Considering the hefty licensing costs associated with producing guitar-based video games, 2010 will be a critical year for both developers and the bands themselves. An extra billion dollars in revenue provides a boost the music industry needs, but the concurrent drop in year-over-year sales leaves the subgenre in a state of flux.

AM I JOHN LENNON OR ME?

Guitar Hero and *Rock Band* raise interesting questions about the influence of video games on users that differ from the existing theoretical literature on the subject. Unlike the first wave of interactive games (such as *Dance Dance Revolution*), which required users to essentially exercise while playing, the guitar games do not require the same level of physical exertion. While one can see the evolution from *Dance Dance Revolution* to the current whole body games, like *Wii Fit*, guitar games are on a fuzzier line, perhaps closer to the handheld devices traditionally used to coordinate the action onscreen. Furthermore, while scholars have done pioneering research on how users think, feel, and interact using online avatars, the music video games ask us to examine the avatar and gamer connection when the avatar is a real person and celebrity.[19]

Music video games, particularly *Rock Band*, which features multiple instruments and players, also make physical requirements on the space used to play them. Scholars Allison Sall and Rebecca E. Grinter from the Georgia Institute of Technology, conducted a study examining the physical environments of typical exergame (video games that require people to physically exercise while playing) users in the Atlanta area. They found that the limitations and multi-functional use of televisions and living rooms played a critical role. As an output device, the television is at the center of the gamer's world, yet "The connection to the television pulled games into the room that was most overloaded with functions: the living, dining, and office space. Consequently, physical gaming seemed to be adding yet another function to a multi-function space."[20] Tying the music video games to issues of physical space naturally leads to questions about the user's socio-economic status, since the play often takes place in a group setting, thus necessitating a space large enough for multiple players.

The celebrity avatar in music-based video games, enabling the player to embody the actual musician or a different icon playing songs outside his genre, is different than the first wave of avatar games, such as *Sims* and *Second Life*. Scholar Bob Rehak says the latter "merges spectatorship and participation in ways that fundamentally transform both activities."[21] Both in games where the player creates an avatar version of herself and typical gun-play games, such as *World of Warcraft* or *Doom*, there is constant interplay between the character on the screen controlled (across life, death, and rebirth) by the user and the player himself watching the action unfold.

Rock Band and *Guitar Hero*, however, differ significantly since the user is transformed into an iconic individual with a real life story and celebrity status. Furthermore, one's choice of rock "character," reveals insight into the user's self-perception and way he interprets the character. For example, in *The Beatles: Rock Band*, the choice of Beatle one portrays provides a glimpse into self, because the life histories of John Lennon, Paul McCartney, Ringo Starr, and George Harrison are also part of the larger popular culture milieu. Similarly, a person who chooses to portray Aerosmith as they climb the ladder to fame at small gigs in the greater Boston area may be in direct opposition to the player who chooses to be Aerosmith at halftime of the Super Bowl. In these instances, the gamer is player, spectator, competitor, fan, and performer, seamlessly weaving between the many guises.

Writer Lev Grossman touches on these issues in discussing the experience of playing the music games for *TIME* magazine. He explains:

> You don't need musical talent to play these games. What you need is a weird combination of vanity and lack thereof: vanity in that you have to really be-lieve, somewhere in your lizard brain, that you are a rock star; lack of vanity in that your human brain still knows you look like an idiot. But when it works, you experience music in a completely new way. Never before have I actually enjoyed Megadeth. Conversely, never before have I hated Dylan's "Tangled Up in Blue." But it's really long, and the drum part is really boring.[22]

"Experience" is the critical term in Grossman's explanation. There is a great deal of entitlement contained in that single word, as if somehow the player is deserving of embodying the rock star's body and feeling the same things. The idea of entitlement and its role among the Millennial generation is much debated as this group ascends to a power position in society as the focal point of mass media and culture.

Then, there is the actual "experience" of hearing the music while playing rock star, which Grossman admits changes his attachment to certain songs and musicians. Indeed, the interaction with music beyond hearing it often transforms the way a person interprets the song and musician, certainly in the video age many people based at least some of their feeling about a song on the impression derived from the video. However, those interactions existed between the musician/song and consumer, not via a person trying to "play" the song or personify the band.

THE FUTURE OF GUITAR GAMES AND THE MUSIC INDUSTRY

The sluggish 2009 holiday sales for music video games may be the first sign of the inevitable slide after the genre peaked earlier in the year or just another shrinking market as a result of the global recession that gripped the latter years of the decade. Regardless of how future observers look back on this critical turning point, the impact of guitar-based music video games is undeniable. The *Guitar Hero* franchise alone surpassed the $2 billion mark in total revenues in early 2009.

The burning question for the video game industry is what is the next step it takes to capitalize on its past successes. Some of the directions seem obvious, though fraught with their own unique challenges. For example, with the launch of *DJ Hero* in 2009, the inevitable move into other genres is under way. Now would-be DJs can create their own hip-hop mashups from famous club music. In addition, after fans and gamers clamored for country music versions of *Rock Band* and *Guitar Hero*, the companies responded with new music. The move into other music forms may follow—perhaps there will follow a Conductor Hero, Jazz Band, or others based on more miniscule subgenres. The heart of the guitar game genre, however, remains the player. This is the consumer developers must excite for the industry to remain strong. If branching into new types of music either reinvigorates the market or draws atypical consumers to the games, the music industry and video game producers will follow.

Given the infinite number of media-based distractions in a converged mass media world, music industry insiders are attempting to "maintain...share of mind" among its "core demographic, the people who play video games 30 hours a week," explains George White, Warner Music Group's head of digital sales.[23] As such, a long-term question centers on whether guitar games will be the focal point of new marketing campaigns or become a tactic within the marketer's strategic launch plan.

When analyzing the potential future for guitar-based games, one must consider the general lack of interest in rock music versus other more popular genres, such as pop music and hip-hop. Looking at *Guitar Hero* and *Rock Band* critically, writer David Hajdu laments the glorification of classic rock and the stereotypical rock star lifestyle that is a reward for playing the game well. The trappings of a rock star—often centered on ego, fame, celebrity, drugs, and sex—are packaged for wholesale acceptance by the impressionable gamer mind, showing that the path to success is lined with debauchery. Basically, Hadju reasons, most parents would not enjoy their young sons (the games' primary target audience) emerging from the basement after a marathon session reeking of "success in these games' schemes—that is, in their opulent glorification of ego-gratifying luxury, idolatry, and easy sex." He continues, "Foremost among those hazards is the delusion that an ego adequate to achieving rock stardom can be gratified by any amount of anything."[24]

The music challenge, explains Hadju, is that the "skills" emphasized in the video games are speed and flash, appropriate to cheesy arena rock, but not altogether necessary for more stylish or stylistic music. Much of the music on the video games, he finds "blandly hyperactive and formulaic. It is music as grotesque as the games' porny electronic girls in the indiscriminate robot frenzy they are programmed, like *Rock Band* players, to enact."[25]

Another potential pitfall for the music games is if there is backlash from the music industry, despite the money it is making from sales via the electronic offerings. Musician and wife of deceased Nirvana front man Kurt Cobain, Courtney Love, threatened a lawsuit over the depiction of Cobain in the *Guitar Hero 5* release. Her outrage over what she claims is unauthorized use led her to publicly criticize Activision, claiming the avatar "denigrate[s] his image." Former Nirvana members Krist Novoselic and Dave Grohl joined Love in blasting the company for enabling users to "unlock" the avatar, basically enabling it to sing songs recorded by other artists. In a statement released by Cobain's bandmates, they said, "It's hard to watch an image of Kurt pantomiming other artists' music alongside cartoon characters."[26] The ire raised by Love could lead to further criticism of the way the games employ real (or deceased) musicians, particularly those who still generate significant profits.

For individuals playing *Guitar Hero* or *Rock Band*, the mix of real and virtual experience opens an amalgamation of perceptions, from how one envisions herself to the performance aspect of "playing" music in front of a real and/or virtual audience. There is also an experience that takes place based on the music fueling the games. Whether the user is a hardcore gamer or casual observer, there are feelings associated with the songs themselves and the individual or group that performs them in the real world. According to Harmonix's Greg LoPiccolo, "We had this debate internally. Like, does anybody care about rock? And then we did *Guitar Hero* and discovered to our great relief that many people cared about rock, including a lot of people who didn't apparently know that they cared about it until they got exposed to the material. So did we create that? Or was it already happening?"[27]

In answering LoPiccolo's question, one need look no further than the absolute pervasiveness of music in American society. Perhaps nowhere else on the planet are people so thoroughly engaged with music on a minute-by-minute time frame. Walking across a college campus, for example, reveals that the student without the ever-present iPod ear buds is the exception, not the norm. The access to music downloaded via the computer has fundamentally changed the way individuals operate within their communities.

It seems at the core of music video games is the notion that individuals care passionately about their music and musicians. Listeners vault their musical heroes to iconic status and allow those choices to say something important about them as people. A person's music persona, for instance, often serves as fulcrum for how that person presents himself to the rest of society, perhaps by mimicking a style of dress or letting one's favorite music play a role in one's worldview. At the same time people use music to present an image to the rest of society, others judge their peers by the kind of music they listen to, regardless of what a person thinks, feels, or believes.

In a society driven by popular culture impulses, guitar-based music games occupy a central role across a variety of channels, from use as a marketing tool by music labels and *Rock Band*s to the way they make players interpret and reinterpret self via celebrity and performance. Certainly, *Guitar Hero*, *Rock Band*, and the countless knock-offs sprouting up in discount stores and drugstore chains provide further evidence of the significant position of music in modern American society. Music and gaming have always been entwined with bands yearning to be featured as part of the game soundtrack, but this tie is even stronger now that players can create and re-create iconic songs. Currently, only anecdotal evidence exists to show that music-based video games are triggering sales of musical instruments and lessons, but real guitars, drums, and keyboards do seem to occupy larger shelves at Target, Walmart, and other chains.

The success of *Guitar Hero* and *Rock Band* proves that given the right impetus, video game enthusiasts will get up off their couches, beanbags, and love seats. The games are easy enough for beginners, challenging for experienced players, and the music theme is broad enough to capture the imagination of them all. In a society driven by celebrity, technology, and consumer culture, the idea of gaming the guitar fuses themes that dominate contemporary popular culture.

For the music industry, the guitar game phenomenon has been a needed boost after more than a decade struggling with various forms of piracy and the general notion that music should be available for free. Aerosmith's success, basically using the popularity of its video game to excite a whole new generation of listeners, and its subsequent move into a broad variety of marketing efforts, proves that the combination of good timing and marketing prowess can push a band far beyond its music.

NOTES

1. Chris Roper, "Guitar Hero: Turn it up to 11 and rock the #@$& out," IGN Network, November 2, 2005, http://ps2.ign.com/articles/663/663674p1.html, (accessed March 30, 2006).

2. Kushner, David. "Hero Worship," *Rolling Stone*, May 3, 2007: 24. *Academic Search Premier*, EBSCO*host* (accessed December 12, 2008).

3. For a more detailed discussion of celebrity obsession in the twenty-first century, please see Bob Batchelor, *The 2000s* (Westport, CT: Greenwood Press, 2009), 35–6, 125–29.

4. For a chart outlining the decline in CD sales from 2000–2007 and analysis of the drop, please see *Ibid.*, 158–60.

5. For more information on the early history of illegal downloading, see John Pareles, "With A Click, A New Era of Music Dawns," *The New York Times*, November 15, 1998, http://www.nytimes.com/1998/11/15/arts/music-with-a-click-a-new-era-of-music-dawns.html?scp=3&sq=mp3+illegal&st=nyt, (accessed March 30, 2005).

6. Matt Richtel, "Napster Charts A New Course After Ruling," *The New York Times*, February 14, 2001, http://www.nytimes.com/2001/02/14/business/napster-charts-a-new-course-after-ruling.html?scp=20&sq=supreme+court+napster&st=nyt, (accessed February 5, 2010).

7. Laura M. Holson, "Lights, Camera, Pixels...Action!" *The New York Times*, October 24, 2005, C1.

8. Seth Schiesel, "As Gaming Turns Social, Industry Shifts Strategies," *The New York Times*, February 28, 2008, http://www.nytimes.com/2008/02/28/arts/television/28game.html?sq=&pagewanted=all, (accessed February 28, 2008).

9. Schiesel, "In the List of Top-Selling Games, Clear Evidence of a Sea Change," *The New York Times*, February 1, 2008, http://www.nytimes.com/2008/02/01/arts/01game.html?fta=y, (accessed February 1, 2008).

10. *Ibid.*

11. Hiatt, "Rock Games."

12. Beth Snyder Bulik, "Console Rock 'N' Roll: Two Video Games Clash," *Advertising Age*, October 29, 2007: 8, *Business Source Premier, EBSCOhost* (accessed March 30, 2008).

13. Quoted in David Kushner, "Hero Worship," *Rolling Stone*, May 3, 2007: 24. *Academic Search Premier, EBSCOhost* (accessed March 30, 2009).

14. Hiatt, "Rock Games Battle for Bands," *Rolling Stone*, August 7, 2008: 11–12, *Academic Search Premier, EBSCOhost* (accessed September 15, 2009).

15. Quoted in Bulik, "Video Games Rock the Music Industry," *Advertising Age*, July 7, 2008: 6. *Business Source Premier, EBSCOhost* (accessed December 1, 2008).

16. Luke Plunkett, "Here, Your Blueness…Have Some Beatles: Rock Band Sales Figures," Kotaku, January 18, 2010, http://kotaku.com/5450681/here-your -bluenesshave-some-beatles-rock-band-sales-figures, (accessed January 18, 2010).

17. Dave Itzkoff, "Beatles Video Game: Sales Not So Fab," *New York Times*, January 15, 2010, http://www.nytimes.com/2010/01/16/arts/television/16arts-SALES NOTSOFA_BRF.html, (accessed January 15, 2010).

18. Ben Fritz, "Beatles: Rock Band Sales Slow Over Holidays as Music Video Game Genre Bombs," *Los Angeles Times*, January 14, 2010, http://latimesblogs .latimes.com/entertainmentnewsbuzz/2010/01/beatles-rock-band-fails-to-make -much-noise-over-holidays.html, (accessed January 18, 2010).

19. Cary Gabriel Costello, "Researching Identity in Second Life," *Communications*, 32 (2008): 19–21; Bob Rehak, "Playing at Being: Psychoanalysis and the Avatar," in *The Video Game Theory Reader*, eds. Mark J.P. Wolf and Bernard Perron (New York: Routledge, 2003), 103–27.

20. Allison Sall and Rebecca E. Grinter, "Let's Get Physical! In, Out and Around the Gaming Circle of Physical Gaming at Home," *Computer Supported Cooperative Work* 16 (2007): 211.

21. Rehak, 103.

22. Lev Grossman, "Battle of the Fake Bands," *Time*, December 2008: 74. *Business Source Premier, EBSCOhost* (accessed December 17, 2009).

23. Christopher Palmeri and Tom Lowry. "Guitar Hero: More Than a Video Game," *BusinessWeek*, October 29, 2007: 86–8. *Business Source Premier, EBSCOhost* (accessed August 29, 2008).

24. David Hadju, "Pretending," *The New Republic*, December 2, 2009, 35.

25. *Ibid.*, 36.

26. Charles R. Cross, "Courtney Love Plots Suit Over Kurt Cobain's Use in New Game, *Rolling Stone*, October 1, 2009, 20.

27. James Parker, "School of Rock," *The Atlantic*, March 2009, 37.

BIBLIOGRAPHY

Batchelor, Bob. *The 2000s*. Westport, CT: Greenwood Press, 2009.

Bulik, Beth Snyder. "Console Rock 'N' Roll: Two Video Games Clash," *Advertising Age*, October 29, 2007: 8, *Business Source Premier, EBSCOhost* (accessed March 30, 2008).

Bulik, "Video Games Rock the Music Industry," *Advertising Age*, July 7, 2008: 6. *Business Source Premier, EBSCOhost* (accessed December 1, 2008).

Costello, Cary Gabriel. "Researching Identity in Second Life," *Communications*, 32 (2008): 19–21.

Cross, Charles R. "Courtney Love Plots Suit Over Kurt Cobain's Use in New Game, *Rolling Stone*, October 1, 2009.

Fritz, Ben. "Beatles: Rock Band Sales Slow Over Holidays as Music Video Game Genre Bombs," *Los Angeles Times*, January 14, 2010, http://latimesblogs.latimes .com/entertainmentnewsbuzz/2010/01/beatles-rock-band-fails-to-make-much -noise-over-holidays.html, (accessed January 18, 2010).

Grossman, Lev. "Battle of the Fake Bands," *Time*, December 2008: 74. *Business Source Premier, EBSCOhost* (accessed December 17, 2009).

Hadju, David. "Pretending," *The New Republic*, December 2, 2009.

Hiatt, Brian. "Rock Games Battle for Bands," *Rolling Stone*, August 7, 2008: 11–12, *Academic Search Premier, EBSCOhost* (accessed September 15, 2009).

Holson, Laura M. "Lights, Camera, Pixels...Action!" *The New York Times*, October 24, 2005, C1.

Itzkoff, Dave. "Beatles Video Game: Sales Not So Fab," *New York Times*, January 15, 2010, http://www.nytimes.com/2010/01/16/arts/television/16arts-SALESNOT SOFA_BRF.html, (accessed January 15, 2010).

Kushner, David. "Hero Worship," *Rolling Stone*, May 3, 2007: 24. *Academic Search Premier*, EBSCOhost (accessed December 12, 2008).

Palmeri, Christopher, and Tom Lowry. "Guitar Hero: More Than a Video Game," *BusinessWeek*, October 29, 2007: 86–8. *Business Source Premier, EBSCOhost* (accessed August 29, 2008).

Pareles, John. "With A Click, A New Era of Music Dawns," *The New York Times*. November 15, 1998, http://www.nytimes.com/1998/11/15/arts/music-with-a -click-a-new-era-of-music-dawns.html?scp=3&sq=mp3+illegal&st=nyt, (accessed March 30, 2005).

Parker, James. "School of Rock," *The Atlantic*, March 2009.

Plunkett, Luke. "Here, Your Blueness...Have Some Beatles: Rock Band Sales Figures," Kotaku, January 18, 2010, http://kotaku.com/5450681/here-your -bluenesshave-some-beatles-rock-band-sales-figures, (accessed January 18, 2010).

Richtel, Matt. "Napster Charts A New Course After Ruling," *The New York Times*. February 14, 2001, http://www.nytimes.com/2001/02/14/business/napster-charts -a-new-course-after-ruling.html?scp=20&sq=supreme+court+napster&st=nyt, (accessed February 5, 2010).

Roper, Chris. "Guitar Hero: Turn it up to 11 and rock the #@$& out," IGN Network, November 2, 2005, http://ps2.ign.com/articles/663/663674p1.html, (accessed March 30, 2006).

Sall, Allison, and Rebecca E. Grinter, "Let's Get Physical! In, Out and Around the Gaming Circle of Physical Gaming at Home," *Computer Supported Cooperative Work* 16 (2007).

Schiesel, Seth. "As Gaming Turns Social, Industry Shifts Strategies," *The New York Times*, February 28, 2008. http://www.nytimes.com/2008/02/28/arts/ television/28game.html?sq=&pagewanted=all, (accessed February 28, 2008).

Schiesel, "In the List of Top-Selling Games, Clear Evidence of a Sea Change," *The New York Times*, February 1, 2008, http://www.nytimes.com/2008/02/01/ arts/01game.html?fta=y, (accessed February 1, 2008).

Wolf, Mark J. P., and Bernard Perron, eds. New York: Routledge, 2003

16

How Much Does It Cost If It's Free?
The Selling (Out) of Elvis Presley[1]

Michael Bertrand

When entertainer Elvis Presley unexpectedly collapsed of a heart attack on August 16, 1977, at his Graceland home in Memphis, Tennessee, his longtime manager, Tom Parker, was occupying a hotel room nearly 1,500 miles away, in Portland, Maine. The Colonel, as he was commonly known, had travelled to the Northeast in advance of a Presley tour that was to begin August 17. As was his usual practice, Parker sought to ensure that all preparations and arrangements for the upcoming concert schedule were satisfactory. Back in Memphis, on a different front, the county medical examiner was satisfied that an emergency unit at Baptist Hospital had done all that it could to resuscitate the lifeless forty-two-year-old singer; at 3:30 p.m. CST, he pronounced Elvis dead. A few moments later a member of Presley's entourage telephoned Parker in Portland. His frantic call was met by an eerie silence. After what seemed an eternity, the Colonel finally responded, "Nothing has changed, this won't change anything. . . . It don't mean a damn thing. It's just like when he was in the Army. . . . Elvis isn't dead. Just his body is gone."[2]

While Parker's seemingly manic jibber jabber may have sounded like aggrieved delirium, closer scrutiny of his actions shortly thereafter indicates that the Colonel's near-nonsensical and fanatical reaction to the grim message was nothing if not calculated. Before returning to Memphis for the funeral of his former protégé, for instance, Parker flew from Portland to New York City. Anticipating that Presley's death would create a rush on the nation's record stores, he visited the corporate headquarters of RCA (Presley's record label) to advise company officials to provide a continuous stream of the singer's audio products. Assured of their compliance, the P.T. Barnum-like promoter next met with Harry "The Bear" Geissler, owner of Factors' Etc., Inc., a merchandising agency whose roster of celebrities represented read like a Who's

Who in 1970s Entertainment: Farrah Fawcett-Majors, Suzanne Somers, John Travolta, Olivia Newton-John, Sylvester Stallone, Donny and Marie Osmond, R2D2, C3PO, and Darth Vader. Geissler's motto was straightforward: "Fame goes hand-in-hand with [the] merchandising of posters, T-shirts, towels, lunch boxes, jewelry—anything you can put an image on—and the merchandising is no small part of the accompanying fortune." The "Colonel" and the "Bear" not surprisingly came to an immediate meeting of the minds. Geissler would later declare, "I didn't even like Elvis's music, but I was a fan of Colonel Parker. He's the king of promoters. I'm the king of merchandisers. It was only natural we get together." Indeed. The Colonel wanted Factors' Etc., Inc., to become the sole marketing representative of Elvis Presley; the company would act against unauthorized entities that produced, distributed, or sold merchandise displaying the singer's image. As the master merchandiser explained, "Colonel Parker knows I'm only in this for the money. That's why he respects me. He needs me to protect his boy." Armed with the Bear's pledge that he would "protect his boy," and with the Factors' contract in hand (unsigned—a trivial point, perhaps, but Elvis was dead and Parker theoretically had no client), the Colonel finally headed to the Memphis wake and funeral.[3]

The Colonel arrived at Graceland the next morning. He refused to view or pay his respects to the body in the coffin that lay in state in the mansion's foyer situated between the dining and music rooms. Dressed in a loud, short-sleeve Hawaiian shirt, seersucker slacks, and a baseball cap, he spent much of his time sitting in the back of the room trying to look inconspicuous, or at least unapproachable. This may not have been as far-fetched as it sounds. In her description of Graceland and the Presley wake for *Rolling Stone*'s death-of-Elvis-issue, special covert correspondent Caroline Kennedy conveyed astonishment (and barely-concealed revulsion) over the ornate décor of the 18-room mansion. She described "floor-to-ceiling scarlet drapes tied with gold tassels, potted plastic palms surrounding the coffin, [and] a clear-glass statue of a nude woman [standing] high off the floor, twirling slowly, adorned by glass beads that looked like water." Given this idiosyncratic atmosphere, it is possible that the not-so-nattily-attired Colonel may have gone mostly unnoticed. When occasional mourners did approach him to express their condolences, he reassured them that "Elvis didn't die, [only] the body did. We're keeping up the good spirits. We're keeping Elvis alive." Parker was much more emphatic on this point to Vernon Presley, Elvis's grieving father. Convening in the kitchen at every available opportunity, the one-time carnival hustler appeared extremely animated as he pressed Vernon to sign the Factors' contract. It was important to seize the moment, Parker reiterated. If they failed to do so, there would be all sorts of people swooping in to take advantage of them. Everything for which he and Elvis had worked all of these years would be lost. He and Vernon, Parker argued, quickly reconfiguring a twenty-two-year-partnership that had come to an abrupt yet temporary halt with the death of Vernon's son, had to safeguard their interests. They had to protect Elvis. The father understood. Vernon signed the contract. He could trust the old carny. After all, years ago the Colonel had vowed he would keep Elvis on top of the pop music world despite his being away while serving in the U.S. Army. Had he not fulfilled that promise? The current situation, although traumatic, would be no different. When asked by a reporter what he would do now that his "meal ticket" was gone, the Colonel did not blink, "Why, go right on managing him."[4]

The purpose of this chapter is not to vilify Tom Parker or linger on the notorious financial arrangements between manager and artist that disproportionately seemed to favor the former over the latter. (Their contract calling for a fifty-fifty partnership agreement was unparalleled in the industry and garnered even more for Parker since his own merchandising company—Boxcar Enterprises—separately controlled all of Elvis's commercial and merchandising transactions.) There have been plenty of works that have addressed this sleight-of-hand con game. Neither is it to examine the evolution of entertainment law as it pertains to dead celebrities and the licensing of intellectual property formerly known as the dearly departed. Many legal scholars and others have delved into this fruitful field. Likewise, no one should expect to find within these pages any sensationalist accounts of Presley's love interests, food or badge fetishes, Nixonian White House wanderings, overdependence on the PDR (Physicians' Desk Reference), fascination with mysticism and the occult, or any documented post-1977 sightings of the King in Kalamazoo. Those subjects, too, have been mined to the extreme elsewhere.[5]

Rather, this is a study that will examine how Elvis Presley was transformed from a human being into a commodity. As the above anecdotal summary suggests, to his manager, Elvis was no more than a product to be sold, merchandise to be marketed. Parker's personal philosophy, as noted by a reporter in the mid-1960s, was "Don't try to explain it; just sell it." Presley's life as a commercial artist did not challenge the Colonel's credo; his dying, strangely enough, merely confirmed it. One observer noted with irony thirty years later that Presley's "career since his death is certainly much more lucrative than his living one ever was." In foreseeing his client's beyond-the-grave appeal and popularity, the seemingly less-than-grief-stricken Colonel, dressed in Hawaiian shirt and baseball cap, had turned out to be a chillingly accurate prophet. Parker's prescience, moreover, serves as a reminder that while they may hold various meanings for consumers, performers in the entertainment marketplace are "things" ultimately intended to be bought and sold. Dead or alive, or more to the point, alive and dead, Elvis was a commodity.[6]

Presleymania, a phenomenon that had scorched the Eisenhower era before smoldering into a somewhat hazy memory in the tumultuous years that witnessed the Vietnam War, Black Power, Woodstock, and Watergate, reignited with a vengeance upon the singer's final curtain call. Initial efforts at exploiting the posthumous interest in everything Elvis adhered to conventional wisdom and a conventional course—targeting aging fans that had grown up with and followed the entertainer during his more than twenty years on the public stage. This niche market represented consumers "bonded together by [their] admiration [for] a man with a useable past." They were willing and eager to visit his 14-acre estate and gravesite in Memphis (as well as his shotgun shack birthplace in Tupelo, Mississippi). They pushed the United States Post Office to issue a commemorative postage stamp, bought an occasional Elvis-themed memento, viewed documentaries, television specials, and motion pictures devoted to their idol, and purchased various repackaged collections of his audio performances. By the dawn of the new millennium, the strategy had worked, famously—dead Elvis represented a $100-million-a-year industry moving music, movies, and memorabilia.[7]

Even in their success, however, the corporate underwriters marketing the Elvis brand could anticipate failure. Without a means to expand Presley's original audience, his shelf-life was finite. Those working on behalf of the Elvis Empire had to cultivate new consumers, as the senior vice president of strategic marketing for RCA Records/BMG acknowledged at the turn of the twenty-first century: "For us, it's about taking a property and figuring out, how do we make him hip, young and irreverent—into a brand that's relevant to this younger demographic." And as Jack Soden, longtime Chief Executive Officer of Elvis Presley Enterprises, added, "We don't want to abandon the original demographic. But to successfully sell that music, you've got to sell the guy, and tell new generations why the music's important, why he's important." At least during the new millennium's first decade, the youth-oriented marketing campaign had succeeded in propagating a positive rendition of its property. Technological advances made it relatively easy to insert the late entertainer into the contemporary pop culture and music marketplace; the performer's (product's?) inherent appeal, evident since the mid-1950s, did the rest: he (more precisely, his video image) frequently appeared "live" in concert with former (albeit visibly older) backup musicians, a technofied-remix of a thirty-four-year-old recording shot to the top of world charts following its inclusion in a series of Nike athletic shoe commercials, the same song served as the signature tune of a blockbuster film set in Las Vegas that starred some of Hollywood's biggest names, a compact disc containing digitally-remastered classics surprisingly outsold acts not even alive when he died, and the Walt Disney Company featured the singer and several of his songs within the plot of a highly-successful animated movie that kids and critics adored. "We're just trying to come up with ways to get Elvis in front of young people," explained the director of media for EPE. "The biggest challenge," an official for RCA admitted, "is to erase the memory of the caricature of Elvis, the one ingrained for so many years as a bloated icon."[8]

Although the Presley marketing machine is unlikely to induce a collective case of aggregate amnesia, it has succeeded in causing many to wonder if the vibrant and charismatic Elvis really ever left the building. As the director of media and creative development for Elvis Presley Enterprises declared on the eve of yet another anniversary that drew thousands of pilgrims to Graceland, "Elvis has this great career going. Elvis is everywhere. He died, but the demand for Elvis did not end. It's as if he's still here with us." Parker, of course, could not have said it any better. But does it sound any less strange and ahistorical now than it did on that August afternoon when the Colonel obviously was overwhelmed by dollar signs rather than grief? "Nothing has changed, this won't change anything. . . . It don't mean a damn thing. It's just like when he was in the Army. . . . Elvis isn't dead. Just his body is gone."[9]

Turning Presley into a ubiquitous commodity that produces a bottom line that most current pop stars would die for has produced a quandary for historians. For the transformation has come with a stiff price, particularly in regard to distorting (or erasing) certain realities of race, class, gender, and region central to Presley's persona and import. Such high costs perhaps were best appraised by cultural scholar Erika Doss in examining the tendencies recently evinced in the official marketing of Elvis by the Presley estate: "EPE's Elvis is hygienically sterile, a specimen of upwardly mobile middle-class normalcy and achievement. He's conservative and controlled, seamless and uncomplicated, fixed—even paralyzed—as not much more than a symbol of monopoly capital."[10]

Doss's assessment implies that the product the estate is selling in the new millennium is a far cry from the controversial young Southern white working-class hip-swiveling and black-sounding "Hillbilly Cat" who challenged the status quo of his era and thereby changed history. She contends that the corporate-induced makeover has removed much of what made Presley not only interesting, but significant. In this, Doss is correct, but perhaps only to a point. For the homogenization efforts that have taken place in the over quarter of a century since Presley's death arguably represent the concluding stages of a trajectory that began as early as 1955, when Presley signed with RCA Records. Although not immediately evident, the initial attempts to neutralize the more extreme aspects of the performer's character and behavior would generate a not-so-subtle tension between reality and perceptions of reality that underlined the remainder of Presley's career. When asked during a 1972 press conference to comment on the way the public perceived him, for instance, Elvis provided a glimpse into this tension, declaring that, "The image is one thing, the human being is another. It's very hard to live up to an image." Certainly the attempts to manipulate the singer's image while he was alive were fraught with the frailties of his own humanity. His no longer being around surely has afforded those who control his likeness much greater latitude to determine how it is presented to the public. Put crassly, Presley's death was a great career move. It has allowed marketing gurus to promote the singer straight out as a commodity rather than as a human being.[11]

Again, however, it is important to remember that Presley's death did not inaugurate a significant departure from the way his handlers had marketed him while he was alive (a major caveat being that in death the image became frozen in time, making it possible to emphasize certain aspects while minimizing or jettisoning others). In addition, there is no doubt that Presley willingly had participated in a long-term process meant to iron out his rough edges and create a "sterile specimen of upwardly mobile middle-class normalcy and achievement." The prize, as both Elvis and the Colonel understood, was to garner the fame and fortune that flowed from becoming an all-around matinee idol that offended no one, a safe and sanitized commodity. The results, however, were ambiguous at best, a situation that suggests a complexity to the process which begs further scrutiny. For historians, it is this aspect of the Presley story that might prove to be the most significant.

The Elvis Presley-as-commodity saga had its beginnings in a controversy that commenced in the early 1950s. Indeed, before Presley emerged in 1956 as the figure most associated (for good and for bad) with rock 'n' roll, the years between 1953 and 1955 witnessed a hostile mainstream adult reaction against rhythm and blues. Of particular concern to critics was the "uninhibited waxing and exploring of filth, passing under the guise of hep lyrics." This "leer-ics" controversy subsumed all of R&B, attaching to the music an immoral and depraved connotation. Consequently, the pop music establishment would develop and employ several strategies to counter the spread of rhythm and blues. After numerous false starts, it ultimately succeeded in instituting authority over the music. Accordingly, R&B eventually gave way to rock 'n' roll; the utilization of Elvis would be instrumental in this conversion.[12]

The adaptation that transpired, however, was neither clear-cut nor seamless. Later depicted and decried as a white and watered-down imitation of R&B, rock 'n' roll in its formative years was a working-class biracial musical force with Southern roots that belied simple categorization. The same holds true in regard to Presley. Yet in the end, the overt commodification of rock 'n' roll and Elvis helped the entertainment industry regain control of popular music while containing the larger and deeper implications associated with each. As a consequence, both began to resemble something they originally were not. It was a significant transition, one tied more to marketing than it was to music. Ironically, it would be the immaterial black-sounding share-cropper's son from Mississippi that the powers-that-be used to eradicate much of the racial, regional, and working-class character of R&B-influenced rock 'n' roll. To comprehend this bizarre progression involves addressing the "leer-ics" storm and the ensuing "birth" of rock 'n' roll followed by the corresponding "death" of rhythm and blues.[13]

Rhythm and blues originally personified groups whose economic and social positions were narrowly confined. They were marginalized African Americans who either had remained segregated in the South or had trekked northward to urban ghettos. Their music, like their backgrounds, occupations, inhibitions, dialects, perceptions, and overall living conditions, failed to embody typical middle-class characteristics and aspirations. As such, rhythm and blues of-fended urbane tastes and sensibilities. As the "popular music of the Negro people," LeRoi Jones noted, "rhythm and blues was hated by the middle-class Negro." It contradicted the expectations of prosperity, contentment, and har-mony that the postwar mainstream fostered. The working-class genre served as a reminder of a past that was far too close in time for those people who recently had experienced upward social mobility. Rhythm and blues, as well as the people who performed and consumed it, unquestionably needed to remain exiled, segregated from middle-class black and white communities.[14]

As the 1940s melted into the 1950s, however, affluence, long-term demo-graphic shifts, and technological advances threatened to break down the walls that isolated the music. These changes led to an increased demand for rhythm and blues. Having eliminated most of their commercial interests in black grassroots music during the Great Depression and World War II, ma-jor recording companies such as RCA-Victor, Columbia, and Capitol found themselves at a major disadvantage when requests for rhythm and blues esca-lated in the latter part of the decade. They had no affiliations or working rela-tionships with the publishers, writers, performers, or insiders located within rhythm and blues circles. In the meantime, local entrepreneurs, responding to the postwar demands of a fast-growing urban black population that wanted to consume more of its own music, formed small record companies that re-cruited and recorded relatively unknown yet modern-sounding black artists. These independent record owners generally were white and wanted to make money. Any collateral benefits that emerged from these operations, such as financially empowering the artists that they recorded, were not intended and were rarely achieved. These upstart businessmen often kept their independent recording outfits together with little more than spit, chewing gum, and baling wire. Exploitation was the name of their game.[15]

Yet at least they were there to record performers who otherwise had no access to the production of commercial music. Taking advantage of specific local, regional, racial, and working-class forms of articulation and talent, independent labels such as Atlantic, King, Chess, Specialty, Sun, Excello, Duke, and Ace were cutting records in New York, Cincinnati, Chicago, Los Angeles, Memphis, Nashville, Houston, and New Orleans. In the process, they gained a hold on the R&B market that the major recording companies could not (and initially seemed unwilling to) break. Completely shut out from recording such working-class black performers—they typically relied on older, more familiar artists—the majors fell far behind their undercapitalized competitors in producing commercially-viable rhythm and blues material. In the late 1940s and early 1950s, independents, assisted by local radio stations that had been accorded greater autonomy as network programming declined in the advent of network television, advanced and exploited the tastes of commonly disregarded segments of the population.[16]

Ordinarily, such music would have stayed sequestered within the bounds of its own working-class African American audience and community. By the early 1950s, record retailers, jukebox operators, and disk jockeys, however, noticed that the number of white adolescents requesting R&B records was growing. Consequently, as the middle of the decade approached, rhythm and blues songs and artists occasionally were entering the upper reaches of the highly-segregated national music popularity charts. Interestingly, despite the restrictive bounds of Jim Crow segregation, the rhythm and blues material fared still better on local pop indicators throughout the South, where working-class white "cat-minded teenagers" were beginning to request and buy rhythm and blues records regularly. Presley, as an unknown and invisible Mississippi migrant relocated to Memphis, apparently was one of those "cat-minded teenagers." Like other white working-class Southern youngsters listening to black radio programming and attending rhythm and blues concerts, Elvis had come under the influence of African American culture. And like many of his peers, he did not see anything wrong with such an inclination. That he eventually became enormously popular performing in a manner associated with black rhythm and blues artists simply confirmed a cultural insurgency that had been quietly developing in the South for quite some time. *Jet Magazine* noticed the trend and reported that "when white teenagers in the South go into a record store and ask for a 'cat' record, they mean one featuring Negro musicians. Down there they call it 'cat music.'"[17]

As R&B swept the country, it ignited a struggle along highly polarized fronts. Labeled a "raw music idiom" that "smelled up the environment," the music posed a serious threat to those who administered custody of the country's musical and moral standards (such "smutty records" contained "thinly veiled by-words like 'squeeze,' 'roll,' 'hug,' 'sixty seconds,' 'all night long' and the rest," as well as constant references to alcohol consumption as a means to deal with everyday life). Although many recognized that such music was not necessarily new, several also appreciated that class and racial boundaries had heretofore contained or "restricted it to special places and out-and-out barrelhouses." Not surprisingly, the controversy did not "shift into high gear" until rhythm and blues songs had made "serious inroads into the white-dominated 'pop' field." Offered as standard popular fare, rhythm and blues suddenly threatened to influence a general middle-class white audience that included highly-impressionable teenagers.[18]

Teenagers had quickly become a force in postwar popular music, the ones who "buy the records and create the fads." This situation presented a dilemma for the popular music industry. If adolescents wanted rhythm and blues, how was the industry to respond? Even if the material was questionable and perhaps morally offensive, it nevertheless represented big business. As one music trade paper columnist advised, "This is inevitable. The consumer—the kid with the 89 cents in his pocket—is ready and eager to lay his cash on the line for what he likes. Those who won't give him what he wants may be well-intentioned, but they will lose out to someone who will. This is a blunt fact." Members of the industry, however, hoped that they could navigate the rough waters of both morality and the market. As one record executive pronounced, "Of course, we must cater to [the youngsters], but we must not give them complete responsibility for our moral standards."[19]

Even if the music industry had been willing to follow the tastes of teenagers completely, older and more politically-connected adults were not. Civic pressure in numerous cities, towns, and smaller communities forced local radio station managers, jukebox operators, and the owners of entertainment venues to amend their positions regarding the music they provided for increasingly youthful audiences. In Memphis, for instance, during the fall of 1954, police confiscated jukeboxes and levied $50 fines on operators who permitted the playing of questionable recordings, prompting white-owned and black-operated radio station WDIA to institute a "clean up the air" policy. Various groups in other cities followed the WDIA example in encouraging "voluntary cooperation" to "keep objectionable records out of the city [insert here offended community]." Newspapers, Youth Study Commissions, Junior National Audience Boards, Parent-Teacher Associations, pastors, priests, preachers and police commissioners all seemed to join hands in combating the rhythm and blues menace. They were adamant in forcing the music industry to police itself, to provide "new songs which measure up to those standards which have been set by perennial favorites." They "badgered disk jockeys, distributors, publishers, and song pluggers" to squelch rhythm and blues.[20]

The music industry's response to such pressure was a complex one. It definitely did not want outsiders to control its pop music output. Leading trade papers representing the entertainment establishment wholeheartedly endorsed self-regulation as a means to curtail external censure. *Billboard* urged the industry to monitor itself less the results be "damaging from both economic and creative points of view." *Cashbox* admonished, "We're happy to see rhythm and blues come into its own. We're happy to see it recognized and accepted. We hope the trend continues to where it is no longer a trend, but an everyday method of operation in the music business. Just don't overdo it." *Variety* argued that the industry could keep governmental and religious groups at bay simply by cleaning up the tasteless mess created by R&B: "In short chums, do it yourself or have it done for you."[21]

Claiming that the rhythm and blues phenomenon was nothing more than a tasteless fad that smaller independent firms were exploiting for quick monetary gains, the major recording companies quickly distanced themselves from controversial material and artists. RCA-Victor, for instance, sought to reassure the public that it had a responsibility to maintain the highest of standards and that it would not jump on any bandwagon simply for financial gain. As a company spokesperson explained, "Because Radio Corporation of America (RCA) occupies an eminent position in American life and industry, we consider any compromise with good taste and propriety unthinkable. Any [product bearing] the RCA insignia . . . must be free from any taint which may be construed as affecting adversely even the smallest segment of society. The Record Department will never sacrifice the principles set for the entire corporation in any effort to gain profit or financial advantage." Columbia, another of the six major recording companies, also proclaimed that profit would be secondary to other more aesthetic and moral concerns. As the president of Columbia emphasized, "It has nevertheless been our view that good business can go hand in hand with good music. . . . Generally speaking, our endeavor is to record music which has popular appeal, sales potential, and is in good taste."[22]

Although many in the popular music establishment were concerned with the issue of taste, there also was another element at play. As the founders of independent Atlantic Records noticed, "It strikes us as unfortunate that R&B records are singled out for censure at this time when instances of questionable material abound in the pop and country music fields as well." Alan Freed, a maverick disk jockey who helped rhythm and blues transition into rock 'n' roll, also took exception to the negative attention given R&B. He gauged the reason to be financial: "The old-timers who formerly controlled the music-publishing business wouldn't even license rhythm and blues until about a year ago. By that time a new group of writers and publishers had got the inside track on rock 'n' roll, and now the newcomers are making the money." Ruth Cage, a columnist for *Down Beat*, agreed, noting that after a long history of being overlooked, "suddenly R&B has been recognized by the vested interests that live off the music business; and as suddenly it is portrayed by them as the most destructive musical force in recent years." Cage concluded that the "vested interests" were anxious about losing control of "their" industry. The public was looking toward new performers and writers, and that fact was "not likely to delight the fellows whose annual stipend depends on the tastes of yesteryear and who apparently can't readjust their skills." The Hollywood-Tin Pan Alley-Broadway entertainment axis that had for a generation controlled popular music had recently "come upon hard times." It had failed to notice that younger consumers were becoming significant trendsetters. It could not relate to the new generation. The major record labels were finding the new realities associated with rhythm and blues to be particularly harsh. They could "no longer rely on artist loyalty among the fans to insure (sic) success of a new top-name entry. The course of the music business. . . . [had] shown that hits can, and do, come from anywhere, and from any label."[23]

Having failed to halt the rhythm and blues juggernaut through evasion, derision, and outspoken attack, the music establishment's next step in containing the threat involved having well-known veteran pop performers "cover" R&B material. As an industry historically defined by its emphasis on music publishing, with the performer merely serving as a song "plugger," the tactic of renowned singers recording pop interpretations of current rhythm and blues or country hits (records that were enjoying success in their primary and thereby limited markets) made perfect sense. Historically, songs that originated in "race" or "hillbilly" markets generally were perceived as the raw material that would be refined in the hands of a pop craftsman. In the age of *Your Hit Parade* and *Billboard*'s "Honor Roll of Hits," if several glamorous and alluring performers were able to etch a tune in the minds of listeners, so much the better for the publisher and the popular music establishment. The focus had always been on the song, not the singer. "It's as simple as this," advised members of the establishment. "If the customer wants rhythm and blues music (and he does), he'll buy it from whomever supplies it."[24]

By the end of 1954, the majors had succeeded in getting their own "R&B-type material into the pop market." This generally entailed having pop singers produce unexceptional vocal performances that "feature[ed] a wailing sax and the R&B beat." Their lack of appreciation for or understanding of the genre was compounded by a refusal of the majors to work with original working-class black artists. Consequently, *Variety* noted, "the major diskeries are not finding it easy to crack the rhythm and blues formula. For one thing, most of the artists and repertoire chiefs can't recognize a potential R&B hit when they hear one. As a result, they are all waiting for the tunes to break through on the indie labels [and on the R&B charts] and then they decide to cover." Although the practice exposed rhythm and blues to a larger and wider audience, it necessarily stifled the pecuniary and pop chart progress of the originals. As Langston Hughes argued, the practice of covering represented the highest form of flattery. The problem, he maintained, was that black artists generally were denied access to the lucrative venues (the best nightclubs, biggest theaters, higher-rated radio programs, television, movies, and highest realms of the pop charts) open to white artists. In what he termed "highway robbery across the color line," the white artist "makes the money, we make the basic music."[25]

Yet the originals, the ones who "make the basic music," did not go away simply because the majors pushed white artists performing "black" music. With the support of independent disk jockeys, many of whom had radio shows whose airwaves reached multi-state audiences, rhythm and blues artists continued to infiltrate the world of the American teenager. Acting as spokespersons that both informed and reflected the views of newly-created adolescent communities, deejays undeniably played a major role in disseminating the music. Connected to working-class communities and audiences whose desires and demands veered toward grassroots originals compelled a growing number of disk jockeys to forgo playing the generally antiseptic white cover records that the majors produced. To the consternation of the industry, as the public and the disk jockeys became "more hip to the big beat, they began to go after the real thing more and more."[26]

Ultimately unable to displace the original rhythm and blues performers (and more importantly, the independent labels for which they recorded) in the minds of teenage consumers, major record companies conceded that their cover tactics had failed. They then pursued a different strategy, one that sought to divert attention away from rhythm and blues. One industry official, although acknowledging that R&B had introduced a new "beat" into popular music, nevertheless contended, "That doesn't mean it's ALL [that audiences] want to hear." The problem called for diversification. Accordingly, Steve Sholes, an artist and repertoire chief for RCA, offered a strategy to blur the various categories in popular music, thus making no one field any more significant than any other. Apparently striving to diminish the influence of rhythm and blues, Sholes advised in 1955 that "audiences [today] are not interested in a country field, a pop field, an R&B field, American or whatever, just so long as the records are entertaining."[27]

Sholes's observation that consumers did not care about musical categories went against the then-current patterns of record buying and seemed strangely out of sync with the larger pop music world. Bob Thiele, Sholes's counterpart for Coral Records, an independent firm, almost simultaneously stressed that "even the slightest survey of the public taste today shows that R&B is what the kids are going for." This was a fact of which Sholes was well aware, but openly did not want to concede. Behind the scenes, however, RCA's A&R chief counseled his superiors that "we must get some of those rock 'n' rollers." Publicly, he continued to maintain that "strict categorization of records is gradually becoming less important."[28]

RCA-Victor, under Sholes's shrewd guidance, intended to counter the popularity of rhythm and blues by developing its own trend. Fittingly, the company was following a somewhat obscure but fast-rising regional performer who recorded for Sun, an independent record label located in Memphis. For a little over a year, Sun had promoted the twenty-year-old white shouter in the country field, but noted that he received "spins on R&B as well as country shows." Not surprisingly, the local press had a difficult time classifying him: "He has a white voice [and] sings with a negro rhythm which borrows in mood and emphasis from country style." Representatives of the little label claimed that his records "were equally popular on pop, folk, and race programs. The boy has something that seems to appeal to everybody." While this may indeed have been the case, it was difficult to be sure. He was hot in the South and Southwest, but had had little exposure in other areas. Reports from the field indicated that he seemed provincial. Still, as an undisciplined performer who recognized no boundaries, he seemed to be just what Sholes was seeking. Consequently, in the fall of 1955, RCA purchased from Sun Records the contract of Elvis Presley. According to the ensuing press release, "Altho Sun has sold Presley primarily as a c[ountry] & w[estern] artist, Victor plans to push his platters in all three fields—pop, r.&b., and c.&w . . . RCA Victor's specialty single's chief, Steve Sholes, will record Presley." Sholes had located the artist who would prove that the strict categorization of records had become insignificant. The company could now develop its trend. The establishment had acquired a figure that, if packaged correctly, would save the industry from the rhythm and blues onslaught. Noticeably, the first advertisement trumpeting Presley's new recording home (a full-page ad in *Billboard* in the same issue that announced the news of his joining RCA) mentioned nothing about any particular musical genre (or by association any region or socio-economic class) with which he could be coupled: "The most talked-about new personality in the last ten years of recorded music: Elvis Presley, now on RCA Victor Records."[29]

From the very beginning, RCA marketed Elvis not as a rock 'n' roll star (which would have connected him directly to rhythm and blues), but as an eclectic entertainer who could appeal to vastly different segments of the population. The company took advantage of the man's talent for singing rhythm and blues, country, gospel, and pop to create a product that defied categorization. His handlers put him on television and in the movies, media that undoubtedly exploited fully the visual attraction of his performance persona. Such settings, however, also worked eventually to contain the more extreme facets of his performance style. And while it would be a stretch to argue that the entertainment industry had conspired to concoct an entity capable of bringing down R&B, it is fair to say that it had stumbled upon one that would do just that. Fulfilling Sholes's earlier vision, the industry's proficient promotion of Presley ultimately assisted in burying or concealing the rhythm and blues roots of rock 'n' roll.

Although his background and personality were far too complex for such an ill-fitting straitjacket, RCA (with Elvis generally willing and acquiescent) attempted to fashion him as the prototypical whitewashed teen idol, an icon that corresponded to the mainstream perception of a youthful and "safe" performer. Such packaging, however, would require time to take, as the following illustrates. In a 1956 promotional record titled "The Truth About Me" that was inserted in selected teen magazines, Elvis told young fans that "I don't smoke and I don't drink, and I love to go to movies. Maybe someday I'm gonna have a home and a family of my own and I'm not going to budge from it. I was an only child, but maybe my kids won't be." While there is little doubt that such feelings and the upwardly-mobile aspirations they represented motivated young Presley, a somewhat off-the-cuff and mischievous comment he furnished at about the same time ("to the consternation of assorted [RCA] vice-presidents") to a question concerning marriage revealed that he was a multi-dimensional individual shaped by his class and regional upbringing: "Why buy the cow when you can get the milk for free from underneath the fence?"[30]

The cow comment indicated that RCA was going to have its hands full in trying to market the young Southern working-class troubadour as an innocuous teen idol. Indeed, during his first year with the company, putting out fires started by the "howling hillbilly" seemed to be taking up much of the firm's time; no one was complaining, however. Controversy only seemed to drive record sales higher. Throughout 1956, inhabitants across the country first took note of Presley on network television. Interestingly, RCA initially had had difficulty getting this accomplished. When Presley's handlers had first approached NBC Television about a guest slot, the network balked. Elvis instead would make his network debut through CBS on the Dorsey Brothers Stage Show. An executive for NBC explained his network's reluctance to showcase the singer despite the fact that RCA had been the parent company of NBC: "Presley isn't as simple a commodity to 'sell' as, say, Peter Pan. . . . Not everybody would buy him. You could bet your boots, for instance, that a company like General Motors wouldn't touch Presley with a ten-foot pole. They want class." After guest starring on six episodes of the Dorsey Brothers program and continuing his dramatic rise up the nation's pop charts, NBC finally relented. The singer appeared twice on NBC's Milton Berle Show. On his last appearance, the hip-swiveling rockabilly seemed intent on validating NBC's initial aversion; bumping and grinding to the final strains of "Hound Dog," Elvis detonated a national firestorm and drew the ire of columnists around the country. The viewpoint of Jack Gould of *The New York Times* was typical, claiming that this "whining virtuoso of the hootchy-kootchy" should in no way be classified as a vocalist: "Mr. Presley has no discernible singing ability."[31]

During his next small-screen appearance, on NBC's Steve Allen Show, the establishment, in the person of Allen, attempted to defuse Elvis and his "hootchy-kootchy" sexuality. The result was humiliating and condescending, with Allen "humorously" consigning inferior status to the singer's regional and class roots. The host placed an always-polite-and ready-to-accommodate Presley in tux and tails (and blue suede shoes) and had him stand still while singing "Hound Dog" to a similarly-attired and stationary basset hound (sans shoes, but wearing a top hat). In a later skit, producers dressed him as a hayseed and scripted him to sound like a rube. For Elvis, the whole show represented "the first time he felt sold out." For his fans, many of whom picketed outside the television studio with signs that read, "We Want the REAL Elvis," the program was an insult. For the industry, however, the incident demonstrated that the amiable Presley would go along with whatever shtick was put before him. It was a lesson that would not soon be forgotten.[32]

For his final venture into 1950s television, Team Elvis turned toward the most influential host of Sunday night variety programming, Ed Sullivan. Earlier in the year Sullivan had sworn that he would not "touch Presley with a ten-foot pole," implying that the singer was a dirty and vulgar spectacle who did not belong before a family audience. After a "detwitched" Elvis helped Allen (and NBC) garner higher ratings than Sullivan for the same time slot, the emcee of the program formerly known as "Toast of the Town" had a change of heart. At a time when the going rate for a "big star" was $7,500 per appearance, Sullivan paid Presley the unprecedented sum of $50,000 for three appearances. As Colonel Parker later explained, "You've always got to think big in this business. A sure way to debase your merchandise is to give it away. They don't want Elvis if he's cheap."[33]

On September 9, 1956, in his highly-anticipated return following the Allen debacle, Elvis playfully engaged viewers with a youthful exuberance and sexual energy that no doubt shocked the older members of Sullivan's studio and television audience. Unfortunately, Sullivan had to miss the performance;

he was recuperating from a recent automobile accident. Undoubtedly, many of the nearly sixty million Americans who tuned in from home—a record 82.6 percent of the nation's television households, including presumably, that of the absent host—were familiar with the uproar Elvis had caused on the Berle and Allen programs. Their resultant curiosity made the occasion the highest-rated program in broadcast history. Presley's second visit to the program, in late October, almost seemed anti-climactic. Unlike many of his critics, the singer did not seem to take himself or the "power" he held over his audience very seriously. Acting like a naughty naïf with a secret, Presley teased the audience, eliciting screams from the teenagers in the crowd. Even Sullivan, who apparently had recuperated from his accident, got in on the act. In retrospect, it all seemed like innocent fun.[34]

It was Presley's third appearance on the Sullivan program, in January of 1957, that has become one of the most well-known moments in television history. This was the episode where Sullivan's cameras televised Elvis from the waist up. Yet only moments after his final performance, Sullivan closed the program by providing Elvis with an impressive endorsement. Putting his arm around Presley, who had just finished singing the gospel number "Peace in the Valley," the genial host declared, "I want to say to Elvis Presley and the country that this is a real decent, fine boy. We've never had a pleasanter experience on our show with a big name than we've had with you. . . . You're thoroughly all right. So now, let's have a tremendous hand for a very nice person."[35]

Sullivan never explained his reasoning for the above-the-waist censorship; it simply may have been a gimmicky response to critics of Presley's first two appearances. The action seems to have taken on a greater significance in retrospect. At the time, what seemed more important was Sullivan's commending of the entertainer. The two had shared an on-stage banter that appeared genuine; Sullivan probably felt a sincere fondness for him. For Parker, RCA, and other show business stakeholders in the Presley property, this was the key. The Sullivan show was a venerable Sunday night institution. It provided entry into the American mainstream. The famed-journalist-turned-variety-show-emcee served as a gatekeeper. In his first two engagements, the show had helped convince open-minded viewers that Elvis was not as horrid as many in the press had made him out to be. His final appearance, in which the performer came across as calm and somewhat subdued, confirmed that he Presley was "a real decent, fine boy." More to the point, perhaps, Sullivan's taming-by-video-edit of the "Hillbilly Cat" did nothing to hurt Presley's status with teenagers, while his open acceptance of the singer gave Elvis's reputation a much-needed boost with adults. Parker, Sholes, and RCA could not have been happier.

Television had done its part both in bringing Elvis to the attention of and then legitimizing him in the eyes of the American mainstream. It had not necessarily been easy, but by the time of his final Sullivan appearance, Presley's image had undergone a positive makeover (at least by middle-class standards). Next in line, to try its hand at refitting Elvis was Hollywood. Producer Hal Wallis had noticed the singer performing on network television and perceived big-screen charisma in the hip-swiveling chanter. Wallis immediately signed Presley to a long-term, multi-picture contract. Not having a project immediately available, Wallis loaned Presley to Twentieth-Century Fox. The rock 'n' roll idol made his movie debut to much hoopla as a supporting member of a second-rate western initially titled *The Reno Brothers*. It eventually was changed to *Love Me Tender* when advance sales of that recording sold more than one million copies.[36]

Like countless anonymous and socially-invisible young people who reached adolescence in the post-World War II American South, Elvis Presley had come under the influence of what Hortense Powdermaker called the "Dream Factory." Growing up in the working-class communities of Tupelo, Mississippi, and Memphis, Tennessee, he spent many an hour in darkened movie theaters imagining himself as the hero he was watching on the big screen. As the consummate popular culture consumer, he created an identity largely based on the motion picture protagonists he so idolized. Anyone vaguely familiar with the Presley saga can recognize within his persona obvious references to actors such as Marlon Brando, Tony Curtis, and of course, James Dean. He dreamed of becoming a movie star. Even after he had conquered the world of popular music, Hollywood remained in his mind the ultimate prize and destination.[37]

Hollywood, for its part, hoped to capitalize on rock 'n' roll for everything it was worth. The popularity of earlier films such as *Blackboard Jungle* (with Bill Haley's "Rock Around the Clock" blaring over the credits) and *Rebel Without a Cause* (the vehicle that turned James Dean into a star) convinced studio heads that teenagers could support the making of motion pictures. In response, studios concocted the rock 'n' roll exploitation film. Quickly-made and cheaply-produced, movies with titles like *Shake, Rattle, and Rock*; *Don't Knock the Rock*; *The Girl Can't Help It*; *Rock Around the Clock*; *Rock, Pretty Baby*; and *Rock! Rock! Rock!*, generally featured threadbare plots and cameo musical appearances by rock 'n' roll and rhythm and blues stars currently popular on radio and records, such as Chuck Berry, Bill Haley, Fats Domino, Jerry Lee Lewis, and Little Richard. The exploitation flicks did what they were supposed to do. They put teenagers in movie theaters, and they presented rock 'n' roll (and its original practitioners) as a bizarre novelty, a rage that would not last. The movie industry, at least in the 1950s, placed Presley's film work in a different category. It marketed him as a bankable star, a figure that transcended rock 'n' roll.[38]

Following the release of *Love Me Tender*, a period piece that shoehorned four songs into the script, three of which had Elvis rockin' and rollin' without reference to historical context, Presley's subsequent producers sought vehicles tailored especially for him. Accordingly, the singer's next three motion pictures, *Loving You*, *Jailhouse Rock*, and *King Creole*, featured contemporary plotlines that centered on the musical rise of the movies' protagonists. Yet, despite each character's uncanny resemblance to a certain current rhythm and blues-inspired hip-shaking shouter, the films contain no mention of rock 'n' roll or R&B. The loosely-autobiographical *Loving You*, for instance, told a rags-to-riches story of a rural lad who joins a country and western troupe and with his unique and rambunctious brand of putting over a tune takes the countryside by storm. The western-attired and blue-jean-clad hero even gets in trouble with the PTA and other civic organizations because of the unsettling affect he is having on his female fans. Fiction and fact begin to blur, but only momentarily, for while the "real" Elvis did tour with country shows like the Hank Snow Jamboree, he always stood out because of his non-rustic look, attire, and appearance. Presley certainly may have emerged from a culture of segregation steeped in country music, but as a "cat-minded teenager" he resided much more on the darker side of the color line than is evident in this film. Likewise, despite the adolescent Presley's much-noted immersion in rhythm and blues, pop, and country, his music in *Loving You* is presented in cultural isolation.[39]

The next two films were similar. In *Jailhouse Rock*, a gritty black and white urban drama, a "serious musical," Elvis becomes the nation's newest singing sensation after having learned the craft in prison from an old-time hillbilly star. This is awkward stylistically, for the movie's leading man demonstrates an approach that is far removed from that of his country mentor. It is closer to rhythm and blues (in fact, the two primary songwriters for the film, Jerry Leiber and Mike Stoller, were veteran composers of R&B material). Yet there is no reference made in the script to the genre recently associated with "leer-ics." The protagonist's performance approach is a stand-alone style that obviously is incomparable and unparalleled. Presley's next picture, the last before he entered the U.S. Army, was set in New Orleans and was entitled *King Creole*. Leiber and Stoller, as in the previous outing, penned many of the songs. As he did before, Elvis offers a solid musical performance. But again, there are no allusions to the contemporary music scene, a travesty in this case since the Crescent City, at the time, was the recording home of rhythm and blues pioneers Fats Domino, Little Richard, Roy Brown, Lloyd

Price, and many others who had been and still were enormously influential in Elvis's development. Contrary to his own background, Elvis is submitted to the public as *sui generis*. It was as if R&B did not exist.[40]

Such cinematic presentations were significant. Shorn of their class, racial, and regional pedigrees, Presley's on-screen musical performances reiterated that youth comprised the primary component of rock 'n' roll. Thus the music symbolized nothing more than adolescent rebellion, a cyclical and safe fad with a known expiration date that could be packaged and sold like any other commodity. In the three films described above, for instance, the initial stages of the plots intimated that Elvis (as Deke Rivers, Vince Everett, and Danny Fisher) was a rebel of some sort—a loner, a self-centered cynic, or a misunderstood juvenile delinquent. As the stories unfold, however, his experiences and relationships with others help him grow into a model citizen who is then accepted and welcomed into the larger community. In such a way did the Hollywood-produced Presley become the "face" of rock 'n' roll, the quintessential good-looking teen idol who could convince adults that the music their kids were listening to was "not so bad after all." As one veteran columnist observed, Hollywood, like the entertainment industry as a whole, "has embraced [Elvis] heart, soul and cashbox. The cigar-smoking geniuses who said rock 'n' roll was strictly race music are now peddling blue suede shoes and blue jeans. For Elvis has lifted rock 'n' roll right out of its [narrow] niche and slipped it into every home in the nation."[41]

The movies played an important role in placing Elvis and teen music (now bleached of its racial, regional, and working-class tinge) smack dab in the middle of the pop music mainstream. It is noteworthy that by the time *King Creole* was released, Presley's film work had increasingly become the major conduit through which his image was presented to the public. After 1956, his personal appearances declined sharply. In that year, he had played 151 concert dates. During 1957, by contrast, he had appeared in concert 40 times, from 1958 to 1960, just once, and in 1961, there were only three instances of his performing live in front of an audience. Obviously the Presley team had hitched its star to a movie career and placed more emphasis in that area. Yet, it is striking how quickly and thoroughly it had ditched its foundational origins. Concert settings had contributed greatly to the singer's honing of a distinctive stage routine; they also had played a role in his growing notoriety as a subversive rocker—"If he did that on the street, we'd arrest him" became as common a rock 'n' roll refrain as "lay off of my blue suede shoes." This was a notoriety that Colonel Parker and Steve Sholes, however, could do without. Apparently the pop music establishment felt the same. By the late 1950s, industry executives were advocating that "the very expression 'rhythm and blues' be dropped now as obsolete." Indeed, from a corporate perspective, rhythm and blues had matured; now called rock 'n' roll, it had exchanged its more "savage" or vulgar qualities for sophistication. This new youth-oriented music promised to "attract more listeners and still retain teenage groups who will still get their rock 'n' roll, but of a better type."[42]

As for Elvis, he often had indicated his belief that motion pictures offered an entertainer the longevity that popular music generally did not. Had not Bing Crosby made the transition? Dean Martin? Judy Garland? Frank Sinatra was a perfect example. And although he possessed no formal dramatic training, critics had noted that his acting in the mid-to-late 1950s had improved with each picture. A future in movies seemed promising. The singer indicated on several occasions that he wanted to make movies that did not include his singing. As he told a group of reporters in late 1957, "I'd like to do a straight dramatic show. I'm betting on an acting career." Thus even before he entered the U.S. Army in 1958 for a two-year stint, Presley appeared set on a course that would take him away from the rhythm and blues-inflected rock 'n' roll that had brought him to prominence. Parker had never trusted it and would continue to steer "his boy" toward a middle-of-the-road career; Sholes and RCA had been ready to strangle it in its cradle, but contented themselves with pursuing a less conspicuous gambit. Ultimately, their decision to purchase Presley had been justified. The newly-crowned "King of Rock 'n' Roll" had helped toll the death knell for rhythm and blues.[43]

When Elvis died in August of 1977, reporters approached John Lennon and Paul McCartney and asked them their thoughts on the late entertainer. Lennon supposedly replied that Elvis had died when he went into the Army; McCartney's answer was similar, maintaining that military service had "tamed him too much." Like many biographies since, the Lennon-McCartney perspective neatly divided Presley's career into pre- and post-Army segments, an interpretation that acknowledges the singer's ground-breaking rise in the 1950s and then accentuates his tragic fall from grace in the years that followed his discharge. It is a narrative which implies that Elvis, the ultimate rock 'n' roll rebel, was corrupted by fame and consequently betrayed his musical roots. Even when he later returned to those roots in various "comebacks" of the late 1960s and early 1970s, it was not enough to alter the substance of the story. In the end, according to the myth, Presley simply sold out.[44]

It is a reasonable interpretation that contains several interrelated grains of truth. Presley and Parker undoubtedly concerned themselves primarily with the bottom line. As a working-class Southerner who considered his success a product of divine intervention and fan favor, Elvis forever remained insecure regarding his artistry or ability to sustain his success. At any moment he believed he could be back in Memphis driving a truck. Thus, attaining financial security was a high priority. Regrettably, financial considerations frequently outweighed artistic ones. It also is true that Elvis was an eclectic popular music consumer who chose songs in the recording studio as if he were making purchases in a record store. He was just as likely to choose a Dean Martin or Ink Spots number to record as he was to select a composition popularized by Clyde McPhatter, Ray Charles, or Carl Perkins. He had never committed fully to any one genre. Finally, from the time that he started performing, Presley was determined to pursue a movie career. Unfortunately, producers manufactured a formulaic product that consistently gratified a prescribed market, but did little to challenge Elvis or general movie-goers. Even more tragic, perhaps, the films attained a financial success that allowed Presley to maintain a celebrity lifestyle to which he had grown accustomed. This cushion of comfort carried over into the latter stages of his career when he returned to live concerts in Las Vegas and elsewhere. For many who had expected more, Elvis indeed had sold his soul to the devil.

Less obvious in this rationale are the impersonal forces that contributed to Presley's evolution from revolutionary rocker to, in the words of Erika Doss, a "symbol of monopoly capital." Specifically missing are the manipulative forces of monopoly capitalism. Like most performers of his era who made their living in the entertainment marketplace, Elvis became a commodity. As such, he lost full control over how he was presented or packaged to the public. In fact, during his lifetime there was a constant and generally unresolved tension that existed between his image and the person that the image was supposed to represent. Once likened to a "jug of corn liquor at a champagne party," the singer no doubt struggled to overcome what the mainstream perceived as a flawed regional and racially-ambiguous working-class background. Along to assist in this endeavor were people like Tom Parker, Steve Sholes, and Hal Wallis, individuals whose agendas were tied to fashioning a product that could be sold to the mainstream while simultaneously strengthening the entertainment establishment. Others, of course, eventually would replace them. But their agendas would be identical to those they had supplanted: create a commodity that appealed to the largest number of consumers. It would take Presley's entire lifetime and then some for such marketers to concoct an Elvis that fit the bill, one who was "a seamless and uncomplicated specimen of upwardly mobile middle-class normalcy and achievement," and who was, in the words of a recent Disney movie character, "a model citizen." If the human being had been lost in the process, well, that was just show business. Paraphrasing Colonel Parker, "Don't try to understand Elvis; just sell it."[45]

NOTES

1. The title refers to a saying that Thomas Parker, Elvis Presley's longtime manager, regularly used. Parker claimed that the phrase was going to be the title of his memoirs, which he apparently never finished. Parker biographer Alanna Nash has argued that the "Colonel" concocted the tale that he was writing his life story to avoid answering controversial questions put to him about his management of Presley. Nash, like many, held a very dim view of Parker's handling of the singer. See Alanna Nash, *The Colonel: The Extraordinary Story of Colonel Tom Parker and Elvis Presley* (New York: Simon & Schuster, Inc., 2003), 6. Ironically, the Country Music Hall of Fame in Nashville in the fall of 2009 opened an exhibit entitled: "The Colonel Says, 'How Much Does It Cost If It's Free.'" Unlike Nash, the corporate-controlled Hall viewed Parker as a "revolutionary music business figure." See the press release announcing the exhibit's opening as part of the museum's "Archive Spotlight Series" at http://www.countrymusichalloffame.org/the-news-room-archive/view/1021.

2. The quoted material is a composite derived from several sources, all of whom had access to Presley's entourage, including the member who called Parker. All of the responses—each is separated by ellipses—are attributed to the Colonel. For the "nothing has changed" line, see Dirk Vallenga and Mick Farren, *Elvis and the Colonel* (New York: Delacorte Press, 1987), 174. The reference to Presley's being back in the Army can be found in Nick Tosches, "Elvis in Death," in Kevin Quain, ed., *The Elvis Reader: Texts and Sources on the King of Rock 'n' Roll* (New York: St. Martin's Press, 1992), 275. On the assertion that Elvis was not dead, see Alanna Nash, with Billy Smith, Marty Lacker, and Lamar Fike, *Elvis Aron Presley: Revelations from the Memphis Mafia* (New York: HarperCollins, 1995), 731. Parker's acquisition of his honorary title, bestowed either in 1948 by Louisiana governor Jimmie Davis or in 1953 by Governor Frank Clement of Tennessee, is described in Amanda Petrusich, *It Still Moves: Love Songs, Lost Highways, and the Search for the Next American Music* (New York: Faber and Faber, Inc., 2008), 58. For time of death, see Charles C. Thompson and James P. Cole, *The Death of Elvis: What Really Happened* (London: Robert Hale Ltd., Publishers, 1992), 7. There has been some speculation that 3:40 may have been more accurate. A good descriptive account of the events occurring on the day of Presley's death can be found in Neal and Janice Gregory, *When Elvis Died* (Washington, D.C.: Communications Press, 1980), 5–21.

3. Geissler's creed is located in a contemporary Associated Press newspaper story that details the success of Factors' Etc., Inc. See "Posters Reflect Star Status," *The Milwaukee Journal* May 24, 1978, 10. Geissler's admiration for Parker is in Tony Schwartz, "The Spoils of Elvis," *Newsweek*, January 30, 1978, 58. The Bear's vow to protect Parker's "boy" is in Bob Greene, "Elvis' Name is a Business," *The Free Lance-Star* March 1, 1978, 2. For more on the meeting between Parker and RCA and Parker and Geissler, see Frank Rose, *The Agency: William Morris and the Hidden History of Show Business* (New York: HarperBusiness, 1995), 363–365; Alanna Nash, *The Colonel*, 309–10.

4. Kennedy's generally negative assessment is in Caroline Kennedy, "Graceland," *Rolling Stone*, September 22, 1977, 40. There was some confusion as to Kennedy's

presence at Graceland. Some Presley family members thought she was accompanied by her mother, Jackie Onassis. Many apparently believed she was there representing the Kennedy family, a perception that she did not bother to dispel. In actuality, she was there on assignment for the *New York Daily News*. She missed her deadline and eventually sold her story to *Rolling Stone*. See Neal and Janice Gregory, *When Elvis Died*, 90. The first quotation attributed to Parker is from Jerry Hopkins, *Elvis: The Final Years* (New York: Berkley Books, 1981), 301.The second can be found in Greg Kot, "But the Legend Lives On: The Big Chill Makes Some Rock Stars Hot," *Herald-Journal* October 22, 1995, 47. The background material for this paragraph can be found in Hopkins, *Elvis: The Final Years*, 292–304; Peter Guralnick, *Careless Love: The Unmaking of Elvis Presley* (Boston: Little, Brown and Company, 1999), 646–661. Also see the oral history collected in Rose Clayton and Dick Heard, eds., *Elvis Up Close: In the Words of Those Who Knew Him Best* (Atlanta: Turner Publishing, Inc., 1994), 335–60.

5. The classic indictment of the Presley-Parker financial relationship is Mary Loveless, "The Selling of Elvis: Who's Taking Care of Business?" *Memphis Magazine*, July-August, 1985, 69–80. At a time when ten percent represented the standard percentage drawn by the managers of entertainers, Presley granted Parker fifty percent. He conceded this to the Colonel in 1967 when they renewed their original agreement. Parker owned fifty-six percent of the stock in Boxcar, Elvis twenty-two percent. Parker's friends and flunkies controlled the rest. Concerning entertainment law and deceased celebrities, see David S. Wall, "Policing Elvis: Legal Action and the Shaping of Post-Mortem Celebrity Culture as Contested Space," *Entertainment Law* 2 (Autumn 2003), 35–69. For an excellent bibliography of books that address various aspects of the Elvis Presley phenomenon, see the exhaustive list of Elvis books in print compiled by David Neale at: http://users.telenet.be/davidneale/elvis/books/Dates.html.

6. Parker's motto can be found in C. Robert Jennings, "They'll Always Be an Elvis," *Saturday Evening Post*, September 1965, 77. The following quotation is in Julie Carpenter, "How Death was the Making of Elvis; Exactly 30 Years after He Died, We Reveal How the King Only Made a Fortune after He had Sung his Last Note," *The Express*, August 16, 2007, 32.

7. The useable past quotation was made by Presley friend Janelle McComb and can be found in Laura Coleman, "Elvis Museum Honors Friend," *Memphis Commercial Appeal*, August 7, 1992, A1. For the $100 million-a-year figure, see Scott Shepard, "Elvis' Career is Booming," *St. Petersburg Times*, August 15, 1993, 8B.

8. The "young and irreverent" and Jack Soden quotations are located in David Halbfinger, "Elvis Lives! (As Marketing Effort, Anyway)," *New York Times*, April 21, 2002, 1. The strategy of getting Elvis in front of younger consumers can be found in Tom Maurstad, "Elvis Lives! The King Left the Building a Quarter-Century Ago, But Thanks to a Flood of Cutting-Edge Marketing, a New Generation Can't Help Falling in Love Again," *Dallas Morning News*, August 11, 2002, 1C. For "bloated icon," see David J. Jefferson, "Elvis Lives," *Newsweek*, August 19, 2002, 54.

9. For the quotation on the dead Presley being everywhere, see Shepard, "Elvis' Career is Booming," 8B.

10. The quoted material claiming the Elvis of EPE (Elvis Presley Enterprises) is the symbol of monopoly capitalism can be found in Erika Doss, *Elvis Culture: Fans, Faith, and Image* (Lawrence: University Press of Kansas, 1999), 227–228. According to the EPE licensing director, "We concentrate on finding products that will preserve the name, image, and likeness of Elvis Presley. We license only companies that support our long-term goals product quality, distribution, creativity and longevity." See Debbie Galante Block, "Elvis: The King of Merchandising: Twenty-five Years after his Death, His Image is Everywhere," *Billboard* June 15, 2002, 74.

11. Presley's response on the difficulty of living up to an image can be heard on the long-play album that accompanied the documentary *This is Elvis*,"Excerpts from Madison Square Garden Press Conference, June 1972," in *This is Elvis* LP Album CPL2-04031, RCA, 1981. While there is a vast number of biographies that address the life and career of Presley, the quality of the works is uneven. The best can be reduced to less than a handful. They are, in no particular order, Jerry Hopkins, *Elvis* (New York: Simon & Schuster, Inc., 1971); Peter Guralnick, *Last Train to Memphis: The Rise of Elvis Presley* (Boston: Little, Brown, and Company, 1994); Dave Marsh, *Elvis* (New York: Warner Books, 1982); Bobbie Ann Mason, *Elvis Presley: A Life* (New York: Penguin, 2007). Still relevant as an interpretive model is Greil Marcus, *Mystery Train: Images of America in Rock 'n' Roll Music* (New York: E.P. Dutton, 1982, rev.ed.).

12. The quoted material can be found in "Negro DJ Raps Spread of Filth in R&B Disks, *Variety*, March 23, 1955, 1, 54.

13. For an elaboration of the narrative that follows, see Michael Bertrand, *Race, Rock, and Elvis* (Urbana: University of Illinois Press, 1995 2nd ed.), 59–92. Other histories of 1950s rock 'n' roll include Jonathan Kamin, "Rhythm and Blues in White America: Rock and Roll as Acculturation and Perceptual Learning," Ph.D. Dissertation, Princeton University, 1976; Arnold Shaw, *The Rockin' Fifties* (New York: DaCapo Press, 2nd ed.); Glenn C. Altschuler, *All Shook Up: How Rock 'n' Roll Changed America* (New York: Oxford University Press, 2003); Charlie Gillett, *The Sound of the City: The Rise of Rock and Roll* (New York: Pantheon Books, 1983, rev. ed.); Linda Martin and Kerry Segrave, *Anti-Rock: The Opposition to Rock 'n' Roll* (New York: Da Capo Press, 1993, 2nd ed.); Craig Werner, *A Change is Gonna Come: Music, Race, and the Soul of America* (New York: A Plume Book, 1998).

14. For the quotation, see LeRoi Jones (Imamu Amiri Baraka), *Blues People: Negro Music in White America* (New York: Morrow Quill Papers, 1963), 169.

15. On the backgrounds and operating procedures of independent recording companies during the post-World War II era, see John Broven, *Record Makers and Breakers: Voices of the Independent Rock 'n' Roll Pioneers* (Urbana: University of Illinois Press, 2009).

16. For more information on independent record labels of the period, see Charlie Gillett, *The Sound of the City.*

17. For "cat-minded teenagers," see June Bundy, "R&B Disks Sock Pop Market; Major Firms Jump into Ring," *Billboard*, January 29, 1955, 56. On "cat" records, see "New York Beat," *Jet*, August 12, 1954, 65. My use of the lowercase in writing out "jim crow" in reference to legalized segregation is intentional. It is based on the belief

that to do so robs the system of its power and "legitimacy," similar to what a group of activists achieved in 1947 when they met at a Fellowship of Reconciliation/Congress of Racial Equality-sponsored workshop in Washington and composed a song that repeated the lines "You don't have to ride jim crow" three times in the first stanza. Based on a traditional Negro spiritual, "There's No Hidin' Down Here," the freedom song was written following the Journey of Reconciliation in the spring of 1947. By the mid-1950s, African American periodicals such as *American Negro*, published independently in Chicago, refused to capitalize the phrase. The *Pittsburgh Courier* likewise utilized the practice of placing the phrase in lowercase in opposition to the "antiquated jim crow setup." See "Editorial: The Temper of the South," *Pittsburgh Courier*, December 17, 1955, A11. For more on "You Don't Have to Ride jim crow," see Raymond Arsenault, *Freedom Rides: 1961 and the Struggle for Racial Justice* (New York: Oxford University Press, 2006), 11, 592.

18. On the various thinly-veiled words, see "Negro DJ Raps Spread of Filth Via R&B Disks," 1, 54; Is Horowitz, "Program Ingenuity, a Keen Eye Lift Deejays to Recognized Prominence," *Billboard*, April 24, section 2, 18. For the assessment that such music had been restricted to barrelhouses and the like, see Abel Green, "A Warning to the Music Business," *Variety*, February 23, 1955, 20. On "serious inroads," see "How DIRTY are Rhythm and Blues Songs? *Jet*, June 9, 1955, 10.

19. On teenagers creating fads, see John Wilson, "What Makes 'Pop' Music Popular," *New York Times Magazine*, December 8, 1957, 24–25. Quoted material on the consumer with eighty-nine cents is in "Don't Lose that Kid!" *Billboard*, March 17, 1956, 18. The industry's not giving in to teens over moral standards was reported in Ren Grevatt, "New York Calling," *Melody Maker*, July 13, 1957, 2.

20. The "clean up the air" policy was announced in "Control the Dimwits!" *Billboard*, September 25, 1954, 33. Also see Paul Ackerman, "Indie Diskers Back WDIA's R&B Ban," *Billboard*, October 30, 1954, 16. On "voluntary cooperation," see "Houston Radio Stations Ask Crime Commission to List Indigo Disks," *Variety*, March 23, 1955, 41. For the quotation that includes "perennial favorites," see "Mobile Station Quotes Variety Leerics, Will Not Broadcast 'Em," *Variety*, March 23, 1955, 62. Also see "WAAB Reports Song Ban in 'Air Editorial,'" *Billboard*, April 2, 1955, 13. "Badgered" disk jockeys and others can be found in "Control the Dimwits," 33. On the various civic groups coming together in opposition to R&B, see "JUV ASSN Gets Jock Support in Drive to Kayo 'Leeric' Platters," *Variety*, July 20, 1955, 47; "Radio Outlets, Disk Jocks Launch Self-Policy Setups vs. Leeric Wax," *Variety*, March 30, 1955, 49. Also see June Bundy, "Obscene R&B Tunes Blasted in New England," *Billboard*, April 3, 1955, 13, 18.

21. On the recommendation for the industry to monitor itself, see "Control the Dimwits," 33. The advice "not to overdo it" was given in "How to Kill a Trend!" Cashbox, February 5, 1955, 3. Also see "Finger Points at You!" Billboard, October 2, 1954, 19; "WDIA's Got a Broom!" *Billboard*, October 30, 1954, 16. On the "chums" comment, see Abel Green, "A Warning to the Music Business," 20.

22. RCA's statement was provided in Abel Green, "Leer-ics, Part III," *Variety*, March 9, 1955, 49. The Columbia Records president's views were given in "On S. 2834," *Hearings before the Subcommittee on Communications of the Committee on*

Interstate and Foreign Commerce, U.S. Senate, 85th Cong., 2nd sess., (Washington, DC: Government Printing Office, 1958), 886, 892.

23. For the "unfortunate" quotation, see "Trade Views Off-Color Disk Situation with Mixed Feelings," *Billboard*, October 2, 1954, 86. For Freed's comments, see George Leonard, "The Great Rock 'n' Roll Controversy," *Look*, June 26, 1956, 48. The last quoted material can be found in Ruth Cage, "Horrors! Recognition Finally Comes to R&B," *Down Beat* April 6, 1955, 1, 17. Also see Paul Ackerman, "What Has Happened to Popular Music," *High Fidelity*, June 1958, 35; Is Horowitz, "Going to Be a Record Fight; Independents Smash Big Labels," *Billboard*, November 19, 1955, 1.

24. On customers wanting R&B, see "Buyers All Right," *Billboard*, January 29, 1955, 56.

25. First quotation is from June Bundy, "R&B Disks Sock Pop Market, Major Firms Jump into Ring," 56. Wailing sax and R&B characterization can be located in "Majors Really Jump with the R&B Beat," *Billboard*, January 15, 1955, 33. Variety story from 1955 reprinted in Charles Gruenberg, "The Negro Issue in Rock and Roll," *New York Post*, October 9, 1956, 50. Langston Hughes, "Highway Robbery Across the Color Line in Rhythm and Blues," *Chicago Defender*, July 2, 1955, 10.

26. See Charles Gruenberg, "The Negro Influence in Rock and Roll," 50.

27. First quotation is in "Kids (and R&B) Here to Stay," *Cashbox*, March 5, 1955, 3. Steve Sholes, "The Customer is Always Right," *Cashbox*, July 2 1955, 82.

28. First quotation is in "Thiele Reaffirms Faith in R&B as Source of Material for Pop Records," *Cashbox*, August 27, 1955, 22. Sholes on getting rock 'n' roll talent can be found in Paul Ackerman, "Presley Period Saw Majors Get Into Rock," *Billboard*, August 27, 1977, 1. Final quotation is in Steve Sholes, "The Customer is Always Right," 82.

29. An early report of Presley's getting "spins" on R&B shows is in Bill Simon, "Boundaries Between Music Types Fall; Deejays Spin 'em All," *Billboard*, November 12, 1955, 36. Local press interpretation can be found in Robert Johnson, "Suddenly Singing Elvis Presley Zooms into Recording Stardom," *Memphis Press-Scimitar*, February 5, 1955, 9B. On the characterization that Elvis had something that appealed to everybody, see Edwin Howard, "In a Spin," *Memphis Press-Scimitar*, July 28, 1954, 23. On announcement that Presley had signed with RCA, see "Double Deals Hurl Presley into Stardom," *Billboard*, December 3, 1955, 15. Full-page ad is "Advertisement," *Billboard*, December 3, 1955, 59.

30. The audio material found on the promotional record, "The Truth About Me," can be heard on the compact disk, *Elvis Presley: The Fifties Interviews*, Compact Disc CDMF074 (Houston, Texas: The Magnum Music Group, Inc., 1990). The cow story can be found in Charles Gruenberg, "The Rock and Roll Story: Elvis Presley," *New York Post*, October 4, 1956, 48. More on this incident is conveyed by Gabe Tucker, an assistant to Parker in the 1950s. Tucker describes the ramifications in Marge Crumbaker, with Gabe Tucker, *Up and Down with Elvis Presley* (New York: Putnam Publishing Group, 1981), 88.

31. The "howling hillbilly" appellation was introduced in "A Howling Hillbilly Success," *Life*, April 30, 1956, 64. The quotation and material concerning NBC's reluctance to book Presley can be found in Marie Torre, "TV-Radio Today: Pres-

ley Pulls His Rating Rank," *New York Herald-Tribune* September 16, 1956, 5. For the critique of Presley's appearance on the Berle show, see Jack Gould, "TV: New Phenomenon," *New York Times* June 6, 1956, 67. All of Presley's television appearances from 1956 can be viewed fully on VHS or DVD. My resources have included the documentaries *Elvis '56: In the Beginning*, VHS, directed by Susan Raymond (Chatsworth, California: Image Entertainment, 1987); *This is Elvis*, DVD, directed and produced by Andrew Solt and Malcom Leo (New York: Warner Brothers, Inc., 2007). In addition, the audio versions of Presley's television appearances have been captured on the multi-record set, *Elvis: A Golden Celebration*, LP Album CPM6-5172 (New York: RCA, Inc., 1985).

32. For Elvis's negative response to his Allen appearance, see Bobbie Ann Mason, *Elvis Presley*, 50–51.The Allen protests by teenagers can be found in Walter Ames, "Sullivan Topped by Steve Allen; Teenagers are Mad," *Los Angeles Times* July 3, 1956, B6.

33. On Sullivan signing Elvis for his show, see Richard F. Shepard, "Presley Signed by Ed Sullivan," *New York Times*, July 14, 1956, 33. Colonel Parker's philosophy on selling his artist can be found in C. Robert Jennings, "They'll Always Be an Elvis," 77.

34. On the ratings, see Cecil Smith, "Elvis Swings Pelvis (and Audience Too) on Sullivan Show," *Los Angeles Times*, September 12, 1956, C10; Howard Pearson, "TV Sparks New Drive to Popularize Color; Presley Sets Record," *Deseret News and Telegram*, October 9, 1956, 10B. For a contemporary assessment that Elvis was not taking his "power" seriously, see James and Annette Baxter, "The Man in the Blue Suede Shoes," *Harper's Magazine*, January 1958, 45. All of Presley's appearances on the Ed Sullivan Show have been captured on DVD and can be accessed through *The Ed Sullivan Shows: Elvis Presley*, DVD (Chatsworth, California: Image Entertainment, 2006). All quotations emanating from Presley's appearances on the show are derived from viewing the various video collections listed.

35. See citation notes 31 and 34 for video collections. Quotations are derived from having viewed the video.

36. All factual information regarding Presley's Hollywood career can be located in the biographies listed in citation note 11.

37. The reference is to Hortense Powdermaker, *Hollywood, The Dream Factory* (Boston: Little, Brown and Company, 1950).

38. In addition to the rock histories listed above that include sections devoted to rock exploitation film genre, see Thomas Doherty, *Teenagers and Teenpics: The Juvenilization of American Movies in the 1950s* (Philadelphia, Pennsylvania: Temple University Press, 2002, rev. ed.); Eric Shaefer, Bold! Shocking! Daring! True: A History of Exploitation Films, 1919–1959 (Durham, North Carolina: Duke University Press, 1999).

39. In addition to viewing each of the movies previewed here, one could also view the documentary *This is Elvis*, which discusses in great detail Presley first four films. Also helpful is the documentary, *In Hollywood*, directed by Frank Martin and written by David Naylor and Stuart Goldman, VHS (New York: BMG Special Products, 1993).

40. My approach to Presley's Hollywood career has been shaped strongly by the following: Susan Doll, *Understanding Elvis: Southern Roots Vs. Star Image* (New York: Routledge Publishers, 1998); Allison Graham, *Framing the South: Hollywood, Television, and Race During the Civil Rights Struggle* (Baltimore, Maryland: The Johns Hopkins University Press, 2003, 2nd ed.).

41. On the music being "not so bad after all," see Ren Grevatt, "Dick Clark – A Fortune Being Shy," *Melody Maker*, May 21, 1959, 16. On the last quotation, see William Steif, "What Makes Presley Tick?" *The Pittsburgh Press*, October 17, 1956, 16.

42. The "arrest" reference can be found in Ralph Gleason, "Perspectives," *Down Beat*, July 11, 1956, 34. The effort to drop the term "rhythm and blues" is from Gary Kramer, "On the Beat," *Billboard*, March 9, 1957, 26. Rock 'n' roll of a "better type" is located in June Bundy, "Censored R&R on New FMBS Disk Service Format," *Billboard*, May 18, 1958, 2. Presley's schedule of appearances throughout this period can be found in Fred L. Worth and Steve D. Tamerius, *Elvis: His Life from A to Z* (New York: Wings Books, 1992, 2nd ed.), 334–36.

43. "Interview with Elvis Presley, October 28, 1957, Los Angeles," http://www.elvis.com.au/presley/interview_with_elvis_presley_october_28_1957.shtml (accessed October 23, 2009).

44. Lennon and McCartney's assessments can be found in Gillian Gaar, "Crossing Paths: When Elvis Met the Beatles, Part I," *Goldmine Magazine*, August 14, 2009, http://www.goldminemag.com/article/crossing_paths_when_elvis_met_the_beatles_part_1 (accessed January 24, 2010). See, for instance, Gerry McLafferty, *Elvis Presley in Hollywood: Celluloid Sellout* (Philadelphia, Pennsylvania: Trans–Atlantic Publications, Inc., 1990).

45. The Disney movie was 2002's *Lilo and Stitch*. For an assessment, see Dave Scheiber, "Move Over Barney, Elvis Still Has Kids Rockin'," *St. Petersburg Times*, July 8, 2002, 1D.

BIBLIOGRAPHY

"A Howling Hillbilly Success," *Life*, April 30, 1956, 64.

Ackerman, Paul. "Indie Diskers Back WDIA's R&B Ban," *Billboard*, October 30, 1954.

Ackerman. "Presley Period Saw Majors Get Into Rock," *Billboard*, August 27, 1977, 1.

Ackerman. "What Has Happened to Popular Music," *High Fidelity*, June 1958, 35.

"Advertisement," *Billboard*, December 3, 1955, 59.

Altschuler, Glenn C. *All Shook Up: How Rock 'n' Roll Changed America* (New York: Oxford University Press, 2003).

Ames, Walter. "Sullivan Topped by Steve Allen; Teenagers are Mad," *Los Angeles Times* July 3, 1956, B6.

Arsenault, Raymond. *Freedom Rides: 1961 and the Struggle for Racial Justice* (New York: Oxford University Press, 2006).

"Badgered" disk jockeys and others can be found in "Control the Dimwits," 33.

Baxter, James and Annette. "The Man in the Blue Suede Shoes," *Harper's Magazine*, January 1958, 45.

Bertrand, Michael. *Race, Rock, and Elvis* (Urbana: University of Illinois Press, 1995 2nd ed.).

Block, Debbie Galante. "Elvis: The King of Merchandising: Twenty-five Years after his Death, His Image is Everywhere," *Billboard* June 15, 2002, 74.

Broven, John. *Record Makers and Breakers: Voices of the Independent Rock 'n' Roll Pioneers* (Urbana: University of Illinois Press, 2009).

Bundy, June. "Obscene R&B Tunes Blasted in New England," *Billboard*, April 3, 1955, 13, 18.

Bundy. "R&B Disks Sock Pop Market; Major Firms Jump into Ring," *Billboard*, January 29, 1955, 56.

"Buyers All Right," *Billboard*, January 29, 1955, 56.

Cage, Ruth. "Horrors! Recognition Finally Comes to R&B," *Down Beat* April 6, 1955, 1, 17.

Carpenter, Julie. "How Death was the Making of Elvis; Exactly 30 Years after He Died, We Reveal How the King Only Made a Fortune after He had Sung his Last Note," *The Express*, August 16, 2007.

Clayton, Rose, and Dick Heard, eds., *Elvis Up Close: In the Words of Those Who Knew Him Best* (Atlanta: Turner Publishing, Inc., 1994).

Coleman, Laura. "Elvis Museum Honors Friend," *Memphis Commercial Appeal*, August 7, 1992, A1.

"Control the Dimwits!" *Billboard*, September 25, 1954, 33.

Crumbaker, Marge, with Gabe Tucker, *Up and Down with Elvis Presley* (New York: Putnam Publishing Group, 1981).

Doherty, Thomas. *Teenagers and Teenpics: The Juvenilization of American Movies in the 1950s* (Philadelphia, Pennsylvania: Temple University Press, 2002, rev. ed.).

Doll, Susan. *Understanding Elvis: Southern Roots Vs. Star Image* (New York: Routledge Publishers, 1998).

"Don't Lose that Kid!" *Billboard*, March 17, 1956, 18.

Doss, Erika. *Elvis Culture: Fans, Faith, and Image* (Lawrence: University Press of Kansas, 1999), 227–228.

"Double Deals Hurl Presley into Stardom," *Billboard*, December 3, 1955, 15.

The Ed Sullivan Shows: Elvis Presley, DVD (Chatsworth, California: Image Entertainment, 2006).

"Editorial: The Temper of the South," *Pittsburgh Courier*, December 17, 1955, A11.

Elvis: A Golden Celebration, LP Album CPM6-5172 (New York: RCA, Inc., 1985).

Elvis '56: In the Beginning, VHS, directed by Susan Raymond (Chatsworth, California: Image Entertainment, 1987).

Elvis Presley: The Fifties Interviews, Compact Disc CDMF074 (Houston, Texas: The Magnum Music Group, Inc., 1990).

"Finger Points at You!" *Billboard*, October 2, 1954, 19.

Gaar, Gillian. "Crossing Paths: When Elvis Met the Beatles, Part I," *Goldmine Magazine*, August 14, 2009, http://www.goldminemag.com/article/crossing_paths_when_elvis_met_the_beatles_part_1 (accessed January 24, 2010).

Gillett, Charlie. *The Sound of the City: The Rise of Rock and Roll* (New York: Pantheon Books, 1983, rev. ed.).

Gleason, Ralph. Perspectives," *Down Beat*, July 11, 1956, 34.

Gould, Jack. "TV: New Phenomenon," *New York Times* June 6, 1956, 67.

Graham, Allison. *Framing the South: Hollywood, Television, and Race During the Civil Rights Struggle* (Baltimore, Maryland: The Johns Hopkins University Press, 2003, 2nd ed.).

Green, Abel. "A Warning to the Music Business," *Variety*, February 23, 1955.

Green. "Leer-ics, Part III," *Variety*, March 9, 1955, 49.

Greene, Bob. "Elvis' Name is a Business," *The Free Lance-Star* March 1, 1978, 2.

Gregory, Neal and Janice. *When Elvis Died* (Washington, D.C.: Communications Press, 1980).

Greil, Marcus, *Mystery Train: Images of America in Rock 'n' Roll Music* (New York: E.P. Dutton, 1982, rev.ed.).

Grevatt, Ren. "Dick Clark – A Fortune Being Shy," *Melody Maker*, May 21, 1959, 16.

Grevatt. "New York Calling," *Melody Maker*, July 13, 1957, 2.

Gruenberg, Charles. "The Negro Issue in Rock and Roll," *New York Post*, October 9, 1956, 50.

Gruenberg. "The Rock and Roll Story: Elvis Presley," *New York Post*, October 4, 1956, 48.

Guralnick, Peter. *Careless Love: The Unmaking of Elvis Presley* (Boston: Little, Brown and Company, 1999).

Guralnick. *Last Train to Memphis: The Rise of Elvis Presley* (Boston: Little, Brown, and Company, 1994).

Halbfinger, "Elvis Lives! (As Marketing Effort, Anyway)," *New York Times*, April 21, 2002, 1.

Hopkins, Jerry. *Elvis: The Final Years* (New York: Berkley Books, 1981).

Hopkins. Elvis (New York: Simon & Schuster, Inc., 1971).

Horowitz, Is. "Going to Be a Record Fight; Independents Smash Big Labels," *Billboard*, November 19, 1955, 1.

"Houston Radio Stations Ask Crime Commission to List Indigo Disks," *Variety*, March 23, 1955.41.

"How DIRTY are Rhythm and Blues Songs? *Jet*, June 9, 1955, 10.

"How to Kill a Trend!" *Cashbox*, February 5, 1955, 3.

Howard, Edwin. "In a Spin," *Memphis Press-Scimitar*, July 28, 1954, 23.

Hughes, Langston. "Highway Robbery Across the Color Line in Rhythm and Blues," *Chicago Defender*, July 2, 1955, 10.

In Hollywood, directed by Frank Martin and written by David Naylor and Stuart Goldman, VHS (New York: BMG Special Products, 1993).

"Interview with Elvis Presley, October 28, 1957, Los Angeles," http://www.elvis .com.au/presley/interview_with_elvis_presley_october_28_1957.shtml (accessed October 23, 2009).

Jefferson, David J. "Elvis Lives," *Newsweek*, August 19, 2002, 54.

Jennings, C. Robert. "They'll Always Be an Elvis," *Saturday Evening Post*, September 1965, 77.

Johnson, Robert. "Suddenly Singing Elvis Presley Zooms into Recording Stardom," *Memphis Press-Scimitar*, February 5, 1955, 9B.

Jones, LeRoi (Imamu Amiri Baraka). *Blues People: Negro Music in White America* (New York: Morrow Quill Papers, 1963.

"JUV ASSN Gets Jock Support in Drive to Kayo 'Leeric' Platters," *Variety*, July 20, 1955, 47.

Kamin, Jonathan. "Rhythm and Blues in White America: Rock and Roll as Acculturation and Perceptual Learning," Ph.D. Dissertation, Princeton University, 1976.

Kennedy, Caroline. "Graceland," *Rolling Stone*, September 22, 1977, 40.

"Kids (and R&B) Here to Stay," *Cashbox*, March 5, 1955, 3.

Kot, "But the Legend Lives On: The Big Chill Makes Some Rock Stars Hot," *Herald-Journal* October 22, 1995, 47.

Kramer, Gary. "On the Beat," *Billboard*, March 9, 1957, 26.

Leonard, George. "The Great Rock 'n' Roll Controversy," *Look*, June 26, 1956, 48.

Loveless, Mary. "The Selling of Elvis: Who's Taking Care of Business?" *Memphis Magazine*, July–August, 1985, 69–80.

"Majors Really Jump with the R&B Beat," *Billboard*, January 15, 1955, 33.

Marsh, Dave. *Elvis* (New York: Warner Books, 1982).

Martin, Linda, and Kerry Segrave. *Anti-Rock: The Opposition to Rock 'n' Roll* (New York: Da Capo Press, 1993, 2nd ed.).

Mason, Bobbie Ann. *Elvis Presley: A Life* (New York: Penguin, 2007).

Maurstad, Tom. "Elvis Lives! The King Left the Building a Quarter-Century Ago, But Thanks to a Flood of Cutting-Edge Marketing, a New Generation Can't Help Falling in Love Again," *Dallas Morning News*, August 11, 2002, 1C.

McLafferty, Gerry. *Elvis Presley in Hollywood: Celluloid Sellout* (Philadelphia, Pennsylvania: Trans-Atlantic Publications, Inc., 1990).

"Mobile Station Quotes Variety Leerics, Will Not Broadcast 'Em," *Variety*, March 23, 1955, 62.

Nash, Alanna. *The Colonel: The Extraordinary Story of Colonel Tom Parker and Elvis Presley*. New York: Simon & Schuster, Inc., 2003.

Nash, Alanna, with Billy Smith, Marty Lacker, and Lamar Fike, *Elvis Aron Presley: Revelations from the Memphis Mafia* (New York: HarperCollins, 1995.

"Negro DJ Raps Spread of Filth in R&B Disks, *Variety*, March 23, 1955, 1, 54.

"New York Beat," *Jet*, August 12, 1954, 65.

"On S. 2834," *Hearings before the Subcommittee on Communications of the Committee on Interstate and Foreign Commerce*, U.S. Senate, 85th Cong., 2nd sess., (Washington: Government Printing Office, 1958), 886, 892.

Quain, Kevin, ed., *The Elvis Reader: Texts and Sources on the King of Rock 'n' Roll* (New York: St. Martin's Press, 1992).

Pearson, Howard. "TV Sparks New Drive to Popularize Color; Presley Sets Record," *Deseret News and Telegram*, October 9, 1956, 10B.

Petrusich, Amanda. *It Still Moves: Love Songs, Lost Highways, and the Search for the Next American Music* (New York: Faber and Faber, Inc., 2008).

"Posters Reflect Star Status," *The Milwaukee Journal* May 24, 1978, 10.

Powdermaker, Hortense. *Hollywood, The Dream Factory* (Boston: Little, Brown and Company, 1950).

"Radio Outlets, Disk Jocks Launch Self-Policy Setups vs. Leeric Wax," *Variety*, March 30, 1955, 49.

Rose, Frank. *The Agency: William Morris and the Hidden History of Show Business* (New York: HarperBusiness, 1995).

Scheiber, Dave."Move Over Barney, Elvis Still Has Kids Rockin'," *St. Petersburg Times*, July 8, 2002, 1D.

Schwartz, Tony. "The Spoils of Elvis," *Newsweek*, January 30, 1978, 58.

Shaefer, Eric. *Bold! Shocking! Daring! True: A History of Exploitation Films, 1919–1959.* (Durham, North Carolina: Duke University Press, 1999).

Shaw, Arnold. *The Rockin' Fifties* (New York: DaCapo Press, 2nd ed.).

Shepard, Richard F. "Presley Signed by Ed Sullivan," *New York Times*, July 14, 1956, 33.

Shepard, Scott. "Elvis' Career is Booming," *St. Petersburg Times*, August 15, 1993, 8B.

Sholes, Steve. "The Customer is Always Right," *Cashbox*, July 2, 1955, 82.

Simon, Bill. "Boundaries Between Music Types Fall; Deejays Spin 'em All," *Billboard*, November 12, 1955, 36.

Smith, Cecil. "Elvis Swings Pelvis (and Audience Too) on Sullivan Show," *Los Angeles Times*, September 12, 1956, C10.

Steif, William. "What Makes Presley Tick?" *The Pittsburgh Press*, October 17, 1956, 16.

"Thiele Reaffirms Faith in R&B as Source of Material for Pop Records," *Cashbox*, August 27, 1955, 22.

This is Elvis,"Excerpts from Madison Square Garden Press Conference, June 1972," in This is Elvis LP Album CPL2-04031, RCA, 1981.

This is Elvis, DVD, directed and produced by Andrew Solt and Malcom Leo (New York: Warner Brothers, Inc., 2007).

Thompson, Charles C., and James P. Cole, *The Death of Elvis: What Really Happened* (London: Robert Hale Ltd., Publishers, 1992).

Torre, Marie. "TV-Radio Today: Presley Pulls His Rating Rank," *New York Herald-Tribune* September 16, 1956, 5.

"Trade Views Off-Color Disk Situation with Mixed Feelings," *Billboard*, October 2, 1954, 86.

Vallenga, Dirk, and Mick Farren, *Elvis and the Colonel* (New York: Delacorte Press, 1987), 174.

"WAAB Reports Song Ban in 'Air Editorial,'" *Billboard*, April 2, 1955, 13.

Wall, David S. "Policing Elvis: Legal Action and the Shaping of Post-Mortem Celebrity Culture as Contested Space," Entertainment Law 2 (Autumn 2003), 35–69.

"WDIA's Got a Broom!" *Billboard*, October 30, 1954, 16.

Werner, Craig. *A Change is Gonna Come: Music, Race, and the Soul of America* (New York: A Plume Book, 1998).

Wilson, John. "What Makes 'Pop' Music Popular," *New York Times Magazine*, December 8, 1957, 24–25.

Worth, Fred L., and Steve D. Tamerius, *Elvis: His Life from A to Z* (New York: Wings Books, 1992, 2nd ed.), 334–36.

17

When Death Goes Digital:
Michael Jackson, Twenty-First-Century
Celebrity Death, and the Hero's Journey

Elizabeth Barfoot Christian and Dedria Givens-Carroll

Michael Jackson is worth more in death than he ever was in life. The pop icon's death seemed to instantaneously reverse Jackson's fledgling image from that of an alleged pedophile quirky recording artist to that of a generous boyhood pop star, who in the public's eye had never grown to adulthood when he died at age fifty.

Death benefited Jackson's image in several ways. CBS News reported that before he died Jackson's net worth was estimated at $236 million and he was deep in debt, but not long after his death, his estate was estimated at $500 million with continued earnings of $50 million a year.[1] One year later, Jackson's estate is reportedly worth $1 billion and counting.[2]

Jackson was a star who was idolized, according to a *New York Times* article appearing the day after his death: "For his legions of fans, he was the Peter Pan of pop music: the little boy who refused to grow up."[3] The famed King of Pop was a "quintessentially American tale of celebrity and excess took him from musical boy wonder to global pop superstar to sad figure haunted by lawsuits, paparazzi and failed plastic surgery."[4]

PUBLIC RESPONSE

He was so idealized in death that the outpouring of grief was almost a religious experience. In his birthplace of Gary, Indiana, people crowded outside the small house where he spent his childhood and there were "tears, loud wails, and quiet prayers.'"Ida Boyd-King, a local pastor, who led prayer for the crowd said, "Just continue to glorify the man, Lord. Let's give God praise for Michael."[5]

Along with that emotional praise, people around the world provided offerings by the millions for his estate. According to Billboard music charts, less than one week after Jackson's death he held eight of the top ten spots—the first for any artist. He also became the first artist to hold six of the top ten (including the top four) in digital album sales.[6] Neilsen SoundScan reported Jackson had America's top three selling albums the week following his death: the *Number Ones* (a 2008 compilation of hits) sold 108,000 copies, the *Essential Michael Jackson* (2005) sold 102,000, and the 2008 re-release of *Thriller* sold 101,000.[7] Jackson's *Number Ones* went on to become 2009's third-highest grossing of the year, with 2.4 million sold—outselling Lady Gaga's *The Fame*, which placed fourth with 2.2 million albums sold for the year.[8]

Of the 422,000 Jackson albums sold, more than half—241,000 were digitally downloaded. SoundScan did not begin keeping track of digital downloads until 2004, but Jackson broke all records set to date. Records that are expected to stand for many years to come barring another untimely superstar death. Within hours of the first reports of Jackson being hospitalized, iTunes listed three of Jackson's albums among its top ten.[9] Prior to Jackson's death, no artist had ever sold 1 million tracks in a single week. Fans bought 2.3 million Jackson songs digitally in that single week. Comparatively, in the first 25 weeks of 2009, they purchased little more than half that number. Fans also purchased nearly 300,000 Jackson 5 tracks.[10] One-third of the *Billboard* Hot Digital Songs list of the top 75 downloaded songs were Jackson titles for weeks after his death.[11]

Jackson's death boosted a bleak year for music sales. In the year following his death, he has sold 9 million albums in America, and 24 million around the world. Additionally, the Jackson 5 and the Jacksons have sold 800,000 albums. Some 12.9 million tracks were downloaded in the United States in the twelve months following Jackson's death in addition to 26.5 million downloads internationally. Ringtone sales of Jackson tunes numbered 1.5 million in the United States and 3 million around the world.[12]

Keith Caulfield, senior chart analyst for *Billboard*, told *USA Today*:

> If anyone can move mountains and shift charts, even in death, it's Michael Jackson. [Sales went up] after the passing of big stars, from Frank Sinatra to Jerry Garcia to George Harrison. The impact was felt on the charts, but not to this degree. The closest might be John Lennon or Elvis Presley. But the impact was spread out because you had to buy a physical album. With Michael, the impact was amplified because you could get whatever you wanted immediately online.[13]

And sales of physical CDs would have no doubt been even higher had stores had the inventory. Most retailers sold out of the stock of Jackson titles within hours of the star's death.[14] Sony Music Entertainment, which holds most of Jackson's music, released about 2 million copies of Jackson music products the week following his death to replenish retail supply and bringing the two-week total of physical albums sold to 794,000.[15] Supply literally could not keep up with demand.

The top fifteen music sellers on Amazon.com all belonged to Jackson, and eBay online auction site had 30,000 new listings of Jackson merchandise.[16] Articles included a newspaper with Jackson's death as headline offered for $50 and a $250 auction for a *Thriller* doll.[17]

Social networking sites reported immediate reaction to Jackson's death, as well. Nearly 10 million queries for "Michael" and "Jackson" were reported across the top 25 search engines, news, and social networking sites for the week ending June 27.[18] Yahoo Music earned 45 percent of Internet surfers looking for Jackson albums, videos, and merchandise. YouTube was second with 23 percent of the web audience. Yahoo reported that it broke its previous traffic records, with more than 800,000 clicks in the first ten minutes after posting news of Jackson's death.[19] And Google reported thirty-six of its top 100 search terms the afternoon of June 25 were related to Michael Jackson, and the site was at times unable to handle the volume of traffic.[20] Traffic to TMZ.com, which broke the story, doubled during the week, to 4.7 million visitors.[21]

So what can explain this kind of record-breaking, as well as groundbreaking, reaction to a celebrity's untimely, if not completely unexpected, death? Jackson was a legend in his own time. His celebrity at a young age, his health and legal problems, his fall from grace, and his return at age 50 are the things of myth. Perhaps the public's reaction to his death is best understood by analyzing Jackson as the epitome of the mythological hero.

Gary Laderman, who wrote *Sacred Matters: Celebrity Worship, Sexual Ecstasies, the Living Dead and Other Signs of Religious Life in the United States*, commented in *USA Today* the day after Jackson's death that the style of mourning carried "the sacred elements of celebrity worship."[22] "Laderman compared the phenomenon of celebrity worship and Jackson's death to take on:

> "mythic dimensions and his life story, though troubling in many ways as it unfolded, will become a morality play of sorts. Like other saints, he will be forgiven by his public . . . an inspiration and role model, in some ways, for those who want to make music, become famous, or leave a mark on this world. Americans look to the stars for guidance and inspiration, intimacy and ecstasy— powerful motives that bear on the sacred and can transform entertainment into revelation, escapism into liberation, and mortals into gods."[23]

Opinion polls for decades have found that celebrities in the music and film industries are among the most admired Americans.[24] Jackson became more than an instant popular cultural icon upon his death—to many he became a larger-than-life hero.

While it can be argued that Americans along with the American media, in particular, overreact to all untimely celebrity deaths, Jackson was a particularly interesting phenomenon to watch. Margo Jefferson, former culture critic for *The New York Times*, said Jackson was a most "spectacular figure" because he contained so many different personas and musical genres. She asked:

> "Who better expressed so many contradictions—struggles, achievements, questions, ambiguities, transgressions—about race and gender? About our obsession with youth, with the innocence and eros of children; that oh-so-American drive to reinvent and transform our bodies, our lives and ourselves? There's almost no major cultural story Michael Jackson hasn't starred in for nearly forty years."[25]

Jackson transcended national borders and racial boundaries. He was a global icon who was plagued by medical and legal troubles, yet always seemed to come across as a child in need of protection. Despite all his issues he was resilient—by most accounts, a loving father, and finally after years out of the music spotlight, was embarking on a highly anticipated and unprecedented fifty date world tour.

Spitzberg and Cupach[26] studied fans' obsession with celebrities and connected celebrity worship and idolization with harassment and actual stalking of stars. Psychologists have coined the term celebrity worship syndrome (CWS) to define fans who become overly involved in a star's personal life. Maltby, Houran, Lange, Ashe and McCutcheon[27] created a Celebrity Attitude Scale to study the relationship between celebrity worship and religiosity. Their study suggested that "many religious people apparently ignore the religious teaching that 'Thou shalt worship no other Gods,' or fail to connect it to their 'worship' of celebrities."[28]

A critical cultural analysis of Michael Jackson's life can be compared to that of the hero in Joseph Campbell's theory of the "monomyth" in the classic *The Hero with a Thousand Faces*,[29] which was first published in 1949. Campbell said: "a hero ventures forth from the world of common day into a region of supernatural wonder: fabulous forces are there encountered and a decisive victory is won: the hero comes back from this mysterious adventure with the power to bestow boons on his fellow man."[30] "Campbell's mythology analyzes several stages along the hero's journey including: the Departure, the Initiation, the Return, and the Keys.

Seeing Michael Jackson as a hero combined with twenty-first-century technology ensures he, even more so than Elvis or The Beatles, will be wanted dead even more than alive. Not only have his supposed sins been washed away—as we martyr people in death—but we can own a piece of Michael's music or celebrity with merely the click of a mouse. The hero Michael can remain with us always—now it's just worth more.

THE HERO'S JOURNEY

The Departure stage for Michael Jackson was what Campbell said was the Call to Adventure. Jackson was born in Gary, Indiana, in 1958, to Joe and Katherine Jackson. Jackson's Departure started as a child at age five when he first started singing with his family. He appeared with his brothers, the Jackson Five, in their first television debut in 1969 at the Miss Black America pageant and their first nationally broadcast performances on *Hollywood Palace* and *The Ed Sullivan Show*.[31] Jackson stole the show and became the face of the group. "Jackson became a self-aware television performer very early in his career . . . he knew how to construct the right performance at the right time to connect with his audience . . . his career came to mean so much for so many."[32] Jackson had departed on his hero's journey as a cute child with a child's voice.

The hero goes forward with his adventure, according to Campbell "until he comes to the 'threshold guardian' at the entrance to the zone of magnified power.[33] Jackson's crossing of the first threshold could be signified by the launch of his solo career when he "ushered in the age of pop as a global product—not to mention an age of spectacle and pop culture celebrity."[34] Jackson's 1983 televised performance of "Billie Jean" as part of the *Motown: Yesterday, Today, and Forever* tribute further set him apart, showing this bright, beautiful young star juxtaposed beside aging and alcoholic has-beens. The public instantly glorified him as the savior (or hero) of Motown.[35] His career hit highs with the release of *Thriller* in 1983—the best-selling album of all time, but as Campbell would note the hero instead of conquering the threshold (solo fame and stardom) is "swallowed in the belly of the whale."[36] In 1984, Jackson, age 26, reunited with his brothers for a "Victory" tour, but continued to maintain a childlike lifestyle. The obsession with his youth and young voice are reflected in his infatuation with Peter Pan, the creation of his home, Neverland, his changes in appearance with cosmetic surgery and his desire to never really mature to adulthood.[37] Like the Biblical character, Jonah, Michael Jackson preferred to stay safely in the belly of the whale.

In the Initiation Stage, the hero faces many tasks and trials and at the most intense moment on the journey, the hero must survive a severe challenge. Jackson's challenges paradoxically came from childlike lifestyle with accusations in 2003 when he was charged with child molestation of a young cancer patient at his Neverland estate. Again, he was accused of molestation in 2005. The Neverland ranch became his sanctuary. After his arrest, he posed on his limousine's rooftop as Peter Pan and some have claimed that his facial surgery was meant to transform his image to resemble Disney's Peter Pan character.[38] "Another study pointed to Jackson's attempt to draw public attention and sympathy, once showing up one hour late for his trial wearing his pajamas.[39]

If the hero survives the challenge, like Jackson's trials, then he may achieve a great gift—Campbell calls the goal or "the boon"—which often results in the important discovery of self-knowledge. In this Initiation stage, two aspects include meeting with the Goddess and Sacred Marriage. Jackson's goddess could perhaps be personified by his brief marriage to Lisa Marie Presley, the daughter of Elvis Presley. The Sacred Marriage symbolized by his second marriage to Deborah Jeanne Rowe, the mother of two of his three children: Michael Joseph Jackson, Jr. and Paris Michael Katherine Jackson; and Prince Michael Jackson II, the son of a surrogate mother.[40] Even while Jackson was reveling in the "sacred marriage" the documentary *Living with Michael Jackson* by Martin Bashir questioned the pop icon's mental well-being and ability as a parent.[41]

The hero must decide, according to Campbell, to return to the ordinary world and he could face challenges on the return journey. Jackson's acquittal of the child molestation charged may have helped him toward his return journey. Johnson[42] argued that through social identity theory that certain stars, like Jackson, despite their failings will be supported by fans who believed in his innocence. If the hero is successful in the return journey, the "boon" or gift may be used to improve the world. This stage is called the application of "the boon."

The hero has attained the keys to the journey, which are the knowledge and powers acquired along the way.[43] Jackson was on his way to a return journey with a 50-concert tour kicking off at the 02 arena in London in July of 2009.[44] The shows were reportedly sold out and Jackson was positioned for a comeback. The Atonement of the Father part of the Return stage comes at the end of the journey. Although Jackson is known to have a trying relationship with his own father, he aspired to be an excellent father to his three children, who actually spoke at his funeral. In some way, Jackson was atoned as a father.

Despite his troubles, specifically of being labeled a pedophile along this hero's journey, most fans never abandoned the pop culture icon. In the Apotheosis part of the Return, the hero is elevated to the rank of a god or the glorification of a person who is ideal. After completing the difficult challenges (trials for Jackson), the hero is idealized or worshipped in some way. Many admirers still supported Jackson and remembered him as the innocent child star who never grew up. "Jackson showed a great deal of care and respect for his most devoted fans and was generous with autographs for those fans and spoke with them whenever possible. The fans knew that he would arrive ahead of a concert through a main stage door and they waited for him there. He always opened the window of his car to speak to or wave to fans that he knew."[45]

Jackson was seen as a "Jung child archetype" and somehow represented a "safe androgynous star."[46] One woman from Gary, Indiana—Jackson's hometown—remembered him after his death, but in his youth. "The older person, that's not the Michael we knew. We knew the little bitty boy with the big Afro and the brown skin."[47] Up until his death, Jackson continued to reinvent himself and use the gift of his music all along the hero's journey.

According to Randy Taraborrelli, in August of 2008 when Jackson turned fifty, he regretted striving to have a youthful appearance: "He has begun to regret having plastic surgery and spends much of his time staring at his reflection in the mirror."[48] Had Jackson finally become the "Man in the Mirror"? To commemorate his fiftieth birthday, a CD called the *King of Pop*, a compilation of his eighteen best songs, as chosen by British fans via the Internet, was released worldwide. But, Taraborrelli contended that Jackson never truly recovered from the trial: "It didn't matter that Jackson was found not guilty. He was ruined—not just his reputation, but his self-esteem, too."[49]

Even after his death and funeral, Jackson's success continued as he was donned the King of Pop. In the past, he had relied on his musical talent to carry him along the hero's journey and he said in 1987: "I can always fall back on what God gave me."[50]

After being acquitted of child molestation charges following a lengthy and ugly court battle, a wounded Jackson withdrew from the public eye as much as possible and focused on raising his own three children. He was the butt of late-night entertainment jokes for months, and his musical career seemed to be over. Surprising the world, however, Jackson—looking healthier than he had in years—held a press conference announcing his final world tour to kick off July 14, 2009, at London O2 Arena. More than 360,000 tickets were sold in the first eighteen hours after going on sale in March.[51] Though purchasers, whose tickets were collectively worth $6.5 million,[52] were offered reimbursement for tickets after his death in June, many remained unreturned after the singer's death—fans choosing instead to hold onto them as memorabilia.

COLLECTIVE GRIEVING OF A HERO IN THE DIGITAL AGE

Jackson's memorial service on July 7, 2009, was a more spectacular event than most of us have ever experienced. Funeral services for elder statesmen and military heroes pale by comparison. When it was announced the memorial would be a public event at the Staples Center in Los Angeles, more than 1.6 million people registered online to win tickets to attend. Network and cable television stations, nearly without exception, aired the 90-minute star-studded event live. European broadcasters cleared regular schedules to air the event during prime time viewing hours.[53] Facebook teamed up with ABC News, CNN, E Online, and MTV to offer Internet users live streams. MSNBC.com and MySpace also teamed up to offer streaming video of the Jackson tribute.[54] MSNBC.com reported 510,000 viewers at its peak. Digital technology also allowed forty-seven movie theaters in twenty-four states to air the tribute for fans.[55] The Internet reported web traffic up nearly one-third during the memorial.[56]

In death, Jackson's star status, it seemed, was larger than it was even at his height of popularity in the early 1980s. This might be explained by the fact that human beings find a satisfying catharsis in coming together in times of tragedy. Whether an act of god or a shared death, people find emotional release a uniting experience. And few in the world were not touched during the past four decades by the life and artistry of Jackson. Because Jackson was such a cross-cultural figure who had been around more than forty years, his passing united several generations. Also, because he remained unconvicted of any crime, he was able to rebound in death from his tarnished image. Bonnie Fuller, former editor-in-chief of *Us Weekly*, said, "The fact that Michael Jackson sang the songs that were the background music for so many of our growing-up experiences, gives us the basis for this connection."[57]

Within minutes TMZ's breaking news of his death reaching fans, people across the world took to Twitter, Facebook, and other social networking sites to commiserate. Radio stations across the country began a round-the-clock vigil of MJ songs. All television stations broke into regularly scheduled programming with the sad news. Hundreds of thousands of Tweets related to Jackson's death were posted within hours of his death, causing the website to crash periodically. Other sites reported similar problems.[58]

Yoshiaki Sato, who teaches on popular music and literature at the University of Tokyo, said Jackson's star power cannot be overestimated. From the moment music went visual, on MTV, Jackson has been a pioneer in our obsession with music as sight as well as sound. We visualize Jackson's red jacket, lone glove, and moonwalking in our minds as quickly as we can hum the lyrics to his hit songs. Sato said:

Michael may have been a bigger force in history than all the unused hydrogen bombs. His moonwalk may have been a bigger leap for mankind than Apollo 11. Just imagine one billion people on earth having watched one minute of Michael every day for 15 years of their lives. Altogether that would make some 90,000,000,000 total hours of attention. This is power. And it's potentially a huge, efficient, cultural—and political power.[59]

Some scholars who study "celebrity" argue there will never be another celebrity death that so affects the global community because the media saturation and digital technologies have diminished what it means to be a celebrity. Daniel Henninger of *The Wall Street Journal* wrote, "Modern media squashed the life out of genuine celebrity."[60] Jackson came to fame prior to the phenomenon of reality television, cable and satellite TV, and the Internet—before everybody could upload a YouTube video and get his fifteen minutes.

In life, Jackson remained a pop culture phenomenon. Thirteen of his solo singles went to No. 1—the most of any male artist, including seven from 1984's *Thriller*. Four of The Jackson 5 songs, too, went to the top of the charts.[61] In death, he became a pop culture commodity of unprecedented status. Sony Pictures paid $60 million for the rights to the "Michael Jackson: This Is It" two-hour concert documentary created from more than 100 hours of rehearsals in preparation of the tour. It debuted October 28, 2009, and grossed $72 million at the box office, becoming the highest grossing concert film ever. It earned another $188 million internationally. U.S. DVD sales as of June 2010 were $43 million and rentals of $24 million.[62]

The circus that had been Michael Jackson's life, is slated to become a real Cirque du Soleil show in death. An arena-touring show is in development for late 2011 to be followed by a permanent Vegas show in 2012.[63] Video game maker Ubisoft has announced plans to license Jackson's image for an upcoming game.[64] Like Elvis Presley, who was worth $10 million when he died in 1977 and whose estate is now valued at $700 million, Jackson's most profitable days still lie ahead. Thanks to the digital technology, the King of Pop surpassed the King of Rock's posthumous value in less than one year."

NOTES

1. "Is Jackson worth more dead than alive?" *CBS News*, July 7, 2009.

2. Gil Kaufman, "Michael Jackson's Estate Has Generated $1 Billion Since His Death," *MTV News*, June 21, 2010. retrieved July 16, 2010 from www.michael jackson.com.

3. B. Barnes, "A star idolized and haunted, Michael Jackson dies at 50," *The New York Times*. June 26, 2009.

4. Ibid.

5. Ibid.

6. Edna Gundersen, "King of Pop reigns over music charts," *USA Today*. July 2, 2009.

7. *Ibid.* The Black-Eyed Peas album The E.N.D. is listed as No. 1, but was actually the No. 4 best-seller with 88,000, because Jackson's titles are not current and ineligible to top the chart.

8. Ed Christman, "Digital Bytes," *Billboard*. January 16, 2010. Vo. 122, Iss. 2, 5.

9. Esrne E. Deprez, "Jackson Death Boosts Music Vendor Sales," *BusinessWeek Online*. June 29, 2009, 14.

10. Gundersen.

11. "Hot Digital Songs," Billboard. July 11, 2009, Vol. 121, Iss. 27. "Hot Digital Songs," Billboard. July 18, 2009. Vol. 121, Iss. 28. Twenty-four of the top 75 songs were Jackson titles the week ending July 11, and 23 the week ending July 18.

12. Kaufman.

13. Gundersen.

14. Gundersen.

15. Ed Christman, "Sound of a Crescendo," *Billboard*. Vol. 121, Iss. 28, July 18, 2009, 4.

16. Shawn Collins, "Marketing the Death of Michael Jackson,"June 26, 2009. retrieved July 16, 2010 from http://blog.affiliatetip.com/archives/marketing-the-death -of-michael-jackson/

17. Deprez.

18. Jenna Wortham, "BITS; Michael Jackson Rocks the Web," *The New York Times*. July 5, 2009.

19. Wortham.

20. Bridget Daly, "Michael Jackson's Death Crashed Google," www.hollywood scoop.com, June 26, 2009.

21. Jon Swartz, "Websites brace for Jackson tribute," *USA Today*. July 7, 2009.

22. "Why do we have celebrity gods like Michael Jackson?" *USA Today*. June 26, 2009.

23. *Ibid.*

24. Marc Baldwin, "Hero as Salesman; Salesman as Hero: The Heroic Art of Representation," *The Journal of Popular Culture*. Vol. 26, No. 3, Winter 1992, 121.

25. What's Driving the Michael Jackson Mania?"

26. B. Spitzberg, and W. Cuach, "Fanning the flames of fandom: Celebrity worship, parasocial interaction, and stalking." Paper presented at the annual meeting of the International Communication Associaton. San Francisco, California, 2007.

27. Maltby et. al., "Thou shalt worship no other gods – unless they are celebrities: the relationship between celebrity worship and religious orientation," *Personality and Individual Differences*. Vol. 32, No.7, 1157–72.

28. Maltby et al., 2002, p. 1157.

29. Campbell, Joseph. *The Hero with a Thousand Faces*. Novato, California: New World Library, 2008.

30. Campbell, 23.

31. M. Delmont, "Michael Jackson & television before Thriller," *The Journal of Pan African Studies*. Vol. 3, No. 7, 64–78, 2010.

32. Delmont, 76.

33. Campbell, 64.

34. Barnes, 2009.

35. Margo Jefferson, *On Michael Jackson*, New York: Pantheon Books, 2006, 9.

36. Campbell, 74.

37. J. Safaer, "The Crystal Ball," *Performance Research*. Vol. 9, No. 2, 2004 118–31.

38. S. Trussler, "Peter Pan and Susan: Lost children from Juliet to Michael Jackson," New Theatre Quarterly. Vol. 23, No.4, 2007, 380–86.

39. S. Silberman, "Presenting Michael Jackson," Social Semiotics. Vol. 17, No. 4, 2007, 417–40.

40. Barnes.

41. M. Gomez-Barris, and H. Gray, "Michael Jackson, television, and post-op disasters," Television and New Media. Vol. 7, No. 1, 2006, 40–51.

42. A. Johnson, "When a celebrity is tied to immoral behavior: Consumer reactions to Michael Jackson and Kobe Bryant," *Advances in Consumer Research*. Vol. 32, 2005, 100–101.

43. Campbell.

44. Barnes.

45. G. Stever, "Parasocial and social interaction with celebrities: Classification of media fans," *Journal of Media Psychology*. Vol. 14, No. 3, 2009, 1–39.

46. J. Izod, "Androgyn and stardom: Cultural meanings of Michael Jackson," *The San Francisco Jung Institute Library Journal*. Vol. 14, No. 3, 1995, 63–74.

47. Barnes.

48. J. R. Taraborrelli, "As he turns 50, is this what Michael Jackson should really look like?" *Daily Mail*, August 28, 2008, retrieved June 30, 2010. (www.dailymail .co.uk/tvshowbiz/article)

49. *Ibid.*

50. *Ibid.*

51. Daniel Henninger, "Michael: The Last Celebrity," *The Wall Street Journal*. July 3, 2009.

52. Gil Kaufman, "Michael Jackson's Estate Has Generated $1 Billion Since His Death," *MTV News*, June 21, 2010. (Retrieved from michaeljackson.com).

53. "What's Driving the Michael Jackson Mania?" *The New York Times*. July 7, 2009.

54. Swartz, "Websites brace."

55. Jon Swartz, "Millions stream Jackson service," *USA Today*. July 8, 2009.

56. Alan Duke and Saeed Ahmed, "Goodbye Michael Jackson: Star, brother, friend, father," CNN.com, July 7, 2009.

57. "What's Driving the Michael Jackson Mania?" *The New York Times*. July 7, 2009.

58. M. G. Siegler, "The Web Collapses Under the Weight of Michael Jackson's Death," *TechCrunch*, June 25, 2009. (http://techcrunch.com)

59. "What's Driving the Michael Jackson Mania?" *The New York Times*. July 7, 2009.

60. Henninger.

61. Mariel Concepcion et al. "Michael Jackson's Top Billboard Hits," *Billboard*. Vol. 122, Iss. 25, June 26, 2010 20–21.

62. Kaufman.

63. Cirquedusoleil.com.

64. Kaufman.

BIBLIOGRAPHY

Baldwin, Marc. "Hero as Salesman; Salesman as Hero: The Heroic Art of Representation," *The Journal of Popular Culture*. Vol. 26, No. 3, Winter 1992, 121.

Barnes, B. "A star idolized and haunted, Michael Jackson dies at 50," *The New York Times*. June 26, 2009.

Campbell, J. *The Hero with a Thousand Faces*. Novato, California: New World Library, 2008.

Christman, Ed. "Digital Bytes," *Billboard*. January 16, 2010. Vo. 122, Iss. 2, 5.

Christman, Ed. "Sound of a Crescendo," *Billboard*. Vol. 121, Iss. 28, July 18, 2009, 4.

Collins, Shawn. "Marketing the Death of Michael Jackson,"June 26, 2009. retrieved July 16, 2010 from http://blog.affiliatetip.com/archives/marketing-the-death-of -michael-jackson/

Concepcion, Mariel, Monica Herrera. Erynn Hill, Gail Mitchell, and Santino Palazzolo. "Michael Jackson's Top Billboard Hits," *Billboard*. Vol. 122, Iss. 25, June 26, 2010 20–21.

Daly, Bridget. "Michael Jackson's Death Crashed Google," www.hollywoodscoop .com, June 26, 2009.

Delmont, M. Michael Jackson & television before Thriller. *The Journal of Pan African Studies*, 3(7), 2010, 64–78.

Deprez, Esrne E. "Jackson Death Boosts Music Vendor Sales," *BusinessWeek Online*. June 29, 2009, 14.

Duke, Alan, and Saeed Ahmed, "Goodbye Michael Jackson: Star, brother, friend, father," CNN.com, July 7, 2009.

Gomez-Barris, M., and Gray, H. Michael Jackson, television, and post-op disasters. *Television and New Media*. 7(1), 2006, 40–51.

Gundersen, Edna. "King of Pop reigns over music charts," *USA Today*. July 2, 2009.

Henninger, Daniel. "Michael: The Last Celebrity," *The Wall Street Journal*. July 3, 2009.

"Is Jackson worth more dead than alive?" *CBS News*, July 7, 2009.

Izod, J. Androgyn and stardom: Cultural meanings of Michael Jackson. *The San Francisco Jung Institute Library Journal*. 14(3), 1995, 63–74.

Jefferson, Margo. *On Michael Jackson* (New York: Pantheon Books, 2006), 9.

Johnson, A. When a celebrity is tied to immoral behavior: Consumer reactions to Michael Jackson and Kobe Bryant. *Advances in Consumer Research*. 32, 2005, 101.

Kaufman, Gil. "Michael Jackson's Estate Has Generated $1 Billion Since His Death," *MTV News*, June 21, 2010. retrieved July 16, 2010 from www.michaeljackson .com.

Maltby, J., Houran, J., Lange, R., Ashe, D., McCutcheon, L. Thou shalt worship no other gods – unless they are celebrities: the relationship between celebrity worship and religious orientation. *Personality and Individual Differences*, 32(7), 2002, 1157–72.

Safaer, J. The crystal ball. *Performance Research*. 9(2), 2004, 118–31.

Siegler, M. G. "The Web Collapses Under the Weight of Michael Jackson's Death," *TechCrunch*, June 25, 2009. (http://techcrunch.com)

Silberman, S. Presenting Michael Jackson. *Social Semiotics*. 17(4), 2007. 417–440.

Spitzberg, B., and W. Cuach, "Fanning the flames of fandom: Celebrity worship, parasocial interaction, and stalking." Paper presented at the annual meeting of the International Communication Associaton. San Francisco, California, May 23, 2007.

Stever, G. "Parasocial and social interaction with celebrities: Classification of media fans," *Journal of Media Psychology*, 14(3), 2009, 1–39.

Swartz, Jon. "Millions stream Jackson service," *USA Today*. July 8, 2009.

Swartz. "Websites brace for Jackson tribute," *USA Today*. July 7, 2009.

Taraborrelli, J. R. "As he turns 50, is this what Michael Jackson should really look like? *Daily Mail*, August 28, 2008. Retrieved June 30, 2010 from http://www .dialymail.co.uk/tvshowbiz/article.

Trussler, S. Peter Pan and Susan: Lost children from Juliet to Michael Jackson. *New Theatre Quarterly*, 23(4), 2007, 380–86.

"What's Driving the Michael Jackson Mania?" *The New York Times*. July 7, 2009.

"Why do we have celebrity 'gods' like Michael Jackson?" *USA Today*. June 26, 2009.

Wortham, Jenna. "BITS; Michael Jackson Rocks the Web," *The New York Times*. July 5, 2009.

Acknowledgments

This is always the hardest part of the process to me, as it is impossible to put into words the contribution of everyone involved in putting together a project, such as this.

I am deeply indebted to all contributing authors. Without your creative ideas, diligent research, and timely revisions, this book would not have come to fruition.

For the contributions of Louisiana Tech University, and in particular Dr. Les Guice, vice president for Research and Development, Dr. Ed Jacobs, dean of the College of Liberal Arts and the Department of Journalism, I am truly thankful for your support of my research project. And to Bill Willoughby, associate dean of the College of Liberal Arts, please accept my gratitude for your continuous assistance and guidance in this and other academic and research endeavors I have pursued while at Louisiana Tech.

To Dr. Reginald Owens, chair of journalism at Louisiana Tech, thank you for your advice and encouragement throughout, and for putting me in touch with some really amazing people.

Flora Stringer, my invaluable copyeditor, thank you does not begin to cover all you have meant to this project. Besides providing an extra set of eyes and thoughtful feedback when things did not quite make sense, your compliance with my comedic breaks to share "just one more video" kept me sane. I appreciate you more than you know.

Fellow members of the Louisiana Tech journalism department and students who kept me motivated with questions and conversation about the progress of this work, I thank you.

To John Shaw, with Select-O-Hits Music Distribution, one of the largest and oldest independent music distributors in the United States—thank you for the hours you spent at the Cutting Edge Music Conference in New Orleans educating me on the current state of the record industry, its history and where it's headed.

To Dr. Fei Xeu, assistant professor of mass communication and journalism at the University of Southern Mississippi—thanks for letting me think outside the box in your doctoral advertising seminar. My fascination with how rock music and KISS used so many of the ideas covered in that course were the impetus for this book.

Lenore Lautigar, assistant editor at Lexington, please accept my humble thanks for the timely attention you gave every question I had throughout this process. I hope I have such luck in all my future publishing endeavors. And to Joseph Parry, the editor at Lexington who got this project rolling, thank you for taking an interest in an offbeat but culturally significant topic and for allowing me so much room to develop the project as I envisioned it.

My friends, who have been so encouraging in offering valuable sources and resources of information, I thank you.

My family has been patient and encouraging during my research, writing, and editing, and I am forever thankful. Who knew my marriage to one of the most fanatical KISS fans would turn into a scholarly obsession for me? Fortunately, my children think it's pretty cool having a mother who studies rock music and popular culture—even if they do find my analysis of every little thing annoying at times. Next time we are home on the Mississippi Gulf Coast, I shall take us all out to Hard Rock Biloxi and celebrate.

Finally, to my parents Will and Marilyn Barfoot, for your encouragement to value reading and writing. I read and I write because you first read and wrote to me. Dad, I miss your postcards with their tiny little factoids of culture, history, and current events more than you could have imagined. While my book might not have been your cup of tea, I might actually have been able to finally teach you a thing or two—instead of the other way around. I wish you were here to enjoy this moment.

Index

AC/DC, 12, 23–38, 344

Adkins, Trace, 220–21, 229

Advertising; advertisement(s), viii, 3–4, 6–7, 9–10, 16, 33, 60–61, 64–67, 69, 80, 82, 107, 177–79, 181, 183, 186–89, 200, 202, 275–76, 280, 303

Advertising Age, 80

A&E, 4, 17

Ailes, Roger, 214

Al Qaeda, 218. *See also* Muslim, terrorist

All-American Rejects, 30

Allen, Kris, 206, 209–10, 265

Allen, Steve, 305

Amazon, 34, 327

The American Dream, 17, 202, 215, 256

American Idol, 5, 206, 225, 255–71; Lambert, Adam, 5, 206, 209, 265. *See also* reality television

American Marketing Association, 9

Anastasio, Trey, 82. *See also* Phish

Apple computers, 5, 9, 30, 32. *See also* iTunes

Arnett, Peter, 219

ASCAP, 60

Atlantic Records, 25, 300

Authenticity; authentic, 61, 153–54, 159, 164, 167–69, 171–72, 202, 219, 243, 246, 259

band as brand. *See* brand

Bashir, Martin, 330

BBC, 219

The Beatles, 7, 16, 24, 87, 89, 142, 179, 273, 280–83, 329

Beck, Glenn, 213, 220–21, 223–25. *See also* FOX News

Best Buy, 30, 33, 280

Bible. *See* Holy Bible

Big Cypress, 83

Billboard, 7, 12–13, 27, 83, 145, 154, 158, 200, 204–5, 217, 225, 263, 300–301, 303, 326

Black Sabbath, 39, 42–45, 51, 273. *See also* Ozzy Osbourne

Blockbuster, 29

Blues. *See* rhythm and blues

Bon Jovi, xi, 139–52

Bon Jovi, Jon, 139–41, 146. *See also* Bon Jovi

Bonnaroo, 83

Bono, 142–43. *See also* U2

Bowie, David, 131, 141

341

About the Contributors

Jeremy V. Adolphson is a doctoral candidate in the Department of Communication at the University of Wisconsin Milwaukee. His research agenda centers on the intersection of rhetoric and popular culture in various ideological, political, and cultural venues including music subcultures, religious extremism, hate speech, and the culture wars.

Bob Batchelor is an assistant professor in the School of Journalism and Mass Communication at Kent State University. He received his doctorate from the University of South Florida. Bob is the author or editor of 10 books, including *The 2000s* and *American Pop: Popular Culture Decade by Decade*. He is also a member of the Editorial Advisory Board of *The Journal of Popular Culture*.

Michael T. Bertrand is an associate professor of history at Tennessee State University. He served as music editor for the *African American National Biography*, and is the founder and moderator of *H-Southern-Music*. The University of Illinois recently released a second (paperback) edition of his first book, *Race, Rock, and Elvis*. Bertrand is working on a manuscript that addresses the 1956 attack on Nat "King" Cole in Birmingham, Alabama.

Dr. Hazel James Cole is a tenure-track faculty member at McNeese State University where she teaches all courses in the public relations sequence. Her academic research interests as a cultural "critical" scholar include: public relations and image restoration, Hip Hop culture and identity, and media criticism. Her professional background includes over 15 years as an award-winning communications professional, working primarily in strategic planning, crisis communication, diversity training, media relations and client service.

Charles Conaway, Ph.D., is an assistant professor of English at the University of Southern Indiana. His research focuses on the afterlife of Shakespeare, particularly in the long eighteenth century and in more recent adaptations and appropriations of the plays into film, theater, and popular music.

Daniel Cochece Davis, who earned his Ph.D. at University of Southern California, is an assistant professor at Marist College in Poughkeepsie, New York. His research focuses on communication and conflict (e.g., culture shock, violence & conflict in schools, social loafing, etc.), as well as technology (e.g., leading virtual groups, music fan communication, student-teacher mediated communication). He teaches Intercultural Communication, Nonverbal Communication, Leadership Communication, Small Group Communication and Research Methods. He consults on organizational culture, diversity valuing, conflict, productivity and leadership issues.

Bryan P. Delaney (B.A., Marist College) works with "at risk youth" in a wilderness therapy program, while living in Atlanta, GA. He is preparing to apply to MSW programs.

Dedria Givens-Carroll, Ph.D., assistant professor in the Communication Department at the University of Louisiana at Lafayette, specializes in teaching public relations. She worked for 20 years in public relations profession in the United States and abroad focusing on the specialty areas of travel and tourism, government and politics, civil and military aviation, business and industry, medical, nonprofit public relations. Her research interests include the study of religious and nonprofit organizations; along with political and governmental entities coupled with the development of communication theory, research methods and new media.

Heidi M. Kettler (B.A., Marist College) lives and works in the San Francisco area. She studied abroad in Ireland, has worked at the Dublin Gallery of Photography, NBC, the Omega Institute, and now spends most of her free time traveling the world, visiting her favorite bands when they perform, and learning as much as she can about nutrition.

Jacqueline Lambiase, Ph.D., associate professor, teaches strategic communication in TCU's Schieffer School of Journalism. Previously, she taught public relations, qualitative research, technology, and writing at the University of North Texas. She has co-edited and co-written two books with Tom Reichert on advertising's use of sexually oriented appeals: Sex in Advertising (2003) and Sex in Consumer Culture (2006). Journal articles and book chapters have focused on ethics, social media, and gendered images in mass media. In 2008, she won a Best of Texas bronze award for opinion writing from the Texas Public Relations Association.

Jordan McClain is a doctoral candidate in Mass Media and Communication at Temple University in Philadelphia, Pennsylvania, where he also earned his MA. His research interests include marketing/branding/positioning, media framing, consumer psychology/behavior, American popular culture, and rock criticism. His dissertation examines media coverage of Phish.

Mary Nash-Wood is a 2008 graduate of Louisiana Tech University in Ruston, LA, where she received her bachelor's in journalism. She has been honored by the Louisiana Press Association in the categories of column writing, news story and features as well as an award from the National Federal of Press Women for sports writing. She is currently employed at *The Times* in Shreveport, LA.

Staci L. Parks is a reporter for *The News-Star* in Monroe, LA. She is a 2009 graduate of Louisiana Tech University in Ruston, LA. While at Louisiana Tech, Parks served as editor-in-chief for the weekly student newspaper, *The Tech Talk*, and as Organizations Editor for the university yearbook, *Lagniappe*.

Heather Pinson, Ph.D., has degrees in Music, Musicology, and Interdisciplinary Arts and teaches courses on art and music history at Robert Morris University. In addition to her training as a classical violinist, she performs rock and jazz regularly and publishes predominately on popular music, jazz, aesthetics, and race theory. Heather is also the author of *The Jazz Image: Seeing Music Through Herman Leonard's Photography* published by the University Press of Mississippi, which examines the photographs of African American jazz musicians during the 1950s and 1960s.

Mary Beth Ray is a doctoral candidate in Mass Media and Communication at Temple University in Philadelphia, Pennsylvania. She earned her MA from Syracuse University's S. I. Newhouse School of Public Communications. Her research interests include new media, online community, ICT&S, popular culture, and cultural studies. Her dissertation examines the impact of digital technology on popular music culture.

Alison Slade earned her Ph.D. in mass communication and journalism from the University of Southern Mississippi. She holds an undergraduate degree in radio, television and film and master of arts in communication from Auburn University. Her work on reality television and media theory has been published in books and journals. She currently does a weekly nationally syndicated radio talk show *The Alison Slade Show* on Genesis Communications Network.

Deborah Clark Vance, Ph.D., is associate professor in and chair of the Dept. of Communication at McDaniel College. She earned her Ph. D. in Intercultural Communication at Howard University in 2002 and her undergraduate degree in Communication at Northwestern University. Her research interests include the interplay of media, culture and identity.

CONSULTANTS

Susan Masino has been a rock journalist more than thirty years and the author of three books, *Rock 'n' Roll Fantasy—My Life and Times with AC/DC, Van Halen, and Kiss*, *Famous Wisconsin Musicians* (featuring a foreword by Les Paul), and *Let There Be Rock—The Story of AC/DC*. She also appears in the Van Halen DVD, The Early Years. She is currently working on *Family Tradition—Three Generations of Hank Williams*.

John "J-DOGG" Shaw graduated from Memphis State University in 1992 with a degree in music education. He has been a clinician, promoter, hip-hop journalist, producer and jazz musician. His articles have appeared in *Murder Dog*, *Rap Pages*, *Grooveline*, *Street Masters*, and *Down* Magazine. Since 1995, he has worked for Select-O-Hits Music Distribution in the promotions department. He has spoken at numerous conventions, including the Southern Urban Music Conference, Omni Music Conference and Mid-Atlantic Music Conference, and is working on a history of Black music in Shreveport, Louisiana entitled "Action Speaks Louder Than Words: Black Music in Shreveport, LA 1948–1998."

About the Editor

Elizabeth Barfoot Christian is an assistant professor of journalism at Louisiana Tech University. She joined the Louisiana Tech faculty in July 2007. She earned her Ph.D. in mass communication and journalism from the University of Southern Mississippi. She also earned her M.S. in political science and B.S. in journalism and political science from Southern Miss.

Christian's professional research interests include literary journalism, popular culture, and journalism history. She has published "Crawfish, Better Biggots, and Hooch Handlers: Mississippi Through the Eyes of P.D. East" in the *International Journal of Regional and Local Studies*. She is also a contributor to the *Encyclopedia of Social Networking*, due out in 2011 from SAGE Publications.

She has presented research at regional and national conferences on topics, including *Framing the Jena Six: A Textual Analysis of Lynching and Racism in 21st Century American Media* and *The Man in the Mirror: How Social Networking and Celebrity Death Helps Us Confront Our Own Mortality*.

Currently, she is revising her doctoral dissertation, *Reading, Writing, and Rabble-Rousing: Willie Morris, A Good Old Editor*, for publication as a book.

Prior to returning to academia, Christian served as the public relations coordinator for the City of Hattiesburg, Mississippi.

CPSIA information can be obtained at www.ICGtesting.com
Printed in the USA
BVOW071818261011

274527BV00001B/2/P